INDIAN NEPALIS

About the Editors

Prof. T.B. Subba teaches Anthropology at North-Eastern Hill University (NEHU), Shillong, India and is an expert on cultural and ethnic studies in eastern Himalayas.

Prof. A.C. Sinha taught sociology at North-Eastern Hill University, Shillong, India for about three decades before his superannuation. He is an expert on Himalayan Studies and ethnic politics of the Eastern Himalayan region. He may be contacted at acoomarsinha@yahoo.co.in

Prof. G.S. Nepal teaches Nepali at North Bengal University, Rajarammohunpur, Siliguri, West Bengal. He is a noted author and creative writer in Nepali. He has received the Sahitya Academy Award for his contribution to Nepali literature.

Mr. D.R. Nepal is a senior bureaucrat of the Government of Sikkim, Gangtok. He may be contacted at the Chief Minister's Secretariat, Tashiling, Gangtok.

INDIAN NEPALIS

Issues and Perspectives

Edited by

T.B. Subba

A.C. Sinha

G.S. Nepal

D.R. Nepal

CONCEPT PUBLISHING COMPANY, NEW DELHI-110059

Cataloging in Publication Data—DK
Courtesy: D.K. Agencies (P) Ltd. <docinfo@dkagencies.com>

Indian Nepalis : issues and perspectives / edited by T.B. Subba.
p. cm.
Papers presented at a national seminar organized by the Government of Sikkim.
Includes bibliographical references.
Includes index.
ISBN 13: 9788180694462
ISBN 10: 8180694461

1. Nepalese—India—Ethnic identity—Congresses. 2. Nepalese—India, Northeastern—Ethnic identity—Congresses. 3. Subculture—India. 4. India—Relations—Nepal. 5. Nepal—Relations—India. I. Subba, Tanka B. (Tanka Bahadur), 1957-

DDC 305.891 495 22

ISBN-13: 978-81-8069-446-2
ISBN-10: 81-8069-446-1

First Published 2009

Published and Printed by
Ashok Kumar Mittal
Concept Publishing Company
A/15-16, Commercial Block, Mohan Garden
New Delhi-110059 (INDIA)

Phones : 25351460, 25351794
Fax : 091-11-25357103
Email : publishing@conceptpub.com

Preface

The editors of this volume endeavoured to assemble representative members of the intelligentsia, opinion leaders, young and senior academics, authors, and concerned citizens for a three-day academic treat at Gangtok. These participants, who travelled from near and far away places, either presented papers in the academic sessions, or took part in panel discussions, or deliberated on the presentations in the various academic sessions. The organizers had a sense of satisfaction that the concerned members of the community and their well-wishers came forward and appreciated the efforts made to raise the relevant issues confronting the community. The editors are convinced that the conference was a right step at right time and with all their inadequacies it was the first effort of its type.

One point must be made very clear at the very outset is that the editors had no individual agenda of their own. Neither did they have uniformity of views on many issues among themselves, not the least because of disrespect to one another but because of a healthy tradition of their professional commitment and a belief in academic freedom. This becomes clear when one looks at their professional background of the editorial team. Professor T.B. Subba is an anthropologist by training and profession and Professor A.C. Sinha is an anthropologist by training and a sociologist by vocation. Professor Ghanshyam Nepal is an expert in Nepali language and literature and is a creative writer himself and D.R. Nepal is a trained government functionary. Perhaps that is why, while Subba has suggested, "Sakhaa" as the new nomenclature of the community, Sinha proposed the term 'Nepamul'/INO' as if they do not bother whether others would approve or not. Professor Ghanshyam Nepal, despite the fact that he heads a university department named "Nepali", would like the present nomenclature to continue only till an appropriate alternative nomenclature is developed. Thus, there is unanimity among the editors that the search for a nomenclature other than Nepali and Gorkha must be pursued vigorously. For the purpose of the present volume, however, the authors have used the nomenclature of their choice and the editors have only tried to make the scripts more readable, intelligible, logical and thematic in presentation.

The conference was an eye-opener to the editors in the sense that a number of revelations took place during the three days. For example, the opinion makers and intelligentsia among the Indian Nepalis appear to be closed minded. They shied away from the debates, and whenever they took part in it, it was more of an advocacy of their stand points. They also appeared to be afraid of taking public stand on the issues of significance, as if they were afraid of conducting experiments.

The editors of this volume have presented perhaps the best that could happen at this juncture of the history of the Indian Nepalis. As one expects of an edited volume, all the articles are not equally strong in argument, documentation, or substance, but they all have something important to say about the Indian Nepalis. Above all, they all reflect some important aspects of the Indian Nepalis, their vibrancy as well as frustration, hopes as well as creativity, and internal churning as well as dialogue with the outside world. We are thankful to all the contributors, and participants, for responding to our detailed queries and bearing with our demands, which were all done with the spirit to make the book truly worthy of the community it is written about.

The editors are particularly grateful to Dr. Pawan Chamling, Hon'ble Chief Minister of Sikkim, for taking a keen interest in the conference and its output in the form of the present book. The conference on "Identity and Nationality of the Indian Nepalis: Issues and Perspectives" was held on April 20-22, 2006 at Chintan Bhawan, Gangtok, Sikkim. We are beholden to the various functionaries of the Government of Sikkim for the support and the Indian Nepali Study and Research Forum, Gangtok, and its president, K.P. Adhikari for constituting the organizing committee for co-coordinating the event. We are grateful to the Indian Council of Social Science Research, North-Eastern Regional Centre, Shillong for funding the conference kits and to the Government of Sikkim for taking care of the remaining and more substantial expenses towards making the national conference possible. This book is based on the papers presented at the conference but includes, fortunately or unfortunately, less than one third of them. We could not publish all the papers because they either did not meet our expectations of quality and standard or we could not arrange to translate them into English. A few of them were left out during the editing process. We are sorry for those participants whose articles did not find place in the volume. However, we do appreciate their efforts and contributions to the discussions during the various academic sessions. Similarly, we are sorry to the panelists of the two panels we had organised for not being able to include their contributions in the volume in spite of our best efforts. Among the Sikkimese intellectuals, we appreciate the valuable contributions made by Shri C.D. Rai and Padmashri Sanu Lama. Lastly, the authorities, faculty and students of Sikkim Government College, Tadong were of great help to us in bringing order in the conference halls and conducting the proceedings. We cannot thank them enough.

Finally, we thank the Concept Publishing Company, New Delhi, for publishing the book in record time and keeping the price within affordable limits for most Indian Nepalis.

T.B. Subba
A.C. Sinha
G.S. Nepal
D.R. Nepal

Contents

Profile of the Contributors

Amena Nora Passah is Reader at the Department of History, North-Eastern Hill University, Shillong. Her area of special interest is history of Christianity in Northeast India.

Anuradha Sharma is Principal Correspondent of *The Telegraph* in Siliguri, Darjeeling District, West Bengal.

Awadesh Coomar Sinha retired as Professor of Sociology from North-Eastern Hill University, Shillong. During his tenure there he has published innumerable articles and several books on eastern Himalayas. He was also former Dean, School of Social Sciences at North-Eastern Hill University.

B.C. Upreti is Professor at the South Asia Study Centre, University of Rajasthan. He has written extensively on various aspects of Indo-Nepal relations.

Bidhan Golay is Lecturer at the Centre for Himalayan Studies, North Bengal University, Darjeeling.

D.B. Chhetry started his career in 1964 as Extra Assistant Commissioner and retired as Commissioner to the Government of Assam in 1998. After his retirement he was on the Assam Board of Revenue till April 2002. Currently he is associated with various social organizations of Assam.

D.R. Chhetri is Lecturer at the Postgraduate Department of Botany, Darjeeling Government College. He is actively involved in research on Himalayan medicinal plants, traditional medicine, Biotechnology and Biochemistry. So far, he has edited a couple of books and published 35 research articles in reputed international and national journals. Dr. Chhetri has also carried out 8 research projects funded by national and international agencies.

D.R. Nepal is Joint Secretary (Home), Government of Sikkim, Gangtok.

D. Sapkota is Associate Professor, College of Veterinary Science, Assam Agricultural University, Guwahati. He is active in various social and literary activities related to the Nepalis in Assam.

Goutam Biswas is Professor of Philosophy at Assam University, Silchar. His area of special interest is Philosophy of Culture on which he has contributed several original articles.

G.S. Nepal is Professor of Nepali Language and Literature at the University of North Bengal.

Jyoti Prakash Tamang has been working for the last 21 years on biotechnology of fermented foods of various ethnic groups living in the Himalayas. He did his post-doctoral research on molecular microbiology in Japan and Germany. Dr. Tamang was teaching at Sikkim Government College, Gangtok before he joined the newly established Sikkim University. He has published more than 60 research papers in international and national journals, filed a patent, produced four Ph.D. students, and guiding several others. He has presented his research findings in Japan, South Korea, Thailand, Singapore, China, Nepal, Denmark, Germany, Italy and Slovenia. He is a Scientific Adviser to the International Foundation for Science of Sweden, a member of Scientific Advisory Committee of the Institute of Bioresource and Sustainable Development at Imphal, and executive committee member of Sikkim State Council of Science and Technology. He is also the Chief Editor of *Journal of Hill Research.* He is a recipient of the prestigious National Bioscience Award of Department of Biotechnology, Government of India in 2005 for his significant research contribution towards improving traditional fermented foods and beverages, and was conferred the Fellow of Biotech Research Society of India in 2006.

K.L. Pradhan is Reader in History at Aizawl Government College, Mizoram.

Madhav Pokhrel is Professor at the Central Department of Linguistics, Tribhuvan University, Kirtipur, Kathmandu. He did his PhD in Linguistics from Deccan College, Pune (1989) and in 2005 attended the courses given by Noam Chomsky at MIT, United States. He has been a Visiting Professor at Beijing University of Communications and Kobe University, Japan. He knows a large number of languages like Nepali, English, Hindi, Sanskrit, Japanese, Prakrit, Pali, Chinese,

Kusunda, Sinhalese and Marathi. He is credited to have discovered four languages and collected data on more than 40 languages. He has helped to develop writing systems for Pahari, Limbu, Tamang, Magar, Sampang Rai, Khaling Rai, Chamling Rai, Mewahang Rai, Dumi Rai, Bahing Rai, Kham, Meche [Bodo], Gurung and Rajbanshi. He has published 4 books on grammar and linguistics, 3 books on literary essays, translated 2 books, edited 7 book and published many articles on linguistics, literary criticism and literary essays.

Michael Hutt is Professor of Nepali and Himalayan Studies at the School of Oriental and African Studies, University of London. His principal publications are *Himalayan Voices: an Introduction to Modern Nepali Literature* (Berkeley: University of California Press, 1991), *Modern Literary Nepali: an Introductory Reader* (New Delhi: Oxford University Press, 1994), *Nepal: a Guide to the Art and Architecture of the Kathmandu Valley* (Gartmore: Kiscadale Publications, 1994), *Bhutan: Perspectives on Conflict and Dissent Valley* (Gartmore: Kiscadale Publications, 1994), *Nepal in the Nineties* (New Delhi: Oxford University Press, 1994), *Unbecoming Citizens: Culture, Nationhood and the Flight of Refugees from Bhutan* (New Delhi: Oxford University Press, 2003) and *Himalayan People's War: Nepal's Maoist Rebellion* (London: Hurst and Co., 2004). Michael Hutt is also co-author, with Abhi Subedi, of *Teach Yourself Nepali* (London: Hodder and Stoughton, 2000).

Nira Devi has taught Geography at Delhi Public School, Digboi, Kendriya Vidyalaya, Siliguri and at BSF Senior Secondary School, Siliguri. Her MPhil dissertation awarded by Gauhati University was "Nepalese in Assam: A Comparative Study of Economic and Cultural Attainment among Different Communities in Gangmouthan Gaon Panchayat, Sonitpur District, Assam". She is at present pursuing her doctoral research in the same university.

Pravesh Jung Golay is Senior Research Fellow at the Department of Philosophy, University of Pune.

Rajendra P. Dhakal was a Reader at the Department of Political Science, Kurseong College, before joining Kalimpong College as Principal in 2002. He did his PhD on "Organisation and Management of Rural Development in the Hill Areas of Darjeeling district" for which he took a special course on 'Methodology on Rural Social Research' from the National Institute of Rural Development, Hyderabad. At present his areas of interest are state and society, politics of identity, literature and politics, and rural development. Besides contributing articles to different journals Dr. Dhakal has been publishing articles in Nepali newspapers and magazines.

Ranju R. Dhamala is Professor of Political Science at Assam University, Silchar. Her doctoral research was on the Panchayati Raj in Sikkim and has ever retained a keen interest in the political developments in eastern Himalayas in particular and Northeast India in general.

Rhoderick Chalmers is SOAS-CNAS Visiting Fellow at Tribhuwan University.

Sharda Chhetri has worked as a journalist for *The Asian Age* for over 10 years in Delhi, Kolkata and Darjeeling. Presently, she is working as a freelance journalist while engaged as the Principal of St Augustine's School, Kurseong. She is also associated with Stree Shakti, Darjeeling, an NGO working for women's empowerment.

Shrawan Kumar Acharya is Professor at the School of Planning and Public Policy, CEPT University, Ahmedabad. After his schooling at Pedong, Kalimpong he completed his graduation from Santiniketan, post graduation and PhD from Jawaharlal Nehru University, New Delhi. He also holds M. Tech. degree in Urban and Regional Planning from CEPT and Diploma in Urban Management from the University of Birmingham, U.K. He was awarded UGC fellowship to undertake his PhD at JNU. He was a SHASTRI Fellow at McGill University and ASIA Fellow at the Chinese Academy of Social Sciences, Beijing and the Institute of World Economics and Politics, Hanoi. Before joining academics Prof. Acharya was involved in the grassroots development work of NGOs in Delhi and Mumbai. He has carried forward this interest and specialises in teaching and research related to participatory planning, urban poor, community development and the role of civil society institutions in urban and regional governance and development. One of his current research interests is related to comparative study of urban transformations and planning issues in China, India and Vietnam. At present he is actively involved in the preparation of city development plans through participatory processes under the Jawaharlal Nehru Urban Renewal Mission in India.

Tapasya Thapa is a Research Scholar at the Central Institute of English and Foreign Languages, Hyderabad.

Tejimala Gurung Nag has specialised in the modern history of Northeast India. Her areas of special interest are of social formation and human movement in Northeast India. At present she is Reader at the Department of History, North-Eastern Hill University, Shillong.

Subba, T.B. is Professor of Anthropology at North-Eastern Hill University, Shillong, India. His research interests include ethnicity, development, culture, and diasporic studies. He has done intensive fieldwork in Darjeeling, Sikkim and East Nepal. His more recent works are *The Anthropology of North East India,* which he edited with Dr. G.C. Ghosh (Orient Longman, 2003), *The Nepalis in Northeast India: A Community in Search of Indian Identity* that he edited with Prof. A.C. Sinha (Indus, 2003), *Between Ethnography and Fiction: Verrier Elwin and the Tribal Question in India* (Orient Longman, 2005), which he edited with Sujit Som, and *Indigeneity in India* (Kegan Paul 2006), edited with B.G. Karlsson. He edits a multi-disciplinary and internationally refereed periodical called *The NEHU Journal* published by the North-Eastern Hill University Publications, Shillong. He has been awarded DAAD Guest Professorship by the Free University of Berlin, Germany and Dr. Panchanan Mitra Lectureship for 2008 by the Asiatic Society, Kolkata.

T.N. Upadhyaya is Lecturer in Nepali at BBS College, Shillong. He is active in Nepali literary activities of Shillong.

Vimal Khawas was a Associate Fellow at the Council for Social Development, New Delhi and Senior Research Scholar, Jawaharlal Nehru University, New Delhi before he joined the newly established Sikkim University. He often contributes research and general articles in reputed research journals, magazines, web sites, and national news dailies. Mr. Khawas is also member of the editorial committee of *Social Change*, a multidisciplinary journal published by the Council for Social Development, New Delhi.

Section 1

Conceptual and Theoretical Issues

1

Introduction

A.C. SINHA

Man as a social being is by nature gregarious and spends most of his life along with other beings in perusing his daily chores. While doing so, he forms a variety of social circles, which turn out stronger, enduring and even binding on him. Family, friendship, neighbourhood, kinship, clubs, associations, and many such formations provide support system and in the process they become so critical for men and women that they live and die for the sake of these social groupings. Ethnicity, nationalism and statehood may be seen as various formations of such human existence today.

Indians of Nepalese Origin or the Nepamul Bharatiya, like other such human multitudes, are engaged in series of activities among themselves and along with other social entities in the vast multi-ethnic Indian Union. Being members of the Indian Union gives them a series of privileges including equal treatment guaranteed by the Indian Constitution. As citizens of India, they have fundamental rights such as free movement within the Indian Union, freedom to choose a vocation, settle down and exercise political rights to vote and get elected to various elective posts in the country. The structure of the Indian Union, divided among the states and union territories, is such that Nepamul Bharatiya feel handicapped, as their name is willy-nilly associated with and tagged to another sovereign state, Nepal. The very nomenclature of the community creates confusion even among them and their neighbours. They are invariably accused of being Nepalese, the citizens of Nepal, who are then charged to be usurping rights and privileges meant for the bonafide Indians. The protestations that they have been living in India for generations and were born and brought up in India are not taken seriously, as open border between the two countries does not ensure an automatic citizenship.

Puzzled Nepamul Bharatiya cast a glance around them and discover that they are underdogs in India. Except for the vague notion of some distant Nepalese ancestry and their common lingua franca with the Nepalese—Nepali—they do not have many things in common even between themselves. They have significant social, religious, linguistic and cultural variations within them. So who are the INO or the Nepamul Bharatiya? What holds them together? How do they identify themselves individually and collectively? How do 'others' identify them? What should be appropriate identity and nomenclature for the Nepamul Bharatiya?

There are a number of real and putative reasons for the INO's nationality becoming a suspect. And for that the common INO not only suffers, but it also confuses him of his status as an Indian. If he is an Indian what type of Indian is he? Like a Marathi, an Oriya or an Assamese? If it is so, then why do 'other' Indians not treat him like they treat an Indian Marathi, an Indian Oriya and an Indian Assamese? The above Indian communities have their home lands (states) within Indian Union, but why do the Nepamul Bharatiya not have their homeland in the Indian Union? Who gives homeland to them? Are they like the Parsis, Sindhis, and Anglo-Indians, who do not have their homelands in India? But these communities are highly developed and economically powerful unlike the community in question here. These and many other questions continue to beg answer. The Nepamul Bharatiya are no doubt Indians, but what type of Indians are they?

With a view to answering some of the above questions, it is imperative to explain terms like ethnicity, nationality, and state prevalent in the contemporary academic discourse.

Ethnicity and Ethnic Identity

The term 'ethnic' is of Greek origin meaning 'a community of common descent', or 'a kinship group linked by ties of blood'. Max Weber defines ethnic groups as 'human groups (other than kinship group), which cherish a belief in their common origins of such a kind that it provides basis for the creation of a community'. His argument centres on 'a set of beliefs, and not on any objective features of group membership such as shared language, religion, and especially biological traits associated with the everyday understanding of race. It is this sense of common ancestry, that is vital, but the identification with the shared origin is largely, if not wholly, fictitious'.[1] For ethnicity to come about the groups must have a minimum of contacts with each other, and they must entertain ideas of each other as being culturally different from themselves. Moreover, the term 'ethnicity' refers to relationships between groups whose members consider themselves distinctive, and these groups may be ranked hierarchically within a society'.

Stefan Wolf finds two distinct schools illustrating the aspects of ethnicity. The so-called primordial school of ethnicity holds that ethnicity is so deeply engrained in human history and experience that it cannot be denied that it exists, objectively and subjectively, and that it should, therefore, be considered a fact of life in relations between individuals and groups, who all have an ethnic identity. The instrumentalist's school of ethnicity argues that ethnicity is by no means an indisputable historical fact. Rather, instrumentalists suggest that ethnicity is first and foremost a resource in the hands of leaders to mobilize followers in pursuits of other interests such as physical security, economic gain, or political power.[2] What both the schools agree on is that ethnicity has a number of tangible aspects such as common history, customs, traditions, language or religion? These are important components of an individual's ethnic identity because these markers make it possible to establish differences not only between individuals, but also between groups.

Sociological tradition displays a conceptual opposition between rationality and emotion. However, Steve Fenton notes that in popular discourse there is little doubt that ethnic attachments and identities are seen as belonging to the realm of sentiments and 'belonging as a psychological bond'. Ethnic sentiments may be seen as not only non-rational, but also as defining rationally—that is, despite the gains to be made by acting in a non-ethnic way, people choose to act ethnically.[3] It is interesting to note that prior to current ethnic studies, it was Soviet anthropologists and American sociologists, who pioneered ethnic studies in their respective countries. While Soviet ethnographers found the study of ethnos at the local and regional levels politically safe enough in the then USSR, Nathan Glazer and Daniel Moynihan in USA popularized ethnicity through their famous work, *Beyond the Melting Pot* in 1970s. For Glazer and Moynihan ethnicity is real and it is the felt basis of political and social actions.

Ilan Peleg drew some general conclusions on ethnicity after evaluating the 'theoretical, comparative and historical analysis of pluralist regimes. They may be identified as the following:

(1) In contemporary world, majority political elites in ethnically divided societies are under increasing pressure to treat minorities equally, democratically, and sensitively. Heavy-handed ethnic oppressions are almost universally condemned and it is likely to backfire.

(2) The pressure on political elites to find new solutions for ethnic problems is especially intense when there is resistance (often among both, majority and minority) to either assimilation or integration. Consociational solutions then become attractive. These are solutions that focus on difference-management rather than difference-elimination and many (moves) are group based.

(3) A liberal solution to the ethnic dilemma—granting all individuals equality under the law—is a necessity but frequently insufficient condition for long term stability in a society plagued by long term division.

(4) What is often required in divided societies plagued by violence is a transformative constitutional settlement granting the major groups in society collective rights: language rights, equal or at least significant share in the polity's economic resources, protected political representation, etc.

(5) Creative solutions of that nature are, of course, not a firm guarantee for long term political stability. In fact, several consociational deals have collapsed over last 35 years. But without consociational solutions, all hopes for stability are gone.

(6) The challenge to consociationism is likely to come from two places:
   (a) Radical groups within the minority that reject any deal with the 'oppressive majority' and demand full independence.
   (b) Conservative groups within the majority that are afraid, often irrationally, of losing power and, even more so, of allowing the polity to change its fundamental character.[4]

Writing in early 1990s, the then Director General of the Anthropological Survey of India K.S. Singh found ethnicity in India generally being interpreted as recognition of rights of the community to maintain its identity, of pluralism, a return to the roots of life and culture, for a participative democracy, and for a genuine federal and decentralized polity. Furthermore, he noted that 'ethnicity in India generally means tribal ethnicity, which is largely concerned with articulation of tribal aspirations for political power through creation of autonomous areas or separate state'.[5]

Nobel laureate Amartya Sen terms human identification as 'solitarist view'. For him it is thought to be formed by the membership to a single social group categorized in terms of religion, caste, class, language, ethnicity, nationality or civilization. He diagnoses that it is the solitarist view that has come to shape and influence much of the dynamics of polity and identity-based violence, especially because one's identity is constructed and sustained by a series of contrasts and exclusions. To further their own selfish ends, politicians, priests and fundamentalists viciously cultivate violence, create factions and set people against one another. Violence is often used not only to hurt, terrorize and kill those who are perceived as enemies or outsiders, but also as a strategy to increase the popular support base for extremist ideology and to convert and convince the moderates within their fold. However, when the governments and their apparatus such as the police and the armed forces are inefficient, partisan or on the verge of collapse, people are forced to turn to identify factions to fill up the lacuna.[6]

Sen proposes a theory of identity, which should be informed and enriched by two important traits: (i) plural and multi-layered identity, and (ii) "reasoned choice" in prioritizing the relevance of various identities. Firstly, the answer to "who are we" and "who are they" may have different levels and layers. In his view it is wrong to define multiple and plural nature of identities in terms of single, unchanging essence. This paves the way for a "miniaturization" of humanity, as if every one is segregated into separate little caves, emerging only to attack each other. It also amounts to a politics of singular identity, which is incapable of appreciating the fact that human beings are able to rise above narrow confines of group identities in order to recognize and respond to fellow human beings. Secondly, by "reasoned choice" in prioritizing the relevance of the various identities, he suggests a catalogue of identities to describe, self and others, but not all of the identities enjoy the same status. Consciously or unconsciously, these identities that a person has come to share acquire a hierarchy of importance and relevance.

Nation and Nationality

The concept of nationality shares with ethnicity the vague notion of a common descent among its members. Benedict Anderson defines nation as 'an imagined community, both inherently limited and sovereign'. The idea of a nation is at first sight a unifying idea across the segmental and regional divides. Historian William H. McNeil argued that nations and nationalism were peculiar phenomena of modern European history from about 1789 to 1945, which he termed as the Age of Western Modernity, when the idea of national unity held sway and modern nation-state was accepted as a political norm. In his view, before and after that phase, poly-ethnic hierarchy was the norm in the history of Europe.[7] It was about 1700 AD that the idea of independent nation-states based on ethnic homogeneity emerged in Europe. There were four factors responsible for such a development: (i) influence of classical humanism, and hence civic solidarity found in classical city-states like Athens, Sparta and Republic of Rome, capturing the imagination of the intellectuals, (ii) growth of reading public verses in standardized vernacular languages such as French, English, German and the like forming the future governing elite, (iii) rapid growth of population in Europe fuelling revolutionary discontent among surplus labour, and (iv) emphasis on modern infantry drill indicative of state allied new sense of civil solidarity and fraternity.

Ernest Gellner believes that nations should have state systems, which give formal expression and autonomy to their nationhood. Conversely, states are nations composed of people with a claim to common culture and ancestry[8] and nationalism is the doctrine of promoting the correspondence of nation and state. Gellner raises three questions with respect to nation-states with a bearing on ethnicity. The first is that the concept of nation raises the same questions as the ethnic groups: how far do we regard nation as grounded in social reality and how far is it the construction or invention of political imagination of the groups whose interest they serve? Second, the formation of the states as nation-states implies the cultural definition of an ethnic majority, that is, within the concept of nation is an idea, which may be more or less explicit, of who and what composes the nation. In a narrow ancestral or even biological idea of the nation, either multiethnicity within the nation is excluded, or minority ethnicities are defined as less than full members. Third, the construction of purportedly homogeneous nation-states has never been perfect. If ethnic identities define nations, ethnicity may define citizenship within nation-states.

Wolf notes that for states and ethnic groups alike, territories possess certain values in itself, which may include ownership of natural resources, goods and services produced by the populations living in the territory, and military and strategic advantages derived from it. Not for nothing, wars have been fought over territories since ancient times. Moreover, nationalism is not necessarily tied to ethnicity. From this perspective, one may distinguish between civic and ethnic varieties of nationalism.

This differentiation often goes hand in hand with a moral judgment: civil nationalism is deemed to be more virtuous and liberal, whereas ethnic nationalism is generally seen as dangerous and explosive.[9]

Moreover, the core nationalist ideology is the conviction that the nations, and the state that represents the nation, embody a people's deepest and most abiding values that destiny of individuals is indissolubly linked to the fate of their undivided loyalty and devotion. Moreover, nationalism has given birth to three different versions, each implying different structure of the state to which it corresponds. The first is the ethno-nationalism, the belief that any people that aspires to political self-determination and self-rule is a nation and as such is entitled to independent statehood. The second version of it is identified with civic nationalism, a territorial concept, defining the nation as all persons regardless of ethnic provenance, who accept the duties and responsibilities of citizenship. What binds them together as a political community is not their ethnic origin, but rather their commitment to a common set of political institutions, political values and way of life. Third, in a multi-national state that includes two or more nations, syncretic nationalism is an ideology that attempts to construct a new, inclusive national sentiment that will subordinate and eventually supplant the original national sentiments of its component peoples. Bi-national and multi-national states encompass within their boundaries two or more peoples, who consider them to be distinct nations, but choose voluntarily or are compelled to function as component of a larger state.

Nation and State

Nationalism is, in view of Ernest Gellner, primarily a political principle, which presupposes that political and national units should ideally be the same. Nationalism as a sentiment and as a movement arouses anger on its violation and satisfaction on its fulfilment. Furthermore, nationalism is the theory of political legitimacy, which is frequently asserted in an ethical and universalistic spirit. Naturally, these stipulations lead us to a discussion on state. And for that, one naturally turns to Max Weber's celebrated definition of the state as that agency within society, which possesses the monopoly of legitimate violence, i.e., only the state has absolute legitimate coercive power with a view to establish social order by controlling the violence. Furthermore, social management all through historical times helped the ethnic groups and nations come under institutionalized state systems. Today state is a universal institution spread all over the world and its various aspects are well established and recognized. Modern state has a distinctly defined territory, legally identified body of citizens, a constitutionally sanctioned government and an internationally recognized sovereignty to take its own decisions within its own boundaries. It is man in society for whom the institution of state has been envisaged, but in the process, it has emerged much larger and powerful in its structure, reducing him to insignificance.

Lord Bhikhu Parikh, while incorporating the above points, reformulates them and also makes some additions, which qualifies the state systems more elaborately:[10]

(1) The state is fixed in space. It is identified with and claims proprietary jurisdiction over a specific area.
(2) It is sovereign, that is, it is an autonomous source of all legal authority exercised within its territory, no area of social life within its bounds in principle is immune to its jurisdiction, and it is not subject to the legal control of an external or internal power.
(3) It is formally independent of society, and mediates the relation between the individual and the society on the one hand and the government on the other.
(4) The modern state is a legal institution, constituted in terms of and speaking in the language of the general and uniform laws of varying degrees of generality and of legal force.
(5) It is not a community of communities but as association of socially abstract individuals, who constitute its ultimate ontological units, enjoy equal rights and obligations, and are subject to a uniform system of law.
(6) It enjoys the monopoly of the authority to use physical force.
(7) The major institutions of the modern states are professionalized and are run like closed corporations by trained men and women in a technical language.
(8) As an autonomous institution, the state relies on its own institutional resources to perform such functions as the maintenance of order, punishment of crime, provision of education and basic social welfare services.
(9) It is constructed and run from top downwards rather than bottom upwards as it is expected in an organization that began as an apparatus of ruling under absolute monarchy.

In the light of the above discussion, one finds that the Indian Union is a universally recognized state, divided sub-nationally among 'states' and union territories. Constitutionally, it is a federal state system with a strong central authority. It prides itself on its multi-ethnic, multi-lingual, plural and secular credentials. It has made special legal and constitutional provisions for enlistment of the weaker segments of the Indian society by identifying them as Scheduled Tribes, Scheduled Castes and Other Backward Classes. The state claims to treat regional, linguistic and religious minorities with care. Its constitution guarantees fundamental rights to its citizens and it is committed to an over-all improvement of the living conditions of the Indian masses through 'directive principles' of the Constitution. The state does not discriminate among its citizens on the basis of ethnicity, language, religion, region or race. Formally, it is a secular, socialist republic committed to the welfare of the Indian masses.

Identity and Nationality of the INO

In view of the above discussion, where do the INOs stand? Are they a distinct ethnic group? How do they identify themselves? How are they identified by others? Are they collectively an ethnic group or are they separately distinct ethnic groups? Are there symptoms/attributes that suggest that they have graduated to a level of nation such as Naga/ Assamiya/Bengali within the state? Are INOs consciously engaged in carving out a distinct Indian identity? Have they charted out a vision for their future in India? If it is so, what does it look like? What are its attributes?

The emergence of nation-states called India and Nepal has created this anomalous status of the INOs, or Nepamul Bharatiya, who are also known as 'Gorkhas' and/or 'Nepalis'. The Nepalese and the Indian Nepalis have been travelling and residing in various parts of India since time immemorial in pursuit of trade, pilgrimage and other vocations. In the past, concepts of state boundary and nationality were flexible enough to overlook the migrants. However, the British colonialists, who adopted a deliberate policy of large-scale recruitment of the Nepalese in the armed forces and constabulary, coolie corps, plantation and forest labour force, also gave birth to the crisis of INOs. From the second quarter of nineteenth century, the British opened up Darjeeling, Sikkim, Duars, Bhutan, and Assam for the Nepalese settlement. And that was the beginning of an organized colonization and extensive presence of the Nepalese in certain pockets of Northeast India.

Most Nepamul Bharatiya writers from Northeast India claim that there was a close ethnic link between the region and Nepal in the past. In their treatment, history of Nepal remained static and ancient Northeast meant the Brahmaputra valley at the most. The problem is that they are not able to prove their point through any conclusive historical data or through a genealogical reconstruction. So, ancient ties remain at best notional. Even if it was historically true, it does not contradict the fact that extensive immigration of the Nepamul Bharatiya occurred during the British period, especially after the Anglo-Nepalese War of 1814-15 and precisely after the Anglo-Burmese War of 1826. They did come as soldiers of fortune to begin with and their settlements could be located on strategically significant landmarks around the British settlements and army cantonments. In the much quoted phrase of the Duke of Wellington, these soldiers from the martial race were, in fact, 'men from the lower classes, who could be bullied, flogged and drilled into subordinating their humanity to rhythm of the guns'.[11] The second set of immigrants were the herdsmen, graziers, dairymen, lumber jacks and other sundry men, who could not be employed in the armed forces. Laws of migration were flexible and issue of nationality was not at all as nagging as it is now. Immigrants, though favoured by the colonial rulers, had to work hard under trying circumstances. Their settlements in the region are success stories of human struggle over natural and man-made obstacles. No doubt, among the coloured underdogs, Nepalese were the favoured ethnic stock of the white colonial rulers. Willy-nilly, they came to be identified as the "sahibs' faithful boys". But it must be added that there were other ethnic groups, which competed for such a distinction.

In the aftermath of 1979 anti-foreigner agitation waged by the All Assam Students' Union (AASU), a seminar was held on "Violence and Conflict in North East India" in June 1980 in Shillong where I presented a paper on the Nepamul Bharatiya in Northeast India. I concluded that 'the Nepalese may get themselves organized to preserve, propagate, and even increase their ethnic solidarity. And this newly acquired Nepalese solidarity would naturally clash with the heightened expectations of the host communities in North East India'.[12]

What hurts the Nepamul sentiments most is to learn that a democratic and predominantly Hindu India does not accord them the status of cultural associate communities like Marathi, Kannad, and Gujarati. The problem is this: India treats the INOs largely the way Nepal treats NIOs in Nepal. Worse still, those born and brought up in India and the immigrants from Nepal are both accorded the same status as a peripheral community, with an opaque status of some one so close, but still not meaningfully connected.[13] Hence, often angry demands are made by the Nepamul

Bharatiya to do away Clause 7 of the Indo-Nepalese Peace and Friendship Treaty, 1950. It appears that the Nepamul Bharatiya presume that once they are separated from the immigrant Nepalese, they will automatically be treated at par with other Indians. One hopes that such expectation comes true, but prejudice, social distance/closeness etc. are irrational and it cannot be formally erased over night.

Echoing the above sentiments, T.B. Subba notes that Nepamul Bharatiya in Northeast India will have to struggle as other Indians to find space for them: 'The political aspirations of the Nepalis in Northeast India are therefore woven around the struggle for equal economic and political rights as other Indian citizens. Such aspirations have often taken very long to be fulfilled or have remained unfulfilled even today. The most important reason for this is lack of a strong ethnic solidarity among them. Their ethnicity is actually much weaker than what is made out to be. The historical, racial, cultural, spatial, and now class and occupational, variations have been successful in acting as a deterrent to the emergence of a strong ethnic solidarity among them'.[14]

Painting rather a depressing picture of the INO's existence in general and in Northeast India in particular, Subba warns the community to get ready for a long drawn struggle for getting their due delivered. 'With more and more indigenous people competing for the various limited resources in the region, the Nepalis will have to prepare themselves to face more hostile environment in future. The possibilities of such hostilities growing in future are fairly certain and they will increasingly have to remain at the mercy of local communities and state governments. New Delhi is not only physically very far, but it is psychologically insensitive. The Nepalis will learn to adapt and live where they are, but not leave (the region). And leave, if they must, they will return soon after, as they did in Assam in 1979 and in Meghalaya in 1987'.[15]

After examining the implications of citizenship and nationality of the Nepalis in Southasia, Michael Hutt finds that a Nepali or a Gorkha born in India is liable to be assumed to be foreign nationals or immigrants in India and all types of sinister political motives are imputed to their leaders for that. Interestingly, he links status of Nepamul Bharatiya in India to that of the Madhesis in Nepal, which none of the Nepamul Bharatiya leaders has considered so far. This is a point that demands serious consideration for the future of the inter-ethnic relationship in Southasia, and what the volume does in this regard is only symbolic of what should be done. Though his concern is much broader, he concludes: 'The simple fact of the matter is that a Newar or a Limbu born in

Darjeeling, Bhutan or Assam will always be considered "Nepali" ', even if he or she adopts the label "Gorkha" or "Lhotshampa", just as Bihari or Marwari, who has no home other than Kathmandu, will always be considered "Indian". Through out this century, Indian Nepalis have struggled to forge an identity for themselves that distinguishes them from the Nepalese of Nepal, so that they might emerge as a distinct ethnic group within India for, ...'ethnic identity had become an organizational form, a weapon, a tool. And/or a means for the attainment of goals'.[16]

The term Lhotshampa has a distinct meaning today and is understood in the same sense by the people who are so referred to, as by the Royal Government of Bhutan, which coined the term. It is, however, unfortunate that although the word was coined in 1975, it came in currency only after the Lhotshampas' flight from Bhutan to the refugee camps in Nepal in early 1990s. The academic, litterateurs, public men, etc all now agree that it has clarified the situation so far as the identity of the Bhutanese of Nepalese extraction is concerned.

Similar clarification is awaited for the INOs. Efforts were made in the past to find a more appropriate term that would largely be acceptable to all INOs and carry adequate, precise, and unambiguous understanding of the community. Subba informs that terms such as Bhargoli and Bharpali were suggested, but they could not catch the imagination of the people. He refers to two more terms: Gorkha and Nepali and describes their context, exponents and opponents.[17] Some of us may recollect the acrimonious panel discussion on 'crisis of nomenclature' in the community on April 21, 2006 at Chintan Bhawan, Gangtok. It is apparent that the community is emotionally and politically divided on the issue. There are strong exponents of term 'Nepali' across India and elsewhere and there are equally strong supporters of 'Gorkha,' especially in the Darjeeling hills. The issue became so emotive that a senior and highly respected academic from the community taking part in the panel discussion felt like signing an affidavit saying that he was neither a Nepali nor a Gorkha. Both Gorkha and Nepali have their strong and weak aspects and it is indeed difficult to resolve the issue.

The writer of these lines has, in course of his researches in Sikkim, Bhutan and the INO, added to the confusion by injudiciously using 'Nepalese' to refer on the INOs. In his recent study, he has tried to rectify the unintended conceptual injury to the theme.[18] He notes an utter confusion about the term 'Nepalese' in literature, every day use and government documents. Naturally, the term 'Nepalese' denotes the people or language of Nepal. But the problem is that the term is used in a very loose sense, referring to any body who speaks Nepali or whose ancestors had been 'Nepalese'. This situation is not confined to the laymen; even the governments of India, Nepal and Bhutan do not maintain a consistent difference between the 'Nepalese' and the Indian or Bhutanese of Nepalese origin. Further more, the members of the community, i.e., the progenies of Nepalese origin themselves add to the problem, as they have not been able to evolve a consensus on appropriate nomenclature for their community. And, there are many 'Nepalese' in Sikkim, Bihar, Uttaranchal and West Bengal who or whose ancestors had not migrated from Nepal and they had been residents of these regions for centuries.

Awareness has dawned since 1970s among the INOs that they must display their distance from the 'Nepalese', the citizens of Nepal. And efforts were made to coin terms describing the INOs as Bhargoli, Bharpali, and Gorkha, but till date consensus has eluded the community. I used the term Nepamul Bharatiya in 2001 but it has not been accepted either. Many of Nepamul Bharatiya scholars and political activists use the term 'Nepali' or 'Gorkha' but unfortunately these two terms have polarized the community in two opposite and even somewhat hostile camps. I think the term 'Nepali' has problems on account of the similarity between the Nepalis in India, Bhutan and Nepal. Whatever is the new proposed term must not send confusing signals and it should be, if not universally, largely acceptable to most of the people concerned. The term 'Gorkha' is strongly projected by people of Darjeeling and a regional political party called Gorkha National Liberation Front (GNLF). It is associated with the Gorkha (Gurkha) soldiers, Gorkha kingdom of Shah dynasty, subjects of Gorkha kingdom, followers of Baba Gorakhnath, and Gorkha watchmen in the Indian metropolis. So, in this chaotic situation, I have referred to the people in question as INO or Nepamul Bharatiya.

History of the INOs

There were several push factors such as the grinding poverty and repressive regime in the Rana-ruled Nepal and a set of pull factors like jobs in armed forces, plantations, forests and a variety of opportunities in the urban centres and a relatively better, secured, and varied prospect compared to Nepal for creating a category I call INO. A considerable number of high caste Nepalese had moved as herdsmen to the marginal forestlands in Northeast India as graziers. In course of time, they turned out to be the industrious peasant cultivators and pioneering dairymen of the region. No doubt, some of the migrants found it more rewarding to stay back in their new place of work in India. When the British withdrew from India in 1947, they left behind a legacy of the Nepalese settlers in Northeast India. This legacy had two types: one in uniform and another in *mufti*.

Unfortunately for the Nepamul Bharatiya, the enlightened Indian public opinion invariably saw them standing behind the British colonialist masters during the Indian freedom struggle. Naturally, the first crop of policy makers tended to develop an attitude of ambivalence towards them. Moreover, lack of an articulate and effective leadership from within, who could have informed the Indian public opinion on the contributions of the community, further added to the postponement of a positive assessment of Nepamul Bharatiya in the eyes of Indian policy makers. And thus, the Nepamul Bharatiya were taken for granted as collaborators in the process of Indian development, and at the worst, an irritant, but they were never considered as a threat to the Indian cause. To add to their woes, Indo-Nepalese Treaty of Friendship, 1950 stipulated that Indians and Nepalese would be permitted to travel, work and settle in each other's country in an unrestricted way. This provision further confused the Indian masses about the century-old Nepamul Bharatiya with transient Nepalese seasonal migrants.

The Nepamul Bharatiyas are alleged to have double citizenship: Nepalese and Indian. It is argued that the Nepamul Bharatiyas invariably look to Nepal as their cultural and social fount and their loyalty to Nepal is unflinching. They are also suspected to be forerunners of the 'Greater Nepal' ambition, nursed by an insignificant segment of the Nepalese. In this context, it will not be out of place to remind our readers the issue of recognition of Nepali language by the Government of India. It was kept hanging for over a decade because of the denial of a reciprocal gesture of according recognition to Hindi, the official national language of the Indian Republic, by the then Royal Government of Nepal. There may be more of this type of litany, but the sane voice among the Nepamul Bharatiya have been ultimately able to convince their fellow Indian citizens of the genuineness of their cause and their concern for the country.

1970s brought a mixed bag of events with far-reaching developments for Northeast India in general and for the INOs in particular: emergence of Bangladesh, UN membership for the Royal Government of Bhutan, death of King Mahendra, anti-Chogyal agitation in Sikkim and its merger with India and a variety of ethnic assertion movements. It was also a period in Indian history that had two "wooden" prime ministers with limited patience to understand the nuances of Northeast India. And thus, they further added to the ethnic muddle already existing by their careless comments on the events and issues without assessing the consequences. One of the outcomes of this confused and uncared scenario was a series of ethnic expulsions of the Nepamul Bharatiyas from the region, GNLF movement in Darjeeling and flight of the Lhotshampas from Bhutan in late 1980s to India and refugee camps in Nepal.

What resulted in was a massive human tragedy. The Nepamul Bharatiya and Lhotshampas suffered untold misery: violence against their life and assets, eviction and forced expulsion from their home and hearth, and denial of basic human rights as ordinary citizens. The community found no effective voice of protest in their favour against their sufferings. They found no spokesmen to articulate their grievances and no body raised the issue of their continuous expulsion from their home and hearth on the floor of the Indian parliament. Moreover, otherwise known for their investigative skills, the Indian communication media also maintained a deafening silence by their near non-coverage. Public men, media, intelligentsia, political parties, civic bodies and other agencies of the open society and vibrant Indian democracy maintained a distance from the plight of the Nepamul Bharatiya and Lhotshampas, as though they are not even human beings. Otherwise, how do we explain the non-concern of the Indian intellectuals and civil society about a hundred and twenty-five thousand Lhotshampa refugees languishing for the last two decades in the eastern Nepal refugee camps?

Why This Book?

Some of us at North-Eastern Hill University, Shillong, decided in mid-1990s to hold a seminar with a view to assemble concerned activists, academics, intellectuals among Nepamul Bharatiyas to assess their existing scenario in Northeast India. We consciously left Sikkim and Darjeeling and other INO-inhabited areas, as those places have their histories and predicaments different from those living in the region in question.

When the event actually took place despite all odds it was an experience to witness the enthusiasm of the first generation young scholars from among the INOs of the region. About two dozen presentations were made and there were a number of issues, which were debated and we came to certain consensus and there were others on which no agreement could be reached. There were senior intellectuals among the participants, who could prevail on a number of emotive issues projected by the young impatient participants. The proceedings were conducted in English and Nepali and there were informed and occasionally emotional deliberations. With a view to disseminating the contents of the seminar to a larger audience, we decided to publish it in English. The proceedings were edited and were published in course of time.[19] That publication turned out to be the first authentic document on the life, literature, history, culture, and economy of the community.

One of the views of the participants of the Shillong seminar was to hold an all India INO meet to deliberate on their identity and nationality on a national level. Thus, a seminar was conceived and organized in Gangtok in April 2006, which would not be successful without the financial and other supports of the government of Sikkim and special patronage of the chief minister, Dr. Pawan Chamling. The present book comprises about one third of the papers presented at the national conference held in Gangtok.

We the editors worked hard to bring out this book because we are convinced that it will fill up a vital gap in the literature on the INOs. It is a fact that no one knows how many Nepalis live in India today—the claim ranging from 5 to 10 millions—but the number is certainly substantial in states like Sikkim, West Bengal, and Assam compared to their population in Meghalaya, Nagaland, Mizoram, and Manipur in Northeast India and Uttaranchal in central Himalayas. The reasons for their migration and settlement are different in different parts of the country, although there are some common strands as well, of which the British admiration for them as brave soldiers in war and hardy and loyal workers in peace times was perhaps the most important. The duration of their settlement also varies from place to place, group to group, and from family to family. So does their legal status as citizens of India, the privileges they have access to, their vocations, their adaptation to local languages and cultures, etc. So also does the perception of the neighbouring communities about them in general, their attitude and character, their identity and culture, their languages and the Nepali lingua-franca, and so on. There is so much of racial, linguistic, historical, and cultural variation in them that it is difficult to make any generalisation about them at all India level. It is not possible to say anything with any degree of confidence until one knows about their number, status, problems, apprehensions, predicament, and opportunities from different parts of India. It is also important to know why they are often evicted en masse from Northeast India and what challenges they face in Darjeeling-Sikkim Himalayas where they are numerically significant.

This book builds on the 'red book' on Northeast India, as the book edited by A.C. Sinha and T.B. Subba are referred to but seeks to widen its scope in terms of issues it seeks to debate on all-India level. Two most important but inter-related issues are their identity and nationality. Howsoever old their settlement in a particular place may be they are categorised together with the ones who arrive from Nepal on any day in search of seasonal employment or for recruitment in India's military or para-military forces. Their claims to historicity, Kirata identity, and sacrifice of lives for their motherland called India, their adherence to a different Nepali dialect from that of Nepal, and the prominent traces of local cultures in their cultures are not at all enough to stake their claim for Indian nationality. They are religiously branded as "foreigners" and "migrants" and deprived even of some basic human rights like right to life and livelihood in times of ethnic conflict between them and their neighbours in Northeast India. They are nicknamed *Daju*s (coolies or porters), *Bahadur*s (chowkidars) and *Kanchha*s (household servants). If they raise any demands—literary, political or economic—they are often told to go to Nepal, as the Governor of Assam did recently. The Indian media, particularly the film media that has such a large presence in Indian psyche, is rarely neutral to them.

Similar is perhaps the situation of the Nepalis of Indian origin in Nepal, and in certain respects perhaps even worse, although in terms of physical eviction they are certainly better off than the Nepalis in Northeast India. Whatever may be comparative status of them their fates are inter-connected, as if by an umbilical cord. What the former suffer from in India the latter suffer from in Nepal. In other words, the issues of identity and nationality not only engage the minds of the Nepalis in India but also the Indians in Nepal. Will they ever be full-fledged citizens of the countries they are living in even if they qualify to be so constitutionally? Will they form a category called "constitutional citizens" whereas they remain foreigners, migrants and outsiders in the psyche of the "real citizens"? The present book seeks to find some answers, no matter how tentative, to such questions as well.

Organization of the Book

In all, the book contains 26 articles, including Introduction and Conclusion. There are three foreigners, seven women, and rest of the authors hail from 10 states of the Indian Union. The book has been divided into five sections on the basis of the thrust of the articles and concerns of the authors, though there are chapters that may conveniently be put in sections other than where they are put in this volume.

The first section is titled "Conceptual and Theoretical Issues", which includes five chapters that address the key issues of the conference. For instance, the first chapter by Michael Hutt takes recourse to about half a dozen literary sources, informs the readers how Lil Bahadur Chhetri (*Basai*), Lainsingh Bangdel (*Muluk Bahiro*), Govinda Raj Bhattarai (*Muglan*), Ganusingh Gurung (*Yatra*) and Indra Bahadur Rai (*Hami Jastai Mainaki Ama*) have tackled the sense of sufferings in Nepal, a picture of better opportunity in India, a sense of migration and a sense of insecurity. He beautifully ends his presentation with Agam Singh Giri's lyrical poem expressing a sense of pride in being a Nepali. In the next chapter, Pravesh Jung Golay addresses three related themes pertaining to Nepali ethnic identity: the way human beings formulate and classify 'things' encountered, relationship between class and identity, and latter's identification by 'others' and one's situatedness in terms of history.

In this context, Goutam Biswas takes up another aspect of identity formation. He talks about a shift from convergence of ideas to lived-in experience in ethics of communication and suggests that the narratives of Nepalis should be seen as 'little narratives'. And for that he cites Pawan Chamling's 'Sky of Nationality' (*Rastriyatako Akash*) as an example. Bidhan Golay finds the question of identity saddled with academic and political discourses. He finds two levels of Gorkha identity: an individual Gorkha as an inseparable part of the colonial discourse and community's historical experience of de-territorialized subjectivity leading to two conflicting impulses of primordiality and demands of modern nation state. By taking recourse to history and literature, he pleads for 'a post-national' or a Southasian Gorkha identity. Tapasya Thapa makes a distinction between 'being' and 'belonging' as a Nepali in India. The author finds Nepalis constituting a minority without any privilege of being a minority like Muslims and Anglo-Indians. She argues that unless the community knows what constitutes being a Nepali/Gorkhali, no solution to the nomenclature crisis of the community will be possible.

The second section is devoted to 'Search for Indian National Identity'. It consists of five papers. In a thought provoking presentation on 'Education, Institutions and Elites Bonding of Nepali Public in Early 20th Century', Rhoderick Chalmers charts out the evolution of Indian Nepali public as an increasingly assertive middle class, challenging the power hierarchy within Nepali society. This process led to inclusion of some and exclusion of other segments of society. Keeping this over-all context in view, the chapter examines three crucial areas: the development of formal education, building of social and cultural institutions and composition of a nascent Nepali civil society. The author exhibits how the development of a modern public culture challenged social structure and models of authority, prompting a struggle for control over language norms and language system. The significant point the author makes at the end deserves serious consideration of the Nepali intelligentsia: 'the process of public negotiation of shared cultural attributes that emerged in this period (in Darjeeling) were both new and crucial to the definition of a modern sense of Nepaliness'. In the next chapter, Rajendra P. Dhakal explains the nuances of the Indian Nepali sub-nationalism in Darjeeling, shows how search for a Gorkha identity is characterized by a strong sense of insecurity, and it is not antithetical to Indian nationalism and national integration, and makes a strong plea for recognition as an equal and proud Indians. Similarly, Ranju R. Dhamala notes two different trends of identity formation in Darjeeling and Sikkim. Further, she finds that various shades of Nepali movements are addressed to identity assertion as a part of broader Indian identity.

Vimal Khawas begins by raising the question: 'Why do the Indians confuse the Nepalis with the Nepalese?' In his view, to address the issues of the two sets of Nepali speakers (Nepalis and Nepalese), certain factors need to be debated. First, the Indo-Nepalese Treaty of Friendship, 1950 need to be looked afresh. Secondly, one has to think how to separate the Indian Nepalis from the Nepalese migrants to Indian metropolitan centres. Shrawan Acharya explores the variety of causes of Nepali ethnic assertion, identifies positive and negative consequences of such developments and suggests a public policy intervention based on cultural planning to mitigate the negative consequences of the Nepali ethnic assertion. He identifies structural inequality, issue of the Constitutional reservation policy and increasing awareness, exposure to media and equalitarian ideas as important reasons for intra-Nepali ethnic assertions. He concludes his presentation with a plea for harnessing the positive public initiatives for treating Nepali sub-cultures as resources and for that Community Based Organizations (CBOs) should be encouraged.

The third section is on regional identities of the Indian Nepalis. The first article in this section by T.N. Upadhyaya notes that though the literary journey of the Nepalis in the region began much earlier, Dhan Bahadur Rai's *Ek Thanga Phool* (1928) is considered to be the earliest Nepali novel in Northeast India. Then he examines Lil Bahadur Chhetri's series of novels as a major source of regional Nepali history depicting their psyche, style of life, economy, family life, stories of exploitation, and a variety of contributions to local economy through their hard labour on the jobs normally not undertaken by the regional indigenous communities. Similarly, K.B. Nepali's *Mero Ghar, Mero-Sansar* depicts gory images of 1987 anti-Nepali communal riots in Meghalaya. At last, he informs how Chandrashwar Dube's novels have described the trials and tribulations of Nepalis in the region. Ultimately, Upadhyaya laments that it has been more than a century since the Nepalis settled in the region, but even today the problems faced by them remain the same. The dominant theme in most of the literary works continues to be the problem of food and shelter. The question of our political identity remains unresolved to this day. In the next article D. Sapkota reports on Nepali settlements and Cattle Rearing in the Northeast region. It is an interesting chapter depicting lives of herdsmen, their economy, ethnography of settlements, rules and procedures for cattle grazing, and introduction of dairy business in the region.

K.L. Pradhan highlights the unique problems faced by the Gorkhas in Mizoram. He notes that the Gorkhas settled in the state prior to 1950 were recognized as bonafide residents of the state with all the rights but the problems emerged when the Nepalese began to come in search of jobs after 1950. The Mizos could not distinguish between the new comers and old settlers and feared being overwhelmed by the migrants. Hence they pressurized the government of Mizoram to withdraw in 1980 the special privileges accorded to the Gorkhas of the state. The old settlers are still fighting to get those privileges restored. Amena Passah enlightens the readers on how the Nepali society was established in Meghalaya and on some of their internal contradictions. She notes that the British intrusion and advent of the Nepalis in Meghalaya went hand in hand. The Nepali adage: 'dress according to the place you are in' is indicative of their extensive assimilation with the local tribal communities at all the levels. She also traces the history of their settlements, anti-Nepali riots of 1987, alienation of the Nepalis from the dominant tribal context and specific plight of the Nepali Christians.

With Nira Devi's chapter on history of Nepali settlements in Assam, the focus of this volume shifts from the hills to the plains. The author provides a brief history of Nepali settlement in Assam and settles down with a field study based data from a village from the Brahmaputra plains. She gives an interesting ethnography of Nepali settlement of Gangmouthan village, its social set-up, economy and interactive pattern between Nepalis and the Assamese villagers. Tejimala Gurung tells the story of Nepali coolies in upper Assam coal fields from 1907. The practice was simply a reminder of old indentured labour conscription from distant Nepal through a fraudulent system of recruitment. Though the number of Nepalis involved as colliers was not large the details provided by the author are indicative of the extent of inhuman exploitation of the Nepalis that took place in Assam during the colonial days.

The fourth section is a significant one. It addresses the issues of 'Nepali sub-cultures: youth, women, food and medicine' and contains four presentations. Anuradha Sharma surveyed the India Born Confused Nepali (IBCN) youths in April 2006 from Bhubaneshwar, Calcutta, Delhi, Goa and Mumbai on a number youth related issues. The findings were eye openers: the IBNC were not proud to be Nepali, had a laid back attitude to life, were reluctant to be part of the mainstream and suffered from an acute inability to dream. They were also critical of their elders, believed that state and the federal governments had not been able to protect their rights and many of them had misplaced loyalties to India and Nepal. They were equally divided on whether they were Nepalis or Gorkhas. With a view to addressing some of the above issues, the author suggests youth net-working. Sharda Chhetri undertook a study sponsored by Terre des hommes Foundation, Switzerland on the Nepali girls in red light areas in the metropolitan India. It was found that out of 200,000 Nepali girls in the red light areas, 25 per cent were from Sikkim, Darjeeling and Jalpaiguri. They are sold for anything between Rs. 70,000 and Rs. 100,000. She shows how the sex workers are in state of bondage, slavery and starvation. Their exodus to red light areas has increased since the advent of Maoist insurgency in Nepal. Among some of the reasons for their exodus were poverty, loss of traditional occupations, broken families, lure of films and easy life. The author's key finding of the study was that almost all Nepali girls had entered prostitution in a situation of slavery or debt bondage under the age of 18 years and at an average age of 14 to 16 years. A majority of them are trafficked by the Nepalese themselves and sold to the brothel owners in India.

Jyoti P. Tamang's chapter on food and identity touches an important aspect of the Nepamul life style. A typical food of an average Nepamul is *bhat-dal-tarkari-achar* (boiled rice, lentil soup, curry and pickles). Then he enumerates more than two dozen food items unique to Sikkim and Darjeeling. Moreover, there are as many as 80 types of common food and beverages found in Northeast region. They are a distinct cultural heritage of the country. D.R. Chhetri's chapter on 'Herbal Medicinal Culture of Nepalis of Darjeeling and Sikkim' finds that the traditional herbal medicine relates to health practices, approaches, knowledge and beliefs incorporating naturally available plants or plant products applied singularly or in combination with minerals, animal products, spiritual therapies etc. in order to diagnose, treat and prevent illnesses or maintain well-being. Traditional systems of medicine attempt to embody a holistic approach, i.e., viewing an individual in his totality with the socio-ecological system. The socio-ecological system remarkably influences the mental state of an individual which in turn alters the secretions of neurohormones etc. These secretions have profound physiological effects. Therefore, it is worthwhile to devise novel methods to evaluate the intriguing aspects of traditional medicine. About 70-75 per cent of Indian population is dependent on herbal medicine for primary health care because of better cultural acceptability, better compatibility with the human body and lesser side effect. Availability and cost-effectiveness are other reasons for its popularity. He identifies some of its drawbacks and makes suggestions to enrich them through research and better managerial styles.

The fifth and the last section on 'India-Nepal Linkages' contains four chapters. First of the four chapters in this section is contributed by Madhav P. Pokhrel on origin and development of Nepali language. It is an intensely researched article by one of the experts in the field. He traces the sources of its origin and informs that while Nepal had termed it "Gorkha Bhasha", it was the literary world of Darjeeling, which gave the nomenclature "Nepali" to the common language. The author acknowledges the singular roles played by educational institutions in Calcutta, Benaras, Darjeeling, and Shillong in development and standardization of Nepali. B.C. Upreti makes an important contribution in the form of chapter on 'India-Nepal Treaty of Peace and Friendship: Nature, Problems and Questions'. The author is of the view that the uniqueness of treaty has worn out and notes that there are demands in Nepal and India to revise, or even to abrogate it altogether. Then, he raises a number of questions: What are expectations of India and Nepal from this treaty? Where has it failed? Is it irrelevant today? To what extent can the treaty ensure identities of the Indians in Nepal and the Nepalese in India? Before trying to find answers to the above, he notes that characteristics of the treaty also has defense and security, economic and social aspects between the two countries to be kept in perspective. The author enumerates various ways in which Nepal violated the terms of the treaty. At the end, he raises two questions: Does the treaty separate two types of speakers of Nepali language: Nepalese and Nepalis? Does

Nepal want to revise/replace or abrogate the treaty? He finds no consensus either in Nepal or in India on these issues.

D.B. Chhetry's chapter on 'Nepalis and Bangladeshis: A Comparative Study' notes how Bangladeshis, who are illegal migrants are encouraged to settle in India whereas the Nepalis who India is treaty-bound to accept as its own nationals are subjected to ill-treatment. Last contribution in this section is on an important issue but utterly lost sight of, that is, 'The Shared Destiny: Indians of Nepalese Origin (INO) and Nepalese of Indian Origin (NIO)' by A.C. Sinha. After a thorough comparison between the Nepalis in India and Madhesis in Nepal, the author concludes:

> Nepal and India both continue to treat Madhesis and INOs in typically colonial style by denying the basic democratic rights and invariably treating them as non-existent citizens. The problem in India is that it is an open system, in which every ethnic group/ sub-nationality is to compete with others for political space and all types of resources. Though there are constitutional and political guarantees for equality among the communities/nationalities, this does not automatically ensure equality to be translated in reality. Thus, in practice, some are more equal than others in terms of their political role, economic affluence, cultural attainments, and over-all indicators of social development. The INOs represent a miniscule community tugged in an economically backward corner in India, who is suspected with Nepalese citizenship in the eyes of many Indians. Their problems too are not taken seriously as worthy of national deliberation, as they are considered transient settlers. Needless to add that the community itself has not been able to help itself by tactfully articulating its grievances in a democratic and peaceful way to persuade others to come round to the community's stand point. The INOs must know that in an open society such as India, no body is ranged against them; rather rest of the ethnic groups/nationalities are engaged in enhancing their own bargaining power. The best people to learn from are their Nepalese counterpart, the Madhesi under-dogs, who have forced the hill Bahun-Chhetri-Newar power wielders during the last six months to take note of the Madhesi demands and ensure corrective steps for their redressal.

'The Last Word So Far...' by T.B. Subba is in lieu of conclusion.

The process of churning that formally began in 2001 in Shillong culminated in the conference held in Gangtok and the result of our common endeavour is before the readers. It is for the readers to ponder over the issues laid bare here in this book, and help the intelligentsia to lead the society towards a desirable direction. The Nepali youths are angry, their intellectuals are confused, and their opinion makers have no clue. The present volume may show some direction to them all.

In the light of the above discussion, there is no doubt that the nationality of the Nepamul Bharatiya is Indian. There is also a consensus that they must be treated and seen as separate from the Nepalese and Lhotshampas. But how it can be achieved is not clear either to our contributors or to the policy makers. And we must evolve ways to separate the two sets of Nepali speakers—the Indian Nepalis and the Nepalese. Similarly, nomenclature of the community, which is crying for an answer, is an issue addressed by Subba in this volume but a consensus on the same is yet to evolve.

I am in agreement with my editorial colleagues, however, that the INO situation is not that bad and the very fact that we sat together to ponder over the issues faced by the community shows how vibrant is the actual ground reality. Perhaps what is not matching is the lack of concerted endeavours on the part of the intelligentsia, opinion leaders and youths to pull the community out of its uncertainty, apathy, and inactivity. May be, we meet again to take stock of the INO situation some years later somewhere.

REFERENCES

1. J. Stone and R. Dannis, 2003, *Race and Ethnicity: Comparative and Theoretical Approaches*, Oxford, Blackwell, p. 32.
2. S. Wolf, 2006, *Ethnic Conflict: A Global Perspective*, Oxford, Oxford University Press, pp. 33-34.
3. S. Feton, 2003, *Ethnicity, Racism, Class and Culture*, London, McMillan, p. 75.
4. I. Peleg, 2004, 'Transforming Ethnic Orders to Pluralistic Regimes' in *Democracy and Ethnic Conflict: Advancing Peace in Deeply Divided Societies*, edited by Adrian Geulke, Palgrave, McMillan, p. 21.
5. K.S. Singh, 1992, *Ethnicity, Caste and People*, New Delhi, Manohar, p. 21.
6. Amartya Sen, 2006, *Identity and Violence: The Vision of Destiny*, New York: W.W. Norton & Co.

7. W.H. McNeill, 1986, *Polyethnicity and National Unity in World History*, Toronto: Toronto University Press.
8. E. Gellner, 1983, *Nations and Nationalism*, Oxford: Blackwell, p. 171.
9. Wolf, *op. cit.*, p. 52.
10. B. Parikh, 1996, 'The Nature of Modern State' in *The Multiverse of Democracy*, edited by Ashis Nandy *et al*., New Delhi: Sage Publication, pp. 41-42.
11. D. Washburn, 2007, 'The Sacking of Delhi', *Biblio*, Vol. XII, Nos. 3 and 4, March-April, pp. 13-14.
12. A.C. Sinha, 1982, 'Nepalese in North East India: Ethnicity and Resource Appropriation' in *Social Tension in North-East India*, edited by J.B. Bhattacharjee, Shillong: North-East India Council of Social Science Research, p. 97.
13. A.C. Sinha, 1990, 'Indian North East Frontiers and Nepalese Immigrants' in *Himalayan Environment and Culture*, edited by N.K. Rustomji and C. Rambles, Shimla: Indian Institute of Advanced Studies.
14. T.B. Subba, 2003, 'Being a Nepali in Northeast India: Predicament of a 'Privileged Nation' in *The Nepalis in Northeast India: A Community in Search of Indian Identity,* edited by A.C. Sinha and T.B. Subba, New Delhi: Indus Publishing Company.
15. *Ibid.*
16. M. Hutt, 1997, 'Being Nepali without Nepal: Reflection on a South Asian Diaspora' in *Nationalism and Ethnicity in a Hindu Kingdom: The Politics of Culture in Contemporary Nepal,* edited by David Gellner, J. Pfaff-Czarnecka and J. Whelpton, Amsterdam: Harwood Academic Publishers, p. 125.
17. Subba, *op. cit.*
18. A.C. Sinha, 2008, *Politics of Sikkim: Direction and Destiny*, forthcoming.
19. A.C. Sinha and T.B. Subba, 2003, *Nepalis in North East India: A Community in Search of Indian Identity*, New Delhi: Indus Publishing Company, rpt. 2007.

2

Where is Home for an Indian Nepali Writer?

MICHAEL HUTT

> For the sake of politeness, they ask me about myself, and sometimes I tell them my profession, sometimes my *jat,* sometimes my religion. I do not feel reluctant to tell them such things. But when in the same context they ask me where my home is, then I am very hesitant.[1]

These lines from a modern short story encapsulate the ambivalent attitude adopted by Indian Nepali writers toward the notion of a 'homeland'. The political leaders of the ethno-linguistic community to which these writers belong have been engaged in a campaign for a recognised Nepali homeland within India for some 100 years (if one takes the first demand for a separate administrative set-up for Darjeeling as a starting point) but the literature the community has produced reflects a more sceptical stance on the part of Indian Nepali intellectuals.

In the Northeast of the Indian sub-continent, the Nepali-speaking community considers that it must struggle for safeguards against discrimination and in some areas physical expulsion, while the political leaders of the communities that neighbour it regard its presence as a growing threat to their control of local economic and political resources. It is perhaps not unusual for members of a minority community to experience a sense of insecurity, while outsiders are simultaneously unsettled by their presence. In autumn 1981, during my first visit to Darjeeling, two students were shot dead by police in the town's lower bazaar during a clash between rival demonstrators; the site of their death was marked by incense and flowers for weeks, possibly months afterward. Five years later, the Gorkhaland movement for a separate state within India began in earnest. One demand of the movement for which those two students, and many others subsequently, gave their lives, was for the constitutional recognition of the Nepali language in India, a demand that was eventually granted in 1992. It was difficult for an uninformed visitor to understand the depth of feeling that underpinned this movement, or the socio-political reasons for it. As Antony Smith remarks,

> Those whose identities are rarely questioned and who have never known exile or subjugation of land or culture, have little need to trace their 'roots'... Yet theirs is only an implicit and unarticulated form of what elsewhere must be shouted from the roof-tops: 'We belong, we have a unique identity, we know it by our ancestry and history'[2]

The ancestors of India's Nepalis left Nepal between 100 and about 190 years (if one counts from the Anglo-Nepal war, which marked the departure of large number of able-bodied Nepalese) ago to seek a better life for themselves. After the Shah kings' conquest of the eastern hills of Nepal during the late 18th century and the imposition of harsh new taxes, district governors used the peasants' growing indebtedness as a pretext for wresting ancestral lands from their control. Gradually, the local peoples came under the sway of high-caste Hindus from the west who moved into the eastern hills in the wake of the conquerors, and many people forsook their native hills for 'Muglan', migrating eastward into British India, where the grass was somewhat greener.

These 'Nepalis' came originally from a variety of Tibeto-Burman ethno-linguistic groups that have traditionally inhabited specific sections of the eastern Nepalese hills and have their own ancestral languages and traditions. They were followed by other Tibeto-Burman speakers (Gurungs, Magars, Sunuwars etc.), by high-caste Hindus (Bahuns and Chhetris) who had Nepali as their mother-tongue, and by a number of Newar traders. Despite the diversity of their ancestors' origins, post-migration generations attained a high degree of cultural uniformity outside Nepal, as well as a somewhat higher degree of equality between castes and ethnic groups than that which obtains in Nepal. The Indian Nepalis are now unified by their use of Nepali as a common tongue, and by the shared experience of living as a minority community in states where they are ever likely to be categorised as foreigners.[3]

By the beginning of the First World War substantial Nepali population existed in West Bengal, Assam, Sikkim and southern Bhutan. The fall of the Chögyal and the Indian annexation of Sikkim in 1974-75 are often attributed to the fact that Nepali-speakers had become the majority community there, though this is a gross over-simplification of a highly complex state of affairs. None the less, since 1975, and particularly since the Gorkhaland movement wrecked much of Darjeeling's economy, Gangtok has taken on Darjeeling's old mantle as the main centre of Nepali cultural and literary activity in India. Nepalis are scattered in pockets across Assam and the other northeastern states, where they work in the logging and coal industries, and also seem to have cornered the dairy market. In southern Bhutan the Nepalis have been the majority community ever since the region was first opened for settlement over 100 years ago. They appear to have remained politically and culturally conservative until long after Indian independence in 1947; they were subsistence farmers who rented the lands they tilled from a Bhutan Agent appointed by the Bhutanese government, and until the 1960s they had no access to education. In contrast, the Nepali community in Darjeeling produced intellectuals who had an important influence on the development of Nepali literature from the 1920s onward. Its political leaders sought to establish an identity for Indian Nepalis that established them as a distinct group within India and also distinguished them from the Nepalis of Nepal. The prime example of political activism designed to meet this end was the Gorkhaland movement, which degenerated into violence between 1986 and 1988 before a compromise solution was reached.[4]

Selected Texts

I wish to argue for the importance of vernacular literature as a means of at least supplementing our understanding of issues that are customarily considered to be more legitimately the concern of social scientists, and perhaps of gaining a more nuanced view of them in the process. As the editors of a recent anthology of essays on literature and migration assert:

> [social-scientific research]... fails to capture the essence of what it is like to *be* a migrant; and be, or not be, part of a community, a nation, a society—cut off from history and from a sense of place. It fails to portray nostalgia, anomie, exile, rootlessness, restlessness... Literary accounts focus in a very direct and

> penetrating way on issues such as place perception, landscape symbolism, senses of displacement and transformation, communities lost and created anew, exploitation, nostalgia, attitudes towards return, family relationships, self-denial and self-discovery, and many more.[5]

A number of published Nepali texts exist that provide unique insights into what it means to be a member of the Indian Nepali community, particularly that which forms the linguistic majority in the Darjeeling district of West Bengal. These insights are unique to this literature because, although self-advancement must be a part of the agenda of any writer who takes his or her work to a printer, the authors of these texts would not have expected them to be read by a non-Nepali readership. While the potential audience for a work of creative literature in English is vast, and a Kiran Desai or a Salman Rushdie must therefore write to and for the world, authors working in regional South Asian languages have inherently limited readerships whose extent and whose boundaries they know. When a non-Nepali reads texts such as those discussed briefly in this paper, it is as if we are eavesdropping on a private conversation. We may not hear all of what is being said, and we may misunderstand what we hear, but some of what we do hear is not being said in any other language. The shared assumptions of author and audience are of as much interest to an eavesdropper as the plot of the story the author tells or the sentiments his poem expresses.

The texts that have informed this paper are as follows:

- the short novel *Basai* by Lil Bahadur Chettri (b. 1932/3), an Assamese Nepali. This was first published in 1957-58 (BS 2014) in Nepal, and had entered a thirtieth edition by 2006;
- Lainsingh Bangdel's novel *Muluk Bahira* ('Outside the Country'), first published 1947/8;
- Govinda Raj Bhattarai's 1974 novel *Muglan;*
- the writings of Indra Bahadur Rai (b. 1928);
- the poetry of Haribhakta Katuwal (1935-80) and Agam Singh Giri (1928-70);
- a collection of short stories by Ganusingh Gurung (1930-65?) published in 1965, entitled 'On the Journey' *(Yatrama);*
- *Sammelan Katha Sangraha,* a collection of short stories first published by the Nepali Sahitya Sammelan in Darjeeling in 1976.

A Legacy of Sorrow

The migration from Nepal took place in a relatively recent past and still has a certain resonance in the ancestral memory. In March 1995, a Kalimpong Nepali family of my acquaintance told me of their feelings during their first visit to Kathmandu. They were, they said, delighted by the way in which the wholly Nepalese cultural environment of the large city reaffirmed their pride in their own ethnicity. But it did not make them feel that it would be a better place for them to live. They explained that this was partly because economic conditions were better for Indian Nepalis, and partly because of their consciousness of the *dukha* ('suffering', 'sorrow', 'poverty') endured by their forefathers in Nepal that had led to their presence in India. This sense of ancestral *dukha* underpins much of the experience of being Nepali in India, and characterises much Indian Nepali literature.

The movement of peasants from the hills of eastern Nepal into British India is the theme of a number of stories and short novels in Nepali, whose *rasa* (aesthetic flavour) is one of overwhelming pathos. The best known of these is Chettri's *Basai.* Its title is a word that denotes settlement in a place other than one's own village or country: in Nepali, to migrate permanently is expressed as *basai sarnu,* 'to shift living-place'. The central character of the novel, which is set in a village in eastern Nepal, is a peasant farmer named Dhan Bahadur Basnet who tries repeatedly to claw his way out of debt. But he is duped, abused and swindled by the landowners and moneylenders at every turn, and eventually the only way in which he can clear his debts is to sell his house and land and leave the village to seek new horizons. These are the last lines of the novel:

> The journey of these three people made a pitiable, utterly pitiable sight. The journey of three people: husband, wife and small son. Time and again they turn to look back, and then they go on. It is difficult to find something that compares with their journey precisely. If there had been an onlooker there at this time he would surely have been reminded of Lord Rama's exile in the forest. Rama had gone into exile in the forest for fourteen years, and had come back as well. But these three have locked up their house and are leaving for ever. Their hearts hold no hope at all of ever returning to this place.
>
> Their journey will not lead them to reside in a forest, nor to reside in a house. The journey is not preplanned. They are

> beginning an unplanned journey. Where is this journey leading, where will it end, and where is its destination? Perhaps even they do not know.
>
> The house, shed, garden and granary: all are still as if the life has gone out of them. Dhane and Maina would always greet the sun from the garden. Maina would rise to bathe very early, and then she would come with a pitcher of water and wait in the garden to offer it to the sun. But today there would be no one there to offer a stream of water from that garden.
>
> With the first rays of the sun today, Dhane and Maina's new life will begin. It may be that that life will be better than their lives in the past, or it could also be that it will be worse. But whatever may be, one thing is certain: when the sun appears to them they will be far, far away from this house, garden and yard where they spent a very large part of their lives. Far, very far away.[6]

A sub-plot concerns Dhane's younger sister, Jhuma, who falls under the spell of a young Gorkha soldier who has returned to his home in the hills on leave, and who eventually forces himself upon her and makes her pregnant, then disappears. Rather than undergo the ignominy of childbirth outside wedlock, Jhuma tries to commit suicide, but she is prevented from doing so by a neighbour who has always loved her unrequitedly, and the two elope to India.

Muluk Bahira is set mainly in the settlement of Ghoom, near Darjeeling; its story begins during the early years of the 20th century, and ends with the 2nd World War and the arrival of Nepali refugees from Burma. It relates the lives of various Nepalis who have emigrated from the Arun Khola, a remote valley in eastern Nepal. Although now somewhat dated and repetitive in its narrative style, *Muluk Bahira* contains further reflections on the *dukha* endured back in the hills (*pahaar*) that led to emigration:

> He remembered the state he was in when he entered Muglan. He had entered Muglan in torn *daura-suruwal* [Nepali national dress], with a *khukuri* knife in his waistband and a *ghum* [bamboo mat to keep off the rain] and blanket on his back. That was all he had owned—others had even less. They came wearing only a

> *dhoti* to cover their shame. Hey Ram! What an uncivilised species of creature they must have seemed to others. What a poor race of human beings! What a miserable state they were in, those arrivals from pahaar! Although there was no land or *kipat* [ancestral land exempt from taxes] in Muglan, one could earn enough to feed one's stomach. It was enough to give you something clean to wear and enough to eat. There was a kind of comfort. You didn't have to go to Bhot [Tibet] for salt, you didn't have to suffer.[7]

Every year thousands of poor, uneducated, lowly people who lived by the plough and the hoe left their country (*muluk*) and entered Bharat [India] and Burma. There they settled down and made a living and in the passage of time they became residents (*raithane*). Once they have come into another land (*pravas*) they have no wish to return to the country (*muluk*). Who would wish to return to a country that is poor, and where one has no happiness, no freedom, where only the lament of the poor labourers' souls can be heard, where there is no flame of humanity or civilisation but only the naked picture of poverty-stricken souls? When they recall the poverty of their country their inner souls are startled. They remember the condition they were in when they left their country and entered another land (*pravas*). Once they have entered Muglan, their eyes open. Their opinions and views change. This is the story of all the poor creatures who leave their country in their hundreds of thousands and enter Muglan.[8]

It was inevitably the case that new arrivals from the hills of Nepal were often vulnerable and naive, and the sense that Nepalis have been and are being exploited for economic reasons supplements the sense of historical *dukha*. In Muglan, for instance, two men employed to porter vegetables and oil to the bazaar at Darjeeling abscond down to Siliguri on the Indian plains to seek a brighter future, intending to head for Assam. As hillsmen, they do not even know how to catch a train:

> 'Assam Mail!' They saw people running towards the train from every direction. 'That must be the *rel* that goes to Assam, brother!' said Kancha, 'Come on, let's get in!' They did not need to wash their faces, nor could they relieve themselves because there were people everywhere. There was nowhere to do it. With empty stomachs and eyes full of yellow dirt, they pushed their way through the crowds in the direction of the

> train. They climbed up and got in. On spotless handsome seats there sat handsome, well-fed people. Some were engaged in conversation, others busy eating, and the rest were just as busy getting in and out of the train, picking up their luggage or pushing it in. Sutar Kancho sat down on the floor, and indicated to his brother that he should do the same, 'Sit here, *dai*, the top seats are for the big Sahebs to sit on.' Both of them sat with their legs crossed. People began to look at them and snigger. Gradually, the whole compartment filled with laughter. All they could do was look at each other, they knew they should be alarmed. Then one of the fat people said, 'Hey, this compartment is reserved, get out of here, where do you want to go?' They looked at one another again. Their innocence was plain on their faces. Oh, if someone in this world is innocent he can only remain so. The man spoke again: 'This is reserved, understand?'
>
> 'We, sir, we are from the hills'.
>
> That is all that Sutar could say in a trembling voice. He began to perspire and his face turned red. When the policeman strolled past with his baton he saw two Nepalis sitting in a reserved first class compartment. In broken Nepali, he asked them for their tickets. What did they know about having to buy a ticket? They must have thought that it was like coming down from Darjeeling on a lorry. The policeman grabbed them by their arms: 'Have to get down, get ticket, not sit here, understand?' And they were put out of the train, as hopeless as could be.[9]

This hapless pair is subsequently tricked into working for a local contractor, believing that he will get them enlisted in the British army. They find themselves as members of a roadgang that is building a road from Paro in western Bhutan over the mountains to Haa; there they work for some two years in appalling conditions on very little pay before finally running away.

Darjeeling and Maina's Mother

The lives of Darjeeling Nepalis provide the themes for much of the work of Indra Bahadur Rai, one of the most distinguished writers of Nepali prose to have emerged since 1960. Rai was one of the three founder members of a modernist literary movement called *Tesro Ayam* ('Third Dimension') that was established in Darjeeling in 1963; he has experimented with non-linear plots and collage techniques, and published theoretical essays that explain his craft. Some of Rai's texts [generally they are categorised as 'stories' (*katha*) but this does not always describe them adequately] are abstracted, poetic reflections upon the nature of Indian Nepali identity.

'*Hamijastai Mainaki Ama'*, ('Maina's Mother is Just Like Us'), one of Rai's most famous 'stories', focusses on a woman referred to only as 'Maina's mother' who sells vegetables in the Darjeeling market.[10] The reader meets her at various stages of her life, arranged unchronologically, in an unconventional, poetic text that articulates the pathos and uncertainty of a single, simple life lived by an old uncomprehending Nepali woman against the backdrop of Darjeeling.

We meet Maina's mother first as a customer enquires after the price of the greens she is hoping to sell, and then decides against buying them, stating 'they've turned yellow'. The narrator points out that the customer 'still remembers living in the forests, where it was possible to get them for nothing'. In the passage that follows, anonymous voices discuss the fact that Darjeeling has become crowded and that there is no work to be found there any more. They agree that it is time to move on to seek new opportunities elsewhere. One speaker recalls that the Nepalis first came there because '[t]here was very little to support them [in Nepal], so they became wanderers, scattered through the great land of India. Bunched together, they would all have died'. Then we return briefly to Maina's mother, who is being scolded for not selling more of her produce by the woman for whom she works.

Maina's mother appears again in the next, lengthier passage, sitting inside a tent beside a woodfire while the rain pours down outside. A man comes running down from the hill above where he has been looking for a new place to live because '[p]eople have covered the hillsides with cow pastures' and 'Darjeeling will be a big town when people have covered it all.' Here, we are plainly in the past—not just Maina's mother's past, but the past of the whole Nepali community in Darjeeling. Water begins to enter her tent, and the man goes out with a piece of wood to dig a channel along which it can drain away. There ensues a brief conversation with passers-by about rumours that a nearby pond might be drained and the land built on, and about the danger of landslides and the need to move further up the hillside.

Next there come hopes and dreams: that all the plants thereabouts are valuable medicinal herbs, that there are copper mines beneath the ground, that the lowlands will pay the hills for the water from their rivers. Then rocks and staves fall down on Maina's mother, symbolising perhaps the dashing of these hopes, and she is made to seem timid and frightened. But,

> [s]uddenly she felt inspired to say— we came here looking for a place where we could see the Himalaya clearly. Now we don't want to go anywhere else. All of us should have a house where we can open the window each morning and look at the Himalaya. Here man is unhealthy; he quickly tires of most things; his thirst is quickly quenched. But with one thing he is never satiated, and that is the Himalaya. Wherever we may go we will take this land with us, wrapped up in little bundles.

Maina's mother reappears as her tired little bunch of greens revives. She contemplates the beauty of a tree, and tends and waters small plants, then she 'goes far across the brown ridges of the fields', walking steeply uphill. She is a woman of the villages, sensitive enough to be moved by the sight of healthy plants and ever alert to their needs. As she wanders up the hill from terraced field to terraced field, Rai invokes a sense of pathos with a line from a famous Nepali song: 'Why then did you come here? Why then did you come here?'

Maina's mother is saddened when she observes household items—dishes, a spice-grinding stone, some medicinal herbs—being sold off in the bazaar. She comes from a pre-capitalist, rural society and believes that such things belong in the home, not out on show in public:

> To Maina's mother, this bazaar looks like someone's home. It's as if a thousand households have been broken open. Why do a thousand households stand neglected here?... Our household things have all been put outside with us in the bazaar. First, man left home, then his belongings came after him, and now they are here in the bazaar, waiting to take him back. Maina's mother tries to go home: suddenly, she is afraid of this bright open afternoon...

The intrusion of political turmoil and an articulation of the Nepalis' general sense of insecurity in India is heralded by a verse from the

19th-century *Nepali Ramayana* which tells of Hanuman watching Ravana from a hiding place as Ravana wonders aloud when Lord Rama will come to rescue Sita from him. Then Maina's mother is surrounded by crowds of people, flags and loudspeakers:

> 'Why did you come here?' asked an invisible person. A man walked by in front of her; he turned and asked her the same question. All the people standing in the street queued up to ask her; all the people inside the buildings opened their windows and asked her the question in high shrieking voices, staring at her from sharp eyes, taking aim with gaping mouths. She hid her face with her dirty shawl and peered out through the chinks of her window: an old fear. The whole bazaar left its work and came toward her. A thousand faces surrounded her, asking, 'Why did you come here?'

But Maina's mother's chief concern is her livelihood: she fears that the vegetables she is trying to sell will be trampled, and she leaps to her feet to gather them up. Despite her fear and bewilderment, Maina's mother (who one feels must be taken to represent all generations of Darjeeling Nepalis) copes with what she knows:

> When night had fallen she covered the spot with a basket and a wooden box, reserving it for tomorrow.

Like most members of her community, Maina's mother plays no active role in the working out of the community's destiny; it is left to others to articulate her sense of insecurity. Conflicts and changes ebb and flow all about her, but she does not comprehend them.

The Old Household in Nepal

Several writers have employed the metaphor of a household to represent the Indian Nepali community. In this representation, the Indian Nepalis' ancestors abandoned an old house back in Nepal, and founded another in India. The Indian Nepalis' relationship with the land of their ancestors' birth is an ambiguous, ambivalent one, and there has arisen among them a nationalist politics that asserts their identity as Indian Nepalis while stressing their separateness from Nepal itself. Rai has recently argued that India is the home of many nations, the Indian Nepali nation among them, and that Indian Nepali nationalism is not incompatible with pan-Indian patriotism:

> Patriotic feeling fastens itself upon more than one expressive embodiment, and the ethnic and/or linguistic consciousness of us Indian Nepalis is certainly one such. One can finally emerge as a pan-Indian nationalist by inductively working one's way up from premises of patriotically loving your own national people and serving one's own national community.
>
> A poet is inalienably a prophet too. He obtains glimpses of that faraway land to which *all* people belong. Before we reach it we must pass through a country to which *many* people belong—our own country and nation.[11]

Within India this nationalism is viewed with suspicion because ever since it was first articulated it has been coupled with a demand for varying measures of political autonomy for Nepalis in India and is thus suspected of being secessionist in its aims.

In Darjeeling, an important part of the vigorous political debate during the late 1980s focussed on the name by which the non-Nepalese Nepali community should be known. The use of the old term *pravasi,* 'dwelling in a foreign/other country' came to be frowned upon, because a central plank of the movement's argument was that the Nepalis in India should not be treated as immigrants or foreigners. Darjeeling intellectuals and their counterparts in Kathmandu began to use the label *bharatiya nepali,* 'Indian Nepali', but the leaders of the Gorkhaland movement (from whom writers and intellectuals became increasingly alienated as the movement progressed) were concerned that the people they aspired to represent should sever all links with Nepal. The title thus chosen was 'Gorkha' or 'Gorkhali': the language hitherto called Nepali began to be called 'Gorkha'; statues of the 19th-century Nepalese poet Bhanubhakta Acharya, who had been a cultural icon for generations of Indian Nepalis, were desecrated and his name was removed from the names of public institutions.[12]

Such measures were considered immoderate by most Indian Nepali intellectuals, who accepted that an act of political distancing from Nepal was in the interests of the Indian Nepalis, but felt that the cultural bond could neither be severed nor denied. Indra Bahadur Rai's story *Akarharu, Chhayaharu* consists of a dialogue between two brothers, the younger of whom, named Puran, is setting out from their home in Nepal for India. His elder brother tells him that he will not be able to leave or forget his home for ever. The 'outside' is hostile and life there will be difficult; ultimately, he will again seek refuge in Nepal:

> 'This is home, are you going to leave it?'
>
> 'Yes'. Puran lifts his resolve and smiles.
>
> Brother's face changes. As Puran smiles, he becomes once more the big brother such a smile has had since Puran was small. His eyes became grey and pitying and the creases ran on the face beneath them.
>
> 'The outside will chew you up', he says, going back into the house, 'You'll need this home later on.'[13]

The rivers of east Nepal, elder brother tells Puran, might prevent him leaving the country, but they will always welcome him back:

> 'If the Arun swells it will stop you leaving, if the Mechi spreads it will prevent you. You are leaving home, and none of us can stop you. But in the winter when they shrink the Arun and the Mechi will always spread out a path for you to return home, that path of yours will not die.'[14]

In Rai's essay 'Hills and Streams' (*Paharharu ra Kholaharu*), two men climb to a temple on a hilltop, and the younger of the two discovers an inscription on a temple bel there:

> 'Read this' he said, calling the old man over. 'It's like a poem' he said, smiling a little. The short man and the tall man read the words together:
>
> *The hills*
> *The green flowers*
> *Do not shift their abode*
> *In vain the rivers pull them.*
> *The streams*
> *The bright birds*

Their movements are not bound
In vain the mountains block them.
Peace. Peace. Peace.

> 'The mountains are we who remain, the rivers are those who are leaving', said the youth.
>
> 'The rivers are always going somewhere, but they always remain' said the old man. 'We hills are always washed along by change'.[15]

Thus, those whose ancestors flowed down from the Nepalese hills still remain there in some part of themselves. Because they know that their forefathers left as a result of hardship and oppression, they need to believe that they have cut all ties with the old place back in Nepal and that life is better where they are. But a young man does go back to see the old house, and is surprised to find it in good shape. As he returns from Nepal, he reflects on his community's relationship with its country of origin:

> As he looks at the hills and streams he is leaving, alone on the path, he recalls something that a Jain guru once said,
>
> 'All day we look at its face, but we have never met it. Many aeons ago we were separated, but we have never been separate for a moment.'[16]

Many Indian Nepalis believe that they must stress their separation from Nepal if they are to be accepted as a part of the Indian nation. Others argue that they cannot deny much of what makes them Nepalis: their language, literature, emblems and icons are still sustained links across the border. Several well known Indian Nepali poets have produced rapturous verse of identification with Nepal. In several poems by Haribhakta Katuwal, for instance, there is an emotional capitulation to a long-suppressed patriotism—an Assamese Nepali's embrace of the country that produced his forebears:

> To gild the tall tall peaks of Himal
> With gold and silver, we only need
> Our own sun and moon,
> Filling our own sky.

Yes, here I have found a sky of my own,
A soil of my own, I have found the Himal:
The Sagarmatha I once found in my dreams
Today I possess in reality.
So I have let loose my hopes:
May they spread from Mechi to Mahakali,
May they rise up as peaks from Tarai to Sagarmatha.
('Banchna Khojirahechu')[17]

Ramlal Adhikari writes of a local Darjeeling man, of the blacksmith (Kami) caste, who in his old age resolves that he must return to Nepal. He pesters his wife about it every day, and, without telling anyone, sells all of his property in Darjeeling. Adhikari tells of the wife's response:

> Then she told me the whole story. 'Nephew, your *Pusain* has been telling me for a year or a year and a half now that he is going to go to Nepal. I was just humouring him, saying '*la, la.*' But then, about two weeks ago, he asked me, 'Shall we go right now, or shall we go tonight?' and he's given me no peace ever since. Then the other night when he was pestering me, I told him. I said I would only go if he took my corpse away with him. Otherwise, I wouldn't go one, I wouldn't go two, I wouldn't go at all…
>
> …I didn't hear that my mother and father in Nepal had died until they had been dead for seven months. I couldn't go then, and now who do I have there that I should go? He says we have land and fields there, and that we have to raise cows and buffaloes and live on the earnings. The old man doesn't even realise that his strength and stamina are all used up. What I say is this: now that I have left the country, this is where I'll die.[18]

Ultimately, Kancha Kami loses his mind. He tries to burn down his house, and is physically restrained. However, he breaks free from the confinement in which his family and neighbours have placed him, and hangs himself from a tree. Again, there is a major ambiguity here about where a Nepali belongs; it is a tension that reaches its peak when the end of his life draws near.

The New Household in India

Indra Bahadur Rai begins '*Paharharu ra Kholaharu*' with a description of the Indian Nepalis' first homestead:

> A high hillridge upon which the Himalaya always gazes. There was a village of Nepalis there, who had come in large numbers. The house that had been there since no one knew when (they called it the *mul ghar* and the *jati ghar*) was on top of a hill. An old house, of rock, soil and wood. Whenever possible it had been extended and added to so that it had become three-storeyed. A neat roof of thatch, bound tightly on. Pretty and strong it stood, that Nepali house on that ridge.[19]

Even after two generations, however, the occupants of this, the house of Nepali settlement in India, still endured a life of insecurity and struggle. They lived together as 'Nepalis' despite their various ethnic origins, but the time was coming when some of them might reap greater economic benefits if they asserted their older identities as 'Scheduled Tribes' or 'Scheduled Castes'; hence their worries in the following extract about who it was that truly owned the site of the house, and about how integrated with one another the various ethno-linguistic groups that comprise the Nepali community (the 'storeys' of the house) truly were:

> But however much that house the forefathers had established was patched up, and however much it was plastered and painted, from far away it was recognisable as the home of people who had struggled to survive. Sometimes, joy would suddenly arrive on a feastday. But otherwise all had to live there in fear of the house being pulled down by a landslip or blown down by a gale. And all had begun to worry about how many of them really owned the site of the house, and how strong the bonds of the storeys were.[20]

One individual decides that he must seek out his own destiny, and make a break from the Nepali community:

> 'We will never succeed if we live together' a young man thought one day. 'This house will collapse, today or tomorrow. None of us will rise if we all sleep in one grave (we live in a living grave). I will choose a separate death for myself. I'll walk out my life alone'.

> He looked at his brothers: 'I am fairer than that one, I am different from him. I am darker than that one, I am different from him. My nose is flatter than that one's, but sharper than that one's: I am different. I am not a pauper like them, I am different. I am not stupid like they are, I am different. I am educated, I am very rich. I have intelligence.'
>
> A fear opens its mouth wide and swallows him up: are we the children of a single race? Are we a single race?[21]

Is the Indian Nepali community welcome now in the house of Indian nationhood? The words of Ganusingh Gurung's essay 'I Have Died' *('Ma Marechu')* are spoken by a ghost who cannot be admitted into its family's home, probably (though this is not stated) because the funeral rites were not performed properly for it. This, at least, is the interpretation offered by Mary Des Chene, who mentions this text in a recent article.

> When night fell... when all that could be seen all around was the kingdom of darkness... when the world was silent all around, I arrived from who knows where at the door of the house. As I reached the door, I called like I always do, 'Mother, open the door, won't you?' When mother did not open the door I knocked loudly on it. And when I made this noise, mother and brothers and sisters all got up and came out holding long sticks to beat me. I was terrified and I ran away, and then when they had all gone back to sleep I came and sat by the door again. Mother never opened the door. She never called me in. I loved the house a great deal and even though the door was not opened I spent the whole night outside in the heart-shaking cold, waiting by the door. But sometimes I arrived home on time. They would have begun to eat at home and I would go and sit beside my brothers and sisters. Mother would begin to serve the food, she would give some to the brothers and sisters, and would herself sit down to eat, but... I would look around, and see that I had not been given a share. I would sit there for a moment, but even so mother would not give me any rice. I would find this unpleasant, and I would get up, go outside and weep for hours. When I saw my mother discriminating between the offspring of a single home in this way, sometimes I would feel hatred even towards my mother. What sort of mother was she, who did not even love her son! And I would think to

> myself that there was no use in loving a mother who did not love me, and I would not wait by the door that night.[22]

Des Chene comments, 'Ganusingh Gurung's short story *Ma Marechu,* written from the point of view of a just deceased person slowly discovering his condition, should be read alongside traditional ethnographic sources by anyone contemplating the significance of Tamu funeral rituals.'[23] However, in view of the cultural and political context in which this Nepali literature was produced, it is difficult to avoid reading this essay as an allegory designed to convey the idea that the Indian Nepali community was not being granted its rightful place at the table. Or perhaps it is just that different eavedroppers hear different things.

Pride, Honour and Duty

The ethnic community confers duties upon the members of its extended, embattled household. These must include upholding the honour of the household when it is living beside others who are ever ready to make capital of its shortcomings. Puran's brother reminds him that he is not wholly free to act as an individual. His choices are constrained by his ethnic origin and domestic ties:

> 'Understand what I tell you' said elder brother, changing the atmosphere like a sudden shower of rain.
>
> 'If you are purely and only a man then you have freedom, you have natural rights, you have everything. But you are not only a man, do not ever forget this, no one is merely a man. By birth you are a Nepali. By your ancestors you are the offspring of this house. Your membership comes to you by birth. Because of this fact, which you cannot scrape off and throw away, there are certainly some duties in you, and probably some rights.' Then elder brother said, with even greater seriousness, 'Society cannot give you the personal freedom you insist on if you must protect home, race [*jati*] and country.'
>
> The lamentation of an era of snatched freedom fell into Puran's consciousness; Jatayu flapped his wings within him as he struggled against abduction.[24]

Freedom is not snatched from Chandra Prakash, the hero of Ganusingh Gurung's story '*Hamro Samaj*'; instead, he chooses to make a sacrifice for the good of his community's reputation. His widowed mother is humiliated and abused for her social presumptions when she goes to the house of the landlord to propose that Chandra Prakash might marry his daughter. Later, however, a rumour circulates that the young woman is 'unable' and this is damaging the big man's family honour. Unaware of his mother's earlier humiliation, Chandra Prakash visits him and offers to marry his unmarriagable daughter, at which the man weeps with gratitude. That evening, Chandra Prakash brings the young woman home:

> 'What to do, mother?' he said, 'This is how our society is today. I have not married, I have covered up society's shame. So many other *jati*s live in this village, what would they say about our society tomorrow if I had not? That's why I have married Jamuna.'
>
> Raini Burhi wept bitterly. But after a while, probably because she has reflected upon it, she says to herself, 'You did well. Our society needs a son like you.'[25]

In the aftermath of the Gorkhaland movement, when efforts were made to sever cultural links with Nepal and carve a Nepali niche within India, many Darjeeling Nepalis turned to the Indian Nepali poet Agam Singh Giri (1928-1970) in their search for a new literary icon. Giri's lyrical poems evoke most perfectly the pathos and pride of being Nepali in India:

> It is coming, it is coming, the unknown future,
> Staggering along, it comes,
> Carrying deep deep silences,
> Inclarities, profundities.
> It is coming to shake and jolt you,
> It is coming to ask you questions,
> It is coming to snatch things from you.
> And how will you shuffle along
> The stony road of your times, my son,
> Bearing such ragged humility?
> Your times will mock and deride you
> With all the sharp satires of the age;
> And in your mind you will curse

The powerlessness of my times:
My helplessness, weakness, poverty.

But for a moment I grab hold of death,
Just for a moment I halt fate's wheel,
I boil up my blood once more,
I make my rotten bones firm and I stand,
I turn up the dying lamp of my life,
And to my son I say:

Dear is this love of identity,
The beautiful pride of Nepaliness,
The honour of birth in a Nepali mother's womb,
The pride of becoming Nepali, just Nepali:
This is life's single unbounded meaning;
These are your wages, this is your wealth.

('Mrtyuaghi salbalauncha jatitva')[26]

A pride in being Nepali infuses much of this literature whenever it touches upon the question of identity. Honour is both familial and communal in the situation in which Nepalis find themselves in Northeast India. But if there is a sub-nationalistic song of ethnic pride to be sung, Indian Nepalis will sing it to a melancholy tune. The literature suggests that an inescapable part of being Nepali in the world beyond Nepal's borders is that Nepalis must struggle for the right to belong. Their solace must be that they are Nepali, with whatever meaning they invest that label, and that no one can take that from them.

NOTES AND REFERENCES

1. Tulsi Apatan, Lakkhidevi Sundas and Jagat Chetri (eds.), *Sammelan Katha-Sangrah,* Darjeeling: Nepali Sahitya Sammelan (2nd edn.).
2. Anthony D. Smith, 1986, *The Ethnic Ancestry of Nations,* Oxford: Blackwell Publishers, p. 2.
3. The use of the term 'Nepali' as an ethnic designation is by no means unproblematic, but this is neither the place nor the time to deconstruct or analyse it. For exhaustive discussions of ethnic and political identities in Nepal, see Gellner *et al.* (eds.) 1997.
4. Tanka B. Subba, 1992, *Ethnicity, State and Development: A Case Study of the Gorkhaland Movement in Darjeeling, New* Delhi: Vikas.

5. Russell King, John Connell and Paul White (eds.), 1995, *Writing Across Worlds: Literature and Migration,* London and New York: Routledge, pp. ix-x.
6. Lil Bahadur Chettri, 1989, *Basai, Kathmandu*: Sajha Prakashan (15th edn.), pp. 69-70. All translations in this paper are my own.
7. Lainsingh Bangdel, 1993, *Muluk Bahira.* Kathmandu: Ratna Pustak Bhandar (9th edn.), p. 84.
8. *Ibid.*, pp. 155-6.
9. Govinda Raj Bhattarai, 1988, *Muglan,* Dhankuta: Rajeshvar Prakashan (3rd edn.), pp. 12-13.
10. *Hamijastai Mainaki Ama* was first published in 1964 and appears in Rai's collection *Kathastha* (1972) and in the anthology *Bharati Nepali Katha,* edited by Dayaram Shrestha Sambhav (1982). The translated extracts given here are from Hutt 1991: 260-5.
11. Indra Bahadur Rai, 1994, 'Indian Nepali Nationalism and Nepali Poetry', *Journal of South Asian Literature*, 29 (1), pp. 150, 154.
12. In Darjeeling, the name of the main public theatre was changed from Bhanu Bhavan to Gorkha Rangmanch. The cover of a 1989 edition of the *Jivani* of Bhanubhakta, published in Darjeeling, bore the subtitle *Gorkha Bhasako Adikari.*
13. Indra Bahadur Rai, 1972, *Kathastha, Darjeeling*: Nepali Sahitya Parishad, p. 49.
14. *Ibid.*, p. 65.
15. Indra Bahadur Rai, 1993, *Pahaar ra Khola,* Darjeeling: Darjeeling Granthakar Sahakari Samiti, p. 63.
16. *Ibid.*, pp. 67-8.
17. Haribhakta Katuwal, 1972, *Yo Jindagi Khai Ke Jindagi,* Kathmandu: Ratna Pustak Bhandar, p. 2.
18. 'Kancha Mijarko Nepal Yatra' in Dayaram Sambhav Shrestha (ed.), 1982, *Bharati Nepali Katha,* Kathmandu: Nepal Rajakiya Prajna Pratisthan, pp. 61-2.
19. Rai, 1993, *op. cit.*, p. 61.
20. *Ibid.*, p. 61.
21. *Ibid.*, pp. 61-2.
22. Ganusingh Gurung, 1965, *Yatrama,* Darjeeling: Nepali Sahitya Parishad, p. 45.
23. Mary Des Chene, 1996, 'Ethnography in the Janajati-yug', *Studies in Nepali History and Society,* 1 (1), p. 120.
24. Rai, 1972, *op. cit.*, p. 53.
25. Gurung, *op. cit.*, p. 85.
26. Agam Singh Giri, 1978, *Jaleko Pratibimba Roeko Pratidhvan,* Darjeeling: Astitva Prakashan, pp. 72-3.

3

Ethnic Identity Crisis, History and Cultural Anthropology: Some Reflections

PRAVESH JUNG GOLAY

My paper is divided into three sections based on the three related themes discussed herein. The first theme pertains to the epistemic ability of the human species with respect to the *necessity and the ability* to formulate and to use 'class' or 'category' when making *sense of* things that it encounters in the world. The second theme deals with the relationship between 'class' and the notion of 'identity' and argues that identities are needed by an individual so that he can be *made sense of* by other individuals. Thus 'identity crisis' stands synonymous with '*crisis of sense*' or the *state of failure to make, and be made, sense of.* The third theme is an explication of the relation between an individual and his history and the importance of history in bestowing sense to one's own *being* in terms of one's *situatedness.* The first theme stands as the foundation of the latter two themes. Ethnic identity crisis of the Nepali individual is mapped unto the latter two themes.

I begin this paper with two comments with respect to the uniqueness[1] of the human species. Human beings have, amongst other accomplishments, faced, successfully endured and adapted themselves to diverse challenges thrown at them in their voyage through evolutionary processes. Amongst the unique abilities that have aided them in this challenge the most fundamental ability has been their inquisitiveness or their ability to try and make sense of things and their ability to try and share this 'sense'. But how do human beings make sense of things? If I, as a human being, try to understand the world, and take the world to be a totality of things, then I can possibly never know much about the world. Taking the stance of viewing the world as a totality of things, whatever I would have managed to know would be highly unsatisfactory as I would have to make an inventory of all the individual things in the world and then make sense of each individual thing. This would be a futile attempt since things in the world are continuously entering and exiting the sphere of existence. This would always leave me with an incomplete and an unsatisfactory knowledge of the world.

But this is not how humans proceed to scale the knowables since we employ our unique human ability to bring into play 'class-ideas' and 'classification' or 'category' and 'categorization'. This unique ability acts as the sharper edges of the tool that continuously aid human beings in their endeavour to make sense of things.

Philosophers right from early times, both in the east and the west, were primarily engaged in the task of building 'categories' or 'classes', which would make it easier for individuals to make sense of the world and acquire satisfactory and complete knowledge about things that furnish it as far as possible, and thereby help him to paint a complete picture of the world. However, though it is somewhat accepted truism that human curiosity knows no bounds and traverses quicker than their potentiality to make sense of things, this quest of painting a complete picture of the world continues and may continue as long as the species continues. Nevertheless, it is also a truism that whatsoever be the degree of progress that has been made in this human quest of making sense of the world, the progress has been indebted to the human ability to formulate and use 'classes' and 'categories'.[2]

Reformulating the above conceptions in a more philosopher-friendly language and terminology, one could say that since *knowledge* is universal, that is, *atemporal* and *aspatial* and thereby, uniform; our attaining of such a knowledge of the world would be impossible in the absence of 'classes' or 'categories', given the fact that individuals are temporal and spatial. 'Categories' or 'classes' are thus needed necessarily and also essentially to bring about the feature of aspatiality and a temporality in knowledge so that even though human beings are spatial and temporal there is uniformity in 'sense' and thereby uniformity in all related activities pertaining to sense, like communication, thought, etc. The 'classes' or 'categories' are, thus, epistemic nets in which the world *(the known world)* is sought to be captured so that one can make sense of reality and that reality becomes both knowable and communicable. That is to say that knowledge and learning are primarily a venture of formulating 'class-concepts', *defining them* and using them in a way so as to make sense of things in the world. Thus, as a connotation one can say that unambiguous understanding[3] results only from a clear understanding of the concepts involved in *that which one undertakes to understand.*

The above discussion brings into our notice a pivotal point, namely, that 'class(es)' or 'category(ies)' is/are essential ingredient(s) of every 'know-claim'[4], albeit it is possible that many variables which may themselves be 'concepts' or 'categories' may go into the formulation of a 'concept' or a 'class' as their defining elements.

Apart from this endowed potential to use 'classes', human beings are unique as they are potentially armed with the awareness of their '*beingness*' (that is the awareness that one *is* or one *exists*) and their '*facticity*' (that is the awareness that one *exists* amongst other things in the world). That is to say, that human beings have the ability to be aware about their own '*isness*' or the ability to know that they '*are*'. Further, human beings are endowed with the ability to be aware of the '*experience of having experiences*'. They are aware that they are experiencing when they experience and this awareness makes them aware that they are 'subjects'—the experiencer of these experiences. A *being* is a subject in so far as it is an experiencer. The constituents of the field of experience of a *being* are what constitute as the *objects* of experience for the *being*. That is to say that any entity that I experience as a subject is essentially a constituent of my field of experience and hence an object of my field of experience. This brings about the most fundamental dualism operative in the epistemic domain, namely, the *subject-object* duality or the duality in terms of *the knower* and the *known*. What requires special attention in the treatment of this duality is the fact of transposition that operates between the two poles of this dualism, with the object as one of the poles and the subject as the other. That is to say, that a subject is also available as an object for some other subject for he is nevertheless, also a *'being in the world'*[5] as are things like tables, chairs and many other entities in the world that furnish it, to name a few. By '*in*' I mean the spatial relationship between two extended entities in a common space. That implies in other words that as all *beings*, a subject is as much as *in the world* as any other entity is *in the world* and is hence essentially available as an object of inquiry to any subject, including the subject himself. In other words, a subject can be transformed into an object for some other subject if the former subject falls in the field of experience of the latter subject. Now as a '*being in the world'*, and with the possibility of being a possible object for other subjects (*others)*, a subject, as an object, like all objects, must belong to a class in order to *be made sense of.*

However, a human being is not merely a *'being in the world'*. For unlike other *beings*[6], he is also a subject apart form being an object thus, human beings transcend the domain of '*being in the world*'. A human being is thus, also, a '*being of the world*'. A *being* who realizes that it is a *'being in the world'*. A *being* that has the ability to, and is bound to recognize the fact that it cannot be taken into account except as being existent in the middle of a world amongst other things and other *beings*. That is to say that as a *'being of the world'*, the '*being in the world'* that is, a human being, is not merely *in* the world but is also a *situated* subject. As a '*being of the world*' it is not merely an isolated subject but rather *an embodied being, anchored and grounded, in a named and a dated physical, historical and social world with a social, natural, political and economic environment environing it*[7]. This environment is what I term as the *situatedness* of a being. A *being* aware of its *situatedness* amongst other things and other *beings* is what I call '*a being of the world*'. That is to say that, as a '*being of the world*', a *being* will always be aware of '*being-with*'. That is, the understanding of the *present-ness* of other beings; the awareness *of others and that they are*. In fact, I take it to be analytical to hold that *'to be a being of the world is to be aware of 'being-with''*. As a '*being of the world*', the *situatedness* of the being, therefore, entails the '*given*'. It implies that in so far as a being is a *'being of the world'*, the physical, historical and the social context of his *situatedness* is given to him. In other words, as Heidegger claimed, a *being*, in this sense of already being given the context of his *situatedness*, is simply *thrown* into the world; into a context, and this '*throwness*' (*Geworfenheit*) is constituted by the fact that the *being* has never prior knowledge nor a personal option of where it is *thrown*. A *being,* thus, is *thrown* into a world that was there before and will remain after. That as a '*being of the world*', the being always has a *'given'*—the '*given*' being the context of his *situatedness.*

Now, a *being* taken to mean both a being '*in the world*' and '*of the world*' is what I term as *individual*. Thus, an individual is not merely a 'being *in the* world' but also a 'being *of the* world'.

In so far as an individual falls within the field of experience of some other individual, it is an object or the known or the experienced for the latter individual and hence views the former individual as a '*being in the world*', and unavoidably, as is the case in all instances of understanding as seen earlier, various 'categories' and 'class-concepts' are bound to come into play in the individual's attempt to understand the *other*. *Identities* are one such category employed in such a quest for understanding of an individual by another individual. Of course, one should not forget that an individual can himself be both the subject and the object at the same time. That is to say that identity-categories[8] are not merely needed by some individuals to make sense of some other individuals or the *other* but the individual himself needs them to make sense of himself in his *situatedness*, as happens in the quest for the sense of one's own *being*. In all such quests for sense, the individual tends to anchor himself to a defined 'category' or 'class'. This anchoring gives him a sense of '*security of sense*'. It gives the individual a sense of *belonging to*. It gives the individual a grounding to identify himself with a 'category' or a 'class' and thereby be made sense of by any *other* inquiring *subject*. It gives the individual his identity. This sense of *belonging to* or the sense of being '*identifiable with*' is of fundamental importance, since as a '*being of the world*' and therefore, due to its sense of '*being-with*' it is forced to abhor alienation from the world where it co-exists with the awareness of its existence in its *situatedness*.

From the above discussion, it thus follows that ethnic identities of individuals are instances of categorizations operative within the framework of a treatment of the individual as a *'being of the world'*. It can hence be argued that no individual can do without identity of some sort for it would lead to alienation of the individual from the net of the knowable and would deprive the individual of his status as a '*being in the world*'. This is the genesis of any identity crisis. That is to say that identity crisis arises when;

(1) An individual in his situatedness finds himself alienated; that is when he discovers that he does not belong to the categories or classes available in his *situatedness,* or
(2) When he finds hazy and weak 'classes' or 'categories' to anchor his sense of *being-with* or *belonging to* and thereby cannot make sense of his own being.

This is when an individual is forced to confront an identity crisis. Identity crisis arises when an individual as a *'being of the world'* is unable to locate himself in the categories available to him in any satisfactory way. When an individual comes across the realization of '*I am neither this nor that*' which leads him to eventually inquire, '*Who am I*?' the question of identities is raised. The question '*Who am I?*' is more often raised than the question '*What am I?*', and one cannot confuse between the two as their orientations are quite different. The latter question leads to ontological and metaphysical problems and pertains to the question of the very nature of '*being*' or 'existence' itself which may be argued to be of specific interest to the subject of philosophy, but the former leads to problems of identity, problems of belonging and the problems of 'what am I identified with' as a '*being in the world*' by other subjects in whose fields of experience I am encountered as an object by them, and 'what do I want to be identified with in my *situatedness* as a *being of the world?'*.

Identity crisis is thus a situation where the individual is unable to situate himself in the *situatedness* of the *given*. It is a situation where an individual fails to make sense of his '*beingness*' and '*facticity*' in the physical, historical, and social world that he finds himself *thrown into* and in the lacuna generated by the absence of this sense, he begins to feel alienated from what is *the given* in his *situatedness*. Thus, as a '*being of the world'*, an individual is already placed in a context. Thus, the awareness of an individual towards his *situatedness* is regulated by the individual's ability to be aware of the two fundamental epistemic categories, namely space and time of which, of prime importance being the category of 'time'. That is to say, that as a '*being of the world*', the individual is *historical* by its very nature. By *historical* we mean the historicity of an individual. That is, the 'time-boundness' of a being and its restriction to experience itself as a '*being in the world*' in relation to the experiential time. *Time*, in the sense of linear succession or cosmological time, that is the experience of time in terms of hours, weeks, months, etc. as well as in the sense of phenomenological time, that is the experience of time in terms of facts and events. It is the latter that is of importance to the individual and as far as the plight of identity is concerned. It is due to time experienced in this sense that one experiences past, present and future. The experience of phenomenological time is what helps the individual relate himself to his own situatedness and the '*given*'. It is in this context that history becomes relevant to the issue of ethnic identity.

Thus ethnic identities of individuals are, as stated earlier, instances of categorizations operative within the framework of a treatment of the individual as a 'being of the world' in the historicity of his situatedness. This brings me to the central theme of my paper, namely, that the ethnic identity crisis faced by the Nepalis[9] is a case of the individual not finding a ground to anchor himself and thereby failing to make sense of his own situatedness. The Nepali youth of Darjeeling is a case in point. The Nepali youth, in this world of vast gathering of various ethnic identities, finds himself alienated from the world for, as an individual, he fails to appear as a '*being in the world'* as a result of a failure to find for himself any sustainable ground or 'class' or 'category' to anchor himself and thereby, to be made sense of, by other *beings* in the world and by himself. The problem soon turns into a crisis for as a *'being of the world'* he finds himself belonging to neither this nor that 'category' or 'class' in his *authenticity*[10] and thereby totally *lacking sense* which will soon lead to the feeling of alienation and a crisis results out of this alienation. Furthermore, the alienation is strengthened by other *'beings of the world'* in trying to make sense of the individual, for they fail to make sense of him as he fails to clearly classify himself as belonging to a defined 'category' or 'class'. To discuss the case in the present scenario, the Nepalis have come to realize that they neither form the class of Nepalis from Nepal[11], nor are they grounded in any other class or category like Bengalis, as their ethnicity bears a distinct mark, but then, as a 'being of the world', they cannot deny that they are 'beings in the world'; that they are entities in the world and have to be *made sense of* and hence, must be hooked onto a legitimately defined 'category' or 'class'[12].

Furthermore, identity cannot merely be established by incessant claiming and by persistently hooking onto a 'category' or a 'class' by an individual until and unless the claim to the *'belong to'* is legitimately agreed upon

(a) by other *'beings of the world'* who would also, as an entailment of the individual's inclusion, be included as members of the class (My belonging to a particular ethnic identity would entail my father and my brother as belonging to the same ethnic category or class),
(b) by *others* or other subjects in whose spectra of experiences the individual appears as an object.

It implies that, in the larger framework of existence, an individual as a *'being of the world'* longs for an identity when he feels that he is being isolated or bracketed from the framework of *that which can be made sense of* and thereby from the framework of knowables which negates the very nature of an individual since an individual is essentially a *'being in the world'* apart from being a *'being of the world'* and thereby essentially an object that can be known by the *others*. Thus the claim of identity is ineluctable since it is a self assertion of one's existence, of one's *being*. Thus, the echoes of questions like 'Who am I?', 'Where am I grounded?', 'How am I to make sense of myself in my situatedness?', and 'How are other *beings of the world'* to make sense of me?' haunt the very sense of a *being* and the cry for an ethnic identity arises.

Assertions of identity are thus expressions of existential assertions. Such assertions, however, make sense if and only if, there is the *other* to reciprocate. Since, as discussed earlier, the notion of the 'subject' can be read in the definition of knowledge itself, knowledge cannot be made sense of in the absence of the *subject-object,* or *the knower-known* duality. This reciprocation is what underlies the *dynamics of recognition.* This general remark on identity when mapped unto the question of ethnic identity implies that given two *beings* where an individual 'A' falls as an object *to be made sense of* in the field of experience of another individual 'B', the recognition of 'A' as *belonging to...* comes not merely from the assertion of 'A' that *it is...* but also from the recognition by 'B' that *'A' is* .... This brings out a crucial facet with respect to an individual's identity namely, that an individual's sense of '*belonging to*' has to be recognized from without; by the *others* or by other subjects in whose experience the individual is *an object and something which is to be made sense of* by the *experiencing subject.* Hence, the sense of '*belonging to*' a 'class' is not an uncontested process.

It is clear thus that an individual's identity poses a question of *acceptance* by *others* but the grounds on which the legitimation of the acceptance is based or the frame of any such structure of legitimate acceptance has its foundations buried in the soil of one's *situatedness* in terms of what is the *'given'* with respect to the individual.

Taking the individual to be a *'being of the world'*, and the notion of his, *'throwness'*, it implies that ethnic identity of an individual is the *given,* in so far as the individual identifies, as well as is identified with, that with which it identifies itself. The locus of this identity as being '*given*' of the individual as a *'being of the world'* in his historicity and *situatedness*. This, however, does not imply that the '*given*' is to be taken to mean as unchanging and constant. For, it must be understood that even the world into which the individual is *thrown* is changing and also has a past, present and a future and thus the '*given*' is also in an incessant state of flux. But change being temporal, the present state of the given to the individual is emergent of the past. That is to say that the '*given*' too is the nascent product of history and socially related domains. Thus it is to be understood that the '*given*' is of an enigmatic nature as it is '*the given to*' as well as '*a continuous construction by*' the individual. This amounts to saying that though an individual is thrown into the world, as a '*being of the world*', that which is *'the given'* in his *'throwness'* is not change withstanding and is also in an ever evolving state. Thus, knowing one's situatedness in terms of knowing the context *that is* in which *one is thrown* plays a pivotal role in one's search or quest of ethnic identities. History and cultural anthropology gain importance in this respect as they execute the function of presenting the individual with a clear '*given*' so that an individual can make sense of himself and also present himself to others as objects that *can be made sense of*[13].

Now, in case of ethnic identity crisis, as is the case with the Nepalis in general, and in particular, the Nepali youths of the twenty-first century, who have started travelling far and wide, in search of better livelihood and career opportunities, is severe, since their identity is challenged in every sphere of life and the need to trace their past roots have become urgent and critical[14] so that they come to understand their *situatedness* in clearer terms. As individuals, the Nepali youths have no clear '*given*' as their sense of history is present only in an implicit and unarticulated form, which seems to get entangled between myth[15] and history as soon as it is articulated. This lacuna, in the '*given*', makes it impossible for them to figure out their own *situatedness.*

There are two ways in which people have tried to confront the challenge and move out of this crisis.

The easier way out, but the more dangerous too, is to look for narrower and microscopic categories which are well defined and therefore less hazier and less vaguer to serve as a well defined *'given' prima facie* so that the individual can be made *sense of.* This way out of the crisis seems to me to be dangerous as it not only fails to address the crisis at its core but rather develops a new brand of problem—the problem of the emergence of smaller ethnic groups. Unfortunately, this seems to be the present general tendency of the people in the recent years, as the sense of *belonging to* one of such smaller ethnic classes is on the increase. In the absence of a clear *given,* individuals are anchoring their *situatedness* in small ethnic classes like Tamang, Rai, Limbu, Newar, etc. This, from a theoretical perspective of what has been discussed above, can be seen as a desperate move for *authenticating* one's being and thereby opening up the possibility of being made *sense of.* These developments can be seen as an attempt to present oneself as a *'being in the world'* to a *'being of the world'*. However, identification of an individual with such microscopic categories would only provide an apparent and a *pseudo relief* to the crisis in hand for they are too small to be noticed by the *others* and does not actually solve the problem unless one is able to identify this 'category' as a sub-class of a larger 'class'. That amounts to say that any such escape route will inevitably fall back to square one. In other words, here, the identity crisis is not resolved, or solved, but rather postponed.

The other way out of this crisis is to work one's way out by understanding the logic of the structure of how *'beings of the world'* make sense of *'beings in the world'*. That is, to take the tedious task of understanding the dynamics of the epistemic relation between the subject and *another subject* which transforms as object in the experiential field of the latter subject or the *subject* and *an encountered object that is also a subject.*

The activity of making *sense of* or understanding, if we recall from the first few passages of this paper, are primarily a venture of formulating 'classes', defining them and using them in a way so as to make sense of things in the world. If so, then the way out is to work towards the building up of a 'class', by distinguishing *myth* from *one's situatedness* and events from imaginative fabrications. That is, to analyze and evaluate and construct or reconstruct the identity of class itself. This would give the individual a defined 'class' to which he can now rope in this *throwness*. Attempts have been made in the past to accomplish such venture though the degree of their success is a debatable issue. The notion of 'Gorkhalis' is a case in point and fresher and more novel attempts are yet being made towards this direction[16].

The basic problem that goes unnoticed when one addresses the problem of ethnic identity of the Nepali people is a critical facet that has already been made in the paper earlier, namely, an individual's claim to an identity is a double-edged process. That is,

(a) the claim of *'belonging to'* must be justifiably grounded in the individual's *situatedness,*
(b) and the *'belonging to'* is arrived at by a *mutual recognition* of the individual and the *'others'* intending to make sense of the individual's identity.

The fact is that none of these two fundamental principles of the *dynamics of recognition* is operative with respect to the Nepalis. The Nepalis as *'others'* understand and *make sense of* has no fair and legitimate grounding in the Nepali individual's authenticity. This explains why that which appears to the Nepali individual as mere myths and fabrications are instead held as history by the *'others'*. The doubt that glares at us thus is that the Nepali individual perhaps has no say in this *dynamics of recognition* as if this identity had been enforced upon him by the *'others'* and *vice versa.* The history that is left both for the Nepali individual and the *'others'* intending to make sense of him with respect to his *situatedness* are those which have been scribbled by *'others'* other than a Nepali individual and hence is the *story* of the *situatedness* of the Nepalis *from the outside* far from being his *history.* They are *stories* of *things as they appeared to them*—and the appearance itself bearing the possibility of being coloured and fabricated to suit the needs of those fabricating them as is evident from colonial histories which adorn our library shelves all over the country declaring to disclose the *situatedness* of a Nepali individual[17]. The Nepali individual's crisis of ethnic identity is thus acute for the 'class' with which he was *identified with* and is still identified to a large extent, was done so without his explicit knowledge or *understanding of being identified thus* by the '*others*' and was itself defined by *'others'*. The Nepali individual who ought to be a member of that 'class' never partook in the genesis of the 'class' with which he is identified with and which is still in vogue till date. Furthermore, the defining elements of this 'class', for which the related members of the colonial rule were chiefly responsible, were based on half studied facts, hastily drawn conclusions, and imposition of their cultural parameters upon the Nepali cultural authenticity.[18] This led to the formulation of an identity class whose members after understanding what *they were identified to be members of,* found it impossible to relate to the identity 'class' with the sense of *'belonging to'* and yet be authentic at the same time.

From the preceding passages one can see the importance of history and the individual's need for a deeper sense of history with respect to one's *situatedness* and the vacuum that lies in its place for the Nepali individual in absence of history and cultural studies based on genuine scholarship and research. Since the *situatedness* of an individual is in terms of the physical, historical and the social objectives, comprehensive and discrete research in historical and cultural arenas of the Nepali people needs to be supported and undertaken by scholars-researches that would replace the present assumptions and presuppositions with respect to the history of Nepali people with facts; that would replace the '*once upon a time'* with dates and figures; that would replace myths with facts; and that would rejuvenate historical, social and political events of significance[19]. But most of all, we need research that will project the *situatedness* of the hill people and *'the given'* as changing and not as something static with no room for growth or air[20] for it has to be noted as stated earlier that history accumulates too.

Keeping the situatedness of an individual, the second measure then, as a corollary of these efforts is the formulating and the making available of, a well-defined 'class' for a Nepali individual to which he can hook up his *beingness* meaningfully and legitimately and also for *others* making sense of the Nepali individual. Moreover, the fulcrum of this effort resides, firstly, in the potentiality to make the Nepali individual aware of this 'class' and its connotations. The yard stick of success towards this end is the ability of the individual to identity himself as *'belonging to'* this class. The potentiality of this 'class-concept' to act as a denoter, of every Nepali, when taken as a *'being in the world'* by other *'beings of the world'* and secondly, the fulcrum of this effort resides in the process of actualizing or augmenting this potentiality.

To suggest a measure to this effect, I intend to hint ardently at the teaching of Nepali history in schools and colleges in the hills to make the Nepali individual aware of his situatedness in the phenomenological time and help develop in them a healthy[21] ethnic identity and draw him out from the lure of pseudo attempts to do away with this crisis, by propagating unhealthy microscopic ethnic identities. Of course, historians can take up issues and proclaim that promoting identity class is generally not considered an appropriate goal of history teaching but then even the class of such historians cannot deny that it is essential for the development of ethnic identity in its historical aspect[22].

NOTES AND REFERENCES

1. By the term 'unique' I mean species-specific attributes.
2. This is justified by the fact that thinkers both in the west and the east have devoted considerable time to the treatment and formulation of such categories or 'class-concept' (universals).
3. I take 'understanding' in its broader denotation to mean 'making sense of'.
4. Now taking into account the vastness of the range of 'know-claims', it is obvious that we have many such categories or class-concepts operative in epistemic realm. Of course, concepts could be simple, complex, open, closed, etc., but a detailed discussion of this classification is not demanded by this paper.
5. Though, I am indebted to the writings of Paul Ricoeur and Martin Heidegger for the ideas expressed herein, I am aware that they would have had problems with some, if not all, of the ways in which I use the term 'being in the world' and readers are not to confuse the terms used here with certain imports these phrases and terms might get in their hands. The senses in which I use them are elucidated in the paper itself. I justify their usage for they are able to express clearly what I intend to express and I beg pardon for the neologism.
6. This is a basic presupposition made in so far as we cannot claim that all

other entities apart from the animals belonging to the higher strata of the animal kingdom lack this ability. To make such a claim unassailably and definitively would be an error of taking ignorance as non-existence.

7. A notion that Ricoeur propounds.
8. Identities like personal identity, fatherhood, brotherhood, motherhood, friends, etc. are other identity categories.
9. The term 'Nepali' in this paper denotes only those Nepalis who are Indian citizens as is obvious for they alone face this identity crisis. Further, following Prof. T.B. Subba's distinction (2003: 56) I use the word consciously in lieu of 'Nepalese'.
10. The way you *actually are* in terms of your customs and social habits and your historicity.
11. The 'Nepalis of Nepal and the Nepalis of India' debate has been there for a long time now. It is more evident in Nepal than in India. Differentiation is strongly made between the Nepalis of Darjeeling and the North-East hills of India and the Nepalis of Nepal. Any individual who visits Nepal for more than a week will neither seek any justification to this claim that I make here nor mark it as uncritical. In the cases of Nepalis from the other parts of the country, especially the North-East, they realize that they are not grounded in the classes or categories of the region like Mizos, Nagas, Assamese, and Manipuris.
12. This strengthening can be instantiated by the almost ready question "Then are you from Nepal?" which any Nepali will be unavoidably asked if he steps into other parts of the world or even into other parts of the country. It is also to be understood that the question is in no way a demeaning one but rather a genuine confusion of the questioner and the questioner's failure to classify the individual in hand into a 'class' or 'category' to make sense of him. The point to be wondered is that nobody has any confusion with respect to Bengalis for that matter, if they are from Bangladesh or not.
13. It is, however, not to be misunderstood that I am claiming 'ethnic identity' as a product of mere history, for it is evident that I do not share this opinion as it is obvious from my treatment of an individual's *situatedness* and *historicity*. What I am claiming here is that history, though not sufficient, is however a necessary element of ethnic identity which has palpably been ignored.
14. There are of course many who either are, or choose to be, oblivious of the issue altogether. They are those who have not yet confronted *'the beings of the world'* as *'being in the world'*.
15. Though recent studies in social and historical sciences do not bother much to distinguish between the two, yet one cannot dilute the distinction between factual-objective statements from speculative subjective ones dominated by unrestricted imagination.
16. Professor A.C. Sinha's coinage and usage of the term 'Nepamul' in his prologue in A. C. Sinha and T. B. Subba (eds), *The Nepalis in Northeast*

India. New Delhi: Indus Publishing Company. 2003, is an example, though it is yet to be accepted by scholars unanimously.

17. The issue here is not whether it was fair on the part of the colonialists to have written a history founded on observations that were already bound in their political motives and cultural impositions, and partially understood cultural institutions of the Nepalis. One is to take into account and also grant that the colonialists were interested only in certain epochs and specific facets of the *situatedness* of the Nepali individual and it can be argued if they were really writing *a history* in true sense of the term and whether their objective was to really *understand* the *situatedness* of the Nepali individual rather than present to the world the *situatedness* of the Nepali individual to suit their premeditated purposes. After all, one cannot sincerely take mere writings on some *personal diaries* and *travelogues* as the primary source of a genuine document of one's *situatedness* without further investigation which unfortunately is the case with the *so called history* written by the colonialists and then by others based on these colonial readings. The issue rather is to treat these writings as history itself in absence of any other alternative. May people come and do better and attempts are now being made to undo this unfortunate error.
18. Wittgenstein, in his *Lectures on Frazer*, accuses Frazer's *The Golden Bough* of committing the same mistake of superimposition.
19. *Significance* as being understood as something resulting in a better understanding of historical, social, economic and political *situatedness* of an individual's *facticity*.
20. This is most needed to come out of the mythical concepts that the hill people associates and are associated with the identity concept of 'Nepalis'.
21. This is not to be confused with an idea of closed teaching of history to generate a Nazi-attitude of being a superior race or to develop any such lines of thought.
22. Other subjects like Cultural Anthropology and Sociology can be equally crucial unfolding and developing the cultural and social aspects of ethnic identities.

4

Possibilities of Cultural Communication: Identity and Nationality across Cultures

GOUTAM BISWAS

Theory of Communication

Communication may be understood as a one-way transmission of certain spiritual-cultural contents to the members of a community from within the community for substantiating and strengthening the socio-political agenda of retaining the differential markers of the community. Communication may also be participatory in nature within the community and in a space created between the particular community and its other. Despite inter-ethnic schisms at various levels and dimensions of social life, particularly in Northeast India, a poly-ethnic ethos and multiculturalism as a philosophical disposition is a cognizable phenomenon. The question of identity of a particular community, particularly from the socio-cultural angle, is often smudged or in an ever extending mode in the face of identities which exist either with an emphasis upon the incorrigibility of a type of self-enclosure and resistance to each other or a self-reflective acceptance of change as a value without any dilution of one's cultural *swaraj*. The practice of cultural swaraj is by definition a self-conscious project of a community—the community that is not oblivious of its own identity, cultural memory and history but at the same time in progress and eager to locate its culture in a larger space. If this phenomenon is stretched to an interactive/participatory model of communication, emergences of disciplines like comparative philosophy and comparative literature become explicable. Increasing communication between literary practices of Bengalis and Nepalis of West Bengal and Assam, Nepali and Hindi literature can be cited as examples in support of this thesis. Interactions between literary activities of Nepali population in India and other Indian communities vindicate the assertion that in the context of Indian society and polity at large Nepalis have been able to mark their existence in a significantly richer fashion and to safeguard their existence against marginalization and hegemonization. Issues related to identity and nationality across the cultures of India and Indian subcontinent can be addressed from this point of view that may succeed in settling conflicts to a certain extent.

There is no single phenomenon called the phenomenon of communication, but there are phenomena of communications. As Raymond Williams, a well-known social scientist and a theorist on communication as a subject of human studies, pointed out,

> "....the study of communication, in its modern forms, is a convergence or attempted convergence of people who are trained, initially, in different fields; in history and philosophy, in literary and cultural studies, in sociology, technology and psychology. What all these people have in common, ultimately, is a field of interest. But it is not only inevitable, it is also in the end useful and necessary, that they should study this field in what are, at least initially, very different ways. For the problems, when closely examined, are neither simple, nor special, and the necessary range of different kinds of knowledge and different kinds of analysis is beyond the scope of any single approach"[1].

If this concept of communication is shifted from the sphere of a discursive understanding of convergence of ideas of different academic disciplines to the context of lived experiences in concrete geographical, demographic and social-cultural situations, the varieties of phenomena of communications remain ineluctable. What are these communications? Do we have to understand them as cases of communication production or communication consumption or manifestations of true human fellowship or derangement derived from an obsessive commitment to 'transmission view' which is oblivious of the 'space' between the others? In fact, a philosophy of communication is not derivable from such exteriorities or factualities of communication. Our choice of any specific type of communication in its socialized sense reveals its axiological parameters as well.

In this connection a distinction between the *transmission view of communication* and the *ritual view* may be relevant. James W. Carey, a theorist on media communication, has explicated communication as a human cultural phenomenon. He says:

> The transmission view of communication is the commonest in our culture—perhaps in all industrial cultures—and dominates contemporary dictionary entries under the term. It is defined by terms such as 'imparting', 'sending', 'transmitting' or 'giving information to others'. It is formed from a metaphor of geography or transportation. If the archetypal case of communication under a transmission view is the extension of messages across geography for the purpose of control, the archetypal case under a ritual view is the sacred ceremony that draws persons together in fellowship and commonality ... It sees the original or highest manifestation of communication not in the transmission of intelligent information but in the connection and maintenance of an ordered, meaningful cultural world that can serve as a control and container of human action.[2]

But, even in this ritual view, what is missing is an adequate emphasis upon the nature of relational space which shapes communication and determines its acceptability in terms of a kind of virtuality. But at the same time a preferential approach can be easily marked in comparing such models. In Carey's own assessment with endorsement drawn from Williams:

> Our minds and lives are shaped by our total experience—or, better, by representations of experience and, as Williams has argued, a name for this experience is communication. If one tries to examine society as a form of communication, one sees it as a process whereby reality is created, shared, modified, and preserved. When this process becomes opaque, when we lack models of and for reality that make the world apprehensible, when we are unable to describe and share it; when because of a failure in our models of communications we are unable to connect with others, we encounter problems of communications in their most potent form ... The wide-spread social interest in communication derives from a derangement in our models of communication and community. This derangement derives, in turn, from an obsessive commitment to a transmission view of communication and derivative representation of communication

> in complementary models of power and anxiety. As a result, when we think about society, we are almost always coerced by our traditions into seeing it as a network of power, administration, decision and control—as a political order. Alternatively, we have seen society essentially as relations of property, production and trade—as an economic order. But social life is more than power and trade, and it is more than therapy as well. As Williams has argued, it also includes the sharing of aesthetic experience, religious ideas, personal values and sentiments, and intellectual notions—a ritual order.[3]

This preference for the ritual order, in a little unnoticed manner, is based upon a sense of human loss an ethical evaluation of which consists in defying the vertical nature of a politics of culture with its network of power, administration, etc. as operative in the transmission model of communication. Still such preferences lack an ethico-philosophical underpinning which would not simply justify preference and/or defiance in terms of a lack of human satisfaction (which may easily be turned down as a sort of human whim) but explicate their ontological and axiological relevance. To do so, the best step is to address oneself to questions like: What is the nature of the space for communication? Is it like physical space? Is such a space created by the social/individual subjects or groups as subjects? Is it outside the subject and therefore expressive of a defiance of the primacy of any subject? Does it have its own ontology, and if so, what is this ontology like? Does it have any moral significance for which we prefer a particular mode of communication as being more human? Questions concerning the space for communication hinge upon the human ontological (i.e., anthropological) and axiological (i.e., having ultimate worthwhileness or counter-worthwhileness) concern over the phenomena of communication. Relation between communication and value is conceivable in the context of posing, discussing and answering these questions.

An ethics of communication is conceivable within the broad spectrum of these questions. The *other* is the primary focus in this conception because the space for communication beholds the communicating selves as *others*, as *those-facing-each-other*. The ethics of communication, in its root, is the ethics of the 'face'. According to Levinas, a French philosopher with original contribution to the domain of contemporary continental philosophy and a well-known name in the field of existential ethics:

> It is with subjectivity understood as self, with the exiding and dispossession, the contraction, in which the ego does not appear, but immolates itself, that the relationship with the other can be communication and transcendence, and not always another way of seeking certainty, or the coinciding with oneself. Paradoxically enough, thinkers claim to derive communication out of self coinciding ... In expiation the responsibility for the others, the relationship with the non-ego; it precedes any relationship of the ego with itself. The relationship with the other precedes the auto-affection of certainty, to which one always tries to reduce communication.[4]

Any justificatory note for a particular model of communication without any link with this relationality is not true to humanity. Martin Buber, an existentialist thinker who introduced dialogical existentialism, held that this relation has its 'own being'. In Maurice Friedman's extension of the philosophy of Buber, 'relational trust' plays a major role in pedagogic communication.[5] A decentering of self in a space for the other and to become an *other* has become a central theme in our time. Here 'de-centering' does not mean 'dis-location'; on the contrary, it is based upon a self-conscious programming of the mode of communication that challenges the transmission view and any politics of culture that tends to usurp the identity of an *other*,—individual, group, community and society. Creation of literary works of art and diffusing them through translation work is a mode of communication that invites dialogue, which cannot deny the *presence* of that self and its *identity*. Here de-centering is explicable more in the sense of disclosure. Such works also bring writers of different communities in proximal terms. The success of practiced Nepali literature is worth mentioning in this connection. It may be considered one important way to reveal the exteriority of the politics of culture or any hegemonic political system.

Cultural Communication and De-centering of Self

A culturally centered self is clearly conscious of its mission of enlarging its own purview with information stock, technical know-how, and its own markers. In the multi-ethnic, multi-lingual and multi-cultural context of Indian subcontinent this theme has gathered momentum in constructing conceptual categories for cultural studies, and the ethics of communication under the control of any master is questioned.

Participatory mode of communication in this case is largely controlled by the communitarian interest, which should not perhaps have any marginal importance in matters of state craft. But state craft alone cannot exhaust the infinite possibilities of human beings. The fundamental philosophical-anthropological presupposition of human sciences today is this infinitude till the time an individual is alive and the cultural self is struggling both for sustenance of its being in deepening its obligation to the tradition and sharpening of its critical power. From this point of view communicative action in participatory mode needs to extend its horizon beyond the point of sheer utility; it then becomes 'dialogical' in a horizontal sense and involves a moral responsibility of projecting the other culture, other person, and the other horizon as such within its own space.

Acceptability of a culture to other cultures is grounded on this process, which can be called a process of '*selfing the other and othering the self*'[6]. This does not however make the cultural being of a self lose sight of its own markers because the very nature of the dialogical space does not permit it. One can explicate its nature in terms of what I have somewhere called 'Cultural *Swaraj*'.[7] Internal logic of the concept of swaraj or self-rule is such that the moment I speak of my swaraj I have to acknowledge the swaraj of the other. By denying the cultural swaraj of the other one cannot have one's own swaraj. This recognition does not simply speak of a neutral co-presence of many cultural selves or more than one cultural self; the very act of recognition here requires one cultural self to be respectful and dialogical to other such selves. Dialogicality is thus an essential component of swaraj. If the participation of the other in public sphere is constricted, inhibited, and finally refused then some 'Self' or 'Selves' who are not others for themselves monopolize participation as policy makers and/or rulers.

At a theoretical level it surfaces as epistemic violence as it denies the very possibility of developing a modality of knowing the other in terms of the categories available with the other. In terms of this recognition, the logic of swaraj speaks for a philosophy of non-closure and possibility of cultural communication across the identities and cultural boundaries. While such communication is a commonplace phenomenon in generating intermediate spaces between cultures in the Indian context a self-conscious projection of it in the public life assigns a philosophical and ethical underpinning to it so much so that it becomes a part of the philosophy of life for individuals and collectivities. It is like a space that is produced out of an interaction or encounter between two cultural spaces somewhat or fully unfamiliar to each other. If it is an intermediate space produced out of an interaction between cultural spaces of say, X and Y, it is a third space not completely identifiable with X or Y but somehow working as a bridge between the two with the ethos of both. It is like the translated version of a literary work of art. In fact spaces of this kind become components of the cultural life of people over the years. As long as encountering an *other* culture is not out of one's choice the interaction is not self-consciously programmed and therefore not dialogical in the truest sense of the term.

The question remains: 'is this choice necessary at all?' Or is there any question of choice at all? It has two answers, viz. the first in terms of the inevitability of the presence of an other before a self, be it an individual or collective; the second answer points to the absurdity of the question of identity of an individual or cultural self without an other. Even then the choice remains to be in a non-dialogical relationship where communication is deeply divided and in a conflictual mode or to be absolutely self-enclosed accepting the existence of others in a non-interactive manner. While the former mode of communicative action can seek correction and improvement upon the situation because inter-subjectivity among communities, though in a conflictual mode, still prevails, the second option is straightway anti-progress and pro-closure endangering the very existence of an individual and/or community as a whole. The distinction between self-determination and self-enclosure is smudged or obliterated in this second context. The political system that generates conflict and divided communication should undoubtedly be critiqued but the system responsible for endangering the very existence of a community should be taken to task.

Victory of Little Narratives: The case of Nepali Literary Communication

Let us not talk about any political system that works more as something exterior to the internal history, tradition and culture of a community. In fact the politics of culture developing out of such system takes a vertical character and looks upon other cultures in a hierarchical fashion. It is rather a question of each and every community in Indian society to be so ethically and rationally equipped that no exteriority can matter to its existence and progress in a significant manner. One principal means to achieve this state is to practise the logic of *swaraj* in every communitarian perspective with regard to other individuals and communities by engaging oneself into developing a translated version of one's cultural reality as an intermediate space that may become the ideal reference point for a community and its *other* too. In this respect the Nepalis of India have made considerable progress by engaging themselves with translation work and inspiring the other Indian communities to take up the same project. Today the richness of Nepali literature and cultural lineage has reached the wider and larger readership in India and abroad. Particularly in the context of Northeast India this in a way has created a major impact by developing an intermediate space of familiarity for India as whole.

The narratives of the Nepalis in India are 'little narratives' like many other communities, but as little narratives they have reached the maximal point of success by questioning any master narrative in a rather unnoticed manner. The proximity of such narratives with other narratives in the country has of course been an advantage for reaching this goal. But proximity speaks of similarity and not of any identical prototype. In fact it is also a matter of amazement that despite such proximity either in terms of a moral search for nationality of the community[8] or alternative of caste-centered approach to life,[9] the hypocrisy of the middle class in the context of individual relationship amongst one's own people,[10] the serious task of retaining the uniqueness of the style of presentation and nurturing the overwhelming philosophy of life for the community is never lost sight of. Translated versions of these works inspire people of different *forms of life* and different traditions to re-understand their own life praxis and traditions. Translations of some such works have offered the third intermediate space to the Bengali intellectual ethos. Contribution of Indian Nepalis to making this third space remains often unuttered but continues to work silently for sustaining and nurturing the 'Sky of Nationality' as the sky of inerasable and rich differences. Transcendence from the trivialities of life and the world is an important component of such translated versions. In fact a literary work of art represents two inter-related facets of life. First, as an art form it disengages itself from such trivialities and fact-ridden nature of the world and simultaneously it transcends them in suggesting a different or virtual order of reality. Thus it becomes an *addendum* to the existing culture and its narratives.

Secondly this disengagement and transcendence do not mean any other-worldliness but points to a deeper perspective of life and the world mostly in a narrativized shape. As Baudelaire said, 'There are moments of existence when time and space take on extra-depth and the feeling of existence is immensely amplified.'[11] In a way it disowns and deconstructs the present reality as an already 'spoken fact'. But in another sense it owns the reality in a transformed and reconstructed form. No translation work can overrule these characteristic features of literary works of art. On the contrary a translation transmits the deep insights and realizations in one form of life to another form of life and enriches the latter. For example, the untold tale of the exploitation of a Nepali woman gathers a new significance in its Bengali translation for the Bengali readers and adds to the stock of narratives they have for further insights into their own social reality[12]. The translucency in every narrative due to its aporia[13] results in a serious hermeneutical effort on the part of its reader, and for its translator the task is double; he has to delve into the depth of the aporia in the translatable text and its narrative on the one hand, and the narrative he is going to make out of it in the translated form based upon his own system of signs but crossing its limits on the other.

One important outcome of this way of working is the spread of identity and national character of a particular community across other cultures. While it speaks of its own cultural *swaraj*, it asserts and establishes the value perspective emerging from it in the wider national context,—the context which can be named as the 'Sky of Nationality' [14] It marks a transition from closure to non-closure, projects a resistance to be definitive in the face of any vertical engineering of the politics of culture and ushers in a new horizon.

NOTES AND REFERENCES

1. Raymond Williams, 1995, 'Human Communication and its History' *in* Oliver Boyd-Barrett *et al.* (eds), *Media, Knowledge and Power,* London and New York: Routledge, pp. 33-34.
2. James W. Carey, 1992, *Communication as Culture: Essays on Media and Society*, New York and London: Routledge, pp. 15, 18-19.
3. *Ibid,* pp. 33-34.
4. Sean Hand (ed.), 1994, *The Levinas Reader*, Oxford and Cambridge, Blackwell, p. 18.
5. Maurice Friedman, 1995, in S.C. Malik and Pat Boni (eds), *Intercultural Dialogue and the Human Image*, New Delhi, Indira Gandhi National Centre for the Arts and D.K. Printworld (P) Ltd., p. 100.
6. I owe this concept to my colleague Professor C. Goswami of the Department of Philosophy, University of Hyderabad, India.
7. I have explicated this concept in my paper "Reason, Normativity and Cultural Swaraj" in Sujata Miri (ed.), *Rationality and Tribal Thought,* New Delhi, Mittal Publications, 2004.

8. This refers to Pawan Chamling's poem "Rashtriyatko Akash", in Pawan Chamling 'Kiran', *Antaheen Sapana: Mero Vipana* (collection of poems), Yangyang, Nirman Prakashan, 1986 (1993), p. 10.
9. This refers to Rupnarayan Sinha's short story *Bigreko Bahun* in Rupnarayan Sinha, *Katha Navaratna*, Darjeeling, Col. Shamsherjung Singh, 1950 (1971). Bengali translation by Haren Ghose, *Raatbhor Jhar Bristi*, Kolkata, Jogmaya Prakashani, 2001.
10. This refers to Rajendra Bhandari's poem *Afna Mancheharu* in Rajendra Bhandari, *Kshar/Akshar*, Gangtok, Nirman Prakashan, 1998, pp. 57-8.
11. As quoted by Roger Cardinal in *Figures of Reality*, New Jersey, Barnes and Noble Books, 1981, p. 129.
12. Rupnarayan Sinha's short story "Dhanmati ko Cinema-Sapana" in Rupnarayan Sinha, *op. cit.*, Bengali translation by Haren Ghose, *op. cit.*
13. 'Aporia' is a Greek concept the literal meaning of which is 'without a gate or entry'. In post-structuralist writings it signifies a paradox or moment of self-contradiction not resolvable dialectically and in which meaning becomes un-decidable. It poses a resistance to be definitive.
14. "Sky of Nationality' is a literal translation of Pawan Chamling's "Rashtriyatako Akash", *op. cit.*

5

Rethinking Gorkha Identity: Outside the Imperium of Discourse, Hegemony, and History

BIDHAN GOLAY

> "Critique is the movement by which the subject gives itself the right to question truth on its effects of power and to question power on its discourses of truth...in a word, the politics of truth."
>
> —*Michel Foucault*

Introduction

The phase we are living in is one of the most crucial in human history. It is a phase marked by contradictions and confusions, and a phase that is increasingly characterised by the interplay of two seemingly opposing and yet complementary forces of essentialism and hybridity. At one end of the continuum is a growing tendency in global political and economic forces towards greater integration—one that is stoked by the continual movement of people and their cultural baggage across the boundaries of nation-states, throwing up new forms of trans-national practices, locations, solidarities, and institutions that do not strictly conform to the demands and logic of the nation-state. In fact, theorists like Arjun Appadurai have already written obituaries of the nation-state.[1] At the other end of the same continuum, still newer forms of micro-politics have secured moral legitimation, marking a distinctive shift towards the fragmentation of the cultural landscape.[2]

In the backdrop of this, the question of identity has saddled itself firmly at the centre stage of both academic and political debates. The argument in essence is that the old identities that had stabilised the social world for so long are in decline, giving rise to new identities and fragmenting the modern individual as a unified subject. The 'crisis of identity' is now increasingly seen as a part of a wider process of change which is dislocating the central structures and processes of modern societies and undermining the framework which had until now given the individual a stable anchorage in the social world.[3] In the rarefied terrain of academics we are witnessing debates that raise significant questions about the very legitimacy of the fundamental axioms of enlightenment and the way 'history' has been conceptualised as an irreversible process of modernity. With this movement, the earlier notion of a universal human subject has come under serious attack and the notion of a 'decentered subject' seems to be acquiring greater salience in academic parlance.

It is in such an academic climate that this paper will try to understand the emergence and formation of the Gorkha[4]/Nepali identity in India spanning a period of over two hundred years and its continuing crisis. The crisis of identity is nothing new to the Gorkhas in India. It was co-opted together with the people as they were introduced to 'Civilisation' and 'History'. And with the passing of time it has only become that much more convoluted and complex. At a much deeper level, the problem of identity is in fact the problem of modernity. One of the most enduring and lasting features of modernity is the necessity of all modern subjects to organise themselves around the normative idea of nation.[5] The modern identities circumscribed as they are by the symbolic boundaries of the nation are mediated by the complex discursive structures of national culture and national identity. In such a situation the problem of Gorkha identity cannot be understood in isolation. The need here is to locate it within the complex matrix of nation, space, territory, culture, race, and history. It is by understanding the nature and dynamics of the discursive formations of these structures that our effort to deconstruct the Gorkha identity may come to fruition. This paper in that sense is a preliminary attempt to theorise the Gorkha identity by locating it in these discursive structures. In what follows, I will make a modest attempt to contextualise the emergence of Gorkha identity in nineteenth century colonial India, tracing its origins in the British colonial discourse particularly in their ethnographies on "martial race". Taking the colonial encounter as the historical moment of its evolution, the paper will try to map the formation of the Gorkha identity through an inter-textual discourse study within the context of the colonial public sphere and the liberal nationalist historiography of colonial India. Further, I shall argue that the problem of Gorkha identity exits at two levels. One, the very idea of Gorkha identity is inscribed on the body of the individual Gorkha by the colonial discourse. At another level, the historical experience of the Gorkha creates a sense of a deterritorialised Gorkha subjectivity, torn between two seemingly conflictual impulses of a primordially constructed notion of Gorkha *jati* (community) and the demands of a modern nation-state.

The Poverty of Academic Research and the Question of Gorkha Identity

The 'life-world' of the Gorkhas in India is located both literally and figuratively on the margins of the imagined nation. This 'marginality' is not merely a location but a byword for the oppressed and dispossessed. It is characterised by the dispossession of narratives, the cannibalistic appropriation and the continuing colonisation of their epistemological grid. For the most part, it occupies a peripheral location in relation to the metropolitan academic research. It remains an under-researched terrain, in which the standards of the scholarship emerging from these locations struggle to measure up to the standards set by the 'mainstream' academia, which on its part forms a peripheral location *vis-a-vis* the metropolitan academia. The Gorkhas who were historically subjected to the Orientalist gaze of colonial humanist anthropology continues to remain the subject of discourse. From such a standpoint, the academic discourses on the problem of Gorkha identity, emerging both from within and without appears skewed and stifled by the disciplinary contours of traditional methods of social enquiry. Their narratives revolve around the idea of the Gorkhas as an exclusive ethnic group juxtaposed with the liberal nationalist imagination of the Indian nation. There exist some commendable works on identity formation, particularly on the importance they have laid on collective memory of home and the experience of migration, and the changing structure of caste and village settlements.[6] However, a comprehensive study of the contributions of social and cultural movements in Darjeeling and elsewhere towards the formation of a distinct Gorkha identity still eludes us. What is clear in these scholarships and other forms of utterances, especially the ones that have come from within, is the evidence of the fundamental fissures that are located in the interstices of the subjectivity of the Gorkha. Barring a handful of works which can be called insurrectionary, majority of these tend to revolve around the celebration of the famed "bravery" of the "Gurkhas".[7] Girdled by the colonial constraints of valour and its validation, the Gorkha subject appears ambivalent towards colonialism. Colonialism is often understood in a periodic sense rather than a well-defined set of discursive practices outliving the formal end of the more brutal forms of rule.

What is completely missed out here is the reality of the continuing discursive colonisation of the Gorkha identity. Similar is the case with the studies on the more recent movements of the Gorkhas for statehood. There is a marked tendency in these works to explain it away as stemming from economic causes like relative deprivation or internal colonialism—one that informs the paternalistic policies of the Indian state—or it is simply pitched as a case of ethnic exclusivism and "separatism". Both forms of scholarship suffer from reductionism. Either it is an instrumentalist understanding of the problem, or worse still, it is about constructing an identity in the most essentialist image. The missing link in both these genres of works is colonialism. It is not as if these interpretative gestures and exercises have ignored the colonial history, but where they have failed is in the diachronic comprehension of the colonial primaries of the Gorkha identity-formation. We shall return to discuss all these, particularly the relations of power as it is reflected in our historiography and nationalist imagination, a little later.

Identities are as much self-constructed as it is constructed by the other. In that sense there appears a fundamental difference in the manner in which the Gorkha identity or the Gorkha *jati* is imagined by the 'self', and the way the Gorkha identity is conceptualised in the metropolitan as well as in the 'mainstream' Indian academic discourses. There appears a significant gap in the meanings of the word *jati*. Even while admitting that the word *jati* is a loose term that allows a wide array of meanings within its semantic field, Gorkha *jati* in the culturally specific sense signifies a cultural identity, expressed through imageries and symbols derived from its composite culture.[8] The Indian 'mainstream' academic discourses in their turn have merely derived from the metropolitan academia. Since the 'mainstream' academia looks at the peripheral identities and their narratives through the Western lenses, it takes a derivative form.[9]

The 'Gurkha' as the *Subject* of Discourse and their History

The 'Gurkha' identity as a 'martial race' is largely the 'discovery' of the ethnographical knowledge of the colonial state. This discovery marks off the colonial state's shift in its emphasis from the brutal modes of conquest to cultural technologies of rule—the production of colonial knowledge.[10]

A lot has been written about the 'short, broad chested, flat faced, snub nosed men with their *khukuris*'.[11] In one of the ironies of history, it was the defeat of the Gorkha soldiers under Amar Singh Thapa that led to the 'discovery' of the 'Gurkhas'. Numerous reasons ranging from the 'run of reverses and deaths of veteran English generals in the war' inspiring awe for the Gorkha soldiers,[12] the (East India) Company's desire to cut down the number of Hindus with 'brahmanical prejudices', to the 'growing Russian threat to the British Empire from the North Western frontiers necessitating the shifting of the base of recruitment from Madras and Bombay towards Punjab and Nepal' have been cited for the Company's decision to enlist the Gorkhas in the British Indian Army.[13]

It is indeed important to contextualise the decision to recruit the "Gurkhas" in the political requirements of the colonial state. The imperatives of Empire building had prompted the British into thinking that it would be better and cheaper to dominate the world if the natives could be induced to shoulder much of the Whiteman's military burden.[14] But to attribute the decision to the political exigencies alone is to over simplify the issue. Furthermore, Lionel Caplan argues that 'the theory of martial race did not emerge *sui generis* to meet specific military needs, rather it was a deeper manifestation of the wider European doctrine of biological determinism or scientific racism'.[15] Hence the search for the best "fighting material".

The discourse on martial race occupies an important place in the larger scheme of colonial knowledge and its relation with power and domination. The underlying idea of "martial race" was elegantly outlined by Lieutenant-General Sir George MacMunn in his, *The Armies of India* (1911) in the following way: 'It is one of the essential differences between the East and the West, that in the East, with certain exceptions, only certain clans and classes can bear arms; others have not the physical courage necessary for the warrior. In Europe as we know, every able bodied man, given food and arms, is a fighting man of sort...In the East, or certainly in India, this is not so...Nor are appearances of any use as a criteria. Some of the most manly looking people in India are in this respect the most despicable.'[16] The theory had two main strands. One, it was based on the idea of natural qualities, emphasising that martiality was an inherited trait and therefore an aspect of 'race'. Secondly, martial thinking introduced an element of environmental determinism. It was argued that warlike people were to be found in hilly, cooler places, while in hot, flat regions, races were supposed to be timid, servile and unwarlike.[17]

Within a short time, martial race enthusiasts not only reshaped the British Indian army but also systematised the new discourse. Towards the end of the late 1890s, the "martial races" began to be codified in a series of official "Recruiting Handbooks" for the different classes of the Indian Army, which were almost invariably written by British officers long acquainted with the troops concerned. Here, Caplan makes an interesting observation about the long existing huge body of literature on the 'Gurkhas'. He senses a strong current of 'consensus and continuity in them, coming across as monolithic and timeless, relying heavily on stereotype, and with little political and historical content'.[18] The atomizing effect of the ethnographic enumeration of the 'Gurkhas' into smallest meaningful component led to the essentialisation of the Gorkha traditions. Furthermore, the working of the Foucauldian 'system of dispersion' is quite clear in the colonial representation of the 'Gurkhas'. In a strange way, the British admiration of the 'Gurkhas' was reserved to the ordinary soldiers only and not to the Gorkha officers. Moreover, the discourse on martial race was as much about the praise of the dogged bravery and masculine qualities of the Gorkhas as it was about highlighting the cultural difference. Thus it was a commonplace belief that the 'Gurkhas' could realize their enormous potential *only* under the tutelage, supervision and leadership of British officers. The 'bravery' of the 'Gurkha' was considered to be a danger to him, forcing the British to keep him under continuous supervision. Eden Vansittart, one of the illustrious recruiting officers, is supposed to have remarked that 'without a strong hand they [the Gurkhas] would very soon deteriorate and become slovenly'.[19] Choicest of racist labels like 'tykes', 'little highlanders', 'little Gurkha', 'little blighters', 'doughty little Mongolian hillmen' were used even as they fetishised him.[20] One of the common jokes about the Gorkhas that did the round was about a mule that went lame when he kicked a Gorkha head while the Gorkha got a slight headache.[21]

Colonialism aestheticised the native Gorkhas in a typically Orientalist image, who squatting next to the white man would add the charm of a simple and unsophisticated native to his prepossessing presence. It was a deliberate policy on the part of the British to recruit from the most illiterate and remote regions of Nepal. The search for the most authentic Gorkha would force the *gallawalas* (local appellation for recruiting agents) go deep into the interiors of Nepal to prise open his pristine habitat. Scientific racism had led the British into believing that an ethnic group could be martial only in one's own territory. It was commonly held that the Magars and Gurungs, who had migrated to east Nepal, would cease to be martial because intermarriage would lead to the contamination of their blood which carried military qualities. Jeffrey Greenhut, while discussing the structure of the racist British Indian Army, says that 'Indians who were intelligent were labelled as cowards, while those defined as brave were uneducated and backward. In such a case, the British Gentlemen stood to combine both intelligence and courage necessary for a man to become officer'.[22] If the Bengalis were 'effeminate' then the Gorkhas had to be 'brave'.

The colonial state through various measures ensured that those who joined the ranks of its army are treated well back in their society. In 1899, Field-Marshal Lord Roberts revived a dormant order granting soldiers precedence in hearing of civil suits. Five years later Lord Kitchener persuaded the Prime Minister of Nepal to exempt former Gorkha soldiers from *corvee* works. Many of them were honoured on public and festive occasions.[23] The discourse on martial race and the subsequent enlistment of the Gorkhas into the British Indian Army changed the entire course of the Gorkha history. At the discursive level, the colonial state firmly placed its control over the hill societies by 'civilising' and 'normalising' the 'frontiers'. It also collapsed multiple identities and fluidities, typical of the Gorkha society then, and represented them as a single identity—the martial identity. The ethnic identities were stereotyped and continuously reproduced through a discursive practice. In fine, colonialism violently disrupted the social-conceptual world of the Gorkhas, taking away his freedom by permanently colonising his body. The Gorkha subject was dislocated by stripping off his past and relocated him back again as a deterritorialised subject of "History".

Three battalions of Gorkha regiments were raised as early as 1815.[24] By the time Sepoy Mutiny was crushed, the Gorkhas had proved their masters right. A series of recruiting depots came up along the long stretch of areas bordering Nepal. By 1864, the British government issued a charter providing for the Gorkha Regiment to buy land for settlement stations at Dharmasala, Dehradun, Almora, Gorakhpur, Shillong, etc. In Darjeeling, the Gorkha Recruitment Depot was opened in 1890, and it continues to draw recruits from in and around Darjeeling and neighbouring Nepal. By January 1904, nearly 57 per cent of the Indian Army (86,841) came from Punjab, Nepal or the Frontier.[25] Though some changes have been brought about in the recruitment policy since Independence, the discourse of martial race continues to be the guiding principle for recruitment of groups like the Gorkhas and Sikhs to the Indian Army.[26]

Colonial Capitalism, Plantation Labour and the History of Darjeeling

Much of the early history of Darjeeling remains in oral form, interwoven with myths and anecdotes, passed down the generations. Nepali history seems caught in a time warp where the same old hackneyed events unfailingly keep appearing in its unchanging form over and over again. For some strange reason the paradigm of social enquiry in the hills remains ossified and immune to the world of social and cultural theories. As a result the scholarship that comes out from here fails to situate itself on the broader canvas of postcolonial theoretical discourses in general and such on India in particular. One way of making amends to these inadequacies is by undertaking a comprehensive inter-textual analysis of the colonial discourse in all its varying forms, particularly the relation between colonial knowledge, power and domination. A cultural criticism of colonialism and its 'technologies of rule' will certainly open up new areas of research.

The most striking aspect of the history of Darjeeling is the issue of "migration". No one seems to be taking the issue head on.[27] The question of "migration" is used as a favourite stick to beat the community on most occasions.[28] The point of contention seems to be centering around an innocuous sounding report by Dr. Campbell, who was appointed as the Superintendent of Darjeeling and who claimed to have raised the population from 'not more than hundred souls in 1839 to about 10,000 in 1849, chiefly by immigration from the neighbouring states of Nepal, Sikkim and Bhutan.'[29] All kinds of theories and counter theories have come up. The entire debate seems to be caught in a dangerous cycle of cause and effect or what is popularly known in migration theories as "push" and "pull" factors. But one feels that by oversimplifying the matter we are doing the greatest disservice to those who experienced it. The question of migration should be properly theorised by rescuing it from this binarism and situating it in the prevailing colonial 'racist ideologies that identified particular sections of the people as intrinsically and biologically suited for particular tasks'.[30] When history is tinkered endlessly with an intention to pass some kind of a retrospective judgment on a community, it only becomes that much more hazier and confusing.

Darjeeling was sparsely populated when the British set their foot there. The boundaries with its neighbouring territories were notional and people from adjoining places would come for grazing sheep and cattle or for cutting firewood. But with the discovery of Darjeeling by the British as an ideal retreat, far removed from the "heat" and "dust" of the northern plains, much of the things changed. With the establishment of a 'modern regime of power' in Darjeeling, this wild frontier was gradually normalized into a "hill station". Colonialism ended its fluidity by putting it firmly under the control of its knowledge system. This production of colonial knowledge about Darjeeling, to borrow from Sudipta Kaviraj, led to the refiguring of the 'fuzzy' identities into an 'enumerated' community.[31] In fact, the production of knowledge later became a necessary tool of domination and control in the hands of the colonial state. This 'anthropolisation of knowledge' by the 'ethnographic state' proceeded slowly in the context of myriad other interests and processes in this period. The decade of 1860 saw a veritable explosion in the production and circulation of gazetteers and manuals that included extensive reports on the manners and customs of the castes, tribes, and religion of the specific regions being studied.[32] Census was one of the most widely used tools for 'transforming barbarism into civilized data, effecting a transformation of moral condemnation into moral basis of both science and state.'[33] What was happening in the rest of colonial India was also happening in Darjeeling. The colonial state with its superior cognitive apparatus set about collecting "facts" and creating knowledge about Darjeeling and its inhabitants. Through an extensive use of, what Bernard Cohn calls the "investigative modality",[34] botanists and naturalists set about conducting studies on the local flora and fauna, local population, the products of which were voluminous treatises on the region's plant species and other information.[35] Survey and cartography were used extensively in the 'geographical arrangement of knowledge necessary for state supervision'.[36] The Darjeeling Municipality, one of the very few municipalities then in India, was established in 1850, and the first official census was carried out in 1872.

Coming back to the question of migration, the colonial state adopted specific theories and administrative practices while dealing with 'frontiers' and margins. The trajectory of the expansion of the colonial state's sovereignty followed a distinct pattern, from the first outlining of territory and subjects to the reconstruction of the state and society. In considering the spread of the jurisdiction of the colonial state, Peter Robb talks about two types of borders and frontiers, viz., internal and external borders, and narrow and broad frontiers.[37] The narrow external frontier was the one the colonial rulers sought to draw on the map. The broad internal borders, on the other hand, represented the one in which there were various layers or zones of contestation and influence rather than a definite line of demarcation between one jurisdiction and another. Moreover, within India the indeterminate zone of authority persisted, and was even encouraged by the colonial rulers for all their claims of sovereignty. The narrow frontier implied a single rule of law within a given territory. However, there were exceptions to this rule, mainly by excluding many aspects of life, classes of people and territories (non-regulation and frontier provinces, princely states and so on) these exceptions constituted the broad internal frontiers of British rule. This demarcation was not only a physical line; rather it was a demarcation of the various realms of transitional sovereignty.[38]

A similar kind of territorial concepts was in practice in Nepal. The entire territorial domain was called *muluk*. The king saw himself as a landlord or *malik* of his territory. Within the *muluk* there was *desa* or realm over which the king exercised ritual authority. The realm was an auspicious icon of the universe centered on the temple of the king's tutelary deity (Taleju) and demarcated on the perimeter by temples.[39] The third concept was the notion of *des*, meaning country. The "country" consisted of unique people who experienced a common moral and natural identity by virtue of their living and interacting in the same region. People of the same country spoke a common language, shared a common lore (of proverbs, stories and songs), and observed certain customary practices that objectified as a way of life of their country.[40] Furthermore, the boundary of the possession depended on the collection of revenue. This boundary extended or receded depending upon the ambition and strength of the kings' revenue collectors. The ritual boundary, on the other hand, was fixed in particular localities which might be outside the administrative boundaries.[41] All these complexities both in colonial India and in Nepal point towards the fuzzy nature of the entire northern frontiers.

But the Nepalese did migrate to *Muglan* (the land of the Mughals), and their numbers kept increasing with the possibilities of starting tea and cinchona plantations in Darjeeling. Migration was encouraged by feeding the oppressed and brutalized people with stories like, *chiyako botma paisa falchha*, meaning money grows on tea bushes. Migration was a painful experience, a tragic event in the lives of most people, even though in the Burghardian sense it was merely an act of 'relinquishing one's tenurial contract in one polity and taking up in another polity within the "country".'[42] Nepal was considered to be the land of the pure, leaving which meant permanent defilement. "Immigration" was encouraged by the colonial state, as it required cheap labour for building infrastructure for its "hill station", and most importantly for its teeming tea gardens, which had by the turn of the century formed wonderful mosaic on those "virgin" hills. There is an interesting parallel between the discourse of "martial race" and the discourses that informed the decision to employ "Hill Coolies". Just as the "Gurkha" soldier, simple and free of religious prejudices was better suited to serve in the British Indian Army, he was also thought to be a useful plantation worker as he was casteless, docile and hardworking hill-man. It was within the matrix of race relations in the colonial situation that the colonial capitalist enterprise (tea gardens) encouraged migration. The British planters did not fail in employing *sardar*s (local appellation for agents) who would go to Nepal and bring back "young" and "healthy" labourers to work in their tea gardens. The *sardar*s in return got commissions from the planters. Along with this, the *sardar*s had the additional duty of enforcing discipline and attendance, for which 'he got one pice (paise) for every worker turning up for work'.[43]

The most significant impact of colonial capitalism was that through its civilizing mission it transformed the docile and hardworking hill-man into a proto-wage labourer. The hill-man was turned into a reified commodity.[44] Like elsewhere, the tea gardens in Darjeeling too provided 'a massive spectacle of order, productivity and enterprise, a constant picture which provided the self-assurance that was so crucial to the European culture of colonial rule?'[45] While the discourse of martial race had succeeded in creating the Gorkha regiments as a domain for continuous disciplining of the body of the "Gurkha", the tea gardens on the other hand created a rival domain in which the "hill-man" was turned into a hard working labourer, disciplined and controlled by colonial science—the Imperial botany. The British Indian Army and the tea gardens while competing with each other completed the process of colonisation of the body of the "Gurkha".

The Emergence of a Community and the Stirrings of an Alternative Identity

Towards the middle of the nineteenth century the colonial state started consolidating its power through a series of territorial acquisitions from Sikkim and Bhutan. By early twentieth century the colonial state had firmly established itself as a 'modern regime of power'. Like elsewhere the expansion of the colonial rule towards the frontiers like Darjeeling led to the 'institution of European forms of civil society even though it always remained an incomplete project'. Furthermore, as Partha Chatterjee observes, the process of legitimation of the colonial state by creating a public domain in the form of civil society was fundamentally limited as it could confer only subjecthood on the colonised. The colonised in response refused to accept membership of this civil society of subjects and began constructing their identities within the narrative of community.[46] Moreover, this civil society did not spread evenly, limiting itself to a small section of 'citizens' which meant that the enlightened elites often engaged in a pedagogical mission in relation to the rest of the society.[47] Darjeeling also witnessed somewhat similar kind of developments. By the middle of the second decade of the last century there had emerged a sizeable middle class in Darjeeling. They often engaged in pedagogical missions, educating the masses for a need to form a strong community. Pratyoush Onta identifies general education and improvement of Nepali language and literature as the two special areas of emphasis of the reform movements of this time.[48] A flurry of civil society organisations like the Nepali Sahitya Sammelan (1924), Gorkha Dukha Niwarak Sammelan (1932), Sri Hitkari Sammelan (1945), Himalaya Kala Mandir (1950) and many others emerged which were actively involved in redefining and creating a new self-identity based on the idea of kinship—Nepali *daju bhai*. Another major factor in this amalgamation was the standardization and universalisation of Nepali language. The efforts of these organisations and many other factors led to a pluralist synthesis of the myriad groups that together constituted the Gorkha *jati*, secured and sustained by a pluralist culture and imagination. In a rather strange way colonialism became, to invoke Marx, the "unconscious tool of history", providing a basis for fashioning a new self-identity. This has led scholars like T.B. Subba to argue that nation building which has been the national goal of Nepal, to have realised itself outside the boundaries of Nepal.[49]

Here, it will be an interesting exercise to study the Gorkha subjectivity. To be sure, the problem of Gorkha subjectivity is not so much the problem of cultural displacement as it is a sense of being deterritorialised. There was a certain sense of lack that kept haunting him as he left his home and hearth. His subjectivity was bitterly torn between the calling of the home and the hard reality of never returning to see it again. There was optimism and hope when he said '*sunako lingo, chandiko ping, ek jieu khana launalai thikai chha Darjeeling*', meaning Darjeeling will take care of me. But there was also a fear of the uncertain. This liminality of the deterritorialised subject was clearly reflected in the cultural production of those times. It was not surprising that it created, to borrow a phrase from Appadurai, a 'diasporic public sphere', in which even while the nascent community was making ceaseless efforts to ground its new self-identity, was also at the same time lamenting the fact of leaving home. Nepal was present everywhere, within the subject as a memory, and more strongly in its literary utterances. The memory of migration was at once an occasion to feel lost, and also a historical moment from where one had to chart a different course of history. It was also a moment for readying oneself to the regimen of new life. People would often say '*ek jhumro launchhu, ek mana khanchhu*', meaning "I will live frugally".

This material history was subjectively reproduced in many famous literary works like Lil Bahadur Chhetri's *Basai* and *Brahmaputrako Chheuchhaumaa*, Lain Singh Bangdel's *Muluk Dekhi Bahira*, Rudraraj Pande's *Prayaschit*, Asit Rai's *Naya Chhitijko Khoj* and many others that were based on the motif of exploitation and migration.[50] This also explains the unprecedented popularity of Man Bahadur Mukhia's *Ani Deorali Roonchha*, a play that captured the plight and oppression of the people caught in the cycle of debt in late nineteenth century rural Nepal. Agam Singh Giri, in many ways, epitomises this double consciousness of the subject that swore by the primordial form of communal self-identity that was beginning to locate itself within a nation, which had just begun its career. In his works one can trace the self-identity constructing its moral ideological foundations on the spiritual conception of *pahaad* (hill), *kamaan* (tea garden), and *maato* (land). These ideological foundations were grounded on the notion of *bir Gorkha jati* which for its own historic reasons became the foundational narrative of a deterritorialised community recreating its home in a somewhat alien place. His poems like *Mayaloo paakha chiyaabaari, Suna hai suna Nepali*, and *Pahaad ki raani Darjeelinglai* exhort his fellow folks to reconcile to the reality of Darjeeling as their new home.[51] But there are also indications of a somewhat diasporic community's yearning for home, located in the interstices of the text. The ambivalences of the subject stand out very clearly in poems like *Meechilai baato sodhera, Shri Panch Maharajdhiraj prati pravasko sadhbhavna*, and *Samachar yahi bhanidinu*.[52]

The process of Gorkha identity formation was the product of the cultural renaissance in Darjeeling. However, this process of formation of a strong cultural identity in the shape of Nepali identity was again unsettled as it was relocated within the matrix of the national culture and identity of the Indian nation. The problem of identity arises when this national culture not only provides resources for defining the identities but also mediates it. National cultures, as Stuart Hall reminds us, are not composed of cultural institutions but of symbols and representations. Furthermore, national culture is a discourse—a way of constructing meanings that influences and organises both our actions and conceptions about ourselves. National cultures, he argues, construct identities by producing meanings about the nation with which we can identify.[53] Furthermore, the process of the formation of self-identity was dislocated by the Nepali historiography which while carving out a political space in the liberal nationalist imagination of India constituted its subjectivity in the pre-colonial Gorkha glory and bravery. It is not that there were no indigenous conceptions of martiality and valour. The problem with Gorkha history is that these very ideas and values were appropriated by the colonial state by giving a scientific sanctity to the great tradition. Thus the narrative of the *bir* Gorkha quite logically conflates with the discourse of "martial race". It creates a peculiar situation in which the *bir* Gorkha is self-idealized and reified into a brave soldier but since the identity is deeply implicated in the colonial history, it remains tied to the white master with feudal loyalties. In such a case ambivalence towards colonialism becomes inevitable. The Gorkha subject while attempting to liberate itself from the hegemony of colonial discourse creates a new subjectivity in the self-identity which is again reconstituted by the same discourse from which it came out. Thus, the emerging cultural identity of the Gorkha remains hostage to the racial identity inscribed on the body of the Gorkha by the white man through colonial state. Colonialism not only created hierarchy of knowledges, it also created a hierarchy of human beings in which the "Gurkha" was consigned to the role of a supplicant, first to the white man and then later to the inheritors of that colonial knowledge.

The Problem of Gorkha Identity and the Discourse of Freedom

The Gorkha identity has been treading a difficult path in which it has tried to strike a fine balance between its cultural identity and the demands of citizenship and national culture of India. The Gorkha identity constituted in the narrative of the community had to submit to the postcolonial state 'embedded as it was within the universal narrative of capital which does not necessarily recognize within its jurisdiction any form of community except the single, determinate, demographically enumerable form of the nation.'[54] The problem of the Gorkha identity arises from everyday experiences and the necessity to carve out a political space for its cultural identity in India. The identity often claims its legitimacy by citing its contribution to the anti-colonial struggles.

This moral claim is often buttressed by the denial of history, the historical link with Nepal. Hence, the lexical juggleries like *Indian-Nepali*, *Bharatiya-Gorkhali* or *Bhargoli*. Part of the problem also stems from the manner in which the Nepali historiography has charted its path. One feels that in these historical works there is no serious attempt to interrogate colonialism. One also senses a subtle fixation of our historians with colonial knowledge. There is an innate feeling that the native's history can be authenticated only when it is culled from Western sources—the Vansittarts, the Hookers, the O'Malley's. In effect, the very colonial discourses have become the canonical texts for the production of knowledge about the community both from without and from within. The native voice is often lost in the cacophony of the metropolitan and 'mainstream' voices. The immediate impact of this historiography is the endorsement of the idealised and orientalised identity as the self-identity. In other words, the historiography orientalises the Gorkha identity. As Edward Said would like to remind us, the Orient was Orientalised not only because it was discovered to be "Oriental" in all those ways considered commonplace by an average nineteenth-century European but also because it could be—made Oriental.[55] The colonial knowledge system at once participates in the construction of reality and also gets itself constructed.[56] The true goal of the Gorkha historiography should be 'to recover their own particular forms of subjectivity from the universalising modes and reconstitute them and restore in history'.[57] There is a need to reconstitute the Gorkhas as a historical character, rehabilitate their consciousness and agency in history. This can be done by engaging with the canonical texts, reading them against their grain and unsettling the discourse. This will eventually liberate the Gorkha identity from the hegemony of discourse and the totalising tendencies of Western history.

The liberation of the Gorkha identity from the colonial discourse should create fertile grounds for further hybridisation of the identity and not towards essentialisation of identity. Identities, we must remind ourselves, are always hybridised. Identities often keep changing boundaries making culture the prime site of contestation of the multiple layers of identities. It should be thought of as a 'production' which is never complete, always in process, and always constituted within, not outside, representation.[58] The Gorkhas are spread across South Asia, most of them hybridised by the local traditions, languages, and cultures. In such a case, it will be more useful to think of the Gorkha identity as a post-national identity or a Southasian identity.

NOTES

1. Arjun Appadurai, "Patriotism and Its Futures", in his *Modernity at Large: Cultural Dimensions of Globalisation*, New Delhi: Oxford University Press, 1997, pp. 158-177.
2. Yogendra Singh, "A Life-World of Disenchantment: Modernity, Ethnicity and Pluralism", in *Sociological Bulletin*, Vol. 4, No. 2. September 1998, pp. 155-65.
3. Stuart Hall, "The Question of Cultural Identity", in Stuart Hall, David Hall, *et al.* (ed.) *Modernity and Its Futures*, Polity Press, in Association with Open University, 1992, p. 275.
4. The word 'Gorkha' comes from the small principality (now a district) in Nepal by the same name. The kingdom of Gorkha was established by Drabya Shah in 1559. It is located 40 miles west of Kathmandu. The names 'Gorkha' and 'Nepali' are used interchangeably in India although political movements at different times have favoured the use of the word Gorkha over Nepali in order to differentiate between the citizens of Nepal and India. T.B. Subba has devised an ingenious way differentiating them. He spells the citizens of Nepal as "*Nepalese*", and the Nepali speaking Indians as "*Nepalis*". See his, *Ethnicity, State and Development: A Case Study of the Gorkhaland Movement*, New Delhi: Vikas, 1992, pp. 67-74.
5. Dipesh Chakrabarty argues that European imperialism and third world nationalism have together achieved the universalisation of the nation-state as the most desirable form of political community. See his "Postcoloniality and the Artifice of History: Who Speaks for the Indian Past?" in Padmini Mongia (ed.), *Contemporary Postcolonial Theory: A Reader*, New Delhi: Oxford University Press, 1997, p. 240.
6. On the factor of migration and memory, see Kumar Pradhan's *Pahilo Pahar,* Shyam Prakashan, Darjeeling, 1982. On the changing nature of caste structure, see T.B. Subba's, "Caste Relations in Nepal and India", in *Social Change*, Vol. 15, No. 4, December 1985, pp. 23-26.
7. In Western writings, the word Gorkha is spelt as "Gurkha" or "Goorkha".
8. Kumar Pradhan talks about the multiple meanings of the word Nepali, viz., a language, a citizen of Nepal, and as a cultural identity. See his *Pahilo Pahar*, *op. cit.*, p. 4.
9. Partha Chatterjee, while commenting on the nature of anti-colonial nationalism says that while nationalism challenged the colonial claim to domination, it also accepted the very intellectual premises of 'modernity' on which colonial domination was based. See his *Nationalist Thought and the Colonial World: A Derivative Discourse,* New Delhi: Oxford University Press, 1996, p. 30.
10. Nicholas B. Dirks, "Foreword", in Bernard Cohn's, *Colonialism and Its Forms of Knowledge: The British in India*, New Delhi: Oxford University Press, 2002, p. ix. Also see, Bernard Cohn and Nicholas B. Dirks, "Beyond

the Fringe: The Nation State, Colonialism, and the Technologies of Power", *Journal of Historical Sociology,* Vol. 1, No. 2, June 1988, pp. 224-229.

11. Kamal Raj Singh Rathaur, *The Gurkhas: A History of Recruitment in the British Indian Army*, Nirala Publications, New Delhi, 1983, p. 33.
12. Kanchanmoy Mozumdar, "Recruitment of the Gurkhas in the Indian Army, 1814-1877", *The Journal of the United Service Institution of India,* Vol. lxxxxiii, April-June 1963, p. 143.
13. David Omissi, "The Sepoy and the Raj: The Indian Army, 1860-1940", McMillan Press Ltd., 1994, p. 12.
14. *Ibid*., p. 2.
15. Lionel Caplan, "Martial Gurkhas: The Persistence of a Military Discourse on 'Race'"in Peter Robb (ed.), *The Concept of Race in South Asia*, New Delhi: Oxford University Press, 2006, p. 261.
16. Quoted in Lionel Caplan's, "Bravest of the Brave: Representation of 'The Gurkha' in the British Military Writings", *Modern Asian Studies*, Vol. 25, No. 3, July 1991, p. 580.
17. Lionel Caplan, (2006), *op. cit.*, pp. 260-261.
18. Lionel Caplan, (1991), *op. cit.*, p. 573.
19. *Ibid*., p. 573.
20. *Ibid*., p. 573.
21. Omissi, *op. cit.*, p. 26.
22. Jeffrey Greenhut, "Sahib and Sepoy: An Inquiry into the Relationship between Officers and Native Soldiers of the British Indian Army", *Military Affairs,* Vol. 48, No. 1, January 1984, pp. 15-16.
23. Omissi, *op. cit.*, pp. 68-69.
24. For details, see Kanchanmoy Mozumdar, *op. cit.*
25. Omissi, *op. cit.*, p. 19.
26. For a detailed discussion on the continuity and change in the recruitment policy, see Omar Khalidi, "Ethnic Group Recruitment in the Indian Army: The Contrasting Case of the Sikhs, Muslims, Gurkhas and Others", *Pacific Affairs*, Vol. 74, No. 4, Winter 2001-2002, pp. 529-52. Also see his, 'No basis in military bias", *The Hindustan Times*, New Delhi, February 19, 2006.
27. Kumar Pradhan has dealt with the issue in part but there is a need for a more comprehensive research on it. See his, *The Gorkha Conquest: The Process and Consequences of Unification of Nepal with Special Reference to Eastern Nepal*, Calcutta: Oxford University Press, 1991, pp. 178-179.
28. See the chapter titled "A Historical Outline of the Migratory Movements", in *Gorkhaland Agitation: The Issues, An Information Document* (A white paper issued by the Government of West Bengal, published by the Director of Information, Government of West Bengal, 1986.) pp. 4-6.
29. L.S.S.O' Malley, *Bengal District Gazetteers: Darjeeling*, New Delhi: Logos Press, 1989, p. 22.
30. Ania Loomba, *Colonialism/Postcolonialism*, London: Routledge, 2001, pp. 125-26.

31. Sudipta Kaviraj, "On the Construction of Colonial Power, Structure, Discourse, Hegemony", in Sudipta Kaviraj (ed.), *Politics in India*, New Delhi: Oxford University Press, 1997, pp. 156-157. Also see his, "The Imaginary Institution of India", in Partha Chatterjee (ed.), *Subaltern Studies*, Vol. VII, New Delhi: Oxford University Press, 1993, pp. 1-39.
32. Nicholas B. Dirks, "The Ethnographic State", in Saurabh Dube (ed.), *Postcolonial Passages: Contemporary History Writing on India*, New Delhi: Oxford University Press, 2004, p. 70.
33. *Ibid.*, p. 78.
34. Bernard Cohn, *Colonialism and Forms of Knowledge: The British in India*, New Delhi: Oxford University Press, 2002, pp. 4-5.
35. For example, J.D. Hooker's *Himalayan Journals: Notes of a Naturalist in Bengal, the Sikkim and Nepal Himalayas, The Khasia Mountain, etc.* (2. Vols.) Ward Lock and Co. Ltd., London, 1891. A. Campbell's, "On the Tribes around Darjeeling", *Transactions of the Ethnological Society of London*, Vol. 7, 1869.
36. Peter Pels, "From Text to Bodies: Brian Houghton Hodgson and the Emergence of Ethnology in India", in Jan Van Bremen and Akitoshi Shimizu (ed.) *Colonialism and Anthropology in Asia and Oceania*, Surrey: Curzon Press, 2000, pp. 66-68.
37. Peter Robb, "The Colonial State and the Constructions of Indian Identity: An Example on the Northeast Frontier in the 1880s", *Modern Asian Studies*, Vol. 31, No. 2, 1997, pp. 248-49.
38. *Ibid.*, p. 250.
39. Richard Burghart, "The Formation of the Concept of Nation-State in Nepal", *Journal of Asian Studies*, Vol. xliv, No. 1, November 1984, pp. 103-05.
40. *Ibid.*, p. 106.
41. *Ibid.*, p. 112.
42. *Ibid.*, p. 108.
43. E.C. Dozey, *A Concise History of Darjeeling District Since 1835*, Printed and Published by the Art Press, Wellington Square, Calcutta, 1916, p. 120.
44. Kaushik Ghosh, "A Market for Aboriginality: Primitivism and Race Classification in the Indentured Labour Market of Colonial India", in Gautam Bhadra, Gyan Prakash and Sussie Tharu (eds.), *Subaltern Studies: Writings on South Asian History and Society*, Vol. X, New Delhi: Oxford University Press, 1999, pp. 13-18.
45. *Ibid.*, p. 14.
46. Partha Chatterjee, *The Nation and Its Fragments: Colonial and Postcolonial Histories*, Oxford University Press, Delhi, 1995, p. 237.
47. Partha Chatterjee, "Beyond the Nation? Or Within?", *Social Text*, Vol. 16, No. 3, Fall 1998, p. 6.
48. Pratyoush Onta, "Creating a Brave Nepali Nation in British India: The Rhetoric of *Jati* Improvement, Rediscovery of Bhanubhakta and the

Writing of *Bir* History", *Studies in Nepali History and Society*, Vol. 1, No. 1, June 1996, p. 39.

49. T.B. Subba, "Nepal and the Indian Nepalis", in Kanak Mani Dixit and Shastri Ramachandran (eds.), *State of Nepal*, Kathmandu: Himal Books, 2002, p. 126. Also see Harka Gurung, "Nepali Nationalism a Matter of Consolidation", *Himal South Asian*, Vol. 14, No. 3, March 2001, p. 22.
50. Michael Hutt, "Being Nepali without Nepal: Reflections on a South Asian Diaspora", in David N. Gellner, *et al.* (eds.), *Nationalism and Ethnicity in a Hindu Kingdom: The Politics of Culture in Contemporary Nepal*, Amsterdam: Harwood Academic Publishers, 1997, pp. 102, 140.
51. See, Mohan Thakuri (ed.), *Agamsingh Giri Rachna Sanchayan*, New Delhi: Sahitya Akademi, 1992.
52. See Bijay Kumar Rai (ed.), *Agam Singh Giri Rachnaavali*, Vol. 1, Namchi: Nirman Prakashan, 1998.
53. Stuart Hall, *op. cit.*, pp. 291-92.
54. Partha Chatterjee, 1995, *op. cit.*, pp. 237-38.
55. Edward Said, *Orientalism: Western Conceptions of the Orient*, New Delhi: Penguin Books, 1995, pp. 5-6.
56. Ronald Inden, "Orientalist Construction of India", *Modern Asian Studies*, Vol. 20, No. 3, 1986, pp. 444-45.
57. Rosalind O' Hanlon, "Recovering the Subject: Subaltern Studies and Histories of Resistance in Colonial South Asia", *Modern Asian Studies*, Vol. 22, No. 1, 1988, p 190.
58. Stuart Hall, "Cultural Identity and Diaspora", in Padmini Mongia (ed.), *op. cit.*, p. 110.

REFERENCES

Appadurai, Arjun. 1997. "Patriotism and Its Futures". In Arjun Appadurai, *Modernity at Large: Cultural Dimensions of Globalisation.* New Delhi: Oxford University Press, pp. 158-77.

Burghart, Richard. 1984. "The Formation of the Concept of Nation-State in Nepal". *Journal of Asian Studies*, Vol. XII, No. 1, pp. 101-25.

Campbell, A. 1869. "On the Tribes around Darjeeling". *Transactions of the Ethnological Society of London*, Vol. 7, pp. 144-59.

Caplan, Lionel. 1991. "'Bravest of the Brave': Representation of 'The Gurkha' in British Military Writings". *Modern Asian Studies*, Vol. 25, No. 3, pp. 571-97.

_______. 1995. "Martial Gurkhas: the Persistence of a British Military Discourse on 'Race'". In Peter Robb (ed.), *The Concept of Race in South Asia*. New Delhi: Oxford University Press, pp. 260-81.

Chakrabarty, Dipesh. 1997. "Postcoloniality and the Artifice of History: Who Speaks for the Indian Past?". In Padmini Mongia (ed.), *Contemporary*

Postcolonial Theory: A Reader. New Delhi: Oxford University Press, pp. 223-47.

Chatterjee, Partha. 1988. "Beyond the Nation? Or Within?" *Social Text*, No. 56, pp. 57-69.

——. 1993. *The Nation and Its Fragments: Colonial and Postcolonial Histories*. New Delhi: Oxford University Press.

——. 1996. *Nationalist Thought and the Colonial World: A Derivative Discourse*. Delhi: Oxford University Press.

Cohn, Bernard and Nicholas B. Dirks. 1988. "Beyond the Fringe: The Nation State, Colonialism, and the Technologies of Power". *Journal of Historical Studies*, Vol. 1, No. 2, pp. 224-29.

——. 2002. *Colonialism and Its Forms of Knowledge: The British in India*. New Delhi: Oxford University Press.

Dash, A.J. 1947. *Bengal District Gazetteers: Darjeeling*. Alipore: Bengal Government Press.

Dirks, Nicholas B. 2004. "The Ethnographic State". In Saurabh Dube (ed.), *Postcolonial Passages: Contemporary History Writing in India*. Delhi: Oxford University Press, pp. 70-88.

Dozey, E.C. 1916. *A Concise History of the Darjeeling District since 1835*. Calcutta: Art Press.

Ghosh, Kaushik. 1999. "A Market for Aboriginality: Primitivism and Race Classification in the Indentured Labour Market of Colonial India". In Gautam Bhadra, Gyan Prakash and Sussie Tharu (eds.), *Subaltern Studies*, Vol. X. New Delhi: Oxford University Press, pp. 8-48.

Government of West Bengal. 1986. "Gorkhaland Agitation: The Issues: An Information Document". Kolkata: Director of Information, Govt. of West Bengal.

Greenhut, Jeffrey. 1984. "Sahib and Sepoy: An Inquiry into the Relationship between the British Officers and Native Soldiers of the British Indian Army". *Military Affairs*, Vol. 48, No. 1, pp. 15-18.

Gurung, Harka. 2001. "Nepali Nationalism: A Matter of Consolidation". *Himal South Asian*, Vol. 14, No. 3.

Hall, Stuart. 1992. "The Question of Cultural Identity". In Stuart Hall, David Hall, *et al.* (eds.) *Modernity and Its Futures*. London: Polity Press, pp. 274-315.

——. 1997. "Cultural Identity and Diaspora". In Padmini Mongia (ed.), *Contemporary Postcolonial Theory: A Reader*. Delhi: Oxford University Press, pp. 110-21.

Hanlon, Rosalind O'. 1988. "Recovering the Subject: Subaltern Studies and the Histories of Resistance in Colonial South Asia". *Modern Asian Studies*, Vol. 22, No. 1, pp. 189-224.

Hooker, J.D. 1891. *Himalayan Journals: Notes of a Naturalist in Bengal, the Sikkim and Nepal Himalayas, The Khasa Mountain*, 2. Vols. London: Ward and Lock Co. Ltd.

Hutt, Michael. 1997. "Being Nepali without Nepal: Reflections on a South Asian Diaspora". In David N. Gellner, *et al.* (eds.) *Nationalism and Ethnicity in a Hindu Kingdom: The Politics of Culture in Contemporary Nepal.* Amsterdam: Harwood Academic Publishers, pp. 101-45.

Inden, Ronald. 1986. "Orientalist Constructions of India". *Modern Asian Studies*, Vol. 20, No. 3, pp. 401-46.

Kaviraj, Sudipta. 1993. "The Imaginary Institution of India". In Partha Chatterjee and Gyanendra Pandey (eds.), *Subaltern Studies: Writings on South Asian History and Society*, Vol. VII, Delhi: Oxford University Press, pp. 1-39.

——. 1994. "Crisis of the Nation-state in India". *Political Studies*, Vol. XIII.

——. 1997. "On the Construction of Colonial Power: Structure, Discourse, Hegemony". In Sudipta Kaviraj (ed.), *Politics in India.* Delhi: Oxford University Press, pp. 141-58.

Khalidi, Omar. 2001-02. "Ethnic Group Recruitment in the Indian Army: The Contrasting Cases of Sikhs, Muslims, Gurkhas and Others". *Pacific Affairs*, Vol. 17, No. 4, pp. 529-52.

——. 2006. "No Basis in Military Bias". *The Hindustan Times*, New Delhi, February 19th.

Loomba, Ania. 1994. *Colonialism/Postcolonialism.* London: Routledge.

Malley, L.S.S.O'. 1989. *Bengal District Gazetteers: Darjeeling.* Delhi: Logos Press.

Mozumdar, Kanchamoy. 1963. "Recruitment of the Gurkhas in the Indian Army, 1814-1877". *Journal of United Service Institution of India*, Vol. IXXXXIII, pp. 143-58.

Mukhia, Manbahadur. 2002. *Ani Deorali Roonchha.* Darjeeling: Shyam Prakashan.

Omissi, David. 1994. *The Sepoy and the Raj: The Indian Army, 1860-1940.* London: McMillan Press.

Onta, Pratyoush. 1996. "Creating a Brave Nepali Nation in British India: The Rhetoric of *Jati* Improvement, Rediscovery of Bhanubhakta and the Writings of *Bir* History". *Studies in Nepali History and Society*, Vol. 1, No. 7, pp. 37-76.

Pels, Peter. 2000. "From Text to Bodies: Brian Hodgson and the Emergence of Ethnology in India". In Jan Van Bremen and Akitoshi Shimizu (eds), *Colonialism and Anthropology in Asia and Oceania.* Surrey: Curzon Press, pp. 65-92.

Pradhan, Kumar. 1982. *Pahilo Pahar.* Darjeeling: Shyam Prakashan.

——. 1991. *The Gorkha Conquest: The Process and Consequences of Unification of Nepal with Particular Reference to Eastern Nepal.* Calcutta: Oxford University Press.

Rai, Asit. 1993. *Naya Chhitijko Khoj.* Darjeeling: Shyam Prakashan.

Rai, Bijay Kumar (ed.). 1998. *Agamsingh Rachnavali.* Namchi: Nirman Prakashan.

Rathaur, Kamal Raj Singh. 1983. *The Gurkhas: A History of Recruitment in the British Indian Army.* New Delhi: Nirala Publications.

Regmi, Mahesh Chandra. 1971. *A Study in Nepali Economic History, 1768-1846.* New Delhi: Manjushree Publishing House.

Robb, Peter. 1997. "The Colonial State and the Constructions of Indian Identity: An Example on the Northeast Frontier in the 1880s". *Modern Asian Studies*, Vol. 31, No. 2, pp. 245-83.

Said, Edward. 1995. *Orientalism: Western conceptions of the Orient.* New Delhi: Penguin Books.

Singh, Yogendra. 1998. "A Life-World of Disenchantment: Modernity, Ethnicity and Pluralism". *Sociological Bulletin*, Vol. 47, No. 2, pp. 156-65.

Subba, T.B. 1985. "Caste Relations in Nepal and India". *Social Change*, Vol. 15, No. 4, pp. 23-26.

——. 1992. Ethnicity, State and Development: A Case Study of the Gorkhaland Movement. New Delhi: Vikas Publishing House.

——. 2002. "Nepal and the Indian Nepalis". In Kanak Mani Dixit and Shastri Ramachandaran (eds.), *State of Nepal.* Kathmandu: Himal Books, pp. 119-37.

Thakuri, Mohan (ed.). 1992. *Agamsingh Giri Sanchayan.* New Delhi: Sahitya Akademi.

Acknowledgements: I would like to thank Pemu for all her encouragement, Saunak and Ranjita for going through the earlier version of this paper and giving suggestions, and Eldho and Jay Shankar for being wonderful friends.

6

Being and Belonging: A Study of the Indian Nepalis

TAPASYA THAPA

> 'If one lacks the sponsorship of a nation state, one can readily come to be regarded merely as a "human being" in general—without a profession, without a citizenship, without an opinion, without a deed by which to identify and specify (one) self.'
>
> —*Hannah Arendts*

The identity of the Indian Nepalis has been a contentious issue for many decades and to arrive at an agreeable consensus seems to be the need of the hour. However, this need encounters a big hurdle at the very onset when one seeks to examine tentative connotations of the term "identity." What is identity? The root of this word comes from Latin which means 'the same'. Logically, therefore, identity invokes the concept of sameness. To have an identity one must have features that are both relevant and enduring. Identity of a person should endure through time.

However, the paradox of the term arises when one probes the praxis of the word "identity". The concept of identity rests on the praxis of difference, i.e., difference of persons or groups from other groups. Difference also includes the prospect of re-identification, that is, the possibility of holding distinct features over a period of time. Thus the term allows space for sameness as well as difference. Also, the human condition is constantly in flux, change is the order of the day. People are encouraged and expected to change constantly. Coherence and constancy do not amount to much any more in a world of instantaneous communication and rampant consumerism. In such a world the human self is everywhere and thus nowhere in particular.

The identity of the human self is thus fleeting and evanescent; giving credence to the "post-modern condition" as postulated by the influential French critic Jean-Francois Lyotard in his book titled *The Post-Modern Condition*. The break in self is a result of trying to negotiate the parameters of sameness and difference.

The identity crisis inherent among the Indian Nepalis today is an off-shoot of their condition in this era of globalization. They inhabit a post-colonial world where the third world countries are trying to create their own "space", free from the appendages of their colonial past. Stuart Hall, in his essay "Cultural Identity and Diaspora" published in *Colonial Discourse and Postcolonial Theory: A Reader*, considers the third world countries as a "juncture point", where diverse cultures meet. The Nepali community in India is also part of the diverse cultural fabric of the country. They have been granted citizenship of the country and thus they try and balance themselves between the internal dynamics of Nepali ethno-nationalism and external pressure of conforming and establishing Indian nationality.

The first issue of the journal *Diaspora* defines the concept as such: '*Diaspora* is concerned with the ways in which nations, real yet imagined communities (Anderson), are fabulated, brought into being, made and unmade, in culture and politics, both on land people call their own and in exile.' The Indian Nepalis cannot overlook their diasporic conditions. Therefore, instead of a sense of "being", the current post-colonial situation involves a sense of "becoming". "Being" "becoming" and "belonging" are three terms that constitute the three dimensions of the identity of Indian Nepalis. "Being" denotes a state or fact of existing in space and time. Identity as "being" offers a sense of unity and commonality. "Becoming", on the other hand, emphasizes the temporality of events that occur in the life of a being, be it an individual or a community. The term "becoming" sums up human experience aptly in a post-modern context where the world is seen as a "fragmented whole". Identity as "becoming" hints at a process of identification which shows the discontinuity in our identity formation. This discontinuity is a result of the consequence of ruptured pasts and the inability of the present world situation to explain the dissonance between the past and present. The concept of identity as "becoming" holds a mirror to our post-colonial condition where the powers-that-be of nation states thrive on the politics of "difference" and thus the contentious issue of "belonging".[1]

Marcel Proust, in his great novel *In Search of Lost Time,* jokes with Shakespeare and gives this new perspective on Hamlet: '[T]he question is not as for Hamlet, to be or not to be, but to belong or not to belong.' Similarly, the human condition today is concerned more with the experience of belonging rather than the existential dilemma of being. We inhabit an insecure world where boundaries, whether real or imagined, between nation-states and people of various origins, are constantly changing resulting in unwarranted conflicts. The anxiety of belonging assumes political overtones. The question of survival forces us into the membership of a nation, gender, profession, sexual preference. What matters is admittance to a clan, alliance with "them" which ultimately serves to confer status, image and power. The personal opinion of a human subject is repressed or subjugated in the effort to belong to someone or somewhere. The New World Order purports the human self or being as a political object. The human being as a subject is neglected.

Why does the term "belonging" assume such importance? The term denotes being a part of something, whether a nation or a particular group of people. The term "belong" denotes a relationship between two entities. For these two entities to enter into a relationship, recognition of the identities of each other is essential. Do particular persons belong to a nation or does the nation belong to particular persons?

Thus, the term "belonging" denotes a process in continuum and posits a dubious relationship between the two entities of a particular people and the nation-state. The people striving for recognition by the nation-state automatically encounter and feel insecure in the process of "belonging" and therefore the questions that arise when the term "becoming" is invoked.

It is therefore inevitable that in everyday usage or, even more, in the way it is used every day by the social, political, and journalistic contexts in which we live the word "belonging"—so crucial in human terms—assumes threatening overtones when we talk about "belonging" to one side "as opposed to" another, about things "belonging to us" in a grim division of goods and spaces. The constant query "to what tribe/ community do you belong?" comes as a major irritant when one is trying to establish one's identity on nationalistic grounds but all one encounters is suspicion that is often embedded with a stranger's interrogation.

There is an inherent connection between belonging and participation. The term "belonging" begins to reveal the sense of a more constitutive relationship. You are a part not only because "you are someone's," but also because you take part in. Widening the field, we can say *to belong to a people*, and here the foundation is a sharing of origins, traditions, needs and aspirations. However, if we take a reductive viewpoint of the concept of belonging then we can say that when we belong to a nation or an ethnic group, there is an automatic exclusion of others, as we introduce a principle of division. The nature of being part of or belonging to a nation hinges on the politics of manipulation because the more number of people there are who belong to a particular nation, the less rich and free do the people become. It is a belonging that diminishes in quality and becomes a form of social envy because of the unequal distribution of rights and resources.

Where does one belong? Can one truly "belong" to a particular nation-state? How does the politics of "belonging" carve identity? When and how did nation-states lose the confidence of their citizens? Nation-states purport responsibility to its citizens. The nation-state is an institution for safeguarding the identity and interests of all its members. "All men are created equal", "but some are more equal than other" follows almost immediately Who constitutes the "men"? Post-colonial studies seek freedom of the individual through a thorough investigation of the past. The dilemma of the "present" as a causal auxiliary of identity/difference is attempted to be explained by postcolonial practices of investigating the past and constructing a present that makes sense of concepts like alterity, difference and subject as agency.

The insecurity posed by the notion of "belonging" brings into focus the Indian Nepalis residing in various parts of India. India and Nepal form integral parts of Southasia. The Indian Nepalis constitute a minority group without any privileges of being a minority in Indian society such as the Anglo-Indians and Muslims in India have. The minority concept proposes a power relationship, a relationship based on the historical relation of an ethnic group (Indian Nepalis) to the dominant culture (Indian culture). What is Indian culture? Is it homogenized or does the culture thrive on diversity/difference? How does equality and difference balance each other out in an evolving Indian identity? How do Indian Nepalis negotiate two kinds of identities? A local identity of "being" Nepali and a global identity of "becoming" Indian. Or on three levels? We may be Assamese Nepalis, Manipuri Nepalis, Sikkimese Nepalis, and so on locally, Indian Nepalis at the nation-state level and simply "Nepalis" at the global level, no matter whether one is a citizen of India, Nepal, Bhutan, Myanmar, or Thailand. Unfortunately for the present author, "being" Nepali immediately associates Indian Nepalis with the sovereign country Nepal in the minds of the larger Indian population. This association creates a perception, however false, that the Indian Nepalis are a population who always has the option to return to their "land of origin". The Indian Nepalis thus "become" space invaders in a post-colonial world. Can the Indian Nepalis ever "become" Indian or Nepalese for that matter? The Indian Nepali identity continually changes with the process of "becoming" Indian. There is a conscious effort to detach themselves from the history of Nepal and assimilate themselves with the history of India. Thus the Indian Nepalis are endeavouring to make a "place" for themselves in the matrix of Indian history and therefore Indian society. The struggle for recognition of their identity as Indians goes on. The association of the term "Nepali" with their "being" Indian creates a dissent in their global identity and the Indian Nepalis have not been able to counter balance their Nepali-ness with their Indian-ness.

Continuing with the thread of a post-colonial approach to understanding the current situation of the Nepali community in India, a discussion of a seminal short story of the Nepali language is attempted. The first model of a post-colonial text seeks to incorporate elements of national and regional culture. The Nepali short story *Hami Jastai Mainaki Ama* is one text that seeks to uncover the "past" through a journey. The journey takes into account the spatial movement of events in "space". This particular text is written by Indra Bahadur Rai, an important literary figure in Indian Nepali literature. Rai spearheaded the "Third Dimension" movement in Nepali literature, also known as "Tesro Ayaam" in the 1960s. The third dimension movement in Nepali literature attempts to define the nature and function of Nepali literature. It is an attempt to create a "space" for Nepali literature through the binaries of modernism and postmodernism, even though postmodernism itself is a theory that tries to undercut the reductionist tendencies of assigning binaries. The completeness or 'totality' of human experience is sought to be written. Nepali literature, according to this movement, lacked definition. The literature was merely there. The third dimension movement sought to explain modern man's engagement and therefore postulation with concepts or entities like "existence" and "experience". The study of these two dimensions further the cause of the third dimension movement as seeking a "place" for Nepali literature in a post-colonial world.

The "existence" of the Indian Nepalis constitutes "being". The crisis of "existence" is discerned in the writings of the third dimension movement. "Experience" connotes "becoming". The "experiences" of the Indian Nepalis in India is a continuous process that is defining and setting new parameters of identity for them. The vagaries of "becoming" occur and acquire meaning in fragments. This fragmentation showcases the division in the identity or "becoming" of Indian Nepalis. "Being" Nepalis establishes, for the Indian Nepalis, a false sense of unity *vis-à-vis* a shared and uniform identity with the people of Nepal. "Becoming" Indian Nepalis invests responsibility on the community—a responsibility to understand the past and thus make sense of the discontinuity in identity in a land where the issue of "belonging" is still contentious.

Past, future and present—the understanding of these three dimensions seeks to provide a "totality" of the experience of the history and cultural heritage of Darjeeling in Rai's story, *Hami Jastai Mainaki Ama*. The story is a series of fragmented events that endeavour to document the 'totality' of Nepali experience in India through the historical and cultural consciousness of the Nepali inhabitants of Darjeeling. The journey is made by a woman selling vegetables in the market square of Darjeeling. The development (becoming) of Darjeeling as a town, the poor labourers that came to the place searching for economic respite, the nomadic past of the protagonist's ancestors, etc. are events constructed within the matrix of ever present time. The story is abstract because it incorporates a thousand years of Nepali time and space. Post-colonial and (neo) colonial find "space" in the trajectory of the story. The first part of the story deals with woman creating an economic "space" for her "self" in the market. This "space" is created through spatial categories. Time is secondary. Thus the aspect of "space" in the space-time continuum emphasizes the post-colonial situation. The second half of the story deals with a journey into the past, through time, back to the modern present—a present that glaringly points to the inability of Darjeeling to develop an independent economic and political identity in the wake of "globalization".

The story moves from modernist to postmodernist and back again. A journey into the past, through time, back to the modern, becoming and evolving, the history of Darjeeling and its people, these events invest the text of the story with a modernist appeal. However, the concept of "space" dominates the narrative. Travelling through time and having gone beyond time, in the sense of having transcended any hope of change or progress, the woman in the story finds herself "lost" in space. The post modern element is discerned here. Place identity becomes important to the story because everyone occupies a space of individuation (a body, a room, a "home", a community, a nation) and how we individuate ourselves to these various "spaces" shapes our identity. Darjeeling, its economic regression, scarce water resources, political upheaval, have all pushed its people out of their "place" of identity.

The cultural journey of the woman is juxtaposed with the natural journey of the streams of Darjeeling. The temporal and spatial movements of the image in motion (the flowing streams) hint at the complication of geographical displacement. The journey of the stream is "corrupted", traveling through industrialized terrains and unsound ecological practices. The marketplace in Darjeeling was constructed over a pond. The pond was emptied and filled with earth to make "place"[2] for an economic establishment (the marketplace). This incident is associated with the "greed" of imperialism and colonialism. The journeys are unidirectional in the story, traveling in the direction of change and progress, a modernist viewpoint. However, the first and last parts of the story emphasize the circularity of motion. The woman in the marketplace constitutes the mediating term between the two kinds of movement. She (a metaphor for Darjeeling and its people) is caught between progress and regress, hope and despair. The "meaninglessness" of the circular journey comes through because this journey brings one back to where one was. This "meaninglessness" is corroborated by the fragmentary nature of the story, a post-modern condition.

The dual nature of the text, oscillating between modernism and post-modernism, brings forth the post colonial condition which contrasts a linear view of evolution with a cynical view of the impossibility of real change. The alienated character of the woman and the fragmentary structure are aspects of a concept of a post-colonial world which has not yet succeeded in discovering a socio-political vision that can balance creativity and artistic impulse. The story effectively puts forward the position of the "wandering" Indian Nepalis in post-colonial India through the many journeys portrayed in the text.

Nepali literature easily lends itself to interpretation according to Indian literary tradition, thus bringing into contention the fact that Nepali literature also belongs to the corpus of Indian literature. If we apply the theory of *rasa* to Nepali literature, we can see that the experience of emotions like love and sorrow by the self abounds in our literature. The *rasa* theory claims that meaning is sought to be conveyed in literary works in the nature of an emotional effect of diverse human experience on man's heart and mind. Through this theory a possibility of enumerating the whole range of emotions or states of experience is discerned. The *rasa* theory is therefore a theory of literary experience that purports the seeming human reality. The *rasa* theory builds its structure around the concept of *bhava* (emotion). *Bhava* is an instrument of being. The *vibhava* or element of *bhava* is rendered meaningful by *rasa* and creates an emotion in the reader. There is never one single emotion or condition. The many manifestations of *bhava* attest to this condition of the human "being". Thus the Indian aesthetic theory of *rasa* gives meaning to the Nepali "being" in literature and can further help to uncover and thus cement the participation (and therefore the belonging) process of the community in the rubric of Indian society.

Why is "construction" of the past important to ethnic groups? Nation-states invariably exclude indigenous populations from the nation-building project. The Nepalis have always been involved in the nation-building project as indentured labourers brought in by the British for establishment of tea estates, construction of roads, and valuable soldiers in the army. The concept of the nation-state is a western or rather British concept established in the Southasian region in the late eighteenth century. The initial post-colonial initiative was to build a nation free from the 'influence' of the colonisers. Therefore the Nepalis whose origin was that of being brought in by the British or rather as 'imports' gave ample ground for the community to be viewed through a window of suspicion. Therefore the linguistic demand for the inclusion of the Nepali language in the Indian Constitution was overlooked time and again until 1992, whereas the demand had been gaining momentum since 1909. Also the need for a federal state for the Nepalis has remained a fading dream till date.

Such people constitute ethnic groups and these groups try to come to an understanding of their own identity in terms of something outside of the nation state—either an alternate history, or in ahistorical terms, or in terms of a connection to another nation-state. Thus ethnic groups are "social constructs".[3]

The concept of a shared common genealogy or ancestry is not a determinant of ethnicity because there is always a "choice" involved. An ethnic group can choose a genealogical line. The members of such a group choose which genealogical line to trace and how far back to go to locate the first ancestor. A shared biology gives an ethnic group the option of choosing distinctive biological traits amongst its members which can function as relevant markers of difference. Thus the categorization process is created socio-politically, via power relations and social practices that offend or repress human dignity.

The concept of "ethnicity" carries with it the notion or implied baggage of myth making. Ethnicity often grounds itself on the myth of common descent. A people share a common ethnicity insofar as they share a myth of common descent, that is, insofar as they believe themselves to be descended from common ancestors. Thus the existence of ethnicity is dependent on the beliefs about its existence, which is derived from the mythical lived experiences of common ancestry.

Myths surround the Nepali community in India. The myth of a "double homeland" was created with regard to the Indian Nepalis. This myth further complicates the notion of "belonging" for the community. Furthermore, the Indian Nepalis are Indian citizens and also struggle with the maintenance of their Nepali ethnicity. This leads to a situation of "double consciousness" whereby the minority group is forced to represent two different identities, never finding wholeness in either identity. The myth of the creation of "Greater Nepal" also gives credence to the large-scale displacement of the Nepali community from various parts of the country in early 1980s. The Gorkhaland movement was seen as an attempt towards the creation of this mythical Greater Nepal, leading to further suspicion and doubts regarding the authenticity of the claim that the Nepali community truly sought to belong to India. The myth-making process has been so effective that the tag of "foreigner" sits uneasily on the forehead of Indian Nepalis even today.

The myth of "double homeland", the trials and tribulations of negotiating the dual identities of local and global and the stipulation that the Nepali community in India be aware of the situation of "double consciousness" makes the Nepali question of identity "doubly problematic" and the negotiation for achieving a balance between all these factors calls for encouragement and support from the nation-state that purports responsibility to all its citizens.

The voice of Indian Nepalis was finally heard when the Gorkhaland movement for a separate statehood within the Union of India turned violent. The proof of this is seen in the establishment of an 'autonomous' body of governance in the district of Darjeeling, West Bengal in 1988. This autonomous body was taken to be the solution to all the problems ailing the Indian Nepali population in India. However, the word "autonomous" is mired in confusion. Autonomy of a governing body alludes to separation or secession; it does not lead to independence. Thus the concept of autonomy is puzzling. According to the Canadian political theorists like Charles Taylor and Will Kymlicka, with regard to their postulations about multiculturalism, their conception of the autonomous individual or body becomes important because there is a dialogic dissension in the very construct of the term itself. The individual or group can demand autonomy but it cannot be complete separation or freedom because the individual or group has no function outside the society which is driven by power politics and an inadvertent push towards homogeneity.

Hence, it is neither possible nor right on the part of the nation-state to treat people as autonomous individuals because the term indicates "hanging in the middle of nowhere". The autonomous individual or body cannot assert complete independence because there is no provision for separation. Thus the term becomes misleading.

The importance of finding one's roots cannot be disputed. However, roots also bind one to a singular place. How can one achieve growth in such a scenario? The routes taken by a particular people in the history of time become markers of growth as well as tradition. No doubt an investigation of the routes taken holds us in places but they do not hold us in the same place. A logical understanding of the various steps or routes taken in the making of our identity needs to be addressed so that we can compare our then and now and logically connect meanings to come to a better understanding of who we are and who we should ideally become.

The concept or idea of "we", as Indian Nepalis, should get a definite perspective before we get into the politics of belonging. The insecurity of being that ails us today is only hampering the process of belonging. Unless we know what is being a Nepali/Gorkhali we cannot find a solution to the dynamics of belonging. The nomenclature crisis should be resolved as soon as possible so that a secure Nepali/Gorkhali "being" can finally work towards participation in nation-building and thus get the fulfilment of "belonging".

NOTES

1. See Hall 1994.
2. We can use Jurgen Habermas' concept of 'the public sphere' as the focal point for establishing collective identity in this regard. Therefore the 'market' in the text of *Hami Jastai*...becomes exploratory as well as consolidating space for Nepali identity.
3. I have already specified in the previous lines why ethnic groups come together to form a collective whole. Thus in this sense the entire concept of the formation of ethnic groups is a social construct...with regard to construction or re-construction (re-membering) of a supposed shared history (past). I have used the quotation marks to emphasise the point that all ethnic groups are social constructs in the necessary endeavour of formulating a distinct identity.

REFERENCES

Smith, Anthony. 1986. *The Ethnic Origin of Nation*. Oxford: Blackwell.

Kapoor, Kapil. 1998. *Literary Theory: Indian Conceptual Framework.* New Delhi: East West Press Private Limited.

Pradhan, Kumar. 1984. *A History of Nepali Literature.* New Delhi: Sahitya Academi.

Hall, Stuart. 1994. "Cultural Identity and Diaspora.". In Patrick Williams and Laura Chrisman (eds.), *Colonial Discourse and Post-Colonial Theory.* New York, NY: Columbia University Press, 392-403.

Cohen, Robin. 1997. *Global Diasporas: An Introduction.* Seattle: University of Washington Press.

Anderson, Benedict. 1991. *Imagined Communities: Reflections on the Origin and Spread of Nationalism.* 2nd Ed. London: Verso.

Rai, Indra Bahadur. 1990. *Kathastha.* Darjeeling: Sajha Prakashan.

Macey, David. 2001. *The Penguin Dictionary of Critical Theory.* London: The Penguin Group.

Tölölyan, Khachig. "The Nation-State and Its Others: In Lieu of a Preface." *Diaspora* 1, 1 (1991): 3-7.

——. "Rethinking Diaspora(s): Stateless Power in the Transnational Moment." *Diaspora* 5, 1 (1996): 3-35.

Section 2

Search for Indian National Identity

7

Education, Institutions and Elites Building and Bounding Nepali Public Life in Early Twentieth Century India

RHODERICK CHALMERS

Introduction

The early twentieth century saw the emergence of Nepali public culture in India and, with it, the definition of a modern Nepali identity and its limits.[1] Newspapers, journals and books published largely in India—from centres such as Banaras and, latterly, Darjeeling—reached a growing audience of literate Nepalis. Patterns of migration out of Nepal, coupled with social and educational changes, were enabling the construction of a new type of Nepali community, one that was increasingly self-aware, sophisticated and concerned at its perceived backwardness in comparison with India's more powerful and assertive groups. The topics that concerned many early Nepali writers contributing to this new form of public debate in print often revolved around an aspirational rhetoric of social progress and reform.

This paper questions the scope and functioning of the emergent Nepali public sphere and the ways in which it institutionalised an initially abstract sense of Nepali identity. It follows two broad lines of enquiry: First, how were the abstract concerns of intellectual discourse translated into practical action? To what extent were rhetorical priorities embodied in Nepali social, cultural and political institutions? Second, how representative was the emergent public sphere? Did it have the capacity to involve a wide social spectrum or was it inherently narrow-based and exclusive?

This paper argues that although participation in the early Indian Nepali public sphere was severely restricted, it exerted an increasing influence over Nepali society as a whole and gradually opened its doors to new participants. The early twentieth century saw the emergence of an increasingly assertive middle class which challenged existing power hierarchies within Nepali society. This altered some patterns of social inclusion and exclusion (for example, bringing non-Hindu and traditionally non-Nepali-speaking groups into positions of prominence and influence) but left others (such as the marginalisation of women) untouched. Following a sketch of these theoretical concerns and their historical context, this paper examines three crucial areas: the development of formal education, the building of social and cultural institutions and the composition of a nascent civil society.

Context

A Shift in Gravity

The developments that this paper traces illustrate a gradual shift in the centre of gravity of the Nepali community in India. From the nineteenth century education, political organisation and publishing had centred on Banaras, with its long-established ritual, political and educational ties to Nepal. However, the start of the twentieth century saw an increase in the significance of Darjeeling, which had been populated largely by economic migrants from hill communities in eastern Nepal in the latter half of the nineteenth century. Darjeeling's Nepali community differed from that of Banaras: it was far more ethnically diverse, contained far fewer ancestral Nepali-speakers and was dominated by poor migrants with few resources. Furthermore, Nepalis were a majority in Darjeeling, unlike their counterparts in Banaras (most of whom in any case actively participated in a broader Hindu culture—as Sanskrit students, practising or trainee priests, or *Kashivasi*s, people who had retired to die in Banaras by the banks of the holy Ganga).

The relatively recent migrants to Darjeeling were able to write their culture on a fairly clean slate. Darjeeling itself was a new settlement and almost all residents—Nepalis and others—were immigrants of the first, second or third generations. They shared an often conscious awareness that they could build a new form of society and reshape models of authority. This shaped the way in which they viewed *unnati*—the term for progress which had dominated the calls for Nepali advancement since the late nineteenth century. To a greater extent than in Banaras they initiated essentially modern projects, which appreciated the value of working within and exploiting the modern state. For example, they pushed for recognition through local government and official institutions such as the state education sector.

Institutionalisation

This paper opens with a discussion of the institutionalisation of the Nepali language in the education system. Language was much more than simply a medium for the transmission of ideas: it became a territory for the contestation of cultural authority and control, a symbol of community recognition, and provided the means for fixing and propagating some fundamentals of Nepali identity. These processes took place through debates over language standardisation, campaigns to gain official recognition for the language, and its deployment in early textbooks. The discursive public sphere came to be embodied in varied institutions and—despite the restrictions of Rana Nepal or British India—to engage in politics.

Most of these developments share common features. First, the institutionalisation described here may have had a wide impact across the Nepali community but control of it remained in the hands of a limited number of people. Second, active participation and leadership in Nepali institutions in India demonstrated the increasing value of formal education and professional qualification over birth and ethnic or caste origin. Third, patterns of Nepali institutionalisation were influenced by developments in other parts of India, and by relations with the British regime which varied from patronage to protest. Each Nepali organisation demonstrated in its own way the public face of a nascent Nepaliness. Such public faces may on occasion have been directed at the outside world, as the political agenda of the All-India Gorkha League suggests. But they were probably of greater significance *within* the Nepali community, as it started to look at itself—self-consciously and self-critically.

Exclusivity

As a more concrete, precisely defined concept of Nepaliness emerged, so did new paradigms of exclusivity. The coexistence of inclusive and exclusive tendencies during the development of Nepali public culture reflected the inherent tension of the public sphere itself—between normative and critical tendencies. Questions of membership and agency were entwined with issues of power and control; the definition of identity markers and community characteristics was approached descriptively and prescriptively.

The fundamental criteria for membership of the Nepali *jati*—the term, with no exact English equivalent, which long predated concepts of Nepalis as a 'nation'—were caste and ethnicity. However much Nepaliness might reflect a supra-ethnic formation, belonging remained primarily dependent on birth within a prescribed set of ancestries. However, participation in public life and the chance to contribute to the further definition and development of Nepali culture was conditioned by more mutable factors, especially class and socio-economic status. Success in business could buy access to cultural power, for example through sponsoring publications or exercising leverage as a major donor to public organisations. Educational status could be a basis for promoting those who might otherwise have had a lesser voice or for excluding from power those seen as not reaching the right standard.

The final section of this paper examines the ways in which dynamics of exclusion from public culture were developed, starting with a sketch of early Nepali civil society. This small core of the wider community established its authority through both traditional social hierarchy and the new capital of formal education. Access to active participation in this limited circle of culturally productive people was neither closed—the key activist Parasmani Pradhan, for example, established himself by study and industry rather than high birth—nor completely open. This section proceeds to investigate the lines of exclusion drawn by both educational and cultural elitism, and the attempt to establish normative standards of moral purity and social order. This paper deals with exclusion on the basis of gender, caste or ethnicity only in passing; these are topics that deserve to be covered at greater length in their own right.

Education: Recognition, Consolidation, Propagation

The development of Nepali education was related to questions of language standardisation and authority.[2] Public debate was central to advancing the codification of Nepali but the power to enforce and propagate standards remained unevenly distributed. A major impetus for the standardisation process was the fact that Nepali's promoters had to exploit new methods for its propagation. The power of mass print production extended the reach of the written Nepali word and changed the context of its reception; even pulp fiction publishers had to acknowledge public concern over language usage. The expansion of formal education was even more important. It brought new opportunities to earn official status for Nepali and to disseminate both 'correct' language and an approved version of Nepali culture.

Early Nepali Textbooks and Teaching Methods

At the start of the twentieth century there were few formal Nepali educational institutions. In Nepal only the Darbar School and, latterly, Trichandra College, offered western-styled education.[3] In the Darjeeling area there were some schools but severe limitations (for example, even a sizeable settlement such as Kalimpong did not have a government high school). In Banaras there were numerous schools and also a university but their intake represented only a limited tranche of (primarily) high-caste Hindus.

There were of course other types of instruction. Foremost among these were varieties of Sanskrit *pathshala*s which existed both within Nepal and in large numbers in Banaras. Effectively limited to male Brahman students, and offering a primarily religious curriculum, they nevertheless ensured the literacy of large numbers of Brahman Nepalis, as well as their familiarity with topics such as grammar and astrology. Elsewhere, some adults also gained literacy opportunities through work, for example as clerks in the army or on Darjeeling tea estates. Pedagogical resources were gradually developed but the more advanced materials took a long time to appear. For example, Rudraraj Pande and Vasudev Bhattarai, teachers of Indian and British history in Kathmandu's Darbar High School, only produced textbooks for these subjects in the 1930s (Onta 1996b: 224). Nepal's history and geography were not taught at all.

In India, the Nepali language crossed a major hurdle when it was approved as a vernacular for composition in Calcutta University examinations in 1918 but this opened up a new set of challenges. The tireless young editor and activist Parasmani Pradhan greeted this achievement with an editorial in the monthly *Chandrika* [1(8-9): 41]: 'Dear readers! You have become joyful hearing this joyous news; but alongside it is another problem...our language has gained a place in Calcutta University but where are the Nepali books for the course of study? ... we must now start to write these or later we will have to suffer great shame.' Some months later, Suryavikram Jnavali (1919a: 20), a key collaborator, echoed Parasmani's sentiment:

> Now I will ask one question of the Nepali *jati* and conclude this letter. We made a movement; our language was recognised; now

> what answer may we give when Calcutta University demands books suitable for teaching? Shall we put forward *Saagardarpan* [a mildly erotic poetry collection]? ¼ it is absolutely essential that we now immediately create 15 or 20 textbooks. We must devote our full attention to this subject from now on or we will suffer disappointment later.

Yet the implication that no Nepali textbooks existed is unfounded: Even before the inclusion of Nepali in formal curriculums became a realistic goal, private sector publishers had reaped rewards from textbook production: there had been a flourishing educational print market from well before the turn of the century.[4]. Rammani Acharya Dikshit had successfully campaigned for the recognition of Nepali in the United Provinces years earlier; when Allahabad University sanctioned its use in examinations, books produced by the Prabhakari Press which he managed were approved as textbooks. By the time of the First World War basic primers had gradually been supplemented with more sophisticated textbooks and an increasing number of English-learning aids. None of these books were officially approved by educational authorities: they would have served a market of private schools, *pathshala*s, home tutoring, and self-teaching. The presence in this market of the major Nepali publishers (joined, for example, by the Krishna Madho Company, whose own language primer dates from at least 1915) indicates that there were profits to be made. At the start of the twentieth century tens of thousands of Nepalis were reading and learning to read.

Apart from the involvement of commercial publishers—whose enthusiasm to enter a sizeable and profitable market is unsurprising—the production of educational materials had enticed authors well known in other fields. Alongside catechisms and other religious materials, the Darjeeling Christian priest Gangaprasad Pradhan had, with his long-standing collaborator Miss Goalen, published a translated history of India (1910).[5] The talented young writer Padmanabh Sapkota had also published a *History of India* in 1914.[6] Similarly, the versatile Sikharnath Suvedi turned his hand to various educational works.[7] These publications illustrate the overlaps between generic popular publishing approaches and the emergent professional pedagogical styles endorsed by government education departments and school inspectors. For example, Suvedi's *Aksharmala* (1913) couches its compendium of information in attractive traditional terms ('*rasila rasila* definitions of each character') but also pays detailed attention to recommended teaching methods.

Other successful popular authors were also drawn into the educational world, their efforts shaped by formal education's particular demands. Ramprasad Satyal acknowledged in his *English Grammar in the Nepali Language* (1915/16) that even as it was struggling to establish itself *vis-à-vis* other Indian languages, Nepali was also forced to compete against the established appeal and status of English:

> Gentlemen! Seeing that our Nepali students studying in schools and other gentlemen of the general Nepali public are having to make a great effort to learn the foreign English language because until now no English language grammar has been made in our Nepali language, this book has been written to alleviate their effort. Nowadays is there anyone who does not want to know English? Who does not have some need to use the English language? As well as students studying in *pathshalas*, the English language is a topic of conversation in everyone's houses. As this book is in Nepali, our country brothers may learn all the rules of conversational and written English grammar conveniently and without great effort and will very quickly become skilled in the English language. This book is written on the basis of very large English grammars. It is the best friend of our students studying English and others who seek to learn English.

In this way educational aids were commercialised as well as being promoted by established writers and publishers. The appearance of more sophisticated publications indicates a maturing market. Advertising his *English Grammar*, Gangadhar Shastry Dravid establishes its academic credentials by emphasising that it is based on the opinions of 'many famous western grammarians'.[8] Its high price (rupees) is justified by its usefulness to 'students young and old ... from those studying in schools and colleges to "private" or home-educated students'.

From Private to Public: A New Pedagogy for a New Society

As the previous section makes clear, Pârasmani and Suryavikram's more dramatic claims about the lack of Nepali teaching must be taken with a pinch of salt: Banaras's Nepali publishing business had been catering to the needs of tens of thousands of students over decades. But the call for a pedagogical paradigm shift was significant. It is this that underlies Parasmani's work to transform textbook production and it is here that he has left his imprint on Nepali schoolbooks to this day. By 1940 he had produced no less than thirty original textbooks (a few in collaboration with other writers) and fifteen translations or adaptations.[9] Their style was radically different from some of their predecessors.

The shift from Banaras to Darjeeling in textbook-writing represented a broader shift from Brahmanical tradition to Western-oriented modernism. The type of mathematics primer that held prime of place in the Banaras publishers' catalogues was the *Ankendukeshar*, 'a treasury of arithmetic ... with the all forms of calculation such as the *trairasik, pancharasik,* etc., given with examples in Nepali *slokas.*'[10] In contrast, Darjeeling's educators aimed to win official recognition for Nepali by producing English-styled texts endorsed by publishers such as Macmillan and Longmans. For Parasmani, the educational field was the perfect testing ground for the social *unnati* projects that he had promoted through his journal. *Chandrika* had printed many articles about education; these now added to Parasmani's drive for textbook-writing.

Moreover, the promotion of Nepali education was only one front in a broader struggle for cultural recognition and community representation. The changing market for language primers reflected not just shifting pedagogical technique but a more far-reaching transformation in the balance between private and public culture. The Banaras market had catered largely to the private: private publishers catering to a core market of private students, often receiving private tuition, for whom the symbolism of the Nepali language was historically constituted privately and within the family. Parasmani's drive, however, was for the institution of the Nepali language in the public realm: public recognition through university and government, public tuition in state schools, public promotion through cultural organisations with open membership. Public approaches to formal recognition were not entirely alien to Banaras or Kathmandu—indeed, the 1918 campaign to have Nepali recognised by Calcutta University succeeded largely because it mobilised support from Kathmandu, Banaras and Darjeeling, the three crucial pillars of the Nepali public sphere. Nevertheless, Darjeeling was the laboratory in which the experiment of incorporating Nepali in the official curriculum took place, and it was here that the challenges of delivering Nepali's public status became apparent.

Six months after Calcutta University's decision, Parasmani penned a celebratory editorial [*Chandrika* 2(2): 52-53]: 'At last the [Nepali] language was approved and everyone was overjoyed. In particular, there were no bounds to the delight of school students.' But the congratulations turn sour: 'But alas! Seeing that the authorities have still not made arrangements for teaching the Nepali language to students of Darjeeling High School one is deeply disappointed.' Parasmani launches a bitter attack on the government school's principal, complaining that 'headmaster Sriyukta Achyut Nath Adhikari has no love for the Nepali language or for Nepali students. If this were not the case then would he not have made arrangements for teaching the language in his own school as soon as it had been approved by Calcutta University?' Refusing to accept the argument that there were no books, teachers or rooms for Nepali classes, he pointed out that there were no problems with facilities for Bengalis or Biharis. He ended with a blunt appeal to the headmaster to mend his ways *(Chandrika* 2(2): 54): 'Guruji, if you have within you the pride that as their head teacher you really love Nepali students and want their welfare then immediately start to promote the Nepali language in school by whatever means. Through this you will gain name and glory for welfare, otherwise not.'

This plea was successful; shortly afterwards Dharanidhar Koirala was appointed to teach Nepali in the Government High School. Meanwhile the month in which Parasmani's editorial appeared, February 1919, turned out to be his last as manager of the Hari Printing Press. While it took some more months to hand over the editorship of *Chandrika* to Rashmi Prasad Ale, Parasmani quickly resigned from his other duties when he was appointed as the first teacher of Nepali to Matriculation level in the Scottish Universities Mission Institute at Kalimpong. The situation for promoting Nepali as an educational medium in the area became rapidly more favourable, and the early 1920s were crucially productive years. Parasmani himself impressed the Education Department with his ability and commitment and two years later was promoted to the comparatively influential post of Sub-Inspector of Schools for the Darjeeling Hill Region, the first Nepali to occupy such a position. Meanwhile, in 1923, Suryavikram also joined the Nepali teaching staff of the Darjeeling High School, thus bringing together the SuDhaPa (Suryavikram, Dharanidhar and Parasmani) three some that was to be a driving force behind many important developments such as the founding of the Nepali Sahitya Sammelan in 1924. By 1926, Nepali had taken more steps towards official status. It was recognised as a 'principal vernacular' of Bengal by the Indian Naturalization Act and Nepali books were approved for use in all classes of primary schools and primary stages of Middle Vernacular Schools in Bengal.

The New Textbooks

The endorsement of Nepali textbooks was of signal importance in providing the basis for propagation of an increasingly standardised language and associated culture and literature. It was also the result of a diplomatic coup by Parasmani, when he persuaded the influential publishers Macmillan to take up their publication.[11] When Macmillan representatives visited Darjeeling Parasmani, deputed to act as their guide, decided to impress them with the majestic views of the Tista river on the road to Gangtok.[12] The representatives were so moved by the twisting hill road that Macmillan's manager, Mr Parkhurst, was sick. Parasmani moved with alacrity to offer his own pullover for the distinguished guest to vomit on. For this somewhat humiliating display of quick thinking he had a good ulterior motive: from the publisher's gratitude Parasmani extracted the promise that he would recommend to his head office that Macmillan publish Nepali schoolbooks.[13]

The significance of this small incident was far-reaching: the reputation and financial clout of a major publishing house gave a great boost to the campaign for producing curriculum materials that would gain official acceptance. The introduction of these books was not without problems—Parasmani incurred the wrath of his superiors by jumping the gun and introducing them without formal approval, and non-Nepali communities were not enthusiastic about the language's new-found status—but they rapidly gained currency and fulfilled Macmillan's hopes of profitability.

These textbooks' form and content both indicate their distance from earlier efforts. Parasmani's first guide to Nepali literature (1924), aimed at second grade students, illustrates the use to which Macmillan's backing was put.[14] Despite the high quality Calcutta printing and a liberal sprinkling of good engravings the price was restricted to an affordable two *anna*s. Its preface (1924: i-ii) contains useful practical advice for teachers on how best to use the book in the classroom. Parasmani's experience as a teacher and inspector enables him to offer guidance quite different to Sikharnath's notes for *panditji*s working in private tuition. Here instructors are offered tips on how to use the blackboard and manage large classes. In short, the directions are in line with his later advice (1927, preface) that 'it is best that *guru*s should follow current scientific methods', with the clear implication that traditional pedagogical techniques should be abandoned.

The lessons themselves are unremarkable but textbooks such as this also formed a platform for selling ideals of social progress to a much wider audience. For example, this reader (1924: 20) features a poem entitled 'Vidya' which presents to young readers an encapsulation of the many benefits of learning as they had been elaborated in journal discourse. The writing and editing of approved textbooks was also a source of great influence: school curriculum materials could disseminate to a vast and impressionable audience the ideas and attitudes that had previously been confined to limited and rarefied literary circles. Meanwhile, the ability to dictate schoolchildren's orthography and grammatical standards would decisively help Parasmani's style of Nepali to eclipse its rivals. The influence of his first series of textbooks also spread through routes other than schools. For example the Gurkha Rifles, which had previously adapted the traditional *Virsikka* tale, staple of Banaras publishers, for use as teaching material, now translated Parasmani's 'scientific' Nepali readers.[15]

Parasmani's books were not adopted by the Nepal government but they were nonetheless influential in shaping the development of Nepalese textbooks. The first full set of graded primary readers (from class one to seven) produced within Nepal was the *Sahayak praveshika* series of the 1940s.[16] Published by the Nepali Bhasha Prakashini Samiti and written in Kathmandu, they were initially printed in Banaras, their typically colourful North Indian cover illustrations representing the lowest common denominator of production values. First editions emerged from a remarkable variety of Banaras printers, presumably in a search for value and reliability but the publication of second editions was entrusted to Macmillan and printing switched to Calcutta.[17] Under the direction of Nepal's Director of Public Instruction, Major-General Mrgendra Samsher, new writers were employed (Badrinath Bhattarai and Syamdas Vaisnav) and new topics were included. This led to some 'Nepalisation' of content (various Nepal-specific topics such as a description of Bhaktapur's Bisket festival were added) but more obviously to a 'Macmillanisation' informed by Parasmani's approach. The balance of subject matter in the new Nepalese editions closely reflected that developed by Parasmani (hence a liberal sprinkling of generically Indian tales, from the story of Valmiki to Akbar-Birbal episodes) while the layout, illustrations and print were also brought into line with this precedent. Even the inclusion of Nepalese topics was not always new: for example, the portrait of Jang Bahadur's character in *Sahayak praveshika* 3 (1946/47: 30-32), while more hagiographic, reflects a similar lesson in Parasmani and Rudramani's earlier *Nepali Sahitya* 2 ([1923] 1949: 70-75).[18]

New Challenges

With the development of the modern education system the abstract ideals of social improvement developed in public discourse were transmitted through teaching materials to an ever-expanding captive audience of young students. The progress of Nepali education remained a vital topic of discussion and activity in the public realm within India as further degrees of recognition and implementation were sought. Following the production of a full range of basic textbooks, the goal of introducing Nepali as a teaching medium—rather than just as one of the vernaculars approved for study—was achieved in Bengal in 1935.[19]

In this year Hariprasad Pradhan, one of the founders of Darjeeling's Nepali Sahitya Sammelan (described below), took the opportunity of his speech as Chair of its annual general meeting to review the progress made by Nepali in the education system.[20] The Sahitya Sammelan had completed its first ten years and Pradhan, having left Darjeeling five years before, was well placed to make a balanced assessment of developments. He recalls that when he was a student, schoolchildren had no choice but to start their studies in Hindi and then some years later transfer to English, meaning that none could pass their matriculation examinations before the age of eighteen to twenty. Reviewing the gradual success of the Nepali recognition movement, he notes that it took fifteen years for the Bengal Government's civil servants to implement Nepali as a teaching language.

Mindful of opposition from some non-Nepali communities, he argues persuasively that no one should object to Nepali-speaking children being taught in their own mother tongue: 'even though we Nepalis are the largest [group] in this district we have never said that students of other *jati*s must study in Nepali.' The use of Hindi was earlier a necessity but 'the difference between circumstances then and current circumstances in the district is like that between heaven and hell'; if the government now tries to force Nepalis to study in Hindi it meets fierce opposition. Pradhan also offers some interesting insights on the progress of Nepali education in different regions. Of students from across Bengal and Assam, those who have worked most on literature are from Darjeeling, because it offers the best arrangements for teaching Nepali. While Shillong also teaches Nepali literature he bemoans the fact that Calcutta—'second city of the

British empire, home to university and knowledge'—has no provisions for promoting Nepali literature or teaching the language. Nevertheless, Nepali has now gained a place in education and it is only in the top two classes that schools cannot yet offer full Nepali language education—a deficiency that new books and some lobbying can surely correct.

Pradhan underlines both the remarkable achievements of the preceding decades and the need for further efforts. Yet the higher status he now targets is more ambitious than his predecessors could have hoped for: 'Now the Nepali people must quickly mount a fierce campaign to register the Nepali language as a "major" language among the various languages of India'. And the campaign should not stop there, for 'all educated men and women' should press on and 'make the Nepali language worthy of comparison with the great languages of the world'.

Indeed, by the turn of the next decade Nepali education had been consolidated and its supporters were looking beyond its survival to an increasing refinement of pedagogical technique. By this stage, increasingly typically for Darjeeling, the District Inspector of Schools was a well-qualified Nepali of non-ancestral-Nepali-speaking origin, Karna Bahadur Gurung BSc, BT, BES. Introducing a translated manual on teaching methodology (1942)[21] he effortlessly reproduces the language of the preceding decades:

> What is 'education'? To whom must it be given? When must it be given? And how must it be given? The *unnati* of each *jati* depends on the answers to the questions asked above and their practical use. The *jati* which understands the meaning of education and has real knowledge of to whom, why, by whom, when and how education should be given will be counted among the world's developed *(unnat) jati*s. But how far behind are we in relation to education? Thinking of the answer to this we are forced to say 'Alas!' ... until hundreds and hundreds of new books in our language about modern teaching methods are written we will indeed remain behind in the right to education.

But while his rhetoric retains the old tropes the context is transformed. For contributors to *Chandra* and *Chandrika* more than two decades before, the situation of Nepali and its speakers had seemed hopeless and prospects of catching up with the progress effected by Bengali and Hindi-speakers bleak. Their acute awareness of Nepali backwardness had been exacerbated by a sense of powerlessness, their cries for *jati* advancement resounding within their own print community but not reaching the ears of authorities in either India or Nepal. Yet by the start of the 1940s, calls for further progress were being backed by solid institutional achievements: while Gurung's phraseology is inherited, the fact that he is able to deploy it from a position of authority within the educational establishment reflects the strides that Nepali had made. Within one generation, Nepali had been standardised, recognised as an educational medium and propagated to new generations of students.

Institutions: From Cultural Expression to Organisation

At the weekly meeting of Darjeeling's Gorkha Samiti on 20 September, 1922, Dharanidhar Koirala read out a new essay. To see through any task, he observed, one needs a combination of *hosh* and *josh*, awareness and enthusiasm: 'work is the outcome of this *hosh* and *josh*; in *vedanta* it is called yoga' (Koirala 1923: 3). His philosophical ruminations on work and progress had a concrete purpose:

> Since the creation of the world until today many *jati*s have arisen and many have been destroyed. Destroyed by what? Only by ignorance. For that reason if we are to prevent rust from appearing on our *jati* then we must make an effort to destroy ignorance. And how to do that? By work ... Now if we do not devote body, mind and wealth to lighting the lamp of knowledge, we Nepalis will be destroyed ... one sees and hears that Gorkhalis from place to place are opening associations, committees and libraries. Among such institutions some are only flickering with life, and seem about to be extinguished.

Dharanidhar offered his listeners a manifesto which explicitly recognised that intellectual exercises producing *hosh* would only produce fruit when coupled with a *josh* that found expression in institution-building. For him, as for many of his leading contemporaries, the urge to build organisations flowed naturally from the priorities of abstract rhetoric.

Even as Dharanidhar was addressing the Gorkha Samiti, the other 'lights of knowledge' of which he speaks were flickering in many locations. Library projects—such as those of Banaras and Kurseong described in detail below—provided one obvious link between the world of print and of community association. Social welfare organisations had also been founded, such as the Nepali Asamartha Sahayak Samiti of Calcutta.

Institutions created by Nepalis in India were pioneering in their voluntarism and their conscious self-justification.[22] In Nepal, government support or *diktat* was sufficient basis for an institution whereas in India even the process of establishment was mediated by a new form of public debate. This is exemplified by the discussion that took place at the meeting called to propose creating Darjeeling's Nepali Sahitya Sammelan (discussed below), in which speakers directly addressed issues of the composition of the Nepali *jati*, a question that was not a subject of public consideration inside Nepal until long after the end of Rana rule.

For early Nepali writers, print not only offered literary progress but afforded new opportunities for publicity and awareness-raising campaigns. Alongside poetry for poetry's sake, the pages of journals could be used to appeal for funds for a building project or to report on the successful conclusion of public cultural functions, to announce committee meetings or to record donations. Allied to the written word was the development of drama, a medium serving both as a vehicle for literary aspirations and as a platform from which to address the public and urge social reforms. Many associations shared similar or overlapping aims even if they were apparently working in different sectors: for example, the social messages of Darjeeling plays could be echoed in the political manifestos of the All India Gorkha League's newspapers from Dehradun. The following sections examine the process of social institutionalisation which enabled abstract ideals to be embodied in concrete programmes and organisations.

Drama: Extension of Medium and Audience

In 1909 the ambitiously named Gorkha National Theatrical Company, the first Nepali theatre group, staged Pahalmansingh Swanr's play *Atalbahadur* (Rai 1984: 34).[23] The playwright was from Nepal—and this work is considered one of the first modern Nepali plays—and the setting was Darjeeling's Hindu Public Hall, constructed in 1906, destroyed by fire and rebuilt in 1908.[24] The same year saw the founding of the Children Amusement Association (CAA), which then incorporated the earlier company.

Darjeeling pioneered drama as a means of taking social messages, wrapped up in pure entertainment, to a wider audience. Nepal's foremost playwright Balkrishna Sama neatly encapsulated the didactic potential of the stage: 'Education should be mandatory in our country. The country cannot move ahead unless [its people] are educated or literate. The most easy means of education is through stage performances of *natak*s. This way education is made tasteful.' (cited in Onta 1996b: 238-39) Of course, the Nepali language had already found expression in different popular media, from hereditary lineages of *gaine* singers to a variety of folk drama forms (Bandhu 2001/02: 266-82). Darjeeling's dramatists, however, envisaged a new role for theatre. And the rapidly changing Nepali society of Darjeeling allowed them to experiment with public performances long before playwrights inside Nepal.

Subsequent plays (such as *Kanjusko dhan*, 1910) were often adaptations from Hindi or Bengali: Sharma (1995/96: 35) observes that notable progress in Darjeeling Nepali dramas coincided in particular with the development of Bengali drama. As Kumar Pradhan (1982: 100-01) notes, this was—as far as other Indians were concerned—the era of Bengali *jatiyata* (loosely, nationalism). In Darjeeling, as elsewhere, the British administration's partition of Bengal was seen as an attempt to crush a blossoming national sentiment. Although Bengali plays may not have been performed locally, the inspiration for leaders of the would-be Nepali *jati* was direct and compelling.[25] The CAA was soon joined by another troupe, the Himalaya Amusement Association, which staged *Rukmani haran* (1913), *Raj khana* (1913) and *Raja Harishchandra* (1916);[26] in 1916 it combined with the CAA to form the Himalayan and Children Amusement Association (HCAA).[27]

These developments, and the history of the birth and development of theatre in Darjeeling, have been the subject of detailed analysis by two valuable works: Kumar Pradhan's 'Darjilingka kehi purana natakharu ra buddha-charitra natak' (1982: 95-176) and Indra Bahadur Rai's *Darjilingma nepali natakko ardhashatabdi* (1984), as well as by numerous literary historians, including Ramlal Adhikari (1977) and Dilliraj Sharma (1995-96); there is no need to recover this ground here. However, it is worth briefly reassessing the relationship of theatrical performance to the worlds of print and social institutions.

Theatre was one of the foundations on which the process of institutionalisation rested; the individuals involved in its promotion were often concerned with other social projects. Dhanvir Mukhiya, who produced that first performance of *Atalbahadur*, went on to form the Gorkha Dukha Nivarak Sammelan, Darjeeling's most enduring social, cultural and charitable association (discussed below). Assam's leading Nepali political activist, Chhavilal Upadhyaya, also worked towards the development of education and drama, converting the school he had studied into a Middle Vernacular School and then a Combined Middle School, supporting the youths of the Mazgaon Nepali Theatre Party in their efforts to build a permanent theatre, and helping to establish the Mazgaon Library (Rai 1992: 47).

In such developments, India-based Nepalis remained well in advance of Nepal, where the first drama staged for the general public was *Madan Mohini* prepared by 'Ustad Narandas' and performed in Kathmandu during 1929's Gaijatra festival. The first ticketed public performance—of Sama's *Mukunda Indira*—did not take place until 1937 (Adhikari 1977: 35).[28] The cosmopolitan influences on Darjeeling's Nepali theatre writers and producers are also noteworthy, as is the inventiveness of their hybrid formats.[29] Sanskrit, Hindi-Urdu and Bengali plays provided rich seams for Nepali translators and adapters to mine, while the British influence on early productions was not limited to the names of companies but reflected the active involvement of at least one resident enthusiast, James Dunne, and the incorporation of English themes from Shakespeare to pantomime.[30]

From the early 1920s Parasmani and others brought a more didactic approach to the theatre.[31] But more low-brow productions offered the means to package the morality of social progress in a populist format. Bhaiya Singh's *Svami bhakti va adarsha nari* (1925),[32] for example, recalls the idealised role of the Indian *sati* but is designed for popular appeal. His worthy subject matter justifies a melodramatic and risqué presentation of prostitution, general licentiousness, theft, betrayal and murder which threatens to overwhelm the virtuous message. The overall effect is far removed from the pompous opining of most essayists and would have reached a larger, and perhaps more genuinely appreciative, audience. But the process in which Singh was engaged was nonetheless an extension of his more earnest counterparts' concerns.

Attempts to entice a wider and less sophisticated audience may have introduced the refined literary values critics were seeking to promote but they were nonetheless effective. Plays were not confined to Darjeeling town itself but were also staged in Singhamari and other villages; the HCAA travelling to perform in further-flung locations such as Pul Bajar and Jhepi (Rai 1984: 17). As Rai enjoins his readers when considering these pioneering plays (*ibid.*: 40): 'Drama is not only literature, not only entertainment, but through both is also a third thing: it becomes an act *(karya)*. Rather than just looking at them in the form of literary works let us recognise those performed dramas also as an act in the Gorkhali *jati*'s upliftment.'

Libraries and Titerary Associations

Libraries were both an incarnation of the rhetoric of learning and progress and a repository for its printed form. For the gentlemen of Kurseong in 1918, the remedy for the miserable state of Nepali society was to establish a library. They stressed that it would be more than just a collection of books: it would be a forum for social interaction and development; providing an environment for strangers to meet would strengthen social cohesion and allow social projects to be discussed. The idea that a Nepali community could be constructed by drawing hitherto unknown members into a common space—both physical and discursive—illustrates the transformations that emerging public culture could effect: 'This building will be suitable for unknown Gorkhalis coming from afar to spend the night and to sit in groups of brothers to debate topics related to *unnati*' promised the Kurseong library's backers [*Chandrika* 1(1): 18-19].

Libraries also offered the passage to information that could help Nepalis make sense of their own society. As Lakshmikanta Arjyal observed (1918: 14), a library could consolidate information without imposing cultural uniformity, and act as a catalyst for a chain of progress:

> It is necessary to complete the task of *unnati* of the government and the people by directly seeing or hearing of the types of place that fall within one's own country, by looking to the geography of that country of Nepal. Alongside this, by printing the writings and books written in the languages of Nepal's various *jatis* and, gathering them together with [other] printed books, establishing a library, people at large will be encouraged to find out what sort of things there are in their own country, what jewels there are ... once a library has been established, some people are certain to gain a desire to learn their own mother tongues, and once the desire has been aroused in society then there can be no doubt that the task will be accomplished.

The relationship between opening the sources of knowledge, bringing together members of society for intellectual interaction, and enhancing the potential for concrete social reform rapidly came to be widely acknowledged. Thus Dipakesvar Sharma's poem entitled 'In praise of libraries' (1918c: 8) is part standard eulogy, part recognition of actual social dynamics: 'The library is an entire object of limitless joy ... The stream of knowledge flows here eternal and forever ... Where great worthy men gather in meetings/holding papers in their hands and considering affairs'.[33]

It was accepted that libraries could form a cornerstone of an incipient civil society, where Nepalis could start to participate in the type of debate enjoyed by Europeans. This was an inspiration for Pratiman Singh Lama (1918: 20): 'Wherever there are large numbers of Gorkhalis, there in each place we must open at least a debating club, if not a library.' Of course, debate might be open but the structure inherent in even such a modest organisation implied a replication of social hierarchy. Lama suggested that clubs should elect 'honourable and worthy gentlemen' as office-bearers and that they should organise a debate on a set topic at least once a week, if not daily: 'with five, ten or twenty people gathering together for this purpose, all sorts of new subjects for society will keep on arising' (*ibid.*: 21). The duty to take the initiative—and the blame for lack of progress to date—lay with the leaders of society, whom Lama (*ibid.*: 21) compares unfavourably to Europeans:

> ... but how would a task such as this endear itself to us Gorkhalis? For our leaders, filling their stomachs is all that counts; where is the "time" for them to look after others, to make the slightest social reforms? Look at the Darjeeling Planters' Association! [Look at] how they are carrying out their work. Look also at their number. If we could only follow their example what advantage we could reap, what honour we could achieve. Honourable leaders of our country! Now arise and arouse your assistants, devote your minds to the reform of society, otherwise the hill of blame for our *avanati* will be collapsing on your own heads.

The call for the establishment of libraries and debating clubs had palpable political overtones, recalling the exhortations of other writers to unite behind a cause and exercise the power of organised society. Even Parasmani's first venture in this field in his schooldays—insisting that the Darjeeling Government High School complement its Hindi Sahitya Samaj with a Gorkha Sahitya Samaj and eventually taking the initiative himself (Pradhan 1997: 9-10)—can be seen as a forerunner of the campaigns for recognition that mobilised Indian Nepalis until the last decade of the twentieth century.

The first Nepali public library project (in Nepal or India) was probably the Gorkha Library in Kurseong, established on 8 June 1913.[34]

However in Banaras, where the Nepali Library was established in 1915, its founders were clearly not aware that they had been pre-empted by Nepalis resident a long way from their traditional seat of learning (*Chandra* 1(7): 19):

> These days the civilised people of various *jati*s have opened many libraries for the sake of the *unnati* of their language. Until now Nepalis had not opened a single library. By our good fortune today the young lovers of learning of the holy area of Kashi have opened with great enthusiasm a Nepali Library for the benefit of those sad, poor people who cannot even buy books and as a service to other gentlemen as well. This library's main duty is to bring about the *unnati* of the Nepali language. It is fitting that Nepalis alone should promote their own mother tongue with body, mind, and money. For this reason it is a good thing for gentlemen to bring about *unnati* of this library by generously donating books, money, newspapers, etc.

The list of contributors consists almost entirely of Brahmans, including the publishers Visvaraj Harihar, Madhav Prasad Regmi, and Madho Prasad (who donated *Chandra* and a large picture of Emperor George V), and the writers Padmanabh Sapkota, Suryavikram, and Dharanidhar. Contributions were not limited to Nepali works: Padmanabh Sapkota sent the *Indian Daily News*, Pandit Ganganath Sharma the Hindi monthly *Maryada*. Three years later, a further appeal for this library (*Chandrika* 1(1): 21) was couched in similar language (some of it copied from the original appeal in *Chandra*). It claimed that poor members of other *jati*s have flourished after gaining access to libraries and thus 'we Nepalis of Kashi' aimed to provide a similar arrangement for the use of ordinary people. Emphasising the poverty of many students from the hills of Nepal, the appeal played on readers' consciences: 'whether or not this institution—opened for the benefit of such students—will be the subject of gentlemen's compassion is something that you yourselves must decide.'

Despite a shortage of funds the library formed a focus for *unnati*-related activities in the city and beyond. While dominated by Banaras-based Brahmans, the library's fourth anniversary ceremony (held on the afternoon of 2 February, 1919) also attracted Parasmani and Mani Narayan Pradhan from Kurseong, the distinguished-sounding Captain Bakhan Singh Thakur Sardar Bahadur and one F.N. Sharma from Parasi in south central Nepal. This occasion also brought together the SuDhaPa trio before they would meet and work together in Darjeeling: Dharanidhar (as previous Secretary and Chair of the library) offered some words, while Suryavikram (as chair of the welcome committee) opened proceedings and gave his own speech on the state of the world today (Jnavali 1919b).

The older Kurseong Gorkha Library could trace its origins to May 1913, when local friends supported J. Paval, a Lepcha,[35] in setting up a reading club in his own house. It was when this became inconvenient that he suggested they should establish a dedicated library building. In June 1916 a building was taken on rent and an organisation called Gorkha Library founded; it attracted enthusiastic voluntary support but suffered from a high turnover of officer-bearers.[36] The library's finances were initially precarious—it survived on small donations and by May 1915 had only around Rs. 100 in hand—but generous patronage transformed its situation. In April 1915 the local philanthropist Sardar Bahadur Lama offered to support the construction of a new library building and eventually his Rs. 500 donation was matched by Kurseong Municipality. Many obstacles delayed the work (not least the cost far exceeding the estimate at over Rs. 3,000 before furnishings) but the building was completed in late 1918, thanks largely to the efforts of Dhan Narayan Pradhan. As well as stocking Hindi, Nepali and English books, the library subscribed to a cosmopolitan range of journals.[37]

As Secretary, Mani Narayan Pradhan reported to the fifth annual meeting held on 18 August 1918 at which Kul Bahadur Pradhan and Moti Chand Pradhan, Sub Deputy Collectors, were elected to the executive committee. The new building was opened to the public in January 1919 with a ceremony that nodded to the traditional and the contemporary. British civil servant H. Quinton was placed in the chair and garlanded by two boys from the Gorkha Amateur Club, who had just performed some welcome songs.[38] In a deliberately anti-communal gesture, one wore Nepali dress and offered a garland of flowers while the other wore Bhutia costume and offered a silk scarf, while a further effort towards inclusiveness—presumably aimed specifically at non-Nepali guests but also demonstrating their hosts' sophistication—was Mani Narayan Pradhan's presentation in both English and Nepali.[39] He urged all to remember their duty to sustain the library, an 'institution was opened for the benefit of our Nepali *jati*'. Dharanidhar spoke enthusiastically of *unnati* and the 'true path' but more exhilarating was his recital of the poem 'Jaga jaga' [*Chandrika* 2(1): 27-28]. The success of the Kurseong project inspired others. Shortly after the opening of its building, the newly formed Darjeeling Gorkha Samiti appealed for donations to help establish the organisation, acquire its own building and set up a school and small library.[40]

However, the major development in institutionalising the Nepali public sphere in Darjeeling, and with repercussions far beyond, was the establishment of the Nepali Sahitya Sammelan in 1924. This institution was inspired by similar Hindi organisations, in particular the Kashi Nagari Pracharini Sabha (founded in 1893), whose first president, Babu Radhakantadas, was a literary intimate and first cousin of the leading Hindi writer Harishchandra (Dalmia 1996: 141, King 1994: 142-145).[41] The founding of the Sammelan has been discussed by previous writers, notably Pradhan (1982), Hutt (1997) and Onta (1996a and 1996b), all of whom have analysed its significance in terms of the debate on Nepali *jati* identity which it engendered.[42] It provided an important platform for the activities of leading writers such as SuDhaPa and a focus for activities—such as public discussions, textbook and literary publication—which implemented social as well as cultural goals.

While the Sammelan's activities expanded in the early 1930s following a few years' lull, Dhanvir Mukhiya was planning the launch of a new cultural forum. The Gorkha Dukha Nivarak Sammelan (GDNS) was formed in 1932 amidst some controversy. Mukhiya was not on good terms with Darjeeling's Deputy Superintendent of Police Laden La—a leading establishment figure whose Hill-Peoples' Social Union was the only major local organisation of which Mukhiya was not an active member—and the GDNS faced opposition from the outset. Following a leafleting campaign which claimed that it was a political undertaking some backers withdrew their support and repeated efforts were made to force the organisation out of its temporary home (Rai 1984: 8). Yet Mukhiya stood firm and fulfilled his vision of creating an institution that linked cultural promotion to social welfare. The GDNS became the undisputed centre for Nepali theatrical productions while pursuing a mission to the poorer members of society by, for example, carrying out funeral rites for destitutes; it carries out these dual functions to this day. The Kurseong Gorkha Library and Nepali Sahitya Sammelan also survived the decades, the latter remaining one of the leading Nepali cultural foundations in India. The lasting achievements of these institutions demonstrate the success with which rhetorical concerns for social progress were transformed into durable reality, and with which public space was occupied and moulded for the promotion of socio-cultural goals.

Constituting the Public: The Composition of Civil Society

Participation in the Public Realm

Active participation in Nepali civil society was not necessarily open to all those who might think of themselves as Nepali. The flagship projects of the civic-minded—such as library projects or the establishment of the Nepali Sahitya Sammelan—could best be supported by those who could contribute intellectually or financially. While the poor and destitute were to benefit from the Gorkha Dukkha Nivarak Sammelan, the great and good were expected to manage it. At the same time, non-Nepalis were key participants in some projects. The Banaras-based proprietor of *Chandra*, Madho Prasad, a Bihari, played an important role in developing Nepali journalism by dint of his capital and press; the Kurseong Gorkha Library emerged from an initiative inspired by the Lepcha J. Paval; DSP Laden La was actively courted for association with prominent Nepali projects despite his steadfast opposition to key demands such as the introduction of Nepali as an educational medium in public schools.[43]

Those who constituted Nepali civil society often represented different interest or privilege groups. Non-Nepalis, such as Laden La, the Bhutanese royalty, or British administrators, could influence institutions through patronage. Equally, establishment figures from within the Nepali community tended to reflect the values of their immediate environment: Banaras-based projects could count on the support of *pandit*s, Kathmandu activities might draw in educated Brahmans, members of the Rana clans or government officers, and Darjeeling could look to retired army or police officers, contractors and entrepreneurs, and the growing class of those who held formal British educational qualifications and positions in government service.

Some evidence of patterns of involvement in social and cultural affairs is available in journals, not least in the frequent public notices and reports on efforts to establish schools and libraries and the lists of donors who are regularly thanked for their contributions. For example, *Chandrika* started publication as the campaign to raise funds for the Gorkha Library in Kurseong was underway. The earliest notices of gratitude for financial assistance illustrate the geographical and social reach of appeals to civic solidarity. Similar evidence is available from the Nepali Sahitya Sammelan and its records. Just over a decade later its Executive Committee (in a meeting on 16 August, 1931) agreed that the Sammelan must aim to sign up one hundred new members that year and must encourage all members to help with recruitment. Minutes record the individuals to whom responsibility for specific areas was assigned; this gives some indication of the spread of active members of the Sammelan. Likewise, records of membership of the Sammelan provide evidence of a wide range of ethnic origin, and also a degree of geographical distribution around the district of Darjeeling and beyond.

Materials such as this give some hints as to the audience for early Nepali publications, although it is easier to gauge the size and extent of readership than the nature of its composition.[44] In Darjeeling there is only limited evidence of sales and tastes and the most useful available statistical information dates from 1931. In this year the first *Nepali Sahitya Sammelan Patrika* (1: 3) gives sales figures for four books it had published under the series title 'Jnana Pustakamala'. These indicate that by the late 1920s a Nepali readership had been established which was sufficiently sizeable and well off to support the publication of a certain number of literary works at both the populist and more highbrow ends of the spectrum.[45] The success of textbook sales and the expansion of education suggest that the number of literate Nepalis was increasing. Institutions realised that they needed to reach out to these readers through publicity.[46]

The range of projects which called for the involvement of an emergent civil society have been examined in the preceding sections. The growth of voluntary participation in various charitable, cultural and political undertakings brought certain individuals and groups a social prominence that they might otherwise never have enjoyed. For as well as drawing on traditional patronage networks, social projects offered benefits to two significant classes of people: providing the opportunity of respectable donations, they enabled the newly rich to buy added social legitimation and prestige through public financial support; and requiring educated, literate leadership they provided further outlets for those who dominated print discourse to wield a different sort of influence in public life. Yet just as a dominant mainstream of rhetoric threatened to drown out peripheral or rival voices, so there were actors in public life who did not conform to the primary aims of the 'social progress' project. Thus developments in Nepali identity and community were also being paralleled by less well remembered progress in the creation of a modern sense of Newar identity. Most prominent in this movement were perhaps Madhav Raj Joshi and his son Sukraraj Shastri, both of whom founded their work on religious reform.

Education and Elitism

The forms of public culture that developed among Nepalis in India were not very representative. The early public sphere encompassed a small number of people and granted the socially and educationally privileged disproportionate influence in defining a community and its agenda for development. However, the patterns of exclusion are not entirely predictable and a study of their workings can be revealing. Onta rightly argues (1996a : 67) that the work of Suryavikram, Dharanidhar, Parasmani and others should be viewed within the local agenda of Darjeeling as a deliberate attempt to distance the educated from the illiterate working classes:

> Their efforts at cultural production through the use of the Nepali language can be interpreted as a project of differentiation whereby a proto-middle class, deploying its educational and cultural capital, separated itself from the larger Nepali coolie population of the Darjeeling area. The confidence of this class...was acquired through educational achievements within the formal academy. Hence the arguments of self-improvement espoused by this group revolved so centrally around the spread of education amongst the Nepali population in Darjeeling and beyond.

However, Onta's 'project of differentiation' cannot explain the determined mobilisation behind the Nepali language. At the very least, the differentiation must have been also from the middle classes of other cultural spheres: were this not the case, these activists and their peers could have easily found their place in existing elites, be it of Brahmans or among their fellow graduates from Hindi, Bengali or English medium schools. The contention that these activists could deploy a new kind of 'capital' and that this set them apart from their uneducated fellows is incontrovertible. Yet the dogged pursuit of status for Nepali and the promotion of its pedagogical potential indicate a more subtle relationship between high and low cultures.

At its simplest, the attitude of language activists was downright contradictory: their stated concerns—as expressed in editorial after editorial, essay after essay—were with society as a whole and yet their medium and message often reinforced a position of detached exclusivity. In the early twentieth century the major markers in a debate on linguistic status were still fluid, at least in terms of their popular understanding and adoption. (Hence, for example, the almost obsessive focus of early writers in using, defining and propagating the phrase *matribhasha,* 'mother tongue,' a term which became part of normal usage within a generation.) This was even more the case with the Nepali language itself, where rigid models of aesthetics inherited from Sanskrit literature were not balanced by grammatical or orthographic precision in the use of Nepali. One major, long-running confrontation over Nepali usage was that between Parasmani and Gangaprasad Pradhan, editor of the weekly *Gorkhe Khabar Kaagat* from 1901 until his death in 1930. Parasmani saw Gangaprasad's language as ungrammatical and ungainly while Gangaprasad in return criticised *Chandrika*'s register as being an unintelligibly elitist 'Kashi' dialect. Beyond the clash of personalities which enlivened this debate, Gangaprasad's criticism served a serious warning that *Chandrika* would alienate itself from many readers through its impenetrable style.

This interpretation received support from the most unexpected quarter: from a woman writing within the pages of *Chandrika* itself. The self-deprecating language in which the analysis offered by Srimati Kumudini of the Kalimpong is couched cannot conceal the boldness of her direct challenge to the assumptions of the journal's (male) editor and writers. Her thesis is blunt: newspapers and journals themselves are responsible for their failings; their lack of success cannot simply be blamed on a philistine public. Moreover, the gap between written and spoken language has led to the development of a prose style that is wholly inappropriate for a wider audience. She is willing to accept the need for standards: 'The pure speech of a language is dependent on grammar. Without a knowledge of grammar it is impossible to speak correctly, this much is evident.' (1918: 11) Yet she is a realist, going on to point out (*ibid.*: 12) that each *jati* within the Nepali *jati* (itself an interesting conceptualisation) has its own language and that most Nepalis are uneducated: 'They have not the least knowledge of correct and incorrect usage of language. Yet the while the language of these peasants and workers may not be pure it is natural, flowing and full of expression.' She underlines her praise for the 'natural', unpretentious vernacular of working people by lampooning writers who translate even the simplest of everyday sentences into a dense mass of Sanskritic verbiage. But she places the blame for sluggish progress on journalism as a whole (1918: 12):

> Our greatest duty is to give language the support of *unnati (bhashalai unnatiko teva dinu)*. In many places one can hear

> even parrots and minas repeating that the development of language depends upon grammar and journals but there is no sign of language beating the drum of *unnati* at home or abroad. Why has the Nepali *jati* not been able to bring about *unnati* of its language?

Although careful to qualify her own competence to provide an answer by emphasising her feminine weakness—'to give a realistic answer to this is beyond the powers of a slow-witted woman such as myself'—she does not shrink from launching a direct assault on the role of journals. She notes other factors such as the dominance of English and the way in which its perception as the sole fount for modern knowledge can breed contempt for other mother tongues. Yet it is the gap between journals' lofty claims for their potential and their demonstrable lack of achievement that forms the primary target for her harsh assessment (*ibid.*):

> While repeatedly expressing the hope that journals will make language flourish, many journals have had to hide their faces. The reason for this has already been expressed in many forms by many educated members of society but I see a great difference between the opinions of those educated members of society and what I have to say. In my humble opinion, the main reason for this is the form of [written] language being different from ordinary speech. The language in journals would generally be very difficult. Many people would not be able to understand the full meaning of the language of those journals. Of course it may be that to use difficult sentences among our half-educated people is like reading the *purana*s to bears. If one does not understand the meaning of the language then however much an article is steeped in the sentiment and sense of knowledge one will gain not the least pleasure from it nor will one's attention be drawn to the language again. This is also the reason that the majority of people have not developed a taste for reading journals.

The argument of Kumudini stands in stark contrast to most analyses of the reasons for the limited Nepali readership: she allocates responsibility—and consequently blame for failure—to publishers and writers rather than the general public. Almost all other writers tended to assume that the virtues of high-minded literary endeavour required no explanation: rather it was the unresponsive market that deserved castigation for its lack of support and appreciation of the selfless efforts of their small band of peers.[47] Kumudini is radical in her willingness to turn the tables and offer the opposite analysis: it is not readers that have let down writers but journals that have failed to cater for their potential readership. She does not abandon the ideal of journals leading the way in cultural advancement but concludes (*ibid.*: 13) with an unambiguous challenge to *Chandrika* to change its ways or face failure in its wider ambitions.

> In order to make its contents more engaging any periodical should first of all make its language extremely straightforward. By gradually increasing the complexity of language everyone will gradually understand its sense... In the future it is by the respectful adoption of simple language that *Chandrika* must make the effort to increase its glory day by day.[48] Only if the learned writers of *Chandrika* pay particular attention to simplicity is there any possibility of language making any progress.

Kumudini's brief essay is one of the most remarkable—and least celebrated—contributions to *Chandrika*.[49] It was original and bold; perhaps her *de facto* exclusion as a woman made it easier for her to look on the clique of highbrow writers from the outside and to empathise with less educated society. Still, her criticism was constructive: she used her sharp satire to highlight practical suggestions for improvement rather than simply to prick others' pomposity. She was able to make a business and an aesthetic case: her analysis recognised the need for marketing but did not seek the lowest common denominator for purely commercial success. This approach bridges the gap between the profitable but tawdry *lahari* literature and high-minded but narrow-based efforts to promote language improvement. Yet most importantly, she may well have been right. Whatever its successes, *Chandrika*—like almost all its predecessors and successors—failed to make itself a viable periodical despite the existence of a growing and lively market. The clearest explanation of this failure may be found not in its own self-pitying valedictory editorials but in the words of an unknown woman writer who saw that the same qualities that fuelled its sermonising were also the seeds of its inevitable demise.

Pratiman Singh Lama picked up on the themes identified by Kumudini in the next issue of *Chandrika*. In fact, he was writing directly in response to the comments of another woman, Vasundhara Devi, his predecessor in stewardship of the 'Prasnottar' (question and answer) column. She had expressed amazement that not one answer had been received to the question posed by Bhimdal Dewan in the first issue. Prefiguring one part of Kumudini's case she had exclaimed (1918: 18), 'If this is the case then how on earth can there be progress in society! Where is the benefit in bringing out journals?' Of course, she was lambasting the readership (implying that pearls were being cast before swine) rather than questioning the role of the journal itself. However, Lama (1918: 20) was prompted to think the issue through and question the assumed importance of journals and the breadth of their reach:

> At this time it is a mistake to imagine that our society will achieve *unnati* just by our bringing out journals and writing essays and poetry because these journals fall into the hands of only a few learned people. These learned people will each have read such essays and so forth in their student days. To claim that journals such as these cause 'language' to flourish and announce the civilisation of society is mere words: they cannot have such an impact on society. Yet it is not my intention to say that such journals are of no benefit and so there is no need to publish them. Until thousands of such journals are published no society at all can reach the peak of *unnati*. But the effort to which we must devote all our energies is to use the influence of journals to have the people educated by establishing a range of educational organisations in every village and town. This is the main duty of journals, this is their main purpose.

At the same time, editors such as Parasmani did not hesitate to berate contributors to their own journals if they made slips of language and style, sometimes going to the extent of publicly humiliating them. Such patronising editorial high-handedness can hardly have encouraged more timid writers. The public message conveyed to the readership as a whole is, however, consistent. The combination of didactic editorials and brutal criticism of inadequate literary efforts reinforced a sense of the editor as unquestionable arbiter of taste and correctness and as gatekeeper to an exclusive public realm. Indeed, the criteria for acceptability of creative writing might suggest that the literary public sphere represented more of a promulgatory than a participatory model, acting as a showcase for display of the editorially sanctioned while warning off unprepared would be contributors. With the exception of the occasional lucid critique, high-minded litterateurs tended to assume that their literary and social ideals did not need to be justified: those who failed to appreciate them had only themselves to blame. This is the tension at the heart of much public discourse: the idealism of self-appointed social pioneers could too easily translate into an arrogant disregard for the more pressing concerns of less privileged fellow Nepalis. This is perhaps why the grand ambitions seen in print were only slowly institutionalised in society at large.

Conclusion

This paper has used a variety of analytical approaches in order to sketch the extent and limitations of an early twentieth century Nepali public sphere in India. The purpose of this exercise has been to question the influence and representativeness of these early manifestations of modern Nepali public culture and, following from that, to consider their significance as a social-historical conceptualisation. The process of institution-building illustrated here shows how ideas initially expressed in narrow print circles came to be embodied in organisations, some of them influential and enduring. At a more abstract level, it throws some light on how paradigms of cultural reproduction and propagation that reached across Nepali society were shaped and promoted. As the latter sections in particular suggest, the development of a modern public culture challenged social structures and models of authority—prompting struggles for control over language norms and the education system.

Participation in the Nepali public sphere in India was limited by distinct patterns of exclusion and intertwined strands of elitism conditioned the formation of mainstream discourse. However, these hierarchies reflected changing social realities within the Nepali community. As the dynamics of Darjeeling indicate, the short space of a few decades saw a radical transformation from traditional power relations to a more open model, where factors such as formal educational skills could trump the advantages of birth. Of course, even new voices could tend to a stifling conservatism in areas as diverse as morality and literary style. But the materials presented here show that a variety of dissenting voices and alternative agendas also managed to play a part in the formation of public culture. The models that were arrived at in the first decades of the twentieth century were not immutable, as present-day challenges to concepts of Nepali identity demonstrate. Nevertheless, the processes of public negotiation of shared cultural attributes that emerged in this period were both new and crucial to the definition of a modern sense of Nepaliness.

NOTES

1. This paper is a heavily revised version of one chapter of my doctoral thesis (Chalmers 2003). Unfortunately events in Nepal prevented me from attending the Gangtok conference in April 2006. I am grateful to Tanka Subba for inviting me to submit this paper, which I was planning to present there, for publication all the same. I am sorry that, among other weaknesses, this revision has not benefited from the critical discussion that it would have received in Gangtok. Access to hard-to-find materials for the original research was made possible by the generous assistance of the Nepali Sahitya Sammelan, Gorkha Dukha Nivarak Sammelan, Dr. Parasmani Memorial Library and Madan Puraskar Pustakalaya.
2. These questions are not examined here. See Chalmers (2003) for a detail discussion.
3. Opportunities within Nepal were not quite as limited as the lack of named teaching institutions implies. Minimal as the scope of Rana government may have been, it did require a class of administrators capable of dealing with legal and financial affairs. Thus, even as school textbooks remained unwritten or unavailable, the Gorkha Bhasha Prakashini Samiti was busy producing many volumes on topics such as court procedure and accounting practices. For example, *Gorakha-adalati-siksha* (Acharya Dikshit 1922/23b) and *Gorakha-srestha-siksha* (Acharya Dikshit 1924-25).
4. In 1908, Kul Bahadur Gurung's *Nepali pahila pustak* ('First Nepali Book') saw a first edition published by the author himself—who was stationed in Quetta, presumably in military service—and printed in 1,000 copies in Banaras; a few months later a new edition of publisher Punyaprasad's *Gorkha bhashako varnamala* (an alphabet) ran to 2,000 copies. 1909 saw an attempt by Visvaraj and Harihar Sharma either to ride on the success of Gurung's book or to eliminate it from competition as their own *Nepali pahili (sic) pustak* was launched with a run of no less than 5,000. An enlarged edition in 1912 had a run of 10,000, unprecedented for any Nepali publication. By 1910 Dravid's mathematics primer *Ganit Chandrika* (whose third edition had been published in 1902), was also producing print runs of 2,000, it too published by Viavaraj Harihar (and still being advertised until at least 1928).
5. This was the *Hindustanko itihasko postak.* I have only been able to see this book briefly in a private collection: it is a sizeable work and, although its language is marked by the idiosyncratic orthography and style for which some have criticised Gangaprasad, it is lucid and readily intelligible.
6. This history, according to a notice in *Jivan charitra* (Vijnanvilas 1916) and later accounts such as Sharma Bhattarai (1993-94: 220-21), was titled *Bharatvarsako itihas;* it was probably a translation of Rameshchandra Datta's work.

7. He produced a *Pahila kitab, Varnamala, Sishubodh* and *Balbodh*. The lengthy preface to his *Aksharmala* ('garland of letters') reveals a sophisticated and cosmopolitan approach which combines scientific validation with typical self-promotion. Suvedi's appeal to 'respected gentlemen' explains that his aim is 'that our Gorkhali children, boys and girls, may well and quickly recognise the fifty characters': to achieve this goal he has not only made a survey of all similar primers available in Nepali, Hindi, and Marathi but has added to this his 'own fresh imagination' (Suvedî 1913: 2).
8. The advertisement appears in Dravid's English-Nepali dictionary (1920). Although he wrote several books for Nepalis, information on Dravid is lacking (cf. Sharma Bhattarai (1993-94: 222-23)). His English guides for Nepali students date from at least 1911. He produced an expensive *Gorkha Pronouncing Dictionary* (priced at Rs. 2½), as well a more affordable English-Gorkha primer (whose first and second parts sold for only four *anna*s each). All of his books were available at Visvaraj Harihar's perennially successful Gorkha Pustakalay.
9. The books are detailed by Nagendramani Pradhan (1991: 360-61; 363-63).
10. This description of the *Ankendukeshar* is taken from an advertisement in Visvaraj Sharma (1928).
11. In fact, Parasmani had already had one primer (the *Nepali pahilo kitab*) accepted by Longmans in 1921 but this was specifically for use in mission schools.
12. The tale was later recounted in print by Parasmani himself (Pradhan 1969: 1-7).
13. As he later put it (Pradhan 1997: 27): 'It is said that Guru Gorakhnath by vomiting gave the great king Prithvinarayan Shah the boon of the Kingdom of Nepal. The manager of the Macmillan Company, Mr Parkhurst, too, vomited and gave the Nepali community in the district of Darjeeling the boon of textbooks. Both these boons should be written in letters of gold when writing the history of the Nepalese people.' Indramani Pradhan (1997: 24-28) gives further details on the introduction of the Macmillan textbooks.
14. This *Nepali sahitya* series was later introduced from the first grade, and the revised second grade reader contained the heroic tale of VC winner Gaje Ghale (Parasmani and Rudramani Pradhan [1923] 1949: 38-43) which is discussed by Onta (1996b: 287-91) as an emblematic depiction of Nepali bravery.
15. For example, Pradhan and Pradhan (n.d.), prepared for use in the 6th Gurkha Rifles and printed by the Army Press at their Abbottabad headquarters.
16. These appear to have been published in 1946/47 but a note inside the frontispiece of the fifth reader states that its first edition was in 1943-44, perhaps implying that rapid turnover of the first edition had led to a reprint. The writers were Pandit Shyamkanta Gautam BA and Pandit Kaladhar Sharma. The Gorkha Bhasha Prakashini Samiti had, however, been active

in textbook production over more than two decades; Acharya Dikshit (1922/23a) lists its textbooks published and approved by the board (15), in press (4) and awaiting approval (7).

17. Each of the first edition parts I have seen was printed in a different location: the Yajneshar Press (part 2), Hitachintak Press (part 3), Khages Press (part 4), and Jnanmandal Press (part 5). Of these, the Hitachintak Press had a lengthy record of producing Nepali books for publishers such as Visvaraj Harihar.
18. A detailed comparison of these early textbooks remains to be done, and would be a valuable undertaking. It may briefly be noted that the Macmillan books prepared for the Indian curriculum were in general more advanced than their grade counterparts for Nepal, and included more advanced teaching aids, such as notes on vocabulary and structured questions on passages.
19. *Nebula* (1(1): 11-12) announced Nepali's approval for primary education and reproduced in full the official confirmation from O.M. Martin, Secretary to the Government of Bengal on 4 January 1935. The government's decision was to recognise Nepali as one of the vernaculars for teaching and examination to all lower and upper primary schools in Darjeeling District. However, conditions were attached: the majority of the pupils in the schools concerned must be 'Nepalese', 'non-Nepalese should not be compelled to learn Nepali', and primary examinations were to be conducted both in Nepali and Hindi. One further disappointment was that discussion of adopting Nepali as the medium of instruction in middle schools was deferred for three years. In a reprise of *Chandrika*'s role in 1918, *Nebula* thanks those who played an important part in the campaign for Nepali recognition.
20. The speech summarised here can be found in Hariprasad Pradhan (1935: 67-73).
21. The unnamed translator was in fact Parasmani (Pradhan 1997: 43).
22. Similar developments were slowly coming to Nepal, as evidenced by the establishment of the Gorkha Bhasa Prakashini Samiti or the later charitable Charkha Sansthan (sponsored by Chandra Shamsher; see Shaha 1990: II, 168-69), but they tended to be government-initiated or more closely state-supervised.
23. This was the first recorded performance of a modern Nepali play in India, although as Rai (1984: 35) points out it is likely that Nepalis were producing dramas before then. Motiram Bhatta had earlier translated three dramas from Sanskrit—*Padmavati* (1889), *Priyadarshika* (1892) and *Shakuntala* (1892?)—while Shambhuprasad Dhungel also later translated *Priyadarshika,* as well as several other Sanskrit dramas, of which only *Ratnavali* and *Shakuntala* are available in printed form (Adhikari 1977: 36). In 1902 Tîrthaprasad Acharya's *Vichitra ratna bhandahar* was published in Banaras; its second section ('Vedantasar: naya upanyas') is

a story in dialogue *(samvadmay katha)* which has dramatic stylistic features but is not intended as drama.

24. Swanr was born in Ridikot, western Nepal, in 1879; at the age of sixteen he left for India where, strongly opposed to Rana rule, he lived as an exile for the next fifteen years. Apart from *Atalbahadur* he is supposed to have written some twenty other books including a Nepali translation of *Shakuntala* (Adhikari 1977: 40-41).
25. According to Kumar Pradhan (1982: 100-01), 'it does not seem that Girish Ghosh's plays were staged here but certainly his name was repeated from mouth to mouth.'
26. This company was formed in 1913 by Purnakumar Singh, Dhanprakash Shah, L.T. Lama and others (Rai 1984: 40).
27. This group underwent a further transformation to become, under the direction of Laden La, the Himalaya and Children Advancement Association; this company put on a theatrical performance to conclude the meeting which established the Hill Peoples' Social Union (*Nebula* 1(2): 7).
28. There is room, however, for some doubt over these assertions. *Ashok sundari natika,* written by Virendra Keshari Arjyal and others (1917-18), was published in Nepal by Dharma Shamsher Jang Bahadur Rana: its publication suggests that performances may also not have been wholly private. A work of 130 pages, its stock characters (such as *apsaras*) and themes (such as *viraha*) suggest that it is probably a rendering of a Sanskrit original. Also dating to just before *Madan Mohini* is a theatre programme from Kathmandu (*Akhaka nasa thietarko programme,* 1928-29) in the Madan Puraskar Pustakalaya collection. A hand-written note implies that it was performed at the rajguru's *nachghar* but the twelve-page programme, printed by the Pashupat Press, at least brought an extended plot summary into public circulation.
29. As Rai notes (1984: 39-40), this is revealed even by the names of the groups. For the Children Amusement Association, for example, the 'Children' element was probably inspired by school performances in the missionary-run Loreto Convent and St Paul's School while the English word 'Amusement' was popularised by the Rink Amusement Hall, a skating rink set up by a German entrepreneur around 1902.
30. Hence HCAA productions of *King Lear* and *King John*, alongside *The Bottle-genie* (1927, Bhaiya Singh) and *Aladdin* (1931, Harkabahadur Shahi); one Tibetan play was also staged.
31. As Secretary of the HCAA from 1921-1924, Parasmani wrote eight improving dramas such as *Sundar kumar* (1920), *Ratnavali* and *Chandragupta* (1922), and *Buddhacharitra natak* (1923).
32. The manuscript of this play, along with many others, is still preserved in Darjeeling's Gorkha Dukha Nivarak Sammelan.
33. This poem is reprinted in Bhattarai (1988-89: 401).

34. See Pradhan (1993: 225) and Sharma (1976: 32) for details. Both of these articles provide useful general overviews of the Gorkha Library, Pradhan dealing with its establishment and early years (during which he became personally associated with the library), and Sharma with the history of the library until 1961.
35. Paval was Lepcha although he has been mistakenly identified as both British (Powell) and Bengali (Pal). He later moved to Kalimpong and became Secretary of the Kalimpong Branch of the Hillmen's Association (Nagendramani Pradhan, interview, 18 May, 2001).
36. For some time the president of the organisation was Dhan Narayan Pradhan. When he was forced to relinquish the post through lack of time he remained as Patron but Hanjit Dewan Rai took over full executive responsibility. As he in turn became too busy to fulfil his duties Chautariya Dhan Prakash Shah took over. At the founding of the organisation Bhakta Bir Thapa had been appointed Secretary; when he was appointed vice-president Mani Narayan took his place running day to day business. Then Thapa had to take his leave and was replaced by Purna Narayan Pradhan; in 1918 elections he was in turn succeeded with unanimous approval by Dikabir Rai. At first the enthusiastic supporter Buddhi Narayan Pradhan had given most books but he died prematurely. Realising that they had to carry on his work somehow they appointed his brother Shiv Narayan Pradhan to look after the collection; when he too died in October 1917 he was replaced by Parasmani.
37. It received the *Amrita Bazar Patrika, Darjeeling Visitor, Sarasvati, Sanatandharma Patrika, Gorkhe Khabar Kagat, Chandrika, Gorkhali, Balsakha, Industry, Indian Daily News* and government publications courtesy of the authorities [*Chandrika* 1(8-9): 33].
38. These were later reproduced in *Chandrika* [2(3): 93-94].
39. The meeting was fairly cosmopolitan: later speakers included Lt. Col. Ansell, Assistant Secretary Parasmani, B.N. Bannerji, Dharanadhar, and Laksmi Narayan Agravala in English, Nepali and Hindi.
40. Parallel developments were also starting to take place in Nepal. Ganeshdatta, Secretary of Sri Gorkha Sharada Bhavan Pustakalaya in Siraha published his appeal for assistance for the library under the title 'A library is itself a school' (*Chandrika* 1(10): 24).
41. On the Kashi Nagari Pracharini Sabha and Harishchandra, who inspired the Nepali poet Motiram Bhatta, see Dalmia (1996: 141) and King (1994: 142-145).
42. The speech given by Parasmani at the founding meeting ('Hamro avastha') is reproduced in Pradhan (1991: 139-43).
43. Thus, for example, the Himalaya and Children Amusement Association was established under the chairmanship of Deputy Superintendent of Police Laden La. In the build-up to the approval of Nepali as a primary school vernacular in 1935, Laden La was persuaded to tone down his

strident public opposition to the campaign during a meeting at the house of Sardar Bahadur Lt. Govardhan Gurung (Pradhan 1991: 194-97). The powerful D.S.P. was talked round by the only local Nepali able to pull rank on him: on his retirement from the army Gurung had been appointed aide-de-camp to the Governor-General of Bengal. Just before this, Laden La had summoned Parasmani to his house to account for what he had interpreted as personal insults in Parasmani's speech to the Nepali Sahitya Sammelan (Pradhan 1991: 191-93; the speech was Pradhan 1934).

44. See Chalmers (2002) for an assessment of early Nepali publishing and readership.
45. One thousand copies of each had been printed. Of these, *Man lahari* sold out, *Naivedya* sold 619 copies, *Vadhushiksha* 691 copies, and *Kavi bhanubhaktako jivan charitra* 759 copies. Meanwhile of three textbooks published, *Nepali sahitya kathamala* sold out; *Nepali hasta lekh Part 1* sold 1571 copies and *Part 2* 1644 copies. Given access to printers' and publishers' records, more work could be done on evaluating the quantity of sales of other works and their patterns of distribution and consumption. In this context it should be observed that the Sammelan's accounts were in the black by 34 rupees (*Nepali Sahitya Sammelan Patrika* 1: 3). This had been achieved despite the remainders of print runs and the Sammelan's failure to recruit a large number of fee-paying members.
46. The Nepali Sahitya Sammelan (*Nepali Sahitya Sammelan Patrika* 1: 15) saw that it needed to bring out a journal to keep its members informed of activities: 'As members are completely unaware of the state of work being undertaken by the Nepali Sahitya Sammelan, this small journal has been published so that the Sammelan can give its members full information about work it has done.'
47. Kumudini was not the sole critical voice. In the opening issue of *Chandrika* Mîn Bahadur Bhatta (1918: 12) had pointed out that fine writing was not inherently a good thing: 'Nowadays many poets in making their poetry or penning prose imagine their principal duty to be to fill their captivating, ornamented "work" *(manoharini Shrngarabhusita "lekh")* with a jungle of pedantry *(panditya jhari)*; they have not spared any black ink in dousing their poor, clean paper. Is our language about to enter the highest class through increasing the honour of writing in this way?'
48. 'Increase its glory' translates *'aphno kala pratidin badhaune'* in which the punning *kala* could also stand for 'art' or 'issues': in its meaning of 'moonbeam' it is the name given to each issue of *Chandrika* (which itself means 'moon').
49. For example, she is not referred to in Kamal Dikshit's survey of women contributors to early journals (1979/80: 1-7), and she is only mentioned in passing by Dayaratna Sha. Bhi. (1982: 28) as being, alongside Shesmani, foremost among Kalimpong contributors to *Chandrika*.

BIBLIOGRAPHY

Acharya Diksit, Rammani (ed.). 1922-23a (1979 B.S.a). *Gorakha-patrabodh.* Nepal/Banaras: Gorkha Bhasha Prakashini Samiti/Punyaprasad Upadhyaya.

Acharya Dikshit, Rammani, ed. 1922-23b (1979 B.S.b). *Gorakha-sresta-shiksha pratham bhag.* Nepal: Gorkha Bhasha Prakashini Samiti.

Acharya Dikshit, Rammani, ed. 1924-25 (1981 B.S.). *Gorakha-adalati-shiksha pratham bhag.* Nepal: Gorkha Bhasha Prakashini Samiti.

Adhikari, Ramlal. 1977. *Nepali Ekanki Yatra.* Darjeeling: Nepali Sahitya Sancayika.

Ankhaka Nasa Thietar Ko Programme. 1928-29 (1985 B.S.). Nepal: Pashupat Press.

Arjyal, Laksmikanta. 1918. 'Unnati', *Chandrika,* 1(10): 12-15.

Arjyal, Virendra Keshari *et al.* 1917-18 (1974 B.S.). *Ashoka Sundari Natika.* Kathmandu: Dharma Shamsher Jang Bahadur Rana.

Bandhu, Chudamani. 2001-02 (2058 B.S.). *Nepali Loksahitya.* Kathmandu: Ekta Books.

Bhattarai, Ghattaraj, ed. 1988-89 (2045 B.S.). *Madhyamik Kalin Kavi Ra Kavita.* Kathmandu: Royal Nepal Academy.

Chalmers, Rhoderick. 2002. 'Pandits and Pulp Fiction: Popular Publishing and the Birth of Nepali Print-capitalism in Banaras'. *Studies in Nepali History and Society,* 7(1): 35-97.

Chalmers, Rhoderick. 2003. '"We Nepalis": Language, literature, and the formation of a Nepali public sphere in India, 1914-1940'. Ph.D thesis, School of Oriental and African Studies, University of London.

Dalmia, Vasudha. 1997. *The Nationalization of Hindu Traditions. Bharatendu Harishchandra and Nineteenth-century Banaras.* Delhi: Oxford University Press.

Dikshit, Kamal. 1979-80 (2036 B.S.) *Kalo Akshar* (2nd edition). Kathmandu: Sajha Prakashan.

Dravid, Gangadhar Shastry. 1920. *A Dictionary: English and Nepali with Pronunciation in Devnagri Characters.* Banaras: P. Vishwaraj Harihar Sharma, Gorkha Book Depot.

Gurung, Karna Bahadur. 1942. 'Parichay' in *Prathamik Shiksha Vidhi.* James Alexander Richey (tr. anon.). Calcutta: Macmillan and Co., pp. v-vi.

Hutt, Michael. 1997. 'Being Nepali without Nepal. Reflections on a South Asian diaspora'. In David Gellner, Joanna Pfaff-Czarnecka and John Whelpton (eds), *Nationalism and Ethnicity in a Hindu Kingdom. The Politics of Culture in Contemporary Nepal.*, Amsterdam: Harwood, pp. 101-44.

Jnavali, Suryavikram. 1919a. 'Hamro Bhasha Ra Kalkatta Vishvavidyalaya' *Chandrika,* 2(1): 19-20.

Jnavali, Suryavikram. 1919b. 'Vyakhyan' (speech given at the fourth anniversary ceremony of the Nepali Library, Banaras, 2 February). *Chandrika,* 2(3): 89-92.

King, Christopher R. 1994. *One Language, Two Scripts: The Hindi Movement in Nineteenth Century North India*. Bombay: Oxford University Press.

Koirala, Dharanidhar. 1923. *Hamro Kam*. Darjeeling: the author, Gorkha Samiti.

Kumudini (Shrimati). 1918. 'Nepali Bhashama Saralata'. *Chandrika,* 1(5): 11-13.

Lama, Pratiman Singh. 1918. 'Prashnottar'. *Chandrika,* 1(6): 20-21.

Onta, Pratyoush. 1996a. 'Creating a Brave Nepali Nation in British India: The Rhetoric of Jati Improvement, Rediscovery of Bhanubhakta and the Writing of Bîr History'. *Studies in Nepali History and Society,* 1(1): 37-76.

Onta, Pratyoush. 1996b. *The Politics of Bravery: A History of Nepali Nationalism*. Ph.D. thesis, University of Pennsylvania.

Pradhan, Gangaprasad. 1910. *Hindustanko Itihasko Postak* (tr. with Miss Goalen). Darjeeling: Gorkha Press.

Pradhan, Hariprasad. 1935. 'Sabhapatiko Bhasan'. *Nepali Sahitya Sammelan Patrika,* 4(1): 66-73.

Pradhan, Indramani. 1997. *Parasmani Pradhan*. New Delhi: Sahitya Akademi.

Pradhan, Kumar. 1982. *Pahilo Pahar*. Darjeeling: Shyam Prakashan.

Pradhan, Nagendramani. 1991. *Ba Parasmaniko Jivanyatra*. Darjeeling: Dr. Parasmani Prakashan.

Pradhan, Parasmani. 1924. *Nepali Sahitya: Pratham Bhag (Dvitiya Shrenika Nimitta)*. Calcutta: Macmillan & Co.

Pradhan, Parasmani. 1927. *Nepali Pahilo Kitab (Pratham Shrenika Nimitta)*. Calcutta: Longmans, Green & Co.

Pradhan, Parasmani. 1934. 'Madhauru [sic] Amako Jokhana'. *Nepali Sahitya Sammelan Patrika,* 3(1): 25-35.

Pradhan, Parasmani. 1969. *Rochak Sansmaran (Pratham Khanda)*. Kalimpong: Bhagyalakshmi Prakashan.

Pradhan, Parasmani. 1993. 'Kharsang Gorkha Laibreriko Prarambhik Itihas' in *Tipan-Tapan*, edited by Parasmani Pradhan ([1969]1993). Darjeeling: Dr. Parasmani Prakashan, pp. 225-46.

Pradhan, Parasmani and Rudramani Pradhan. [1923] 1949. *Nepali Sahitya Dosro Bhag* (2nd or later edition). Calcutta: Macmillan & Co.

Pradhan, Parasmani and Rudramani Pradhan. n.d. *Nepali Reader Part Two. Translated from the Nepali for Use in the 6th Gurkha Rifles*. Abbottabad: The Army Press.

Rai, Indra Bahadur. 1984. *Darjilingma Nepali Natakko Ardhashatabdi*. Darjeeling: Sajha Pustak Prakashan.

Rai, M.P. 1992. *Vir Jatiko Amar Kahani*. Gangtok: Ajako Sikkim Prakashan.

Sha. Bhi., Dayaratna. 1982. *Sandarbha Sahitya: Kalimpong*. Kalimpong: Upasak Prakashan.

Sahayak Praveshika Bhag 3. 1946-47 (2003 B.S.). Nepal: Nepali Bhashanuvad Parishad/Nepali Bhasha Prakashini Samiti.

Sharma, Dilliraj. 1995-96 (2052 B.S.). *Nepalbahira Nepali Sahitya Ra Sanskriti*. Kathmandu: Sajha Prakashan.

Sharma, Dipakeshvar. 1918c. 'Pustakalaya Prashamsa' *Chandrika,* 1(2): 7-8 [first published in *Gorkhali*].

Sharma, Shantiraj. 1976. 'Gorkha Pustakalaya: Pachi Pharkera Herda'. In Shantiraj Sharma (ed.) *Kharsang: Hijo Ra Aja*. Kurseong: Gorkha Pustakalaya, pp. 31-48.

Sharma, Visvaraj. 1928. *Nepali-bhasha Ko Sachitra Thulo Varnamala*. Banaras: Shivaprasad Urpha Raghorama.

Sharma Bhattarai, Sharadchandra. 1993-94 (2050 B.S.). *Madhyamik Nepali Gadyakhyan*. Kathmandu: Royal Nepal Academy.

Satyal, Ramprasad. 1915-16 (1972 V.S.). *Angreji Vyakaran Nepali Bhashama*. Kashi: Krisaprasad Dhungana.

Shaha, Rishikesh. 1990. *Modern Nepal: A Political History* (Vol. I 1769-1885, Vol. II 1885-1955). New Delhi: Manohar.

Suvedi, Shikharnath. 1913. *Aksharmala*. Banaras: Shikharnath Suvedi.

Vasundhara Devi. 1918. 'Prarthana'. *Chandrika*, 1(4): 18-19.

Vijnanvilas [Padmanabh Sapkota]. 1916. *Jivan charitra*. Banaras: Krishna Madhav and Company.

8

The Urge to Belong: An Identity in Waiting

RAJENDRA P. DHAKAL

The idea of the nation in the Westphalian sense never grew in India. It was never welded into a single political entity during the period of the Mughal emperors. It was the British who forcefully made a patchwork of India into a single political entity. The political fragmentation notwithstanding, India existed as a civilization through centuries. The politico-geographical boundaries did not hinder the flow of various cultural forms of art, literature, music, dance, religion and philosophy from one community and region to another. The neo-traditionalist, Marxian and the predominantly political analysts despite taking diametrically opposite views on their analyses of early Indian nationalism agree that the pre-British India had absolutely no sense of a nation.[1] To Valentine Chirol, India was merely a 'geographical expression which could never develop into a nation in the western sense of the term, and that whatever political movement, with a pseudo-national colour, existed in India, had their roots deep in traditional, instinctively anti-western sources.'[2] Desai, an eminent historian, comments that religious as well as non-religious secular culture and art that thrived in India were not 'inspired by any national spirit' and that the 'rich, complex, cultural life bristling in towns of pre-British period' lacked 'a national form and scope...which did not and could not exist in that period.'[3] The great M.N. Roy in this context observes: [4]

> ...the economic and political evolution of India was such that her people could be called rather a number of nationalities inhabiting a continent, than a composite national unit. It is quite possible to imagine that but for the intervention of capitalist

> imperialism, which while obstructing the economic growth of her people, forced on them political unity, Indian would be today in a socio-political stage corresponding to that of modern Europe—a continent composed of a number of free nationalities in different grades of economic and social development, but not one united nation.

R.C. Majumdar summarizes the issue by stating that 'the conception of India as a whole, was to be found only in the literary works of a past age and still survived in theory, but had no application to actual politics till the sixties and seventies of the 19th century.'[5] Bipan Chandra also regarded Indian nationalism as an 'entirely new organizing principle and ideology', which was 'clearly recognized by the early nationalist leaders such as Surendranath Banerjea and Lokmanya Tilak, who referred to India as a nation in the making.'[6] The dynamics of a nation in the making has been succinctly described by A.K. Danda in the following words: [7]

> In India sharing of heritage and experiences is as much as the existence of distinct physical and cultural types, the contrast between are not only apparent but evident. They not only manifest widely different cultural expressions, they are also organized social systems that lend to provide support to the maintenance of discreet identities of the people and thus perpetuations of their apparent differences.

The making of the Indian nation was a modern phenomenon necessitated by its independence. According to Bipan Chandra, 'the basic objectives of the early nationalists were to help the process of unifying Indian people into a nation..., and in the end to create a broad all India national movement.'[8] The project of nation-building based on the western liberal paradigm was undertaken to create legitimacy and a base for national integration. It was an attempt to translate a design meant for homogenous states of Europe in a heterogeneous Indian society. Describing the process of nation-building as mimetic construction of the past, Krishna Shankaran writes.[9]

> The story of what once happened in Europe constitutes the knowledge that empowers state elite as they attempt to fashion their knowledge in the images of what are considered successful nation states...premised on this narrative of what once happened

> 'out there', post colonial elites attempt to remake the recalcitrant clay of plural civilization into lean, uniform, hyper masculine and disciplined nation states.

This kind of pronounced engagements of the state elite with the enterprise of nation-building and national integration centered around the putative majoritarian ethos and have excluded the minorities, dalits and tribals. It was around this exclusion that their resistance was often built. The resistance can be explained in terms of a desire to be included in the process of nation building without having to lose the roots of distinctiveness and a search for a dignified place in the system.

In fact, in a nation where such diversity and distinctions are 'so evident in terms of ethnicity as well as cultural variations, the practicality of forging imaginary affinities without ensuring equality of rights as well as sharing of resources and authority is a matter of serious concern, if not doubtful of merit.'[10] It is inevitable for a country like India with its ethno-cultural and religious heritage to experience 'a certain amount of particularistic tendencies which are often referred to as parochialism or regionalism,'[11] which are inherent in the system. The scholars believe that, 'particularism may be an essential precursor' for the purpose of generating sentiment of nationality.[12] B.K. Roy Burman has shown in his study of the process of territorial ethnic mobilization of the hill tribes of Northeast India that 'sub nationalism leads to development of nationalism' as the elites 'consciously promote the search for new identity, new world view and new horizon of mind, so as to come to terms with modern world' giving place to a 'unified command and new institutions.'[13] As we will find in the case of Indian Nepalis the voice of resistance is in fact the voice of an assertion of their loyalty and belief in the democratic process of the country.

The rise of various regional and ethnic groups and their politics of identity in recent years may also be seen in this perspective and not necessarily as leading to disintegration and instability. This also may explain the politics of coalition in the newly emerging federal paradigm. The coalition politics has facilitated the effective participation of regional political parties at the highest political level of the Indian federal polity. According to a study on politics of ethnicity in India it is 'characteristic of most regional parties that each of them represents a distinct ethnic interest group. In India, the traditional and racial groups and caste are the most important ethnic groups and their various combinations have provided a social basis of many regional parties.'[14] The study further shows that '...the existence of several territorial ethnic groups has provided a favourable social basis for many territorial ethnic parties.'[15] Since these regional parties play decisive roles in the formation and governance of the central and the state governments there is also a need to understand the dynamics of federalism and "coalition politics" from the perspective of the regionalization of political parties and the politics of identity.

I have used the term "sub-nationalism" to refer to "politics of identity", following Sanjib Baruah in his interesting study of the politics of Assamese sub-nationalism. He points out that 'ethnic politics is radically different from the politics of identity that is not grounded on homelands—the latter is often easily incorporated within a larger ideology of state nationalism... Since Assamese and other nationalism coexist with a pan Indian nationalism'.[16] The term "sub-nationalism" is described as identities that 'meet some of the criteria of politicization and mobilization associated with nationalism but are not firmly committed to separate statehood.'[17] In fact, an objective analysis of the Nepali sub-nationalism shows that their mobilization was never for secession from India.

This paper intends to explain firstly, the formation of the ethnic sub-nationalism of Indian Nepalis, especially in Darjeeling. Secondly, it will try and show how the politics of identity of the Gorkhas, which is characterized by a strong sense of insecurity, is not antithetical to the existence of pan-Indian nationalism and national integration. It will further try and show that their voice was for recognition as equal Indians and to demonstrate that Indian nationality to them is 'a matter of privilege and proud possession, not a liability.'[18]

The terms 'Gorkha' and 'Nepali' are used here synonymously to mean the nationality of those who are Indian citizens either by being indigenous people of the region or those who migrated from Nepal to India and adopted Indian citizenship and nationality. The British encouraged their migration for fulfilling their colonial interests. First, their migration met the need of workers in the tea gardens. Second, the British adopted the policy of large scale recruitment of the Gorkhas in the army. Third, their migration was encouraged because they were skilled agriculturalists and were needed to develop agriculture in Northeast India and Sikkim. Fourth, due to social, economic, and cultural reasons people to people contact had taken place facilitating to and fro migration between the peoples on either side of the border between India and Nepal.

The Making of Nepali *Jati*

In the context of Indian Nepalis the word *jati* refers to the assimilated identity of heterogeneous groups of people speaking the Indo-Aryan Nepali language and the speakers of various Tibeto-Burman languages for whom Nepali is the *lingua-franca.* The word nationalism is translated in Nepali as *rastriyata* and sub-nationalism as *upa-rastriyata* and not as *jatiyata*. *Jatiyata* in some other languages such as Bengali and Assamese is used to mean nationality which is *rastriyata* in Nepali. Internationalism would be translated as *antarjatiyata* or *antarjatik* in these languages whereas in Nepali it would be *antarrastriyata.* The Nepalis have used the word *jati* to mean Nepali as a community and *rastriyata* to mean their nationality. Therefore they are Nepali/Gorkha *jati* whose *rastriyata* is Indian. The word *jat* refers to castes though not in the rigid hierarchical sense as in the orthodox Hindu society.

The acceptance of 'Nepali' as the *lingua franca* in Darjeeling, Sikkim and other parts of India by various ethnic groups like Rai, Limbu, Gurung, Magar, Tamang (Murmi), Newar, Sunuwar, Thami, etc. facilitated the development of collective consciousness of these peoples.[19] It was not difficult for these various groups of people living together in villages, towns and tea gardens to adopt Nepali as their *lingua franca* as an eminent historian of Darjeeling Kumar Pradhan writes:[20]

> The numerous ethnic tribes like Rais, Limbus, Tamangs, Magars, Newars and Thamis living separately in their own villages and speaking their own languages in Nepal had no opportunity of living separately in the changed environment of Darjeeling. Although the few place names give evidence of them living separately in different villages initially, in towns and in the tea gardens they worked and lived collectively. Not only because Nepal had a State language after the Gorkha conquest but much before that the mingling of the Bahuns, Chhetris, Kamis, and Damais had made other ethnic tribes familiar with the Nepali language (then Khaskura, Parbate, Gorkhali). The migrants, who shared Nepali as the middle or second language with their primary Tibeto-Burman languages in their own homeland, adopted Nepali as the common medium or second language in their mutual conversations in the shared life of Darjeeling. Because of the social need the other languages phased out as those were used less and less and Nepali emerged as the first

> language or the mother tongue... The collective consciousness that was germinating among the Nepalese in Darjeeling found its support in the Nepali language. Here, the language became the strong foundation for Nepali *jati.*

Once, this collective consciousness grew amongst them it was easy to identify others who did not belong to this linguistic confederacy called Nepali. The process was facilitated by the political socialization under colonial rule. The social, economic and political exigencies of the colonial political economy provided congenial background in which a political culture of the Gorkhas developed that was remarkably distinct from that of Nepal. An integrated homogenous Nepali community with Nepali as *lingua franca* emerged in India whereas in Nepal Nepali language was a state-imposed national language. Ramakrishna Sharma,[21] a well known literary critic from Darjeeling, observed that a Nepali society had come into existence in Darjeeling much before Nepal. In fact one still finds a Newar society, a Limbu society, a Gurung society and so on in Nepal.

Thus, the British were identified as the colonialists and the plainsmen as government officials, teagarden *babus*, and as traders. The traders from the plains also served as money lenders and bankers. The extent to which 'disputes' and discontentment developed on account of money lending can be judged from the fact that as many as 808 cases were registered on disputes of loan repayment in Darjeeling Court in 1902. Of these, agreements were made to pay interest rates of 30 per cent in 97 cases, 37.5 per cent in 458 cases, 48 per cent in 93 cases, 60 per cent in 38 cases, 108 per cent in 113 cases, 150 per cent in 3 cases and 300 per cent in one case.[22]

The sense of identifying the self and others gradually developed along with the realization that they belonged to economically and administratively oppressed class, which I call 'ethno-class consciousness'. Darjeeling passed through a historical phase in which almost all Nepalis were 'have nots'. The *jati* in the making consisted of soldiers, coolies and the ordinary farmers. A semblance of middle class grew only after the second half of the 19th century as a result of the introduction of some educational institutions in the hills of Darjeeling by the British missionaries and administrators. The newly created middle class was engaged in various social-political reforms since the early 1920s as is evident from the activities of Hillmen's Association, Kalimpong Samiti, Nepali Bhutia Lepcha Association, Nepali Sahitya Sammelan, Gorkha Dukha Niwarak Sammelan and a host of other associations. This was the time of rising Indian nationalism and the freedom movement was gradually gaining momentum elsewhere in India. It did influence the people in the hills who wanted to be part of the freedom movement as well as political reforms that were being introduced by the British government. The growing collective consciousness of the hill people was also bolstered by the British policy of keeping them outside the reform process as well as the apathy of the Indian National Congress, the political party that spearheaded the freedom movement and ruled the country for many decades after the freedom was achieved. The concerns and apprehensions of the community of soldiers and coolies were ignored by the British Government and by the Indian National Congress as well. Thus, by 1920s, the amalgamation of the myriad groups of hill people was almost complete.

A Nepali *jati* had by now grown into adulthood. There started a language movement that demanded introduction of the Nepali language in the educational institutions and subsequently for making Nepali a medium of instruction for education. The language movement culminated into a bigger movement for demanding the language to be recognized as official language in the hills of Darjeeling in 1961 and into a movement for inclusion in the eighth schedule of the constitution in 1970s with a larger and wider participation of Indian Nepalis. In fact it is the dynamics of the language movement that disseminated the issue of 'identity and insecurity' amongst the masses creating a support base for the movement for a separate state by the Pranta Parishad and later, the Gorkhaland movement by the Gorkha National Liberation Front. Thus, one of the most important factors that have sustained the Nepali/Gorkha identity over more than a century is the socio-political activities centering around Nepali language. Thus the ethno-class consciousness that developed in an atmosphere of colonial polity and administration was a primary determinant in the process of the formation the Gorkha identity. The process was accelerated by the emerging Nepali middle class under colonial hegemony who were exposed to modern education and rational way of life and had experienced an acute sense of subalternity.[23] The perception of a Gorkha as a doorman, a coolie, a soldier, a peon and a guard still continues with absolute indifference to and ignorance of the changes that have taken place in the Gorkha community. One glaring example can be taken from the Bollywood film industry which stereotypes a Gorkha as a *darban* whereas a number of them who are working as cinematographers, musicians, technicians and photographers are ignored. This stereotype is perpetuated by literary narratives of some regional languages as well. For instance, one is amazed by the Bengali literary narratives and films which still stereotype Gorkha in the same image though Bengalis and Nepalis share the same state and there is a continuous social, cultural, economic and political interaction between the two communities.

State Policies Before and After Independence

At a time the Nepali *jati* was in the making the British kept the hill areas of Darjeeling outside the purview of constitutional reforms that were taking place in the rest of India in the direction of allowing larger participation of Indian citizens in the governance of the country. The British policy regarding the administration of India did not provide a uniform system of administration, the division of areas into 'regulated' and 'non-regulated' having started prior to 1861. It was brought under general regulation system during 1861-1870[24] but certain administrative reasons weighed heavily in favour of bringing the district of Darjeeling under non-regulation system.[25] From 1874, within the purview of the Laws Local Extent Act, 1874 (also known as the Scheduled District Act), Part III, Sixth Schedule, Darjeeling district was made a schedule district and kept outside the ambit of general laws in operation throughout the rest of India.[26] The Indian Councils Act of 1909 did not bring about any change in this respect. The Government of India Act 1919, besides retaining all the provisions for Scheduled District and their corresponding administration, brought all the Scheduled Districts under a new terminology, 'the Backward Tracts'. So, Darjeeling became a backward tract till the passing of the Government of India Act, 1935, which declared the district as a 'Partially Excluded Area'. Thus, an Act, either of the federal legislature or of the provincial legislatures, would not extend to either the excluded areas or the partially excluded areas, unless the Governor of the province concerned would give his assent to the application of the Act in its entirety or with such modification as he thought necessary.[27] The district remained a partially excluded area till the attainment of independence by India.

The British policy of segregating the people of this area had far-reaching political implications. The justification given for such segregation was the 'backwardness' and 'distinctiveness' of the region which needed protection. But the demand of the people for the exclusion of the area from Bengal and to provide separate administrative arrangements on similar grounds of backwardness and distinctiveness was rejected time and again.

On realizing that the hill people would never be able to avail themselves of the rights enjoyed by the people in other areas under the reforms, a demand was placed by them expressing their 'wish to remain in Bengal as they are now and have the reform scheme in total'[28] with 'positive and negative safeguards'.[29] Neither the demand for the exclusion from Bengal nor the demand for remaining in Bengal under constitutional reforms with positive and negative safeguards were conceded by the British authorities. The reforms were introduced partially depending upon the convenience of the colonial state. The intention, it appears, was to keep the Indian Gorkhas isolated from the wave of freedom movement that was gaining momentum elsewhere in India and at the same time prevent them from growing politically conscious. According to Randhir Subba, an eminent politician from Darjeeling, the British taught in the Gorkha Regiment that, 'You are different from Hindustanis, their (freedom) movement is not yours.'[30] However, this did not hinder many of them, including those from Nepal, from participating in the freedom movement.

The attitude of the central and state governments of independent India towards the Indian Nepalis do not appear very different from that of the British. One glaring example of this is the decision of the then Dr. P.C. Ghosh government in West Bengal to continue the system of 'nominated membership' in the District Board of Darjeeling whereas the system of election was introduced in all other District Boards of Bengal within a month of the independence.[31] Further, out of 20 members of the District Board in Darjeeling, only 3 members were from the hills.[32] The justification given for such segregation and discrimination was that the region has distinctiveness or peculiarity. But, when the Gorkha League placed the demand for autonomous district council on similar grounds of 'distinctiveness', the same Dr. P.C. Ghosh said during his visit to Darjeeling that there is no need for providing special rules and safeguards to this area.[33]

The language used by the Deputy Prime Minister, Sardar Ballavbhai Patel on 14th December, 1949 in Parliament replying to a question by Pandit Thakurdas shows the insensitivity and indifference with which the Indian Nepalis were treated. According to him, the proposal of making Darjeeling a province is harmful to the welfare of Hindustan, and the Government of India is ready and determined to crush such a proposal which is against national integration.[34] The perception reflects his suspicion about the integrity of the Indian Nepalis as if they were planning to disintegrate the country. The perception has not changed much, as even in 1979, after 30 years of such comment by the Deputy Prime Minister, the Prime Minister of India Sri Morarji Desai declared Nepali as a foreign language when a delegation of Akhil Bharatiya Nepali Bhasa Samiti met him to appeal for the recognition of Nepali language in the eighth schedule of the Indian constitution. In a bid to convince the Prime Minister Desai the delegation tried to draw his attention to the contribution of the Nepalis, particularly in defending the country to which he responded very rudely stating that the Gorkha regiment can be thrown into the Indian ocean. Mrs. Indira Gandhi exhibited a very ambiguous and unsympathetic stand on the Nepali language issue with her rhetoric of "vehicle is moving forward". It was the compulsions arising out of the merger of Sikkim into India in 1975 with about 75 per cent of its population as Nepali-speaking and the concerted efforts of the former Chief Minister of Sikkim Nar Bahadur Bhandari and Sikkim's representative in Indian Parliament, Mrs. Dil Kumari Bhandari, that the Nepali language was granted recognition in the eighth schedule of the constitution.

A subtle shift in the attitude of the Central Government was discernible when Rajiv Gandhi's government did not consider the Gorkhaland Movement as anti-national as opposed to insistence of the Left Front Government's stand in West Bengal to do so with the purported motive of brutally crushing the movement like the Congress government did to the Naxalite movement in the state. Historically, the undivided Communist Party of India had viewed these problems with open mind as the following excerpts from its resolution passed at the Party Congress in 1943 show:[35]

> Every section of the Indian people which has a contiguous territory as its homeland, common historical tradition, common language, psychological make-up and common economic life would be recognized as a distinct nationality with the right to exist as an autonomous state within the free Indian Union or federation and will have the right to secede from it if it may so desire. This means that the territories that are homelands of such nationalities and which today are split up by the artificial boundaries of the present British provinces and the so called "Indian States" would be reunited and restored to them in free India...

But the recognition of the right of separation in this form need not lead to actual separation. On the other hand by dispelling

> mutual suspicion, it brings about unity of action today and lays the basis for a greater unity in the free India of tomorrow...

Towing the above principles the leaders of the Communist Party of India from Darjeeling and the plains of West Bengal demanded 'A Free Gorkhasthan in a Free India'[36]. Even after independence, the Communist Party of India in the state of West Bengal and its District Committee in Darjeeling had favoured—since its inception till its coming to power—special administrative arrangements for the areas inhabited by the Nepalis in Darjeeling and Jalpaiguri, thereby recognizing their distinctiveness. But, there was a turn around once the party formed the government with other Left parties. It opposed the demand for the creation of a state carved out of the Nepali-speaking areas of Darjeeling and Jalpaiguri and even threw its own earlier proposal of regional autonomy for Darjeeling into oblivion. Either the Gorkha leadership failed to convince the Left Front government or the latter refused to accept that the demand of Gorkhaland did not, to borrow a phrase from the sociologist A.R. Desai, 'conflict with conception of a single Indian state.'[37] The label of 'anti-national' or 'separatist' did not do any good to remove mutual suspicion of the two communities, i.e., Nepalis and Bengalis. The Government of West Bengal dubbed the demand for Gorkhaland as 'partition of India'.[38]

The politics of convenience was always manifested in the policies of the successive state governments in West Bengal. The Sidhartha Shankar Ray government, apparently recognizing the distinct social, economic, cultural and geographical characters of the hills of Darjeeling, created the Hill Development Council. The Council was a face-saving centralized device with nominated members and a senior cabinet minister as its chairman. Even after the revitalization of the Panchayat Raj in West Bengal the Hill Development Council with nominated members and Chief Minister as its Chairman remained in the centre stage of planning and development relegating the elected Zilla Parishad into political wilderness. It was the nominated Hill Development Council that shaped decision-making whereas in every other district in West Bengal, the Zilla Parishads were empowered to take up developmental works at the district level. The resistance shown by the elected Zilla Parishad of Darjeeling and its demand to be instrumental in district planning was always sidelined. During the course of the Gorkhaland Movement the members of the Hill Development Council and the Zilla Parishad resigned *en mass* and after the tripartite accord signed in June 1988, Darjeeling Gorkha Hill Council was formed. It was for the first time a semblance of autonomy with extraordinarily limited powers was provided in the hill areas of Darjeeling.

People's Response

The Gorkhas appealed to the British government for justice through a series of memorandums. As the freedom movement gathered momentum, they became very apprehensive about their fate in free India. Their apprehension, which came from the fact that their appeals were rejected one after another, is clear in the following words:

> (T)heir social solidarity and the very existence as community is being threatened with serious disruption owing to various factors coming into play chiefly the realization by many of them that their welfare is now dependant on the exigencies of party politic in the Bengal Assembly and their utter helplessness to make their voice heard and their interest completely lost on the whirlpool of various conflicting party interests in which they have very little concern.[39]

Their sense of deprivation, insecurity, rejection and the desire to be recognized as Indian is reflected in the resolution of the Gorkha League in its Tejpur Conference held in 1947.[40] It states that the 'Gorkhalis' have a share in the history and culture of India like any other 'Hindustani'. They have their own distinct lifestyle, history and culture like that of Bengali, Bihari and others. Therefore, the 'Gorkhalis' have equal rights in 'Hindustan' in the matters of language and culture like any other Indian community. The conference resolved to accept the principles of the Indian National Congress on foreign and economic policy but the Gorkha League would not come to an understanding with any political party compromising or surrendering Gorkha interest in India. The President of All India Gorkha League submitted a memorandum to the Congress High Command and also to Lord Mountbatten on 15 May, 1947 stating that the Act of 1935 had not recognized the Gorkhas as a community in India and pointed out that even the Reforms of 1919 made no mention of them whereas the Act of 1935 'recognized the right of every small community but the three million "Gurkhas" in India and Burma were ignored.'[41] Commenting on the policy of the British government and the attitude of Indian National Congress, and reflecting the Gorkha sense of insecurity an eminent leader observed, '...every community which fought under the leadership of the Congress for India's freedom did fight also for their own province, community and collective self. The Bengalis, the Madrasis, the Punjabis saw their own freedom in India's independence. The Indian Gorkhas without a province of their own were apprehensive of the protection of their culture and identity. The Congress had declared that the language and culture of the minorities will be protected but it never recognized Gorkhas as minority.'[42]

Dissatisfied with the extant situation the All India Gorkha League submitted three alternate proposals regarding the Nepali-speaking hill areas of Darjeeling and the adjacent plains of Siliguri and Duars in Jalpaiguri in 1952 to Pandit Nehru, the then Prime Minister of India, during his visit to Darjeeling. The proposals were:

(1) Separating Darjeeling from Bengal and making it a union territory.
(2) Creating a separate state of Nepali-speaking areas of Darjeeling district and Duars region of the Jalpaiguri district.
(3) Separating Nepali-speaking areas of Darjeeling and Jalpaiguri districts from West Bengal and including them in Assam.[43]

In fact, the League gave a call for 'Assam *Chalo*' which was objected to by the Communist Party of India's Darjeeling Committee which in turn gave its own proposal of a "Free Gorkhasthan in a Free India".[44] Ideologically, the League was closer to Indian National Congress but shared a common perception with the communist party of India as far as the Gorkha question was concerned. The abiding concern of protecting the identity of the Gorkhas had forced the league to allow some of its members to join the Congress which facilitated the beginning of the Congress Party in Darjeeling. Almost all political parties of West Bengal had raised the issue of some kind of homeland for the Gorkhas to survive politically. The concepts of "Uttarakhand" of the Gorkha League, "Gorkhasthan" of the undivided Communist Party of India, "Regional Autonomy" of the Communist Party of India (Marxist), "Hill Autonomy" and "Union Territory" of the Congress primarily formed the plank on which these political parties fought election.

The whirlpool of party politics, politics of expediency, opportunism and factionalism gradually eroded the base of most of these political parties. A general feeling among the Nepalis of the region was that the political parties had sidelined the Gorkha ethos and aspirations for limited political ends. The people felt that political leaders had failed to espouse the cause of the region and its people at the appropriate forums like parliament, state legislature and other national institutions of importance. Simultaneously, the people's perception about national and state level elite, press, academicians and others was and still is that they are insensitive, apathetic and hostile to the Gorkha/Nepali aspirations for being treated as fellow Indian citizens because of their lack of understanding of the Nepalis/Gorkhas.[45] The failure of the language movement at that time to realize the inclusion of the Nepali language in the eighth schedule and the statement of the Prime Minister Morarji Desai declaring Nepali a foreign language made the Indian Nepalis feel insecure. During the language movement a general thinking in the hills of Darjeeling was that the recognition of the language would assert Nepali identity and acceptance of the Gorkhas as Indians.

The experience of the past and the concern for the future sustained the 'demand for a separate state for the protection of the community existence'. At a conference held in April 1980 and attended by the representatives of various political parties, intellectuals, social organizations and others, the Pranta Parishad was formed with the objective of fighting for separate statehood. In the same year in July, the Gorkha National Liberation Front was formed, which ultimately launched a mass movement for Gorkhaland. The basic premise of the Gorkhaland Movement was the identity of Gorkhas in India. The belief was that by the creation of the Gorkhaland, a home for the Gorkhas in India, their identity as Indians would be established.

Thus, the essence of the politics of sub-nationalism of the Gorkhas lies in their desire to be recognized and treated as equal citizens in India. Their social and political demands reveal that they are not willing to be excluded from the history of the making of India. The search for a dignified place in the polity of India from the days of Morely Minto reforms continued.

The experience of Indian Nepalis in other parts of the country and in erstwhile Sikkim before the merger was not very different from that of the Gorkhas of Darjeeling and adjacent areas of the Jalpaiguri district. The systems of *Kuruwa, Jharlangi, Kalobhari* and the revenue system in Sikkim explain the way they were deprived and discriminated. The Sikkim National Congress and Praja Sammelan demanded the removal of the separate rules and regulations between the Nepalis and Bhutia-Lepcha community,[46] and bringing uniformity in the system of land revenue collection[47] and in the purchase and sale of land.[48] The demands made by the Gorkhas settled in Punjab also manifest their desire to be treated as equals and recognized as fellow Indians, as evident from the following lines:

(i) We should be treated as backward communities.
(ii) We should get rights like other communities in Punjab.
(iii) We should be given the status of the agriculturalists like other communities in Punjab.
(iv) We should have equal rights like other fellow citizens and should be given similar employment opportunities.[49]
(v) The concern for insecurity, discrimination and deprivation of the Nepalis in Northeast India is no less than the Nepalis elsewhere. They have become the worst victims of ethnic conflicts there. Their contribution to the economic development of the region has not been recognized. Their feisation[50], eviction from their homes, and the denial of their existence explain their sense of being left out. Such exclusion and isolation have created a sense of inferiority among the Indian Nepalis living there.[51]

The dominant neighbouring communities in India obviously do not like to change the status quo for they benefit from it. The victims who resist the status quo like the Nepalis are careful about their resistance because they apprehend more discrimination and repression.[52] The Gorkhas have tried their best to bring about changes in the administration of the hill areas of Darjeeling and Duars region of Jalpaiguri through a series of memoranda but they were never heard. Paul Brass has aptly pointed out that since Nehru period policies were such that granted 'recognition to language groups whose spokesmen were able to demonstrate strong political support... The decisions finally made were, therefore, political decisions, not linguistic ones.'[53]

The demonstration of such political support often depended on the numerical, administrative and economic strength of a community. This is evident in the reorganization of states and granting of recognition to different languages. It is observed that whenever the interests of the linguistic majorities are affected, the linguistic states function like a pressure group representing such interests. Thus, West Bengal and Bihar could agree to transfer the territories without consulting the people living there, but the former refused to apply the same principle to the minority linguistic groups in the state like the Nepalis. Thus, the state often promotes majoritarianism in its design of nation building and national integration.

Conclusion

Integration is a process which facilitates cooperation and consensus among the members of diverse social backgrounds through the medium of communication, social values and social institutions.[54] It is also defined as a process that binds the diverse cultural and social units within the boundaries of a state and establishes national identity. It depends on the ability of the political system to establish linkages between the political elite and diverse sub-nationalisms through political socialization that facilitates accommodation.

An objective assessment of the politics of Gorkha sub-nationalism reveals that in spite of their strong political will to preserve their distinctive identity they always aspired to be integrated to Indian nationalism. A proposal by the Hillmen's Association of Darjeeling in 1938 demanding the creation of a North Eastern Frontier State for the hill people inhabiting the sub-Himalayan region justifies such state because it would form 'a formidable bulwark and a vast military ground for the military protection of India.'[55] One of the main objectives of the All India Gorkha League established in 1943 was to support the Indian National Congress, especially its economic and foreign policy. The Gorkha leaders in Assam in 1941 mobilized the Gorkhas to enumerate themselves as Assamese speakers at the call of the Assamese leadership and intelligentia.[56] The Gorkhas actually returned Assamese as their mother tongue at that time. This was done due to the perceived threat of being overtaken by the Muslim population and being included in Pakistan. The protest shown against the Indo-Nepal Treaty of 1950 by burning its copies during the Gorkhaland Movement was in fact an assertion of Gorkha loyalty to the Indian nationhood. The demand of the Gorkhas to be distinguished from Nepali-speaking citizens of Nepal is also clearly an expression of their desire to be recognized as Indian nationals.

We have seen in India that whenever the ruling elite has responded to the aspiration of sub-nationalist movements and recognized 'their distinctiveness, the result has been a strengthening and enriching of a pluralist sense of identity.'[57] But negotiation for settlement of the sub-nationalist mobilization should take into account 'the collective memories and aspiration that shape' its policies.[58] Baruah rightly observes, 'Fire fighting tactics might lead to a short term peace that might steal the momentum from a particular group of leaders, but they are unlikely to achieve long-term resolutions.'[59] In Assam, as he points out, the Rajiv Gandhi-AASU Accord opened the space for the rise of the United

Liberation Front of Assam—a major militant and radical organization ready to avenge the perceived betrayal of the Assamese people by the central government.[60] But according to the analysts, the vibrancy of sub-nationalism does not mean that they have a telos that must inevitably lead to a separation.'[61] Two ways of solving the problem of national integration have been suggested by the scholars. The first is to crush the diversity[62] or to adopt the 'authoritarian resolution to destroy through relentless modernization and political repressions, the social space that sustains subnationalist politics.'[63] The second is the democratic way that facilitates dialogue through institutional arrangement, opens up communication channels, makes the government and the political leadership accountable, enhances political capacity to articulate and aggregate conflicting interest for achieving national integration amidst diversity.[64] Indian constitution has adopted the second method. The responsibility of removing obstacles on this road lies with the political leadership.

REFERENCES

1. Rajat K. Ray, 1983, "Three Interpretations of Indian Nationalism" in B.R. Nanda (ed.), *Essays in Modern Indian History*, New Delhi: Oxford University Press.
2. Valentine Chirol, 1910, "Indian Unrest," London, pp. 322-23 Adapted from Rajat K. Ray, *Ibid.*, p. 2.
3. A.R. Desai, 1998, (Reprinted) (First Published 1948), *Social Background of Indian Nationalism,* Bombay: Popular Prakashan, pp. 26, 28.
4. M.N. Roy, 1971, *India in Transition* (Ch. 1), Bombay, Cited by Rajat K. Ray, *Ibid.*, p. 5.
5. R.C. Majumdar, 1961, *Three Phases of India's Struggle for Freedom*, Bombay, pp. 1-2, cited by Rajat. K. Ray, *ibid.*, p. 5.
6. Bipan Chandra, 1969, "Historians of Modern India and Communalism", Romilla Thapar, Harbans Mukhia and Bipan Chandra (eds), *Communalism and the Writing of Indian History,* New Delhi, p. 37.
7. A.K. Danda, 1987, "*Ethno-Cultural Diversities of India and National Integration*", Rasheeduddin Khan, *Composite Culture of India and National Integration*, Shimla: Indian Institute of Advance Study, pp. 195-231.
8. Bipan Chandra, 1979, *Nationalism and Colonialism*, New Delhi: Orient Longman, p. 124.
9. Krishana Shankaran, 2002, *Post Colonial Insecurities, India, Sri Lanka and the Question of Nationhood*, New Delhi: Oxford University Press.
10. Ajit K. Danda, *op. cit.* p. 201.

11. *Ibid.*
12. *Ibid.*
13. B.K. Roy Burman, 1970, *Demographic and Socio-Economic Profiles of the North East India,* New Delhi: Census of India.
14. Tatu Vanhanen, 1991, "Politics of Ethnic Nepotism in India", Diethelm Weidmann (ed.), *Nationalism, Ethnicity and Political Development,* New Delhi: Manohar Publication, pp. 83-84.
15. *Ibid.*, pp. 89-90.
16. Sanjib Baruah, 1997, "Politics of Sub Nationalism: Society *versus* State in Assam", Partha Chatterji (ed.), *State and Politics in India*, New Delhi: Oxford University Press, pp. 497-98.
17. Crawford M. Young, 1976, *The Politics of Cultural Pluralism*, Madison: University of Wisconsin Press, p. 72.
18. A.K. Danda, *op. cit.*, p. 201.
19. Kumar Pradhan, 1982, "Darjeelingko Nepali Jati: Aouta Aitihasik Adhayan", *Pahilo Pahar*, Darjeeling: Shyam Prakashan, p. 32.
20. Kumar Pradhan, 2005, "Agamsinha Giriko Kawitama Jatiya Bhawana," *Adhiti Kehi*, Siliguri: Purnima Prakashan, p. 121.
21. Ramakrishna Sharma, 1978 (2036, Bikram Sambat), "Nepali Sahityako Pragati", *Nepali Gadya Sangraha,* Bhag 3, Kathmandu: Sajha Prakashan.
22. A great deal of literary narratives contain the issue of high rate of interest charged by the money lenders to the poor Gorkhas.
23. Suranjan Sinha, 1993, "Construction of Identity", *Seminar*, 412, p. 41.
24. In 1866 Kalimpong and the adjacent plains areas (now in Jalpaiguri district were acquired by the British Government under the Treaty of Sinchula.
25. Dyutis Chakrabarty, 1988, "Gorkhaland: Evolution of Politics of Segregation", Special Lecture No. X, Centre for Himalayan Studies, North Bengal University, p. 26.
26. D.B. Gurung, 1983,"Darjeeling District: Struggle for Administrative Status", *The Calcutta Journal of Political Studies,* Summer, Calcutta University, pp. 56-58.
27. *Ibid.,* p. 57.
28. From the minutes of the meeting of the Kalimpong Samiti held in Kalimpong on 10th July, 1920 under the Chairmanship of Prem Singh Kumain, Vice-Chairman of Kalimpong Central Union.
29. Proceedings of a Conference held at the Municipal Council Chamber, Town Hall, Darjeeling on March 4th, 1933 vide proceedings: "Safeguards could be of two kinds, i.e., negative which would protect the district against innovation or changes in the system of administration with personal concurrences of the Governor, but would not guarantee the receipt of any particular grant form provincial finance, to guarantee this, safeguards of a positive type would be required. Some of those in the best position to know were of opinion that would have nothing to fear from illiberality on the part of a provincial government. On the other hand fears had been expressed in this point for the future (from the files of AIGL).

30. Randhir Subba, 1955 *Gorkha,* 7th February, Darjeeling.
31. N.B. Gurung, 1971, *Darjeeling Kata*, Darjeeling District Cooperative Press, Kalimpong.
32. *Ibid.*
33. *Ibid.*
34. N.K. Lama, 1950, "Agni Pariksha" in *Gorkha*, 7th January.
35. Quoted in A.R. Desai, *op. cit.*, p. 426.
36. See for Details, Memorial of the Darjeeling District Committee of Communist Party of India on "Gorkha National Demand for a Free Gorkhastan" quoted in "Why Gorkhaland?" 1998, Darjeeling: Pranta Parishad.
37. A.R. Desai, *op, cit,* p. 388.
38. *Ibid.*
39. Memorandum submitted on 11th December, 1938 (from the files of AIGL).
40. Randhir Subba, 1955, *Gorkha,* 7th January, Darjeeling.
41. Memorandum submitted to the Viceroy and Governor General of India by the President of AIGL on 1st May, 1947 (from the files of AIGL).
42. Randhir Subba, 1955, *Gorkha*, 7th February, Darjeeling.
43. From the files of the Gorkha League.
44. From the letter of Sri Ganesh Lal Subba, Secretary, the Communist Party of India to the President, Gorkha League dated 9th May, 1946.
45. P.C. Joshi, 1995, "The Voice of the Himalayas", Seminar, 425.
46. Reported in 1950, *Gorkha*, 26th January, Darjeeling.
47. Reported in 1949, *Gorkha* 7th January.
48. *Ibid.*
49. "Bhagsu Dharmasala Diary", *Gorkha*, 26th January, 1955.
50. Sajal Nag, 2003, "Fei-sation of Indian Nepalis in the North East", A.C. Sinha and T.B. Subba (eds), *The Nepalis in the North East: A Community in Search of Indian Identity*, New Delhi: Indus Publishing Company.
51. Prakash Louis, 2004, "The Meaning of Subaltern—A Socio-philosophical Discourse", Thadathil George (ed.), *Subaltern Perspectives Philosophizing in Context*, Bangalore: Asian Trading Corporation, pp. 47-72.
52. *Ibid.*
53. Paul Brass, 1992, "Language, Religion and Politics", Subroto Roy and William E. Jones (eds), *Foundation of Indian Political Economy: Towards an Agenda for 1990s*, New Delhi: Sage.
54. Donald G. Morrison and H.M. Stevension, 1972, "Integration and Stability", *American Political Science Review*, 103.
55. N.B. Gurung, *op. cit.,* p. 12.
56. Sajal Nag, *op. cit.*
57. Krishna Shankar, *op. cit.*
58. Sanjib Baruah, *op. cit.*
59. *Ibid.*, p. 520.
60. *Ibid.* p. 518.

61. *Ibid.*
62. Myron Weiner and Joseph Lapalambora (eds.), 1966, *Parties and Political Development*, Princeton: Princeton University Press, p. 418.
63. Sanjib Baruah, *op. cit.*
64. Myron Weiner and Joseph Lapalambora, *op. cit.*

9

Identity Formation and Identity Maintenance: Nepalis in India

RANJU R. DHAMALA

Introduction: Understanding Identity

Identity study caught the attention of scholars from the latter half of twentieth century though it constituted the bedrock of national or ethnic mobilization throughout the nineteenth and twentieth centuries. Identity assumes significance in social science discourses as it lays the very foundation of group mobilization in order to achieve certain goals which may be social, economic or political in nature.

According to Norbert Wiley, a Professor of Sociology at the University of Illinois, identities individuate and allow us to recognize individuals, categories, groups and types of individuals. They can be imposed from without, by social process or from within, in which cases they are often called self-concepts. Identities then are nested within and express the qualities of selves and collection of selves.[1] Social identity theory explains relations between communities from the group perspective. It assumes that part of an individual's self definition is the knowledge of membership in a social group (or groups) together with the value and emotional significance attached to that membership.[2]

There are various approaches to understanding of identity such as primordialist, instrumentalist, communitarian, etc. The primordialists like Clifford Geertz, Harold Isaacs and van dan Berghe emphasize the ascriptive identities, ties of kinship, common history, collective experiences etc. as influencing a person's loyalties and behaviour. They argue that ethnic or ascriptive identities are mobilized in modern era in order to overcome the strain that modernity has created in the otherwise traditional and homogenous people. The instrumentalists like Benedict Anderson do not consider identities as "given"; rather they consider these as artifacts, changeable constructions of 'kindredness' elicited under particular circumstances and discarded, adjusted, or traded for others under other circumstances.[3]

When identity is taken as social construction its formation or transformation remains fluid and subject to the role of political entrepreneurs who play critical role in attuning the alternative identity in keeping with changing circumstances and the demand, more often than not, to favour their own political prospects.[4] This implies that a given political community may crystallize around one identity at present and around a different identity in future. Such constructions may even incorporate identity which was once counted as the 'other'. Political entrepreneurs seeking political gains may often manipulate that identity.[5]

Studies on identity are multi-faceted in that they include not only individuals but also collective beliefs and values within the framework of social/cultural boundaries. In spite of the differences of opinion among scholars on whether ethnic or national communities are created more or less consciously, or they grow organically out of pre-existing cultural communities, identities are a way of uniting disparate individuals and groups to achieve goals of common interests. Most of the struggles in recent times are characterized by the use of identity as a political ideology.

Identity formation goes through different stages, mostly starting with a search for identity, preference for dominant identity, awakening to one's own ethnic status onto a period of identity and cultural exploration, and finally ending in a time of ethnic identity conflict resolution and incorporation of ethnic identity into one's overall social identity. Broadly speaking, it involves stages such as unexamined ethnic identity, ethnic identity search and achieved ethnic identity.[6] Identity, including national identity, is thus, about inclusion and exclusion, and the ability of a group to assert its distinctiveness. Such distinctiveness is asserted either to overcome a disadvantaged position or secure its control over the resources vis-a-vis other minority groups.

The present paper is an attempt to explore the issues of identity of the Nepalis settled in India within the broader framework of Indian nationality, and the 'self perceived' and 'other perceived' images of the community. The paper argues that despite the multiculturalism and plurality of the Indian society and in spite of the fact the Nepalis have been living in India for almost two centuries now and have made significant contribution to the security and development of India, the country in general fails to recognize the community as an integral part of the Indian cultural milieu. The question of nationality and citizenship erupt every now and then and the Nepalis have become target of dominant groups' anger especially in areas where they are in minority. The community is now going through a kind of self-interrogation about their national identity. The movements for inclusion of Nepali language in the eighth schedule of the Constitution of India and for a separate state within the Indian union, the concern and controversy pertaining to nomenclature of the community, the issues raised in various conferences and seminars indicate this search for identity—an identity which will hopefully enable them to exist in a plural society without carrying the stigma of belonging to an inferior or foreign cultural group and which will grant them status as legitimate and equal citizens of India.

Nationality of the Indian Nepalis

The Nepalis are scattered all over India, but they constitute a sizable population in Assam, Sikkim and the Darjeeling district of West Bengal. In the initial years of settlement, they were engaged primarily in armed forces, agriculture, animal husbandry, and tea gardens. At present they are employed in almost every sector of the country's economy.

Understanding national identity of the Indian Nepalis is by no means a simple task. First of all, it relates to the integration, disintegration and reintegration of the group identity. The Nepalis who migrated to India ignored the primacy of caste identity and integrated themselves to form a larger Nepali identity subsuming Newari, Rai, Limbu, Tamang, and other such identities but since 1990s one finds a revivalism of latter identities. This is discernible, to a greater or lesser degree, among the Nepalis in both Nepal and India. The difficulty in grappling with their national identity also arises due to the confusion over nomenclature—Nepali or Gorkhali—that has stirred their minds for several years now. Finally the difficulty arises due to lack of clear boundaries between the concepts of nationality and citizenship.

In the identity formation process of Indian Nepalis two different trends are discernible. In the Darjeeling district and Sikkim the lasting contribution of these settlements is the integration of the disparate ethnic groups and the emergence of a unified identity of them as a community despite the variation in language, custom and cultural practices.

It was the policy of the British to encourage the Nepalis to settle in various parts of India both as economic and political strategy. Since they settled mostly in forests and waste lands the Nepalis initially did not encounter any resistance from the communities living nearby except briefly in the Khasi hills in early twentieth century. In the initial years what one notices is the attempt of the community to adapt to the physical and social environment of the place of their settlement. They learnt local languages and married with local men and women. They sent their children to local vernacular-medium schools, participated in social and political movements of the local people, and made significant contribution to the local language and literature. The recognition of all this came when in the presidential address of the Mongoldoi session of the Assam Sahitya Sabha in 1979 it was remarked 'for all practical purposes the Nepalis are Asamiyas'.[7] However, the All Assam Students' Union Movement (1979-1985) that sought to drive away "foreigners" gravely affected the fellow-feeling between the Assamese and the Nepalis. Soon they became target of irredentism in Meghalaya, Manipur, and Mizoram. They began to be labelled as 'encroachers' and 'foreigners' everywhere in Northeast India. Despite the ability to adapt to local cultural environment, their tenacity to hold on to their language, literature and their own cultural roots deepened the xenophobic tendency of the people of the region.[8]

The emergence of a common identity as Nepalis or Gorkhas paved the way for the consolidation of the community for political mobilisation. In 1917, the Hillmen's Association came into being and petitioned for the administrative separation of Darjeeling—a demand that was repeated in 1928 and 1942. In 1928 the Akhil Bharatiya Gorkha League (All India Gorkha League) was formed in Dehradun. During 1940s, the Communist Party of India (CPI) organized the Gorkha tea workers of Darjeeling hills in West Bengal. It was marked not only by the spread of political awareness but also by identity and cultural exploration.

In Assam the concern about the rights of the Nepalis is seen early in the formation of Graziers' Association. As early as 1913, the formation of such an organization was mooted as a reaction against the atrocities on the tax-paying Nepali graziers of Kaziranga though the association came into existence only in 1933. The main objectives of the association were: (1) protection and preservation of grazing land in Assam, (2) stop cultivation in professional grazing reserves, (3) prevention of immigration in Burachapori, (4) protection of forests of Assam for the survival of Nepali community in Assam, (5) involvement of domiciled Nepalis in Assam in the freedom movement of India, and (6) preservation of social integration between the Assamese and Nepali communities.[9] The objectives of the association show that the Nepalis of Assam were mainly concerned with protecting their economic interests though the participation of individual Nepalis in the political activities of the state or the nation, especially in the freedom movement.

The demand for inclusion of Nepali language in the 8th schedule of the constitution of India was the most prominent issue raised by the community in the post-independence period. This is interpreted by some as indicative of their desire to be integrated with Indian nationhood. It indeed expresses the desire to be recognized as bonafide citizens of India.

There are a number of studies[10] that show that resource competition lies at the root of the attack on the Nepalis and their subsequent displacement from Northeast India. There was hardly any protest against their settlement in the initial years when land was abundant. There was no resource competition then nor was there any question about their political status as Indian citizens. They had become part of the social fabric at least in Assam if not elsewhere in the region. The All Assam Students' Union movement about which a mention has been made earlier changed the entire ethnic climate of the region and turned it hostile for the Nepalis living there for over one hundred years. They began to be evicted in thousands. For someone who is born and brought up in India, who grew up listening to the stories of the contribution of his forefathers to the development of the region, and for whom there is no other motherland except India it was traumatic suddenly to come across the label of foreigners and encroachers. The psyche of the people is seriously affected when they are considered as foreigners and identified with Nepal. It also bespeaks of ignorance of historical facts and of treaty obligations between India and Nepal.

When one analyzes the different movements launched by the Nepalis in India one finds that it is done primarily to assert their identity as a part of the broader national identity, which is that of Indian nationality. Perhaps it is because of the existence of Nepal as an independent country that frequent reference is made to that country while dealing with the Indian Nepalis. Such questions need serious consideration in the context of national identity. It is quite common to see other Indians living with multiple identities without any visible problem. However, in case of the Indian Nepalis this confusion exists due to fact that there are Nepalis in Nepal and Nepalese in India as well. It is so ingrained in the minds of both policy makers and the rest of the population of the country that one wonders if even the former are aware of the ethnic composition and history of Nepal leave aside the implication of the Indo-Nepal Treaty of Peace and Friendship, 1950. It may not be out of place to mention here a statement made by a former prime minister of India, Rajiv Gandhi, at the height of the Gorkha National Liberation Front (GNLF) movement for Gorkhaland: 'If the Nepalese of Darjeeling wanted Indian citizenship, there was no harm if they write to their king'.[11]

While dealing with the issue of national identity of Indian Nepalis it is important to understand the views of other Indian communities as well. There are questions that stir the minds of a majority of Indian citizens. As one scholar has pointed out, 'the actual status of the Nepalis, a large immigrant community from another sovereign state, has to be determined. How do they belong to the Indian commonwealth of cultures and religions? In what ways do their history, culture, language, and traditions become Indian? Will the efforts of Nepalis to seek an Indian identity be construed as the extension of the genuine policies, programmes and traditions of Nepal? What will be the economic cost and political implications of the transformation of the Nepalis into Indians? Apprehensions are expressed on their ability to get double citizenship, their easy access to Tibet as Nepali citizen and the associated defense interest of India.'[12]

There is no confusion over the identity of Indian Nepalis as a social and cultural group as it is primarily based on their shared history, their common cultural roots, and their collective memory. The struggle for their national identity pertains mainly to the recognition and acceptance of their national identity by other Indian communities and the desire of the community members to cast aside the 'foreigner' label. This desire has been manifested in different forms at different times. The movement for recognition of the Nepali language in the Eighth Schedule of the Constitution can be seen as one of them. The agitation for statehood spearheaded by the GNLF can be seen as another. The distinction that the GNLF leadership drew between Nepali and Gorkha is aimed exactly at resolving the confusion over the political status of the people. Whatever may have been the political achievement of the movement one cannot deny its contribution in spreading the need to properly understand the identity of the community within the broader national framework. Unlike several regional or autonomy movements which are founded on a sense of deprivation and marginalization and are basically economic in orientation, the struggle of the Indian Nepalis mainly relates to the political issues such as citizenship and the legitimate right to be Indian and their recognition as Indian citizens by the people of India.

REFERENCES

1. Norbert Wiley, "The Politics of Identity in American History" in Craig Calhoun (ed.), *Social Theory and the Politics of Identity,* Oxford: Blackwell, 1994.
2. N. Tajfel (ed.), *Social Identity in Inter Group Relations, Cambridge: Cambridge University Press, 1982,* cited *in* Jack Jedwab "Leadership. Governance and the Politics of identity in Canada" Commissioned by the Dept of Canadian Heritage for the Ethnocultural Racial, Religious and Linguistic Diversity and Identity Seminar, Halifax, Nova Scotia, November 1-2, 2001, available online at www.metropolis.net
3. Ian S. Lustick, "Hegemony and the Riddle of Nationalism: The Dialectics of Political Identity in the Middle East", *Ethnic Conflict and International Politics in the Middle East,* Leonard Binder ed., Gainsville, FL: University Press of Florida, 1999, pp. 332-59.
4. *Ibid.*
5. Abner Cohen, cited by Thomas Hylland EriksenIn in "*Ethnic Identity National Identity, Intergroup Conflict: The Significance of Personal Experiences.*" Ashmore, Jussim, Wilder (eds), *Social Identity, Intergroup Conflict, and Conflict Reduction,* Oxford: Oxford University Press, 2001, pp. 42-70.
6. Lucy Tse, "The Effects of Ethnic Identity Formation on Bilingual Maintenance and Development: An Analysis of Asian American Narratives", *International Journal of Bilingual Education and Bilingualism,* Vol. 3, No. 3, 2000.
7. Lopita Nath, "Conflict-Afflicted Nepalis of Assam: The Reality" in A.C. Sinha and T.B. Subba (eds), *The Nepalis in Northeast India: A Community in Search of Indian Identity,* New Delhi: Indus Publishing Company, pp. 212-14.
8. *Ibid.*
9. Sajal Nag, "Fei-isation of the Nepalis of Northeast India" in A.C. Sinha and T.B. Subba (eds), *op. cit.*
10. Sinha and Subba, *op. cit.*
11. Lal Bahadur Basnet, Nepalese or Gorkhas? Namchi: Sikkim-Nepalese Unity, n.d.
12. A.C. Sinha, "The Indian Northeast Frontier and the Nepali Immigrants" in A.C. Sinha and T.B. Subba (eds) *op. cit.*

10

Nepalis in India: A Neglected Discourse

VIMAL KHAWAS

One of my associates recently complained to me of being verbally abused by a lady in New Delhi on the pretext that her sari accidentally happened to mesh with the edge of his motorcycle. She, allegedly, hurled at him very improper and unfounded statements as far as the Nepali speaking Indians are concerned. She told him, 'You Nepalis! Foreigners! I know you people! You people don't know how to behave!' Although she did not know him personally she lived in the neighbourhood and ran a nursery school in a flat located just below the one where the Nepali boy lived. So she knew him to be a "Nepali", which was enough for her to know about him. The problem in Delhi is that people often assume any hill man/woman to be a Nepali and in majority of cases their assumption is correct possibly due to the presence of a large number of Nepalis in Delhi.

The point here is not a mere abuse of an individual by another individual but it signifies a much larger issue that needs to be seriously debated among the Nepali-speaking Indian citizens. The victim is a bonafide citizen of India and a permanent resident of Kalimpong located in the district of Darjeeling, West Bengal. Like many other Indians he too is struggling in Delhi in search of better economic opportunities. There are Bengalis and Punjabis, for example, with their counterparts residing in other countries like Bangladesh and Pakistan respectively. However, they have never been taunted as Bangladeshis or Pakistanis. In this case, however, the term Nepali or foreigner has often been used by the mainstream Indians. The above instance is one of the examples of the serious situation prevailing across the Indian territory, possibly excluding Darjeeling and Sikkim Himayala. Why are Nepali-speaking Indians often confused with the Nepalis of Nepal? Why do the mainstream Indians not appreciate the fact that there are about five million Nepalis who are *bonafide* citizens of the Republic of India?

National Identity Issue of Indian Nepalis

The nationality issue is something that Nepali speaking Indians have been facing since generations. Finding the solution to this problem was one of the major objectives of the Gorkhaland movement of 1980s led by the Gorkha National Liberation Front (GNLF) under the leadership of Subhash Ghising.[1] The primary objectives of that movement are pertinent here in the context of identity and citizenship issues of Nepali-speaking Indians. The objectives read thus:

- A separate state of Gorkhaland within the Indian Union;
- The question of citizenship of the settled Gorkhas to be resolved on the basis of incorporation of territories (as provided for in Section 7 of the Indian Citizenship Act, 1955[2] and for this purpose a notification to be issued by the Government of India;
- A separate Indian Gorkha regiment exclusively for the India Gorkhas to be created;
- Inclusion of Gorkha language in the Eighth Schedule of the Constitution.[3]

Further, demand for the abrogation of Article 7 of the Indo-Nepal Treaty of 1950[4] found place among the prime demands of GNLF at a later stage of the movement. Since Article 7 allows the Nepalese to cross over to India, reside and own property and also participate in trade and commerce the GNLF alleged that the clause had jeopardized the position of Indian Nepalis or Gorkhas, for they were often confused with the Nepalese of Nepal and consequently faced eviction. To stress the distinction between the Indian Nepalis and Nepalese of Nepal the term 'Gorkha' and 'Gorkha Bhasha' were increasingly used in place of Nepali and Nepali language, respectively. Hence, one of the main reasons behind using the term 'Gorkha' by the proponents of the agitation was to differentiate themselves from the Nepalese and avoid the overlap of the term and subsequent negative impacts.

The agitation, however, subsided without achieving any of its primary goals. Two memoranda of settlement were, nevertheless, signed in this connection in 1988. The first memorandum was signed on

22nd August, 1988 at Calcutta while the second memorandum was signed on 23rd August in New Delhi.

The Memorandum of Settlement signed in Calcutta on 22nd of August 1988 envisaged the setting up of an autonomous hill council covering three hill subdivisions of Darjeeling district, namely, Darjeeling, Kalimpong, and Kurseong and thirteen *mouzas*[5] of Siliguri subdivision contiguous to Kurseong subdivision. By this agreement Subhash Ghising agreed to drop the demand for a separate state of Gorkhaland and withdraw all agitational activities and also to extend full cooperation to the state administration for the maintenance of peace and normalization of the political process. Towards this end, the Darjeeling Gorkha Hill Council Act was enacted in October 1988 under Part III—Act of the West Bengal Legislature. The aim of this Act was to provide for the establishment of an autonomous council for social, economic, educational and cultural advancement of the Gorkhas and other sections of the people residing in the hill areas of the district of Darjeeling. This Act led to the formation of Darjeeling Gorkha Hill Council (DGHC) consisting of the hill areas and a dozen odd *mouzas* of Siliguri subdivision of the district.

The second memorandum between the Government of India and GNLF clarifies the position in respect of the three demands, that is, the citizenship issue of the settled Indian Nepalis, formation of a separate Indian Gorkha regiment and inclusion of Gorkha language in the Eighth Schedule of the Constitution. It was decided to issue a gazette notification clarifying the citizenship status of Gorkhas who have settled in India. With respect to the issue of separate Indian Gorkha regiment, it was decided not to raise any new regiment. It was thought that the Gorkhas settled in India have no obligations to join only specified Gorkha regiments for they have the option to join the regiments of their choice. The GNLF further accepted the Government of India's position on non-inclusion of more languages in the Eighth Schedule of the Constitution on the plea that it would create repercussions and reactions. The Government of India, however, assured to develop the cultural and literary heritage of all languages irrespective of their inclusion in the Eighth Schedule. However, Nepali language was included along with Manipuri and Konkani languages in the Eighth Schedule of the Constitution of India in 1992. This gave the Nepali-speaking Indians some relief. But the objective was to register the language as Gorkha and not Nepali, as some argued that Nepali is the national language of Nepal. The debate is still on.

A new chapter was added to the history of Darjeeling hills on December 6, 2005 following a tripartite agreement between the DGHC,

West Bengal government, and the Government of India. It was formally agreed upon by all three parties to include the Darjeeling hills in the Sixth Schedule of the Constitution with two more *mauza*s of Sevoke Hill Forest and Sevoke Forest to be the part of the updated Council. The objective of this agreement is to replace the existing Darjeeling Gorkha Hill Council to be known as Gorkha Hill Council, Darjeeling, and to fulfil economic, educational and linguistic aspirations and the preservation of land rights, socio-cultural and ethnic identity of the hill people and to speed up the infrastructure development in the hill areas. Although, the agreement and its resultant negotiations are not without criticisms it should be regarded as a constitutional recognition of the Indian Nepalis in Darjeeling region in particular and all Nepali-speaking Indians in general.

Two Sets of Nepali Speakers

One cannot disagree with the fact that India is a multi-ethnic, multi-cultural and multi-lingual country. The societies across the country are made up of various elements drawn from diverse origins. The social groups with diverse ethnic and linguistic origins representing various racial stocks and social status have found places for themselves in India at different points of time adapting themselves to different ecological niches offered by the physiographic and climatic settings of the country. The waves of immigration drew the ancestors of the majority of present population of the country from surrounding territories and across the Himalayas. Their dispersal across the geographies of India led to the evolution of social mosaic that is quite unique in the world.

Many Indians are not aware of the fact that there are two sets of Nepali speakers in India. The first set of Nepali speakers belong to the permanent inhabitants and *bonafide* citizens of the country. Their geographical distribution can be seen across the country with their major concentrations in the hilly pockets of the states of Himachal Pradesh, Uttaranchal, Darjeeling Hills of West Bengal, Sikkim and all other Northeastern states. They have been residing in India for almost two centuries now and hence are bonafide citizens of the country. Within India, their concentration is particularly noteworthy in the hills of Darjeeling district of West Bengal where they constitute about 52 per cent of the district's population and the State of Sikkim where they comprise about 64 per cent of the state's population. In Northeast, Assam accommodates sizeable number of Nepali populace.

The second category of Nepali speakers comprises those who are citizens of Nepal but are residing in India on temporary basis. The feeble economy of Nepal and associated socio-cultural and political forces have compelled them to leave their country in search of employment in India. They are scattered across the length and breadth of India and are mostly engaged in menial jobs in hotel industry, as domestic helps, in canteens/ *dhabas* and security services. Their presence in India has increased significantly in the last 10 years or so, as Nepal was gripped by the Maoist violence.

Impact on Indian Nepalis

Unfortunately, the Indian Nepalis have to face the wrath of various Indian communities on variety of occasions. Abuses, both physical and oral, are often inflicted upon the Nepali speakers in the mainland India even on small pretexts as the one cited in the beginning of this article. Such offences are often meted out to the Nepali speakers on the assumption that they are the citizens of Nepal and have crossed the border for economic reasons. Two important factors need serious debate here both of which are crucial in the context of the confusion about and the resultant negative impact on the Indian Nepalis. First, India and Nepal signed a 'Treaty of Peace and Friendship' on July 31, 1950. Among other things Article 7 of the treaty grants, on reciprocal basis, to the nationals of one country in the territories of the other the same privileges in the matters of residence, ownership of property, participation in trade and commerce, movement and privileges of a similar nature. The treaty is, however, silent with respect to the impact of such agreement on the already settled Indian Nepalis. Over the years, on the strength of this treaty the Nepalis from Nepal have been crossing the border for various blue collar jobs in India. For example, over 100 fourth grade employees at Jawaharlal Nehru University, New Delhi, consist of the Nepalis bearing the citizenship of Nepal. They are mainly engaged in security, hostel messes, canteens and *dhabas* of the university. Likewise they are found all over Delhi, Mumbai, Ahmedabad and other cities of India. They have also settled in rural areas of India. For instance, most of the seasonal labourers for potato and pea cultivation in Lahaul-Spiti region of Himachal Pradesh and Ladakh consist of seasonal migrants from western Nepal.[6]

Second, the crux of the problem has been the ill-reputation of the Nepali speakers coming from Nepal. And the situation is becoming worse with time. The following reports that appeared in the leading news daily in the capital provides us with some examples in this connection: 'A Nepalese servant strangles 60 year old woman', 'A Nepalese servant killed 62 year old businessman', 'A retired lieutenant colonel and his wife were murdered by their Nepalese servant'. The media further cautions the citizens of Delhi: 'Avoid employing servants from areas like Nepal as Nepalese servant is fraught with danger'. What are the repercussions of such activities of the seasonal Nepalis of Nepal on the settled Nepali speaking Indians? They look identical, speak the same language with some dialectical variations, and bear similar names!

In this connection, the cleaning up operations across Northeast India in the last couple of decades has also been the result of the massive influx of the Nepali migrants from Nepal encouraged by the so-called Indo-Nepal Friendship Treaty of 1950. These Nepal Nepalis come and go depending upon the economic situation of the region where they work and also their own economic health. The consequences of their deeds and misdeeds have, however, to be borne by the Indian Nepalis. This has been the case in the whole of India. And the recent abuse of my friend by a mainstream lady in Delhi is the result of one such negative image of the Nepali speakers coming from Nepal.

The Way Ahead

(1) One of the most important factors contributing to the plight of Indian Nepalis is the Indo-Nepal Friendship Treaty of 1950. Thus India and Nepal need to take stock of this treaty and either abrogate or amend the treaty.

(2) Subhash Ghising has been successful in bargaining for the Sixth Schedule status for Darjeeling. The new arrangement may not only benefit the Indian Nepalis of Darjeeling hills but also other communities living there.

(3) Decision makers should accept that mere institutional and legal empowerment of the local communities does not address the issues of social justice, identity and inequality and certainly does not lead naturally or necessarily to better status. At the same time they also need to come to terms that devolution and decentralisation of decision-making are an indispensable component of any move towards social justice, peace and sustainability. Hence, the challenge ahead is to re-conceptualise the very concept of community representation and the institutional arrangements that we often envision with reference

to their relevance to the region and the people therein so that inter-regional as well as intra-regional disparities are reduced and sustainable development is attained.

(4) Last but not the least, although some scholars argue the need to rewrite the history of Indian Nepalis so as to clear some common misconceptions in mainstream India about Indian Nepalis and also to remove such misconceptions recorded in the archives of the country one should not overlook other equally pertinent issues. The statements of Pawan Chamling, Chief Minister of Sikkim, in his speech delivered in Gangtok on 20th April, 2006 deserve a mention here, 'Indian Nepalis should think big, think positive and work towards that end in order to be recognised by mainstream India. They must recognise their weaknesses and know how to act positively while striving to get into the national mainstream. Indian Nepalis cannot afford to live in their past laurels as brave fighters. They need to engage themselves in the present socio-economic and political reality of the country. The need of the hour is to work for the social, economic and political development of the country. Identity issue can be solved only by thinking big, positive and contributing to the advancement of the country. Sindhi is a small minority but a very powerful social group in India. Who can question their identity and nationality in the country?'

NOTES

1. The autonomy claim was the central theme of Darjeeling politics long before independence of the country. Different local political groups raised repeated demands at different points of time starting from the year 1907.
2. The section reads as follows: "If any territory becomes a part of India, the Central Government may, by order notify in the Official Gazette, specify the persons who shall be citizens of India by reason of their connection with that territory; and those persons shall be citizens of India as from the date to be specified in the order.
3. There was increasing demand for constitutional recognition of the Nepali language, more importantly since 1972, in order to maintain ethnic and linguistic identity.
4. The document of the treaty is attached in the appendix.
5. *Mouza* refers to the lowest revenue collection unit in West Bengal. During the Mughal period, the term was extensively used in the sense of the revenue collection unit in a *pargana* or revenue district. A group of *mouza*s

made a *pargana*. In the 20th century, mouza became popularly synonymous with the *gram* or village, which is indeed a social unit.

6. Based on field work in the year 2000 as part of the Post-Graduate Course, CSRD, JNU, New Delhi.

REFERENCES

Chakrabarty, S.R. 2005. "Silence under Freedom: The Strange Story of Democracy in the Darjeeling Hills". In R. Samaddar (ed.), *The Politics of Autonomy: Indian Experiences*. New Delhi: Sage Publication.

Chattopadhyay, S.S. 2005. "Ghising's Game". *Frontline*, 23(1): 43-44.

Compilation of Government Orders/Notifications relating to Transfer, Creation of Offices/Establishment under DGHC published by the Council House, DGHC, Darjeeling, n.d.

Ghosh, Kunal. 2001. "Darjeeling Gorkha Identity is based on False Premises". *Mainstream*, 39(16): 18-23.

Goyal, S.K. 1983. "Policies for Uplift of the Hilly and Backward Districts in India—A Critique". In T.S. Papola *et al.* (eds), *Development of Hill Area—Issues and Approaches*. Bombay: Himalayan Publishing House, 55-64.

Joshi, P.C. 1983. "Perspective of Planners from Above and People's Perception from Below". In T.S. Papola *et al.* (eds.), *Development of Hill Area—Issues and Approaches*. Bombay: Himalayan Publishing House, 30-41.

Khawas, Vimal. 2002. "Environment and Rural Development in Darjeeling Himalaya—Issues and Concerns". *Spatio-Economic Development Record*, 10(2): 27-33.

Khawas, Vimal. 2005. "Nepali *Vs.* Nepalese". *The Hindu*. June 19.

Khawas, Vimal. 2006. "Relevance of Autonomy". *The Statesman*. April 5.

Khawas, Vimal and Shrawan Kumar Acharya. 2003. "Autonomous Development Councils as a Spatial Planning Unit in India: A Case of Darjeeling Gorkha Hill Council". Working Paper No. 23. School of Planning, Ahmedabad, Gujarat.

Pradhan, R.M. 1996. "Continuous Political Struggle for a Separate Constitutional Status of Ceded Land of Darjeeling and Leasehold Land of Kalimpong". Darjeeling: Department of Cultural Affairs, DGHC.

Subba, T.B. 1992. *Ethnicity, State and Development: A Case Study of Gorkhaland Movement in Darjeeling*. New Delhi: Vikas.

Tripathi, N.P. 1983. "Administrative Imperatives for Development". In T.S. Papola *et al.* (eds) *Development of Hill Area: Issues and Approaches*. Bombay: Himalayan Publishing House, 80-87.

Verma, H.S. 1983. "Ethno-Linguistic-Religious Background, Identity Issues and Development of Hill Areas". In T.S. Papola *et al.* (eds). *Development of Hill Area: Issues and Approaches*. Bombay: Himalayan Publishing House, 65-79.

Ackknowledgement

I take this opportunity to thank Prof. A.C. Sinha who encouraged me to write a paper on the subject and participate in the national conference held in Gangtok on 20-22 April, 2006.

Appendix

Indo-Nepal Treaty of Peace and Friendship, July 31, 1950

The government of India and the Government of Nepal recognizing the ancient ties which have happily existed between the two countries for centuries;

Desiring still further to strengthen and develop these ties and to perpetuate peace between the two countries;

Have resolved therefore to enter into a treaty of Peace and Friendship with each other, and have, for this purpose, appointed as their plenipotentiaries the following persons, namely, the Government of India, his Excellency Shri Chandreshwar Prasad Narain Singh, Ambassador of India in Nepal; The Government of Nepal, Mohun Shamsher Jang Bahadur Rana, Maharaja, Prime Minister and Supreme-Commander-in-Chief of Nepal, who having examined each other's credentials and found them good and in due form having agreed as follows:

Article I: There shall be everlasting peace and friendship between the Government of India and the Government of Nepal. The two Governments agree mutually to acknowledge and respect the complete sovereignty, territorial integrity and independence of each other.

Article II: The two Governments hereby undertake to inform each other of any serious friction or misunderstanding with any neighbouring State likely to cause any breach in the friendly relations subsisting between the two Governments.

Article III: In order to establish and maintain the relations referred to in Article I the two Governments agree to continue diplomatic relations with each other by means of representatives with such staff as is necessary for the due performance of their functions.

The representatives and such of these staff as may be agreed upon shall enjoy such diplomatic privileges and immunities as are customarily granted by International law of a reciprocal basis. Provided that in no case shall these be less than those granted to persons of a similar status of any other State having diplomatic relations with either Government.

Article IV: The two governments agree to appoint Consuls-General, Consuls, Vice Consuls and other consular agents, who shall reside in towns, ports and other places in each other's territory as may be agreed to.

Consuls-General, Consuls, Vice Consuls and other consular agents shall be provided with exequator or authorization of their appointment. Such exequator or authorization is liable to be withdrawn, if considered necessary. The reasons of the withdrawal shall be indicated wherever possible.

The persons mentioned above shall enjoy on a reciprocal basis all the rights, privileges, exemptions and immunities that are accorded to persons of corresponding status of any other state.

Article V: The Government of Nepal shall be free to import, from or through the territory of India, arms, ammunitions or warlike material and equipment necessary for it and this arrangement shall be worked out by the two Governments acting in consultation.

Article VI: Each Government undertakes, in token of the neighbourly friendship between India and Nepal, to give to the nationals of the other, in its territory, national treatment with regard to participation in industrial and economic development of such territory and to the grant of concessions and contracts relation to such development.

Article VII: The Government of India and Nepal agree to grant, on reciprocal basis, to the nationals of one country in the territories of the other the same privileges in the matter of residence, ownership of property, participation in trade and commerce, movement and privileges of a similar nature.

Article VIII: So far as matter dealt with herein are concerned, the Treaty cancels all pervious treaties agreements and engagements entered into on behalf of India between British Government and the Government of Nepal.

Article IX: This treaty shall come into force from the date of signature by both Governments.

Article X: The treaty shall remain in force until it is terminated by either party by giving one year's notice.

Done in duplicate at Kathmandu this 31st day of July 1950.

Sd/-
Chandreshwar Prasad Narain Singh
For the Government of India

Sd/-
Mohun Shamsher Jang Bahadur Rana
For the Government of Nepal.

11

Consolidating Nepali Identity: A Cultural Planning Perspective

SHRAWAN ACHARYA

Nepalis/Gorkhalis are a people characterised by diversity of culture, language, religion, etc. They have a high degree of mobility especially within Southasia, which has further enhanced their diversity. The Nepali diaspora issues raised in the present paper refer to the commonly understood categorization of the Nepali community into 'Aryan' and 'Mongoloid' and their sub-categories like Bahun Chhetri, Kami, Sarki and Damai (Aryan groups) and Rai, Limbu, Tamang, Sunwar, etc. (Mongoloid groups) and their identity questions, which at present is a major intellectual[1] and practical concern for scholars, politicians and policy makers.

The main argument of the paper is that because of various reasons ethnic assertions have become important and cleavages and conflicts have increased within the Nepali community, threatening the very basis of Nepali plurality and shared identity. The paper intends to explore the causes of these assertions, identify the positive and negative consequences of such development and then suggest public policy interventions based on cultural planning paradigm to mitigate the negative consequences of the same for the benefit of larger Nepali identity. It is intended to highlight that the question of assertions of identities and rights through careful planning can be used as a positive and integrative factor for which the state and civil society institutions through social engineering initiative can play an important role. There is still a possibility of "retaining" or "sustaining" the Nepali identity provided we see the various identity assertions within the Nepali society as positive elements in its social development process. Assertions lead to cultural regeneration. Cultural assertions will also have to be looked in the context of globalization. Globalisation permits pluralism and the possibility of linking the local with the global, mediated through technologies and market. It is also being realised that cultural consideration in public policy actions alleviates poverty, reduces inequality[2] and is an important development strategy for place making and marketing. However one also has to realise that globalization has negative consequences on indigenous local culture.[3] Such contradictory processes of globalization demand careful cultural planning initiatives.

Causes of Ethnic Assertion

History of the Nepali society indicates that the following factors have led to increasing assertion amongst different Nepali/Gorkhali sub-groups in India.[4]

(a) One of the principal factors leading to resurgence of identity issues among the Nepalis in India and Nepal is related to the issue of structural inequality amongst the different groups. There is no denying the fact that the elite in Nepali society mostly consist of Bahuns, Thakuris and Chhetris. The other groups like Rai, Limbu, Magar and Gurung are economically and politically marginalised. The Nepali dalits like Kami, Sarki and Dami are in the lowest economic and social stratum and still suffer from various social and other disabilities. The failure of the states in both Nepal and India to address the genuine grievances of the latter two categories alienated them from the elite and they started asserting *janajati* and *dalit* identities since the early 1990s, especially after declaration of 1993 as the year of the indigenous peoples.

(b) In Darjeeling and Sikkim one of the principal factors leading to the resurgence and demand for separate ethnic identities is related to issues of reservation policy of government of India. In order to get the benefits of reservation, some Nepali groups belonging to the "Mongoloid" category started re-asserting their tribal status, whereas even the "Aryan" category people demanded the status of Other Backward Class.

(c) Lastly increasing literacy, awareness, external contacts through migration and easy access to information have made the various ethnic groups within Nepalis aware of their distinctiveness, cultural richness and also of their rights.

Consequences of Ethnic Assertion

Demand for rights and identities have always been viewed as a disruptive and negative force and a threat to social solidarity. As a result such movements have been ridiculed by the dominant groups and suppressed leading to further alienation of the groups involved and aggravation of conflicts. In a democratic society conflicts are inherent and are not necessarily destructive. One has to realize that assertive movements have important social processes which can be effectively harnessed not only to address the grievances of the groups but also to enhance social solidarity amongst the contending groups. This is especially true of the Indian Nepalis whose assertiveness has not taken the form of violent conflicts except briefly during the Gorkhaland movement. Groups still co-exist and have considerable degree of interaction amongst each other. It is this attribute which provides opportunity to harness the positive aspect of such movement for greater common good. For instance, a reading of group assertions amongst the Nepalis in the hills of Darjeeling and Sikkim indicates the following positive and negative aspects.

In an effort to identify their distinctiveness various ethnic groups are discovering some of their lost cultural heritages. Lost values, rituals, festivals and other cultural elements are being documented and in some cases revived (*Lochar*, for instance, by Tamangs). Such a process is enriching the cultural diversity and plurality of the Nepali society and not weakening it. Awareness about one's culture and sense of history is a positive development so long it is accommodative and tolerant of other groups. The fact that various Nepali groups have made efforts to develop their languages and literature has also to be seen as a positive development. The fact that history of Sunuwars and Bhujels are being written certainly indicate vibrancy of the plural traditions and needs to be appreciated rather than taken as a threat to the high caste domination, as it is usually seen. In a way it is community empowerment process.

Resurgence of group identities in the Indian Nepali society has led to the establishment and reinvigoration of community associations.[5] They have emerged to protect the interests of the respective groups but in the process they have evolved to undertake a number of community welfare activities, which ultimately serve the interest of the Nepali society as a whole. In many cases there is also an attempt to do away with conservative and traditional practices of the groups in order to make it more contextual and relevant both in space and time. These are certainly positive developments and need to be nurtured through appropriate social engineering processes.

Resurgence of traditional ethnic cultures also enhances spatial attributes through eco-and cultural-tourism. In pure economic terms the development potential of the area increases along with the earning capacity of the people. Tourism, more so cultural tourism, is one of the fastest growing sectors in the world and India, including the hills of Sikkim and Darjeeling. Therefore there is tremendous potential to use it for the benefit of the people in addressing some of their felt needs. This strategy has been very effectively used by many South East Asian countries like Thailand, Vietnam, Malaysia and Indonesia, which have rich and diverse cultural resources.

But there is no denying the fact that identity movements have negative consequences as well. The most important negative consequence is accentuation of conflicts between groups threatening to destabilize the society, disintegration of space and loss of social solidarity. "We" is replaced by a division of "they" *vs* "Us" and is often misused and manipulated by vested interest groups. All this may lead to a sense of "cultural apathy" and ultimately lead to "cultural failure".[6]

In order to be "different" and "unique" groups resort to myth-making while writing and documenting their history. Such a practice is universal but when it is pushed beyond a point it ignores their shared history and geography. This is a threat and has the potential to create conflicts between groups. The problem is further compounded by the limited availability of anthropological, social and geographical studies on many of the Nepali groups in India.

Cultural Planning

As indicated above it is important to build on the positive aspect of the movement for building and consolidating common Nepali/Gorkhali identity. Cultural planning and social engineering approaches provide us with an opportunity to look at the problem from a new perspective. It is based on the premise that 'cultural rights are, no less than other human rights, an expression and requirement of human dignity'.[7] The cultural identity of a community comprises who the people are and their backgrounds, tastes, rituals, experiences, diversity, talents and aspirations for the future. The cultural richness of a place is also governed by local heritage attributes and the natural as well as acquired qualities that attract residents to an area. Cultural planning seeks to identify and confirm such values with the help of the local community and provide information to the government for planning and management purposes. It aims to ensure that the values people hold are protected and reflected in the way government plans, approves and provides infrastructure and services. Therefore, expression and movement to promote culture and identity assumes importance. It is important for the state and international community to see cultural assertions as a positive social process and promote/preserve the cultural rights of local communities. In this context it is important to highlight that the World Bank has recently initiated a Culture and Sustainable Development Programme. "Cultural Planning" is an important development strategy in USA and Europe. The importance of culture in development has also been highlighted by different schools of thought like the Berkley School in the USA, Annales School in France and the local history school in the UK.[8] The state's role in conserving and promoting culture is important in the context of growing global forces which might otherwise augur the demise of indigenous communities if opportunities provided by these forces are not capitalised. Globalisation with all its inherent contradictions also benefits local and indigenous cultures by disseminating information, creating awareness about cultural heritage and by marketing cultures through tourism[9] and other marketing strategies. Planning for culture adopts industrial and economic resource planning and distribution. Cultural economy has supported arts and crafts production, innovation and thriving cultural industry which has created comparative advantage for many ethnic groups for upward mobility and facilitate their global integration processes. This has enhanced their entitlements, bargaining capacity, a sense of dignity and identity.

The following section tries to identify few areas where positive public policy can be initiated for enriching and consolidating Nepali identity.

First and foremost, there is a need for an appropriate and innovative institutional system, either by creating new cultural institutions[11] or by reorganising the existing ones, to address the danger of fragmentation of Nepali community along ethnic lines. The problem of identity issues and its resolution should be included in the institutional agenda. Such an institution should conduct research and document information on different ethnic groups and communities in the hills of Darjeeling and Sikkim (Nepali, Bhutia, Lepcha and others). It should have a museum profiling different communities, their traditions and cultures. Instead of having museums of different communities in different places it may be beneficial to represent all communities together at one central place like Gangtok. A central location representing all groups provides cultural interface, gives viewers an integrated perspective and facilitates interaction between the curators and people. In fact a hierarchy of interlinked institutions at the state, district and subdivisional levels can be thought of. The lowest level can also be effectively linked with the ethnic associations at the panchayat level. Such an approach will also facilitate a participatory, bottom-up cultural planning through institutional structure.

Oral histories, traditional/vernacular architecture, traditional knowledge, folk arts, dance, paintings, crafts, food habits, technologies can find space in such museum. Monitoring and verification of documented histories by the communities should also be made the mandate of such institutions. Autonomy does not ensure secularism. However Sikkim, along with other national and international agencies including universities and civil society institutions, can facilitate the creation of such institutions and also participate in its activities. Given the increasing number of local intellectuals and experts manning such institution will not be difficult.

Cultural planning also requires adequate and appropriate information base on different subgroups and their demographic, cultural, social and economic attributes. Since Indian census does not publish caste data planning becomes a problem. For the hills of Darjeeling and Sikkim information on caste groups is available in old sources like the gazetteers of Risley, O'Malley and Dash or in the writings of T.B. Subba, one of the editors of this volume. These sources may be supplemented with periodic sample surveys of different caste and ethnic groups in the Darjeeling-Sikkim Himalaya.[12]

Such an institution should also act as a forum for different communities and their representatives to interact and share information with each other through regular workshops, seminars etc. It should facilitate interaction amongst different groups and initiate constructive dialogue. It has been observed, after the 1990s, that information on different ethnic groups are being generated in the form of ethnographic reports. Critical assessment of this information involving other communities is limited leading to misunderstanding even within a community.[13] Institutions can facilitate information sharing and discussion between the various ethnic groups in order to create trust and mutual understanding. An institutional approach in understanding cultural identities and assertions may also lead to rectification of some group narratives that are sometimes thought to be "regressive".[14] Such a collaborative and consensual initiative can help in fostering larger Nepali identity by revitalizing the social capital[15] which has eroded over a period of time.

All caste and ethnic groups should have equal access and representations in state-sponsored institutions. In case of marginal communities and groups there may even be a need to target them as special categories needing special protective measures. Resources need to be provided to all based on some criteria and implementation of the same needs to be monitored constantly. Women from different groups should be encouraged to participate in such initiatives because in most communities women are the repository of culture and tradition.

Two important aspects on which such an institution can concentrate are education and tourism. Inter-community fellowship can be fostered by educating the masses especially the school children regarding the diversity and cultural richness of Nepali society. The school system should not shy away from these issues. Sensitizing students on cultural resources and history should be given positive consideration, if not through formal curriculum at least as a part of extra-curricular activities. In the absence of such an effort 'denominational identities will deprive children of any opportunity to get acquainted with diverse cultural resources and make a reasoned choice'.[15] The institution and the museum can facilitate the development of such extra-curricular activities and also act as an awareness-building and exhibition centre. Such an approach will go a long way in establishing a sense of sharing and belonging between the communities in future.

Such an institution can also help promote cultural tourism. At present cultural tourism has developed without much documentary and research support from institutions. The proposed institution can bridge this gap and help promote tourism substantially through research on folk culture, vernacular architecture, costumes, traditional medicines, dance, music etc. Such an organised effort will help heritage conservation and promotion along with economic empowerment of the local communities. In this context local tourist guides and tour agencies should also be considered important stakeholders.[16] While encouraging such initiative effort should be made to counter the negative consequences of cultural tourism through appropriate state, public and civil society actions. The community association can be very effective in promoting cultural tourism and controlling its adverse consequences.

The other important aspect that needs consideration is the need to make the informal institutions like community association more relevant and useful to the village community in development work. Such institutions can act as a Community Based Organisations (CBOs) and can be an important actor in the social and economic development of villages. As indicated earlier they are playing important but limited role. With a progressive policy their role can be substantially enhanced. Unlike in other states the role of NGOs in Sikkim and Darjeeling hills is still limited. Can the CBOs substitute for the NGOs and work with the panchayats in development work? Possibilities exist if appropriate public policy is evolved to integrate them and involve them in the developmental activities of the panchayat or any other development institutions like the state and private sector. The community associations can also be organised as a network of federated institution linked with various government and non-government institutions. Such associations should also be encouraged to document and publish information on their community and also other work they are undertaking. In fact they should be part of the larger institutional set up and should be linked with cultural tourism projects. Such an initiative will create awareness amongst the people and will also counter the centralizing, and sometimes "corrupting" tendency, of global cultural forces which may not be appropriate to the society. It is also possible to integrate and network the functions of such institutions through "information kiosks" which is being planned and promoted by the government in many states especially in Northeast India. In this respect the possibility of using local FM radio clubs for information dissemination and awareness generation is tremendous. The government of India's favourable policy on expanding the FM band for developmental work needs to be capitalised.[17]

The important initiative that needs urgent attention is the preparation of a "regional plan".[18] Traditionally regional plans are basically spatial economic plans. But as indicated before the concepts are changing and cultural elements are important components of regional plans. Such plans should demarcate cultural regions and spatially locate the ethnic groups, their environment, lifestyle and development constraints and potential. Such an approach will provide avenues to integrate economic plan with cultural development so that the aspirations of different communities are properly addressed. As a part of the regional planning settlement initiative "*hats*", "festivals" and "fairs" should also be identified and promoted in a planned manner. Tourism promotion will also benefit from this strategy.

Preserving shared identity is difficult in a rapidly changing world. But it is important to realise that the collapse of the shared and collective identity entails social, economic and political marginalization not only of larger group but also of the sub-groups. At present Nepali/Gorkhali identity has a wider acceptance and recognition and gives a pan-Indian identity vis-à-vis other identities like Tamangs, Rais, Bahuns, etc. Sub-group identities are virtually absent except for categories like tribes, backward communities or castes. The historically consolidated identity of Indian Nepalis is important for political engagements. Decimation of larger Nepali identity will adversely affect the smaller communities, except for some benefits of reservation. Therefore it is important to evolve strategies to minimize the conflicts between larger Nepali identity and smaller group identities. There should be no conflict because it is possible for communities to exist with various identities simultaneously. As Amartya Sen writes, 'identities are robustly plural, and that the importance of one identity need not obliterate the importance of others'.[19]

The scattered distribution of Nepali population in India creates a problem for state action. However, given the concentration of population in the Darjeeling and Sikkim Himalayas action can be initiated in this area. Especially Sikkim can play an important role. The state is already, through its culture department, doing substantial work in promoting local culture and therefore has the capacity to take the lead in this direction. Such efforts in Darjeeling is however limited.

Though the idea has been presented in the context of Nepali community in the hills of Sikkim and Darjeeling the model can encompass other hill communities including the Lepcha, Bhutia and others in the region. The question of Nepali identity is important but a plural and unique identity of the hill areas cannot ignore the existence of other communities in the region for peace and sustainable development. This will facilitate cultural plurality and consolidate shared identity of the hill people.

Conclusions

The paper has briefly tried to highlight the identity issues amongst the Indian Nepalis. It takes a positive approach to the issues and contends that identity issues can integrate community and strengthen shared identity amongst the Nepalis through positive public policy initiative. For this the Nepali sub-cultures should be considered as resources rather than potential threats and planned to optimize the social capital of the region. Cultural planning will facilitate empowerment of the communities, enrich plural tradition and enhance bargaining capacity of the community in a fiercely competitive national and global space. There are inherent dangers in such an approach but with appropriate regulatory mechanism and active participation of the state, civil society and the people the negative effects can be minimised. Such an inclusive approach will make the problem a common concern of the citizens and the state leading to the convergence of the interest between the two. There is a need for new institutions and also more information on different communities and cultural diversity of the Nepalis and other hill communities as well, especially in the context of rapid socio-economic changes taking place in the region. There is also a need for more systematic and substantive research in this direction.

NOTES AND REFERENCES

1. Categorisation is a sensitive issue and there are differences of opinion regarding the categories and basis of such categories. However, the scope of the present paper does not include all that.
2. See Rao and Walton 2004.
3. Negative consequences of globalization, or "cultural pollution" are a serious concern especially for the smaller cultural groups and may even lead to their extinction.
4. The study is in the context of Sikkim and Darjeeling where there is substantial concentration of Nepali population in a geographically contiguous region.
5. Often termed as "Samaj" (or its equivalent in respective languages) like "Bahun Samaj", "Newar Samaj", "Rai Samaj" etc. in villages across Darjeeling and Sikkim.
6. See Appadurai 2004.
7. See UNESCO 1995.
8. See Crang 1998.
9. Many view 'commodification' of culture as the negative impact of globalization. However culture has been one of the most important marketing strategies in the world.
10. Institute of Ethnology, for instance.
11. In this context the occasional census monographs published by the Registrar General of India is very useful. However work in this direction needs to be conducted on regular basis and longitudinal profile of the communities will be able to provide insights into the socio-economic changes in the communities.
12. Interestingly such misunderstanding and conflicts can also take place within a community as reflected in the controversy surrounding the All India Tamang Buddhist Association and "denouncing of the Hindu customs and leanings towards Tibetan culture and tradition" amongst the Tamangs in Darjeeling, *The Telegraph*, April 3, 2006.
13. It is a tendency to regress into the status quo of their past and adhere to their past irrespective of its contextual/contemporary irrelevance. Progressive implies rectification and corrections to be relevant in a given geographical and temporal context. It may imply giving up of practices and rituals which may not be relevant in the present context of time and space.

14. The term, coined by Robert Putnam, implies "the stock of active connections among people: the trust, mutual understanding and shared values and behaviours that bind the members of human network and communities and make cooperative action possible" (Cohen and Prusak 2001). It is important for development because of "increasing evidence that social cohesion is critical for societies to prosper economically and for development to be sustainable" (World Bank, 1999).
15. Amartya Sen as quoted in *The Economic Times*, 28th March 2006, p. 12.
16. Tour guides and agents should be properly trained and educated regarding local culture so that they can effectively transfer knowledge to visitors. They can also be trained to collect information from the field on various cultural aspects. Since their visit is in regular intervals it becomes possible to document longitudinal profiles of cultural groups with whom they come in contact.
17. The importance of local radio clubs in information dissemination and community action is being used quite effectively in Kathmandu, Nepal and has also been documented.
18. Sikkim and Darjeeling still do not have a Regional Plan for cultural development.
19. See Sen 2006, p. 19.

BIBLIOGRAPHY

Appadurai, A. 2004. "The Capacity to Aspire: Culture and the Terms of Recognition". In V. Rao and M. Walton (eds) *Culture and Public Action.* New Delhi: Permanent Black, pp. 59-84.

Cohen, D. and L. Prusak. 2001. *In Good Company. How Social Capital Makes Organizations Work.* Boston Ma: Harvard Business School Press.

Crang, M. 1998. *Cultural Geography*, London: Routledge.

Evans, G. 2001. *Cultural Planning: and Urban Renaissance.* London: Routledge. http://www.worldbank.org/poverty/scapital/whatsc.htm

Rao, V. and M. Walton. 2004, "Culture and Public Action: Relationality, Equality of Agency, and Development" in *Culture and Public Action* (eds) V. Rao and M. Walton, New Delhi: Permanent Black, pp. 1-35.

Sen, Amartya. 2006. *Identity and Violence: The Illusion of Destiny.* London: Allen Lane.

UNESCO. 1995. *Our Creative Diversity.* Report of the World Commission on Culture and Development, Paris.

Section 3

Regional Identities of Indian Nepalis

12

Identity in Nepali Historical Novels from Northeast India

TEKNARAYAN UPADHYAYA

A community's historical contribution must almost always begin with an understanding of that community's history. The Nepalis/Gorkhalis today have spread to almost every corner of the world earning a living by carrying out diverse professions. There is no reliable figure on the actual population of the Nepalis in India but the figure is estimated to be four to four and a half million. A sizeable number of them consist of Nepalese citizens engaged in different vocations in India. The relation between India and Nepal dates back to Vedic times and this has been testified by texts of those times. However, one cannot make a secure statement on the actual movement of people between the two countries prior to the British period. Hence the only definitive record of movement of people is after the signing of the Treaty of Segowli following the Anglo-Gorkha War (1814-1816). One of the most significant impacts of signing of the treaty was that a huge portion of Nepal's territory on its south, east and west was ceded to the East India Company. Peace was restored and with this began the recruitment of the Gorkhas into the British Indian Army, many of who went on to settle in India after retirement.

The movement of people between the two countries, however, cannot be attributed to the signing of the treaty alone. Actually various historical, religious, cultural, and political affinities are responsible for this free movement of people between the two countries. It is a well known fact that: (i) India and Nepal share the same cosmological world views including gods, goddesses and rituals, (ii) the Vedas, Puranas, Ramayana, and the Mahabharata occupy the same spiritual space in both the countries, (iii) people from both the countries visit the same pilgrimages and holy sites, (iv) Indian pilgrims visit places like Pashupati, Guheshwari, Gorakhnath, Manokamna, Swargdwari in Nepal while the Nepalese travel to places like Varanasi, Bodhgaya, Prayag, Haridwar, Vaishnodevi, Mathura, Kamakhya, Tirupathi, Dwaraka, and Parshuram Kund in India, (v) the boundaries between the two countries are notional, (vi) Sanskrit as a classical language commands the same space in both the countries, (vii) The Nepalese have been serving mainly in the Indian Army and carrying out professions in India while Indians are engaged in different vocations like agriculture, trade and commerce in Nepal, (viii) Indian Nepalis have contributed to the anti-colonial struggles of India and have actively participated in her development process as well, (ix) Many books from Nepal can be found in India and Indian books are readily available in Nepal, (x) Nepal and India have strong trade relations, (xi) Nepal and India, inspite of being two independent countries, have a treaty legitimizing movement of people between the two countries.

Besides the above factors there are other reasons that have bounded the two countries together. One of the reasons is the birth of Sita in Janakpur in Nepal and her subsequent marriage to Rama. Lord Buddha was born at Lumbini in Nepal and later attained enlightenment at Bodhgaya in India. King Ashoka's daughter Charumati was married to the Kshatriya Prince Dewapal of Nepal. The Ashoka Pillar at Lumbini also stands testimony to this historic relation.

Notwithstanding the movement of people dating back to the prehistoric times the real moment of mass movement came after 1816. Huge chunks of territory in the terai region and other places like Garhwal, Kumaon, Dehradun, Bhagsu, Nainital and Darjeeling were ceded, along with the people living there to the British India. Moreover, Gorkha soldiers in the British Army played a major role during the First World War, serving in Austria, Mesopotamia, Afghanistan and elsewhere. During the Second World War the Gorkha soldiers participated in wars in Italy, Egypt, Burma, Singapore, England, and Hong Kong. Many are believed to have stayed back in these countries and eventually married and taken citizenship of those countries.[1]

The Nepalese have settled in different parts of the world of which a major section has settled in India. Places like Darjeeling, Kalimpong, Patna, Dehradun, Kashi, and Assam have sizeable number of Nepalis. There is no clear record of the entry of Nepalis in Assam but it is generally believed that they came to this place along with the British.[2]

It was around 1824-1833 that the British won over the Jaintia King of present-day Meghalaya and secured their position in Cherrapunji, near

Bangladesh. The Gorkhas, having enlisted themselves in the Sylhet Light Infantry, are believed to have played a crucial role in defeating the Jaintia and Khasi kings. The bravery of the Gorkhas during this war is well documented in *The History of Eighth Gurkha Rifles* thus: '...in 1824 Mr. Scott captured the areas lying between Sylhet and Jaintia Hills, brought the Brahmaputra Valley under his control and once the whole of Assam was under his control, courtesy the Yandaboo Treaty, the creation of a road link between Surma and the Brahmaputra Valley became a strategic imperative.' (p. 80) There is also a reference to 'Nepali milkmen settling in an around Shillong, Mawlai, Laitumkhra before 1874' in the same book.

With the increased activity of the British in Northeast India the number of Nepalis moving towards Assam increased. On page 20 of *The Gazetteer of Lushai Hills* there is reference to a large number of Nepalis crossing the hills of Manipur and Chittagong and settling down in Lushai Hills. Most of them had joined military police battalion.[3]

Here it is interesting to note that there are a lot of geographical similarities between the hills of Nepal and Assam. The fear of malarial fever had always ensured that there was no movement of Nepalis towards the warmer regions, forcing them to settle in hilly regions and some of them eventually settled in the banks of Brahmaputra, Manas, Dhansiri, Pagdaliya, Kalank, Peeli, Budi, Deehi, and Shillong rivers. One of the characteristic features of colonial modernity is the spread of education. Nepalis were for the first time exposed to western liberal education after they came in contact with the British. *Padi lekhi ke kaam, halo joti khayo maam*, meaning there is no point in educating oneself; one has to plough the field to earn a living, is how they once thought about life. But the colonial encounter was in many ways an enabling moment for the Nepalis. For a community steeped in ignorance, colonialism quite ironically brought with its modern education a certain brand of liberation and empowerment. Enlightened individuals like Manisingh Gurung became a pioneering figure in establishing Gorkha Pathsala in Shillong, Meghalaya. Similarly Chhabilal Upadhyaya set up Behali School at Tezpur in Assam in 1941. Tezpur's Parshuram Karki established Darrang College. Prajapati Rijal started Teligaon High School. Capt. Bhuvan Singh Rai led the way in Upper Shillong by establishing Gorkha High School. Bhim Bahadur likewise established Bhim Bahadur Vidyapeeth. Education certainly became a great leveller and this fact is testified by hundreds of schools that have come up in Northeast India since then. Today Meghalaya alone boasts of over thirty such schools.

A history of any community is given credibility only when that history is documented. Identities more often than not hinge upon its history. History, literature or any text is a child of its time. It is still not very clear as to when the Nepalis in India started their literary journey but according to Hari Bhakta Katuwal it started along with the Nepali settlement.[4] The researches up till now have shown that Dhanbir Bhandari's poem '*Abber Pahadko Sawai*' written sometime in 1894 is considered to be the earliest literary work from Northeast India. The following verse in the poem itself testifies this fact:

Thiyo san attharai chauranabbe saal
Alikati sunahai dushman ko haal...

The year was eighteen ninety four
Let me tell you something about the enemy...

The literary journey of the Nepalis in Northeast India started off with poems. Novel writing started much later. Novels are rightly regarded as epics of the modern age. Novels undoubtedly have a broader canvas, capturing all the vagaries of life. Since the present paper proposes to explore identity in Nepali historical novels from Northeast India, an exploration of the texts is presented in the following pages.

There is a huge corpus of writing on the history of the migration and settlement of Nepalis in Northeast India, and a lot is still being written on it. Some of them have actually managed to come out with outstanding works on the entire history of the community. But we still need to do seminal works on the subject.

Even though the history of Nepali literature is quite old, novel writing itself is a recent phenomenon. Dhan Bahadur Rai's *Ek Thunga Phool* written around 1928-29 is generally regarded as the first novel published from Northeast India but the book being not available there is lot of doubt about this claim. *Sapna Ya Bipanana* (1948) is generally regarded as one of the first Nepali novels from the region. There is now a general consensus among scholars to regard Lil Bahadur Chhetri's *Basai* (1957) as one of the early novels in Nepali literature. The following is the list of novels along with their dates of publication:

1. Dhan Bahadur Rai—*Ek Thunga Phool* (1928-29)
2. Baburbahadur Rana—*Sapna Ya Bipana* (1948)
3. Lil Bahadur Chhetri—*Atripta* (1956), *Basai* (1957),

Brahmaputrako Chheuchhau (1986), *Pratidhwaniharoo Bismrtika* (2004)

4. K.B. Nepali—*Mero Ghar Mero Sansar* (1965), *Samarpan* (1965), *Tasbir Ek Raatko* (1973)
5. Arjun Niroula—*Shishirko Bataas* (1971), *Ghaam Dubepachhi* (1977)
6. Kashiram Subedi—*Pratidaan* (1974)
7. Gahin Upadhaya—*Khojima* (1978)
8. Dr. Chandreshwar Dube—*Deshko Maato* (1978), *Jindagiko Baato* (1978)
9. Sherman Thapa—*Patthar Bolchha* (1981)
10. Bikram Bir Thapa—*Bigatko Pariveshbhitra* (1983), *Teesta Dekhi Sutlejsamma* (1986)
11. Mohan Kumar Shresta—*Saani Aamaki Chhori* (1985)
12. Prakash Subedi—*Dobharoo* (1686)
13. Gunu Gharti Bairagi'—*Prayaschit* (1989), *Sindoor Binaki Aardhangini* (1989), *Sapna* (1990), *Chokho Maya* (1991)
14. Hari Adhikari—*Mutubhitrako Tirsana* (1994)
15. Loknath Upadhyaya 'Chapagai'—*Aandhi* (1999)
16. Sant Kumar Dewan—*Pahad Parvat* (2000), *Kathaa Balla Suroo Hoonchha* (2002)
17. Rohit Gautam—*Agnishnan* (2002)
18. Nayadevi—*Yugsandhi* (2002)
19. Pradip Rai—*Paraalko Ghar* (2005)

Lil Bahadur Chhetri's *Basai* is one of the first literary works from the region that qualifies as a novel. Even though the novel is not set in Northeast India, Dhane and Maina, the two protagonists in the novel, chart an unknown path towards this region. This plot has a touch of historical reality as majority of Nepalis left their home and hearth to flee from the oppressive moneylenders. The flight has in many ways highlighted the totalitarian rule of the Ranas in Nepal.

His other published novel is *Atripta*. In this novel the writer takes a socio-psychological approach. He tries to bring out the psychological problems of a sex-starved young man who has left his home and come into an alien world. This is not the story of the protagonist in the novel alone but a story of countless and nameless Nepalis who have come out of their homes. In fact, *Atrpta* can be regarded as the first psychological novel based on Northeast India. It moves away from the socio-historical approach and heralds a new method in novel writing. Lil Bahadur Chhetri who had already built a reputation with his *Basai* and *Atripta* came out with his third novel *Brahmaputrako Chheuchhau*. This novel has wonderfully captured the social, economic, political, educational and cultural problems of the Nepalis in Northeast India.

Since then many have attempted writing the history of migration of Nepalis to Northeast India and their settlement there. Many more have written biographies of freedom fighters like Chhabilal Upadhaya and Bishnulal Upadhaya but none of them has so far attempted to write anything about lesser mortals like Manbir, Gumane, Kesharbahadur, Khulal, Headmaster Suryaprasad, Tope Master, Bombahadur Limbu, Ghorsane Kaila, Keshav Karki, Malati and others described in Lil Bahadur Chhetri's third novel. Thousands of nameless Nepalis living in Kachhu Village, Mahakhutti, Gamiri, Behali, Garhpal, Shingri, Budachhapdi, Mangaldai, Badpeta etc. have found their voice in this novel. The differences, problems and the political intrigues in the novel are part of the life of the Nepalis in this region. The author writes—'much before anyone had set their foot in the dense forest of Bagechhapadi, the Nepalis had been struggling with their lives here. The entire settlement is neatly divided into small villages with interesting names like—Khadka Pal, Dakhin Tapu, Kulbire Tol, Marasine Pal, etc.' (p. 40).

The contribution of the Nepalis to the Indian freedom struggle has often been ignored by historians. But the innumerable lives laid by them in the nationalist struggle can hardly be erased from history. Chhetri makes this point when he says, 'Like many other freedom fighters Jayprasad Subba was also one of the freedom fighters. Like any enlightened individual he was also aware of the importance of organization in social life and strived hard towards social reform. He can be counted as one of the first to begin animal husbandry and was instrumental in popularizing Gorkha League in the Northeast. He along with the founder of Gorkha League Dambar Singh Gurung played an important role in putting forth the problems of the Nepali graziers before the Assam government.' (p. 51)

The novel also has references to the general elections of 1952, 1957 and 1962: '(I)n the first general election of independent India Dalbir Singh Lohar became the first Nepali to win the assembly election on a Congress ticket.' (p. 57) '...Bishnulal Upadhaya became a member of the Legislative Assembly as a Congress member.' (p. 150)

The names of places certainly indicate early Nepali settlement in the region. The author suggests that the name Paltan Bazar in Guwahati was named after the settling of retired Nepali soldiers. He writes, 'It is only after the settling of Nepali soldiers that the place came to be known as Paltan Bazar' (p. 78).

In the context of the Gorkha League's politics he writes, 'Everyone supported Gorkha League. Dambar Singh was next only to a king in the Northeast.' (p. 90) In fact a pan-Assam organization known as the Assam Gorkha League which was lying dormant from 1955 became active in 1961 and came to Lanka from Dimapur (Nagaland). From then onwards the organization kept low till 1966.' (p. 136)

On the bravery displayed by the Gorkha soldiers he writes, 'Gorkha soldiers saw major action during the Chinese aggression in 1962. Major Dhansingh Thapa made a name for himself with his heroics in the western front of Ladakh. In the eastern front of Aalang, Tawang and other places, Bajiram Thapa, Ravilal and many others endeared themselves with their valour and bravery. It is of course tragic that Nepalis are treated as mercenaries and one does not know whether or not their heroics will ever be documented.'

It is a well known fact that at Aalang in North East Frontier Agency Bajiram single-handedly ran over the enemy camp injuring him seriously in the process. As he was lying on the ground the enemy left him thinking he was dead. It is said that Ravilal before paying the price with his life hacked as many as 17 enemies to death. (pp. 148-149) The novel is strewn together with a series of historical narratives and the author has missed no opportunity to highlight the contributions of the Nepalis.

Lil Bahadur Chhetri's last novel is *Pratidhwaniharoo Bismrtika*. The novel does not provide a space for a hero or his opposite. It is merely a recollection of past events in the life of Commandingba. The novel captures the vagaries of life as it unfolds without any order or pattern. The novel has strong biographical elements, beginning much the same way as life had begun for Commandingba or Prem Bahadur Chhetri struggling up his way from the hills of Nepal. The novel travels to places like Guwahati and Shillong, talking about the establishment and development of these places: 'a huge mass of land has become an island on which one can find Nepalis setting up buffalo sheds'. 'Most of the soldiers are Nepalis. Moreover, most of the Bodo Kacharis would understand Nepali and speak as well…' (p. 45) 'It is around 1926, the year I enlisted myself in the armed branch of Assam Police.' (p. 47) 'Another major place of Nepali concentration is Paltan Bazar. The very name would suggest that "Paltan" was mainly a Nepali settlement. In fact the very name Paltan Bazar was given by the Nepalis settling sometime in 1928-29.' (p. 66) 'During those days Guwahati and all other places where Nepalis had settled had institutionalized panchayat system (village council). The historical Radhakrishna Mandir which later became an important place of worship for the Gorkhas was established by the Gorkha Panchayat in 1932.' (p. 74) 'The land for this temple was given by one Jaychandra Thakur from the Gorkha army. A Gorkha school has come up next to the temple. The Nepalis had settled here long before the coming of the Marwaris, Garhwalis or Bengalis. Nepalis would join the army and police; one could find them working as coolies, watchmen, peons and even as milkmen.'(p. 129) 'There used to be a time when 70 per cent of the police force in Shillong came from the Nepali community.' (p. 132)

K.B. Nepali's first published novel is *Mero Ghar Mero Sansar*. The novel is based on the story of a poor farmer. Set in rural Nepal, the novel has striking familiarity with *Basai*. Just as Dhane Basnet in *Basai* was forced to leave Nepal after losing everything to a ruthless moneylender, Ram Singh in this novel also meets a similar fate. The author's second novel *Samarpan* was published in 1962. As the year would suggest the novel is based on the stories of Gorkha soldiers' valour and sacrifice during the war with China. Ambar Pradhan, the chief protagonist of the novel, represents thousands of faceless and unsung Gorkha soldiers forgotten by history. Like in most other cases, Ambar's father had served in the army and had paid the price of his life. Born in a family of such tradition as most Gorkhas are, they are more than willing to lay down their lives for the cause of the nation.

The author has prepared a long list of martyrs who have sacrificed their lives fighting for the Azad Hind Fauz. He writes, 'inspired by Netaji Subash Chandra Bose's call, "give me blood I'll give you freedom", people like Purna Singh Thakur, Ghambir Singh Thakuri, Suryaman Chhetri, Balbahadur Pradhan, Babulal Pradhan, Dilbahadur Rai, Tulbir Singh, Gopal Singh Majhi, Tezbahadur Subba, Ramsingh Thakuri, Babulal Moktan, Babusingh Lakandri, Harkabahadur Gazmer, Shital Bahadur, Prem Khadka, Jagat Bahadur, Krishna Sunar, Dhan Bahadur Thapa, A.B. Yonzon, Parshu Thapa, Khadka Bahadur Bista, Chandrabir Gurung, Tek Bahadur, Ram Kishen Chhetri, Narayan Thapa, Aita Gurung, Dileep Singh Rana, Sherbahadur Thapa, Ganga Pradhan, Manbahadur Rai, Gulab Singh Thapa, Ganga Thakur, Narbahadur Gurung and many others joined Azad Hind Fauz.' (p. 44) Gopal Singh Nepali penned inspirational verses during the war with China. His contribution to Nepali literature was in no way less than his bravery but it is really sad that very few people know about him today. K.B. Nepali has brought back the memories of those forgotten heroes. (p. 49) Birbikram Thapa's novel *Bigatko Pariveshbhitra* set in

Shillong is the first romantic novel. The novel brings back memories of Hindi literature's famous novelist Faneshwarnath Renu's *Maila Aanchal*. The novel in many ways can be regarded as the first novel from Shillong. The writer is critical of the depraving state of the Nepali society. He writes, 'The identity of the Nepali society will be secured only when individual Nepalis become conscious of their identities. The social and individual are strongly tied to each other.' (p. 30)

To this novelist, drinking *rakshi* (country liquor) has been the greatest nemesis for the Nepali community. This is precisely the reason for their backwardness, loss of honour and identity. It is not just the men but also the women are increasingly taking to drinking. He writes in a satirical style, 'A few days ago Anna Chhetri's wife Pushpa was found in an inebriated state lying in the drain behind Gorkha Pathsala with all her clothes stripped off.' (p. 40) The writer appears aggrieved by the fact that the present generation has almost forgotten the stalwarts of their community. He emphasizes the importance of historical figures for a community. Recalling the contributions of Mansingh Gurung and many others he writes, 'the headmaster of Gorkha Pathsala Mansingh Gurung's efforts in uplifting the Nepalis of Shillong is matched by very few. In fact Gorkha Pathsala is itself his brainchild. His magazine *Gorkha Sevak* served as a beacon light for people steeped in ignorance. But how many among the present generation would know about Mansingh Gurung?' '...while other communities are rediscovering their histories, the Nepalis have been erasing theirs. We have even forgotten about the life of late Capt. Bhuvan Singh Rai, the founding member of the Gorkha High School.' (p. 40)

The Nepalis are suffering from the problems of unbridled westernization. Their language and literature are getting extinct by the day. History testifies the fact that once the history of any community is erased then very soon the community itself gets wiped out. The novel has dealt with this issue at length.

The Nepalis had settled in different parts of Shillong but after the communal riots of 1987 most of the Nepalis were forced to flee from these places leaving back ruins and memories in Umlanka, Nakshe, Lambuwa, Shillingum, Mawlai and many other places. The novel travels to these forlorn and desolate places reliving the now lost serenity and joyfulness of the Nepalis. On reading the novel the reader gets a clear picture of the entire setting of Shillong. Even though the novel revolves round the love relation between Ramesh and Manjula, it nonetheless touches upon the social and cultural awareness of the Nepalis in Shillong.

Birbikram Thapa's novel *Teestadekhi Sutlejsamma* raises the important issue of the loss of identity of the Indian Nepalis. The novel can surely pass off as a work of historical research. Prakash, the main protagonist of the novel stands for thousands of Nepalis serving in the Indian Army. Among the many historical events narrated in the novel, pages 19 to 23 are specifically devoted to the history of Nepali movement and settlement in Northeast India. Writing within this historical context the writer asks, 'I have doubts as to whether the future generation will remember the sacrifices of my friend because the present generation has already forgotten the past.' (p. 25) It is said that many Nepalis worked as labourers during the construction of the Burma Road. (p. 26) He furthers writes, '...not all coming to this part got employment. Those who were left out were forced to earn their living by clearing forests and taking up agriculture.' (p. 27) '...the problem of food and shelter was always there but the condition has only become worse today.' (p. 28) '...in fact most of them settling down in Bishnupur are Nepalis.'

It was in 1980 that a large number of Nepalis were driven out in the "oust foreigners" campaign. The novelist writes, 'The Nepalis living in Assam had never imagined that such a day would come in their life—but today they are labeled as "foreigners". Many died during those tumultuous times, rendering many homeless. Did the government of the day listen to the cries of "we are not foreigners" by the Nepalis? Was the Treaty of Segowli remembered?' (p. 4) '...a generation has passed since the Nepalis started settling in Assam. During the Second World War, Nepali soldiers steadfastly held their posts putting up a brave fight in preventing the Japanese from running over the forests and hills of Northeast India. For this reason alone the present generation should salute their forefathers. (p. 48) 'Our forefathers entered the dense forests of Assam in search of peace and joy, worked in tea gardens of Darjeeling but that peace and joy still eludes the Nepalis.' (p. 50) '...when the Nepalis were clearing forests no one labeled them as "foreigners", the government did not ask for their land deeds.' (p. 54) On pages 60 and 61 Kamal, another protagonist in the novel, describes the problems faced by Nepalis in Northeast India.

The Nepalis living in Shillong witnessed communal tensions and forced eviction in mid 1980s. Ruing these developments the author writes, 'Shillong is the heart of Nepalis in Assam. This is not because of the sheer demographic presence of Nepalis here but because of their awareness and efforts in preserving the essence of their religion, culture and other forms of everyday practices that are well secured within the sanctified space of their homes. It is very clear that the Nepalis living in other parts of Northeast India were inspired by the Nepalis of Shillong. It was because of this that Shillong was known in Nepal, Darjeeling, Dehradun and Benaras. Even today the Nepalis of Shillong have preserved this legacy. On pages 78 and 80 the author gives historical details of their settlement in Shillong. The novel remains within this historical context till the very end.

The objectives of the novel are clearly spelt out by Abhinash Shresta in his "Foreword". He writes, 'The location, time and characters in the novel certainly open up new horizons. Beginning from Upper Bishnupur (Jagun) to Shillong, the novel travels to different corners of India including Northeast India depicting with ease their localness, cultural variations and details of everyday practices.'

One of the biggest challenges facing the Nepalis in Northeast India today is the question of constructing as well as preserving their identity in a somewhat alien as well as multicultural settings. The novel is primarily concerned with the problem of Nepali identity.

The novel takes up the encounter of the author with an elderly Liladhwaj Thapa and his youngest daughter Chandra. Liladhwaj is settled in Chitranna Valley in the interiors of Kerala and has a Malayali wife. There are many Liladhwaj Thapas who have moved to distant places. The novel has wonderfully brought out the pangs of separation and the silent sufferings of territorial as well as cultural dislocations experienced by numerous Nepalis in different parts of the world.

Gahin Upadhaya's novel *Khojima,* even while taking up a common theme, makes it interesting with his powerful narrative style and structure. The novel is about the search of Gomani Rai who has gone missing. But even out of this seemingly simple story the author has been able to come out with an engaging portrayal of Nepalis living in the banks of Brahmaputra. As the novel travels to different places in search of Gomani Rai, it also talks about the nature of relation the Nepalis share with the Mikirs, Bodos, Mishings, Assamese and others. Somewhere the author writes, 'look at my youngest son-in-law, Hewang Pegu (a Mishing). He is like my right hand. Once he takes up a task he makes it a point to finish it.' (p. 70)

Sant Kumar Dewan's novel *Pahar Parvat* takes up the everyday life of the Nepalis living in Arunachal Pradesh. Not much is known about the history of the settlement of Nepalis in Arunachal Pradesh. This is true not just of Arunachal Pradesh but the whole of India. A comprehensive study of the movement and settlement of Nepalis in different parts of India is not only desirable but also necessary at this stage. *Pahar Parvat*'s female protagonist is certainly not a Nepali but the person who scales the hills and mountains is a Nepali. This Nepali teacher finds a Nepali watchman in the new school where he is transferred. This shows that there are many Nepalis living in Arunachal Pradesh. The author writes, 'Most of the government porters I saw are Nepalis from Nepal. One is awestruck to see the Nepali porters walking for almost three days carrying things for the *sahib*s for nominal wages.'

Seeing the Nepali porters sweating with their head loads, one is reminded of a song the lines of which run as follows:

Sahebko bhari bokera
Sukha roti khaera
Hamro Tenzing Sherpale
Chadyo Himal chuchura...

Carrying the Englishmen's load
Eating *chapati*s
Our Tenzing Sherpa
Conquered many a mountain peak...

But the analogy of these porters with Tenzing ends there. Unlike Tenzing who earned a name for himself with his feat, many anonymous porters disappeared in the mountains carrying head loads, many died and are dying. Far from earning money and name for themselves they could hardly secure one square meal a day (pp. 14-15).

Sant Kumar Dewan's second novel is *Katha Balla Suroo Hunchha.* The novel primarily centres in and around Assam. Even as the author makes clear that the story and the characters in his novel are creation of fiction and resemblance to any person dead or alive is a mere coincidence, he narrates the stories of valour and courage shown by Gorkha soldiers during the war with China. He writes, 'Dashera is celebrated in a big way in the Assam Rifles. This is so because in the initial days when the regiment was opened by the British the Gorkhas made the numbers.' (p. 33) He also narrates the stories of Nepalis leaving Nepal and coming to this part of India thus: 'the swearing and abuse of my step-mother hurt me more than anything so I left for Kathmandu where I worked in a small hotel cleaning dishes. Before long I came across a contractor who took me to Bhutan where GREF (General Reserve Engineering Force) was constructing a road there. And I moved from Bhutan to Darjeeling, to Assam and here I am working as a watchman.' (p. 35)

Arjun Niroula's *Sishirko Bataas* is the first absurdist novel published in Northeast India. The novel explores the illegitimate relation between Lalita and Chetan and the problems arising from it. *Gham Dubepachhi* is an existentialist novel published from the region. These two novels have opened up new dimensions in Nepali novel writing. Niroula is probably the first novelist to write on such an important theme. Lil Bahadur Chhetri's *Atripta* had inaugurated this theme but it was Niroula who gave it its present form.

Born in 1936 in Muzafarpur, Bihar, Chandreshwar Dube served as a Hindi teacher in Manipur Government College. Though a non-Nepali he soon developed a taste for Nepali literature and contributed over a dozen novels. His novels *Deshko Maato* and *Jindagiko Baato* trace their roots to Nepal. The first novel is quite critical of the then existing panchayat system as a form of governance. His second novel is a story of the struggles of Kamala. Both the novels are creative in narrative style and structure. Gunu Gharti "Bairagi" has published four short novels. *Sapna, Prayaschit, Sindoor, Binaki Ardhangini* and *Chokho Maya* deal with the theme of love. Hari Adhikari's *Mutubhitra Trishna* takes up the theme of love between Bhaskar and Jyoti. Bhaskar, a penury stricken artist, is falsely convicted for trafficking his ladylove Jyoti. Jyoti, on her part, wanders around in search of Bhaskar. The novel ends with their happy reunion.

Aandhi may be regarded as the first feminist novel published from Northeast India. Namrata is the main protagonist in the novel. Loknath Upadhaya "Chapagai" has placed the internal conflicts and strains of Namrata before the readers. Not many will deny that women constitute an important foundation of any society. Strong, steadfast and courageous women can single-handedly provide leadership for the society. So much is taken away from women by representing them as merely sensual and emotional objects of fanciful imagination. Perhaps the greatest service to women would be to restore their dignity by portraying them as brave, strong and resolute. The novelist has quite naturally shown her as brave and strong willed but the incidents that occur in the life of Namrata are too real to be true. Along with her struggle the novel travels through the Nepali villages narrating their problems. He writes, 'Most of the Nepalis work as milkmen and porters.' (p. 47) 'We have struggled, worked hard but because of lack of consciousness we are still languishing here. Our future would have been lot brighter had we been little more thoughtful.' (p. 47)

The world has seen development and discoveries. Machines have replaced men long ago but sadly the Nepalis are still struggling with the basic problem of food and shelter. Nepalis have been around in places like Gamiri, Behali, Gahpur, Charali, Sadiya, Goliya, Siri, Dekiyajuli, Tejpur, Chandmari for quite sometime now but one would hardly come across them in administration. There was a serious problem of political consciousness and getting into Assam Civil Service itself was a major challenge let alone making it to Indian Administrative Service (p. 91). The struggle of Namrata becomes the struggles of the Nepali community itself. Had all Nepali women struggled the way Namrata did their struggles would have historical value. In fine, *Aandhi* stands for the struggle of the Nepalis and their attempt to construct their history in a new light.

Naya Devi is perhaps the only woman novelist in the region. *Yugsandhi* is the title of her novel. She has certainly become a literary celebrity. Commenting on the novel Padma Dhakal writes in the "Foreword" to the novel, 'perhaps this novel is the first novel in Assam that has taken up the theme of women's suffering.' Laxmi is the main protagonist in the novel. She is energetic, courageous and confident. The only impediment before her is her uneducated and conservative parents. For Laxmi education was the only way to emancipation from ignorance and darkness. The theme of the novel is certainly new and the prose is very readable. There are many things to learn from Laxmi.

Rohit Gautam's *Agnisnan* also focusses on the problems of Nepalis living in Assam. It narrates the problems of their livelihood and brings out their close interaction with other communities in Northeast India. On the role of Chameli, the protagonist in the novel, Lil Bahadur Chhetri writes, the main protagonist in the novel is Chameli who could never live long enough to understand the meaning of life. She was exploited at the very prime of her life.' *Agnisnan* is a connotative word. One cannot bathe in fire but the real meaning of the word is to learn through suffering. Just as gold becomes finer by heating in fire so does Chameli through her suffering. The novel is based on the story of a family in a small village in Goalpara district of Assam. Providing the details of the story Nav Sapkota writes, '*Agnisnan* is a realistic novel that brings out the social, economic, educational and cultural realities into light.'

It has been more than a century since the Nepalis settled here but even today the problems faced by them remain the same. The dominant theme in most of the literary works continues to be the problem of food and shelter. The question of our political identity remains unresolved to this day. Science has opened new horizons and conquered new heights. The newer discoveries of the world are matched by the continuing ignorance in the Nepali society.

REFERENCES

1. Vikramvir Thapa, *Teesta Dekhi Sutlejsamma*, Guwahati: Nepali Sahitya Parishad, 1986, p. 21.
2. Bishnulal Upadhyaya, *Asame Nepaliharoo*, Kathmandu: Bhanuprakashan, 2028 (B.S.), 1971, p. 4.
3. *Ibid.* p. 5.
4. Hari Bhakta Katuwal, "Assamma Nepali Sahityako Gatibidhi", *Himali*, Year No. 4, *Jeth/Asad*, 2025 (B.S.), 1968.

13

Nepali Settlement and Cattle-Rearing in India's Northeast

D. SAPKOTA

Enough historical evidences[1] exist to show that there was matrimonial alliance between the royal families of Nepal and Kamrup (Old Assam) on the one hand, and Nepal and Manipur on the other Contiguity of land between India and Nepal facilitated easy migration from one country to another. Further, many Gorkha soldiers of the East India Company who served in India's Northeast settled in the region after retirement. Most early migrants adopted cattle-rearing for their livelihood. Constitution of professional grazing reserve (PGR), village grazing reserve (VGR) or village grazing ground (VGG) by the then government in 1920s and 1930s must have encouraged the Nepalis to raise more animals and the success of the early settlers obviously enthused others to follow. They practised animal husbandry on the riverbanks and river islands of Assam, which explains why many such islands carried Nepali names. Though most of these have disappeared in the mighty Brahmaputra, the names are still etched in the minds of the community.

Though the Nepalis of Assam reared both buffaloes and cows, more emphasis was laid on the former in the plains of Assam because of their capacity to produce larger quantities of milk as well as for their sturdiness. It is possible that the buffaloes they reared were bred with Assamese local breed (*Bubalus bubalis,* i.e., swamp buffalos). They were basically raised under free-range system wherein they were let loose most of the time and were driven out to surrounding jungles. One especially built bell was hung in the neck of a prominent she-buffalo of the herd (*Bathaan).* The entire night the herd kept itself busy grazing in the jungle. The herds were disciplined and they maintained their hierarchy. Listening to the jingling sound of the bell the herd-man tracked down his herd even in dense forests. The bell, popularly known as *Goalparia bell*, perhaps owes its origin to Goalpara.[2]

The buffaloes returned early in the morning. They were milked only once in a day. The yield ranged from 8 to 10 litres per day. The calves were kept in the shed and milking was carried out after the animals were fed salt. No supplement of any kind of feeds was provided. The jungles had abundant grass, which met the required nutrients. The buffaloes were of semi-wild type. Those who did not return to herd and remained in jungles for several days slowly turned wild. Needless to emphasize, many of the wild buffaloes presently found in Kaziranga and Manas sanctuaries are in fact off-springs of the domestic herds that once belonged to the Nepali pastoralists.

The Nepali graziers had to pay grazing fees (taxes) for raising buffaloes and cattle in PGR to the British government. The buffaloes, older than 3 years, or whose length of horns was more than that of its ears, or longer than one foot, were taxed. The cows aged more than 3 years were also taxed. Sometimes debilitated or older animals were exempted from taxes. A Mohsirdar, who was appointed by the government, made the assessment of taxes.

A Grazing Superintendent, whose rank was equivalent to that of the Sub Deputy Collector, supervised the work of each Mohsirdar. A Mohsirdar used to get commission on the tax collected. However, the Grazing Superintendents, being government servants, were paid their salary from the state exchequer.[3] In 1888 the yearly grazing tax for buffaloes was *8 annas* per head and for cow 4 annas. The tax was raised to Re. 1 per buffalo in 1907 and still higher in 1912, though available records do not reveal the extent to which the tax was raised. The grazing rules that were framed in 1911 were somewhat modified after an official enquiry in 1915 under the pressure of the public to not raise the grazing tax further. Thereafter the grazing fee was increased to Rs. 3 per buffalo and 6 annas per cow, which continued even after the British left.[4] In the hill districts, a rate ranging from Rs. 4 to 6 per buffalo was in force since 1917. However, the milch buffaloes in the vicinity of towns were taxed at a concessional rate of Re. 1 per head until 1916 and Rs. 2 thereafter. Though initially an insignificant source of government revenue, these grazing fees were indeed an expanding source because of a steady rise in the immigration of Nepalis and other graziers along with their cattle. The total number of buffaloes and cows in the Brahmaputra valley between 1895 and 1960-61 is shown below:

1. Tax paying buffaloes:

Year	*No.*
1895	15,640
1900	18,735
1905	24,346
1910	40,000
1915	42,000
1920	86,325
1960-61	44,492 (Estimated)

2. Tax paying cattle: 3,442
3. Non-tax paying buffaloes: 4,36,538
4. Non-tax paying cattle : 43,53,199

Due to constant increase in the number of buffaloes and the rate of taxation as well as tightening up of the collection machinery by the government the revenue increased substantially as shown hereunder:[5]

Year	*'0000 Rs*
1916-17	183
1917-18	342
1919-20	277
1920-21	341

Since most of the graziers were Nepalis the constant increase in the buffalo population and higher revenue collection through tax are, no doubt, clear indications of a growing Nepali population. The burden of tax payment was practically limited to the Brahmaputra valley, which abounded in grazing grounds. For example, as against the total collection of Rs. 2,77,356 as grazing fees from this valley in 1919-20 only Rs. 25,841 were collected from the Surma Valley and the hill districts.

In 1917-18 only 622 cattle owners of local domiciles were treated as professional graziers. The total revenue of Rs. 277 thousand collected in 1919-20 from grazing fees were accounted for by only one and a quarter lakh of cattle actually assessed in that year under the rules. The overwhelming bulk of these cattle again belonged to 6,319 professional graziers of whom excepting a few hundreds all were Nepalis.[6] A steady influx of Nepali graziers into the Brahmaputra valley led to an increased cattle population and milk production. The number of Nepal-born persons in Assam increased from 21,000 in 1901 to 88,000 by 1931.[7]

Though there is no documentary evidence available on the history of graziers of Assam plains, it is believed that most of the early Nepali settlers in Brahmaputra valley had their *Khuti (Goth)* in Kaziranga area. Among the graziers Chabilal Upadhyaya was a prominent figure who fought for the cause of the graziers in 1921. He was an outstanding leader of the Indian National Congress Party, Assam branch and was a freedom fighter. Mackenzie[8] in 1885 gave the statistical accounts of Nepali settlers in Assam as follows:

Surma Valley	*Brahmaputra Valley*	*Hill Tracts*	*Total*
499	2,521	1,465	4,485

However, in 1920 they were driven out from Kaziranga by the forest authorities. They shifted to the riverbanks and islands of the Brahmaputra along with their cattle for their survival.

Among the PGRs Burachapori was predominantly occupied by traditional Nepali herdsmen for cow and buffalo farming. It is believed that the settlement commenced in 1860.[9] Burachapori is an island of the Brahmaputra river, located south of the present Tezpur town in Sonitpur district but north of Solong and Longiabasti of Nowgong district. In the Brahmaputra, south of Lowkhowa Reserved Forest, some other small islands existed which were also occupied by Nepali graziers. The milk produced at Burachapori was brought to Tezpur by boat for sale. Owing to sound economic condition and also due to the vicinity of town most of these cattle owners could impart good education to their progenies and some of them later settled in the town, mostly in Chandmari area. The graziers started Tezpur Graziers' Association in 1933 for collecting, processing and marketing of milk in town.

The Nepalis entered the Cachar area of Assam much before 1886-87[10] when the construction of Badarpur-Lumding railway line was taken up. Many goths existed along the proposed railway line. To solve this problem the state government arranged an alternative site, located in the western side of the area. The new place, known as Badolouka, was covered with thick forest and the settlers had only their *Khukuries* (sharp cutting implement) with them to clear the jungles and protect themselves against wild animals. There were around 5000 Nepalis[11], though in the official census of 1961 the number recorded is 2070 only. In 1967 a dairy farm was started in Harinagar of Silchar.[12] Nepali herdsmen produced abundant milk, curd, butter etc. and supplied them to the town. The quality of ghee they produced was excellent for which the product was popular not only in Assam but also in other parts of India.

Sadiya, located at the northeastern corner of Assam plains, was also a famous milk-producing pocket developed by early Nepali settlers since the British era. Digaru, Sisne Basti, Saikhowa Ghat are other areas where cattle rearing and dairy activities were prominent. It was learnt that the British rulers encouraged cattle farming by permitting mutation of 2 bighas (28,800 sq.ft.) of land in favour of each grazier.[13]

After the World War II when the demand for milk marked a substantial increase it prompted many Nepalis to set up Khutis adjacent to Guwahati after importing cattle from Shillong. A section of the Nepalis, who in course of time came to be known as *Paikari* (wholesale milk trader) used to collect milk from these dairymen (Khutiwallas) and distribute the same to army personnel. Among such Paikaris many were also prominent social workers. Today, dairy farming in Guwahati is mostly concentrated in Bonda, Birkuchi, Basistha, and areas extending from Khanapara to Jorabat. As one passes through Guwahati-Shillong road, one's attention is drawn immediately to the long cowsheds made up of thatched roofs on both sides of road or on distant hill tops amidst exotic Para or Guinea grasses (fodder). Breeds like Holstein-Friesian, Jersey, Red Dane and Shillong local are common. The farmers' day starts at 4 am and ends at 11 pm. All day long they are busy taking care of their cattle, cutting grasses, milking and nursing them like their children. Everybody in the family is involved in the rearing activities. Even the primary school-going children do their bit. Everything from cattle feed to their daily ration has to be carried up the hills, where their homes are located. Though the farmers are in the dairy business for generations, most do not own *patta* land. Seasonal fluctuations of milk production (Flush season: October to March; Lean season: April to September) affects the economy of farmers. The areas inhabited by the herdsmen lack basic amenities, like safe drinking water, communicable roads, sanitation, school, health care centre etc. According to the private census done by the *Brihattar Guwahati Go-Palak Sangstha*—an apex body of the dairy farmers—there are nearly 3400 dairy units with a population of about 34,000 in and around Guwahati city.[14] They produce about 98,000 litres milk per day, much less than the actual demand of 2.5 lakh litres a day in the city. Though the government has fixed the selling price of milk, the control over the price of feed is lacking. Further, it is alleged that most of the cattle feeds are adulterated affecting the milk production and cattle health. Though there is no government support in whatsoever form, of late the State Bank of India has come forward to sanction loan assistance to 90 dairy farmers under the Dairy Plus Scheme amounting to Rs. 1 crore.

Dairy farming was adopted in other places too. Many Nepalis are known to have started cow and buffalo rearing in the villages of Naduar and Sootea Development Block of Sonitpur District since 1840.[15,16] Some of them had large herds of cattle numbering more than 1500. Many of the farmers were also influential people in the society. Among them mention may be made of Sriman Timsina who was a freedom fighter and Bahadur Karki, whose son Prabhu Ram Karki donated the highest amount (Rs. 5000) in establishing Darrang College of Tezpur in 1945.

In 1929,[17,18] nine Nepali grazier families migrated to Amelighat, about 60 kms away from Guwahati and started dairy farming, adopting intensive system (stall feeding) with modern high yielding cows. They started producing and marketing milk under the name of Sitajakhala Prathamik Dugdha Utpadak Samabai Samiti Limited (Sitajakhala Dairy) in 1958 under the chairmanship of Nanda Lal Upadhyaya. Today, the Sitajakhala Dairy has not only acquired name and fame in dairying but it has also given a boost to the socio-economic conditions of the graziers of the area. The Nepalis continued their cattle rearing and milk production even after the formation of new states in the sixties and seventies of the twentieth century, viz., Arunachal Pradesh, Meghalaya, Mizoram and Nagaland, which were parts of erstwhile Assam.

Arunachal Pradesh

Many Nepali graziers shifted to Pasighat and Tezu areas of the state after the devastating earthquake in Assam on August 15, 1950 from Burachapori in search of greener and extended pasture land for buffalo.[19] In 1962 many Nepali graziers shifted their buffaloes to northern part of Kabbu Chapori (river bank) of the Brahmaputra which forms part of Arunachal Pradesh from Burachapori and other parts of Assam, with 500 to 800 heads of animals. They used to sell milk, curd, ghee and butter in Dhaula (Assam) ferrying across by boat. However, presently most of the descendents of original graziers have switched over to other vocations.[20] Today, the cattle-rearing and milk production in the state of Arunachal Pradesh is centered around Tezu, Itanagar and Pasighat. In Tezu the milk production is carried out with local breeds of cattle adopting free-ranging system (pastoral grazing) while in Itanagar and Pasighat areas the same is done through stall-feeding high yielding cattle. Here, the state government has come in a big way to assist the dairymen through Lohit Farmers' Cooperative Society at Tezu.

Manipur

Cattle rearing commenced sporadically in the state of Manipur in the British era but it took shape only after the Indo-Burmese War of 1824[21] when retired army personnel took up the profession. They were soon joined by others brought by the British, especially for cattle rearing. After World War II many Nepalis from Nepal and Burma engaged in dairying. Initially, British rulers encouraged cattle rearing by providing professional grazing grounds in certain places. Among these, K.K. Reserve (Kangpokpi-Kanglatombi Reserve), also known as Gorkha Grazing Ground, was granted in 1919, which spread up to an area of 15 miles in length and 10 miles in breadth.[22] In this reserve more than 200 goths were located. In the same year another ground in Irang valley, extending to 12 miles was given to graziers to establish cattle farms. It is believed that there were 165 goths in this valley. The cattle rearing activities of Nepalis settled in the state in late 1930s is distinctly known from various documents. Among these, one such order issued on March 10, 1938 to the Headman Sri Bishnulal Upadhyay by Mr. C. Gimson, Political Agent, Manipur limited the number of cows and buffaloes in the Irang Valley, K.K. Reserve, Maram Khulen area to 1500 and 3000; 2100 and 1500; 500 and 10, respectively; whereas the number of buffaloes in Taphau area was limited to 250.[23]

The Nepalis were reported to have settled in Mantripukuri before 1815[24], Pangai before 1880[25], Toribari before 1910[26], Kalapahad before 1934[27] and in Laimakhong before 1961.[28] There are enough records that prove that Nepali herdsmen and retired army personnel were allowed to rear cattle in the reserved grazing ground, Mao-Maram subdivision, vicinity of Imphal and other free lands. However, on 31.07.1946 Mr. F.F. Person, President, Manipur State Darbar (HQ) issued an order de-reserving the K.K. Grazing Reserve and opening the same to settlement and colonization. Each grazier was given 1.5 *Paris* (acre) of land. The graziers were given opportunity to shift their herds to Irang Valley, located about 13 kms to the west of Imphal. Many graziers shifted their flocks to Ukhrul district after the de-reservation of K.K. reserve.[29]

The graziers had to pay two types of taxes annually, i.e., Rs. 4 per animal as grazing tax and Re. 1 per person as foreigner tax. It was stated that at one time total collection of grazing and foreigners tax was

Rs. 22,295 and Rs. 35,144, respectively. The Nepali graziers were substantial in number among the tax payers. The cattle farmers were also enthusiastic to start a Graziers' Co-operative Society. This is known from a letter issued to the President, Irang Panchayat in November 26, 1936 by Mr. C. Gimson, Political Agent in Manipur. However, a dairy co-operative came into being much later, i.e., in 1971 as the Ideal Milk Producers' Co-operative Society started by 25 active members in Manipur town to collect, process, pack and market milk and milk products.[30] But after the social unrest there in 1980s on the foreigners' issue the activities of the society have slowly come to a halt.

Meghalaya

The British introduced the 8th Gorkha Rifles in Shillong in 1829. They also brought many Nepalis with them, who along with the retired army personnel started cattle rearing. *Ghee* (purified butter) was primarily produced for sale to local people and the army. In this state the milk production mostly centered around Shillong and Nayabangla areas adopting the method of stall-feeding of high yielding cattle, i.e., Jersey and Holstein Friesian by Nepali herdsmen. The dairy activities picked up momentum after the formation of Harihar Dairy in 1940, Hill Green Dairy in 1945 and Assam Dairy in 1947.[31] In olden days buffalo-rearing in free-range system was also practised especially in the West Khasi Hills. Since the human habitation in the hills was thin, the herdsmen used to keep flock of buffaloes on high, elevated, practically virgin land. Foraging was practised for 3 to 4 months after which the flock would be taken to another hill for grazing and this trend would continue. Among the prominent dairy farmers were Talke Mahajan, R.B. Chhetry and Bhanu Bhakta Subedi.[32] However, social unrest and agitation on foreigners' issue in mid 1980s crippled the dairy activities. Presently, most of the dairies are defunct and the cattle rearing as an occupation has received a serious setback.

Mizoram

The Nepalis set their feet in Mizoram around 1891[33] as members of the British Army. After retirement they settled in the state rearing cattle for milk production. However, as years rolled by, their progenies did not continue the family tradition. Presently, nearly 90 per cent of total milk production of the state is contributed by those Nepalis who are exclusively engaged on the job and who entered the state much later. These herdsmen produce milk through cattle-rearing in the land of local Mizos.[34] At present the milk produced by these farmers is collected by the Mizoram Union of Co-operative Society and processed, packed and marketed by the society. High yielding cattle, Jersey and Holstein Friesian imported from Shillong are used in milk production.

Nagaland

It is learnt that almost 95 per cent of milk production in the state of Nagaland is dominated by Nepalis. Milk production is mostly centered around Dimapur, Kohima, Mokokchong, and the Phuthero subdivision of Wokha district. Initially, milk production commenced with the local breed of cow, *Thotho*. In early seventies of twentieth century upgradation of this breed was started by crossing with imported high yielding breeds of Jersey and Holstein Friesian from Shillong. Since most of the available land of the state is privatized, the Nepalis involved in cattle breeding had to come into an informal agreement with local landowners in which the milch cattle are supplied by the owner and the management, feeding etc. is done by the farmer. The rearing is done by stall-feeding them and the owner would get certain quantity (1-2 litre/day) of milk and offspring. Among the early herdsmen, Purna Bahadur Pradhan of Aradhura of Kohima was prominent.[35]

It has been noticed that there are distinctly two categories of Nepalis in Northeast India—settled (*raithane*) and dairy farmer (*dudhwala*). The former started cattle-rearing and milk production nearly 200 years ago, but most of their descendents are no more following the traditional profession and have opted for government/private employment after acquiring essential skill and education. Presently milk production is carried out by those Nepalis who migrated to the state in the latter part of the twentieth century. They have taken up this business commercially, nearly for last 20-30 years. Along with milk production they have also engaged themselves in supplying milk to the consumers.

It may be concluded that though cattle rearing and dairying was an exclusive profession of early Nepali immigrants, their progenies are no longer in their "family business". This might be due to the gradual shrinking of fodder area, encroachment of grazing land, PGR, VGR, VGG or river islands because of encroachment, insurgency and depredation by wild animals. Difficulties are compounded by non-availability of suitable hands (*gothala*) to look after the animals in free-grazing land and sheds.

Nevertheless, looking into the national and global market scenario *vis-à-vis* demand for organic and processed food, time has come to change the mindset of the new generation. It is high time that traditional graziers switch over to modern system of dairy farming, adopting newer technologies so that animal husbandry practice is not only retained but new avenues are also opened up for employment generation.

REFERENCES

1. According to the historian Kanaklal Barua, Rajyamati, daughter of Harsha Barman, the famous king of Kamrup (653 *saka*) was married to Jayadev II, king of Nepal. Whereas, Surya Bikram Gyawali, another historian also mentions that Rupamati, a princess of the Koch dynasty was married to Pratap Malla, king of Nepal. On the other hand, Ratnakumari, a princess of Nepal was married to King Biswa Singha, who established the Koch dynasty of Kamrup.
2. Durga Prasad Ghimire, 1996-97, *Purbanchaliya Nepali Sahityako Bikash* (1986-1994), *Parishad Patra*, Vol. 6/7, No 3-4, mouthpiece of Nepali Sahitya Parishad, Assam, ed. Gopal Bahadur Nepali, Guwahati, p. 31.
3. As per statement of Ganga Nath Upadhyay, 85 of Chitalmari, Dist. Sonitpur, Assam on April 10, 2006.
4. *Report of the Estimate Committee of Assam Legislative Assembly*, 1960-61, under the Chairmanship of Siddhinath Sarmah, Govt. of Assam, p. 26.
5. Amalendu Guha, 1977, *Planter Raj to Swaraj*, New Delhi: People's Publishing House, p. 93.
6. *Ibid.*, p. 93.
7. *Ibid.*, p. 102.
8. Alexander Mackenzie, 1885, *The North-East Frontier of India*, Delhi: Mittal Publications, Rpt. 1957, p. 548.
9. Durga Prasad Ghimire, 1983, *Mero Dristiko Seropheroma Budachapodi*, Tezpur: Mrs. Vidya Ghimire, p. 13.
10. Somnath Sastri, 1970, Uttar Kachad Pahadma Nepaliko Basobasa Ra Byabasaya, *Assam Gorkha Sammelon Bulletin*, Vol. 12, p. 12.
11. *Ibid.*, p. 12.
12. J. Pandey, 1970, Kachadbashi Nepali Tatha Uniharuko Arthik Samashya, *Assam Gorkha Sammelon Bulletin*, Vol. 11, pp. 5, 10-11.
13. As per statement of Ramalal Upadhyay, 85 of Hahkati, PO Saikhoa, Dist. Tinsukia, Assam on April 3, 2002.
14. Gokarna Mishra, 2006, The Plight of Dairy farmers in Guwahati: How long will they exist? *The Sentinel*, January 8, pp. 10-11.
15. As per statement of Tilak Sarma and Loknath Thapa of Gamiripal, Dist. Sonitpur, Assam.

16. As per statement of Guruprasad Upadhyay of Madhupur, PO Jamugurihat, Dist. Sonitpur, Assam.
17. As per statement of Ramalal Upadhyay, 85 of Hahkati, PO Saikhoa, Dist. Tinsukia, Assam.
18. Premsingh Subedi, 1998, *Asomka Pashupalak Ra Dugdha Byabasaiko Aitihasik Brittanta,* Guwahati: Nepali Sahitya Kala Niketan, p. 14.
19. As per statement of Amar Upadhyay, 75 of Chandmari, PO Tezpur, Dist. Sonitpur, Assam on April 14, 2006.
20. As per statement of Ganga Dhar Ghimire, 75 of Chandmari, PO Tezpur, Dist. Sonitpur, Assam on April 14, 2006.
21. As per statement of Tulshi Adhikari, 68, M.K. Avenue, Imphal, Manipur on April 9, 2006.
22. C. Dubey, 1970, Manipure Gorkhalihari, *Assam Gorkha Sammelan Bulletin*, Vol. 11, pp. 2-3.
23. M. Gautam, 1999, *Manipurma Nepali Janajeeban,* Kanglatombi: Nepali Sahitya Parishad, p. 16.
24. *Ibid.*, p. 61.
25. *Ibid.*, p. 64.
26. *Ibid.*, p. 37.
27. *Ibid.*, p. 40.
28. *Ibid.*, p. 59.
29. *Ibid.*, p. 32.
30. A. Niroula, 1970, Khasia Bhasa Ra Sanskriti Mathi Nepaliko Prema, *Assam Gorkha Sammelon Bulletin,* Vol. 11 and 12, p. 9.
31. D. Sapcota, 2003, Animal Husbandry Practices Adopted by the Nepalese in Assam, *History of Assamese Nepali*, manuscript submitted to the Directorate of History and Antiquarian Studies, Govt. of Assam, Panbazar. Guwahati.
32. As per statement of Bashanta Raj Joshi, B.B.S. College, Mowprem, Shillong on April 15, 2006.
33. Pradip Sunar, Jeevan Kawar and I.K. Subba, 2000, *The Gorkhas of Mizoram*, Vol. 1, Aizawl: Mizoram Gorkha Students' Union, p. 9.
34. As per statement of Dr. H.S. Thapa, Department of Botany, Pachunga University College, Aizawl.
35. As per statement of Dr. Buddhi Lama, Asstt. Director, Department of AH and Veterinary, Kohima, Nagaland.

14

Mizoram Gorkhas: Issues and Problems

K.L. PRADHAN

The present paper tries to analyse in detail the issues and problems faced by the Gorkha community[1] in the State of Mizoram from the latter part of the nineteenth century. The Gorkhas who settled down permanently in the state before 1950 and their descendents did not face any problems either from the natives or the government. Before 1980, there was no restriction at all for them with regard to trade, employment, higher education, allotment of Post-Matric Scholarship, land settlements etc. It was in early 1980s that the permanent Gorkha settlers began to face the problem of their identity. The main reason behind it seems to be the migration of the Nepalis from Nepal and elsewhere, who are engaged as labourers, cowherders, lumberjacks etc. Since there are no specific differences between the permanent Gorkha settlers and the recent Nepali migrants, it is natural for the native people and the government to treat them as one. The native people refer to this community as Gorkha or Gorkhali rather than Nepali.

The history of Gorkha settlement in the present state of Mizoram began in the latter part of the nineteenth century. They initially migrated from Nepal and later from different parts of the British India. The reasons behind their coming to Mizoram are many. It is said that the migratory waves from Nepal were caused by increasing fragmentation of land-holding, indebtedness, rising population and declining land availability and unemployment of skilled labours.[2] There is another important aspect, which is universally accepted about their movement particularly in this region and that was the allurement of military adventures[3]. After the Anglo-Gorkha War of 1814-16, the British had enrolled the Gorkhas in the British army and posted them to different parts of their dominion. Series of columns, expeditions from 1844 to 1889 were dispatched against the Lushais or what the Mizos were called till 1952. And it was in 1891 that peaceful relation between the British and the Lushais was permanently established and the Political Officer was appointed to look after the administration.[4]

Once peace prevailed in the hills, the government required manpower for developmental works. This was the beginning of the settlement of the Gorkhas in the state. Nirmal Kumar Pun, in his article on the community, has concluded that the Gorkhas began to settle in Mizoram in 1891 while others opine that it was either 1865 or 1871.[5] The conclusion of Nirmal Kumar Pun regarding the year of Gorkha settlement in Mizoram rings true and I substantiate it. In 1896, when the Chin Hills Regulation Act was enforced, the government prohibited the influx of foreigners within the Lushai Hills district except in very special circumstances.[6] The amalgamation of the North and South Lushai Hills districts as one administrative unit called the Lushai Hills Distrct in 1898[7] and the early part of the twentieth century further opened opportunities for the Gorkhas to migrate and settle here. These Gorkhas who were skilled in various trades were immediately engaged according to the needs of the district administration. Some of them were even employed by the Mizo chiefs in their villages. The Gorkhas, right from the beginning of their settlement, found the geographical location and climate similar to that of Nepal and felt at home. The natives belong to the Mongoloid race as most of the Gorkhas do, and their hospitable, carefree, fun-loving, friendly, straight-forward nature helped in developing a close and harmonious relationship between them and the Gorkhas, which later cemented the bond of friendship and brotherhood between the two communities. The Gorkhas, in course of time forgot their place of origin while the Mizos embraced them wholeheartedly. The bon-homie continued till the 1980s.

According to the available records, the first Gorkha families who settled down permanently were found in Maubawk, Khagdiya (Rangvamual) and Kolasib. With the beginning of twentieth century, there was rapid growth in the number of non-Mizo settlers. In case of Gorkhas, they were the direct descendents of the discharged military personnel of long services with good conduct, originally recruited in the Lushai Hills. Apart from above villages, the Gorkhas settled at Aijal (Aizawl), Sairang, North Vanlaiphai, Lunglei, Dhemagiri, around 45 miles of Dwarband Road (now Thingdawl). Gradually, they shifted to other villages, viz., Bairabi, Chhimluang (Aizawl-Silchar Road) North Chaltlang, Kawnpui, Sialsuk, Thenzawl, Tlangnuam, Tuikhaw vengthar, Bualpui, Neihbawi,

Vairengte, Champhai, etc. They were also found in the southern part of Mizoram, i.e., Saiha and Lawngtlai and Dhemagiri. Those Gorkhas who settled in other villages in smaller numbers are not known. It is presumed that many of them subsequently became Mizos.[8]

Within Aizawl town areas, the settlements of the Gorkhas are found in Survey Tilla (now Dinthar II), Sriman Tilla (now Zotlang) Khashibanjiang (now Vaivakawn) Patharkhani (Hunthar) Zemabawk, Bawngkawn, Durtlang, Sihphir, Bungkawn, Venghlui, Khatla Lane and Gairigaon (Tuikual). Before the independence of India, the Gorkha population in and around Aizawl, the capital of the District was in majority. It is recorded that in Aizawl sub-division, 25 per cent of the taxed houses belonged to the Gorkha permanent settlers.[9]

With the passage of time, the Gorkhas of Mizoram no longer live a life within the ambit of their tradition. Their socio-religious life has undergone a sea change. As this community forms a small minority group in Mizoram and lives in scattered areas, they can hardly be of any threat to the majority tribe. As stated above, they have coped with the living style of the Mizos and have certain obligations towards the same community.

To supplement the above statement, it is pertinent to examine the social life of the Gorkha community prior to 1966. Almost the entire community professed Hinduism barring a few who professed Buddhism. Among the Hindu Gorkhas, the principle of the caste/*varna* system was rigidly practised. Those belonging to the lowest stratum were referred to as 'untouchable', and were not permitted to perform any rituals. In every Hindu society, members of higher caste have upper hand in all affairs of the locality and enjoy many special opportunities and privileges. Such a situation prevailed among the Gorkha community of Mizoram till 1966.

In 1966 the movement led by the Mizo National Front[10] and subsequent economic hardship resulted in transformation of their society from traditional to modern. The policy of the government to regroup the villages under one administrative control for security purpose led to mixing up of all sections of people, irrespective of castes, creed or religion. The moot question at that time was survival by setting aside the traditional social system. The other factor which hastened the changes in the social system of this community is their long and uninterrupted stay in Mizoram. The Mizo society is a tribal society and free from caste prejudices. Taking cue from them the Mizoram Gorkhas also gradually reformed their traditional system by doing away with the caste system. Another aspect is the development of education within the community which influenced the transformation. From 1970s onwards visible changes have been noticed in their socio-religious practices, which are as follows:

(1) Untouchability has ceased to exist among the Gorkhas in Mizoram.
(2) Inter-caste marriages and inter-dining have started among them.
(3) Free access is available for the 'untouchables' to the Hindu temples etc. Even a Shudra member of the community is elected to the post of President of the Local Durga Puja Committee and Mandir Committee.
(4) Women's position in the society is relatively higher than among other Hindu societies.
(5) And, finally, total prohibition law enforced by the State government has the desired effect on the community.

It is also found that a few Gorkhas have embraced Christian religion at their own will and built a church at Aizawl town. However, their number, at present, is negligible.

Inspite of all the changes, the Gorkhas are close-knit community as far as Mizoram is concerned. They are highly conscious about the welfare and well-being of their community. Though they constantly mix with the native people, they have preserved their language, culture and identity as Gorkha.

From the beginning, the Gorkhas have formed a good work force. As they live a hard life, they go out in search of work. Being diligent, perseverant and hard working the Gorkhas of Mizoram have contributed a good labour force for the development of the state. They were also pioneers in the fields of settled agriculture, horticulture and animal husbandry. Way back in 1898, wet-rice cultivation and terrace system was introduced by a Gorkha retired personnel at Champhai, North Vanlaiphai and other parts of the State. They were also engaged as labourers, lumberjacks, cowherds, chowkidars, dak-runners, peons, etc. In their professions, the Gorkhas earned good names.[11]

Economically, the Gorkhas of Mizoram are not lagging behind the natives. 60 per cent of them are engaged either in government or private sector services as teachers, lawyers, administrators, medical practitioners, white-collared job holders and in defense services. 15 per cent are engaged in cultivation, cattle-rearing and animal husbandry. Of these cattle-rearing is the most important occupation, as they produce about 60 per cent of milk in the state. Some Gorkhas are also serving as petty businessmen and government contractors.

The Gorkhas of Mizoram can boast of 95 per cent literacy. It is largely due to availability of free education in 10 provincialised Nepali primary schools, 3 Nepali middle schools and 2 Gorkha high schools in the Gorkha-concentrated areas. Considering the total population of the Gorkhas in Mizoram (approximately 5000) and number of educational institutions, the government has been generous towards the Gorkha community, and there is no discrimination against them. The Gorkhas have also proved themselves to be good friends of the local people and both the communities have been living side by side with cordial relationship for more than a century.[12]

Socio-political Organisations

In 1936, a Gorkha Mauzadar was appointed for the purpose of exercising some administrative coordination over the Gorkha inhabitants for the purpose of collecting foreigners' taxes on commission basis. In the case of a dispute where the Gorkhas were involved, the case was tried by the native Chief and the Mauzadar was to be present for consultation of the Gorkha customs. And those Gorkhas who settled down under a Lushai Chief's control, were subjected to Lushai customs and chief's order. With the abolition of the institution of Mauzadar in 1953, a Gorkha Panchayat was established at Aizawl. Rules and regulations were laid down with "the intention to give right of control of their social customs to the Gorkha community as far as possible with least interference by the Magistrate of the District".[13] Internal disputes among the Gorkhas were referred to the Gorkha Panchayat for disposal. When the institution of Village Council was introduced in 1954, the Gorkhas were represented fairly well through election or nominations and held important posts.[14] At present there is one Gorkha rajya panchayat and 13 gaon panchayats.

The Mizoram Gorkha Nari Samaj, with its headquarters at Aizawl looks after the affairs of Gorkha women. The main function of this Samaj was to train the jobless Gorkha women in various trades, uplift their status and to eradicate the social evils that exist in their society. The Samaj is affiliated to the Mizo Hmeichhe Insuihkhawm Pawl (MHIP). The Mizoram Gorkha Youth Association (MGYA) is the apex body established in 1976, following the pattern of Young Mizo Association. It looks after the social, cultural, literary and other needs of the youth. There are other associations like Mizoram Gorkha Students' Union (MGSU), Nepali

School Teachers' Association, Gorkha Karmachari Kalyan Sangh, Prabhat Nepali Evam Sanskriti Pariwar etc. These organizations have played their respective roles for the betterment of the community. The Mizoram Gorkha Welfare Association also plays a significant role in the welfare of the community. In fact, national Gorkha organizations like the All India Gorkha Students' Federation and Bharatiya Gorkha Parisangh were established under the initiatives of MGSU and MGYA in 2000 and 2001 respectively to safeguard the interest of the Gorkhas of India.[15] Almost all the Gorkha elders are members of the Mizoram Upa Pawl (Elders' Association). This association looks after the welfare of aged people.

Even with a marginal and scattered population, the Gorkhas have played an important role in Mizoram politics. The votes of the Gorkhas play a pivotal role in winning the elections. One scholar wrote, 'the Gorkha residents, who are considered as permanent inhabitants of Mizoram, have a right to vote and exercise their franchise in elections. Though they do not contest elections with a separate candidate the Gorkhas always play a significant role in the elections. For this reason, some local candidates sometimes put baits to the people with a view to win their votes. Normally, this community cast its votes for a particular candidate en masse, thus allowing one candidate to win'.[16] In fact, the Gorkhas have affiliated themselves with various national and regional parties of the state. The only Gorkha political party in the state is the Gorkha Sangh, which plays a significant role in moulding public opinion in the interest of the community.

Brewing Troubles: Issues and Problems

The question of Gorkha identity cropped up in the early part of 1980s, when the influx of people from Nepal increased. They lived in the outskirts of Aizawl as cowherds and supplied milk to the city. Though they did not constitute any threat to the people of Mizoram economically, the latter perceived demographic threat with the multiplication of the Gorkha population in the State.[17] It alarmed the permanent Gorkha settlers too. The Mizoram Gorkha Youth Association along with the Gorkha leaders immediately took up the matter. They appealed to the government to recognize the permanent Gorkha inhabitants as one of the tribes and extend facilities at par with the natives. They also demanded to the government to undertake census of this community to identify the permanent Gorkhas. Accordingly, the government of Mizoram has ordered state-wide Gorkha census.[18]

Meanwhile the then Congress Government had thoroughly examined the demands of the Gorkhas and accorded the following facilities: granting of post-matric scholarship. Extension of facilities in the matter of education, land settlement certificates including transfer of ownership, employment and trade and commerce at par with their Mizo counterpart, and issue of permanent residential certificate. For the purpose of extending these facilities, the census of Gorkhas who were permanently residing in Mizoram prior to 26-1-1950 as furnished by the Deputy Commissioner was taken as the basis of the genuineness of their claim.[19] But it was vehemently opposed by the Mizo Students' Joint Action Committee by burning the official gazette and demanded immediate cancellation of it.[20] The Gorkha leaders, on their part, continued to apprise the government with the plight of their community and urged for reconsideration of their demands.

When the General Assembly Election of 1998 was announced, the Mizo National Front, in its election manifesto made the following promises to the Gorkhas provided they formed the government:

(a) As per Indian Constitution and Ministry of Law, Notification No. SRO of 10 August, 1950, the permanent Gorkha settlers shall be given the status of Other Backward Classes and extend all the facilities enjoyed by this section at par with other Indian States.
(b) The Mandal Commission recommendations once accepted by the government shall be applied to the Gorkha community.
(c) The District Council Rules and Regulations adopted by the government of Mizoram in regard to land, issue of passes, periodic *patta* and Land Settlement Certificate would continue to be practised.
(d) As per Peace Accord of 1986, the Gorkha community shall be included in Mizoram State Minority List and their rights and privileges shall be protected.[21]

In May 2001, on the basis of the recommendations made at the meeting of the Council of Ministers held on 31-3-1998, the government of Mizoram had decided to accept the final figure of 4453 as the number of Gorkhas who have been in Mizoram prior to 26-1-1950 and their descendents. The government has further directed the concerned departments for issue of Land Settlement Certificate/Passes in respect of the lands traditionally held by them.[22] However, other facilities are yet to be extended to them.

Another problem is the rules and regulations (of 2002) for selection of candidates for higher and technical (medical, engineering etc.) courses which do not accommodate the children of all sections of permanent Gorkha residents of Mizoram in the Category II of the Mizoram Gazette. Because the clause states, 'but serving under the Government of Mizoram, Corporation or Autonomous Body under the State Government or other recognized organizations under the State Government who are regular employees of such organisations'[23]. This clause debars the children of the permanent Gorkha residents of Mizoram who are not employees of the government of Mizoram from being selected as candidates for higher and technical courses. The Mizoram Gorkha Youth Association appealed to the government to modify the clause by adding 'Non-Local Permanent Residents' and making reservation of 5 per cent in the category. The matter is still lying pending with the government of Mizoram.

One other problem was related to the 'right to vote' in the Village Council elections. By the 4th Amendment of Mizoram (Election to Village Councils) Rules 2004, Sub-Rule (4)(d) of Rule 3, the permanent Gorkha residents were debarred to cast their votes in the Village Council election. The operative part of the rule reads as, '...belonging to a Scheduled tribe whose affairs are triable by the Village Councils Court under Rule 14 of the Lushai Hills Autonomous District (Administration of Justice) Rules, 1953'.[24] In fact the Gorkhas of Mizoram have been exercising their franchise in the Village Council elections since 1954 as per a provision made in the Assam Autonomous Districts (Constitution of District Council) Rule 1951 (as amended upto March 1969) part IV, Chapter II, Rules 128 (3), ever since the Village Councils were constituted. In fact the North-Eastern Areas Reorganisation Act—Mizoram) Adaptation of Law Order, 1972 too has made provision vide Rule 110, for the permanent Gorkha residents of Mizoram to cast their votes in the village councils. The matter was immediately taken up by the MGYA and other organizations. With their concerted efforts, the government has re-amended the said rule and extended the voting rights to the permanent Gorkha inhabitants in the Mizoram village council elections.[25]

The most crucial problem of the Gorkha community in Mizoram at present is the question of the status of the Other Backward Classes (OBC). When the Mizo District was a part of Assam, the Gorkhas living in the State of Assam were categorized as "Other Backward Classes" under Nepali in 1961. With the attainment of the Union Territory and Statehood, the Government of Mizoram issued OBC Certificate to the permanent Gorkha residents of Mizoram, under the Mizoram Category of the Backward Classes under the Constitution (Scheduled Caste) Order 1951.[26] However, the Government of Mizoram, without giving any reasons, has stopped the issuance of the Other Backward Classes certificates to the bonafide children of Gorkha permanent settlers as a result of which the young Gorkhas are facing problems in various fields. In fact, the Gorkha Community of Mizoram has been identified as Other Backward Classes by the Second Order Backward Commission (Mandal Commission) and the Government of India has approved it in 1990.[27] To substantiate their claim as one of the Other Backward Classes, the Gorkha leaders approached various State Governments, viz., Assam, Nagaland, Meghalaya, Haryana and Punjab where the Gorkhas are awarded the status of the OBC category and requested to forward their notifications to the Mizoram Government for necessary action.[28] On the basis of their findings on the subject, the MGYA has submitted a memorandum to the Government of Mizoram to recognize the permanent Gorkha inhabitants under the Other Backward Classes irrespective of their caste, creed and religion. Several petitions have been submitted to the Government on the issue. Meanwhile, the Mizoram Gorkha Welfare Association has taken up the issue with the National Commission for Backward Classes for inclusion of "Gorkha" community in the Central List of OBCs for Mizoram.[29]

On 23rd January, 2006, the MGYA met the members of the National Commission of the Linguistic and Religious Minority here in Aizawl and apprised them of the problems faced by the Gorkhas of Mizoram. The Commission has asked the representatives of the community to settle the matter of OBC status with the state government. The MGYA and other organizations are pursuing with the Government of Mizoram for early finalization of their demands. The Chief Minister of Mizoram, in his speech on the occasion of the 29th Annual Assembly of MGYA, held on 10th February, 2006, has assured the permanent Gorkha residents that his government is looking after the issue and is under active process. He promised to finalise the matter as soon as possible. Thus, once the OBC status is granted, the problems of this community would be greatly reduced even though the Gorkhas of Mizoram have not faced any serious problems and threats in the fields of education, economy, politics, legal or cultural matters from the native people. The community maintains cordial relations with the Mizos by speaking their language, mixing up with them while keeping their own culture and identity alive.

NOTES AND REFERENCES

1. K.S. Singh (Gen. Ed.), 1995, *People of India-Mizoram*, Vol. XXXVIII, Calcutta: Seagull Books, pp. xii-xiii. It shows that Mizoram has 18 communities, 14 Scheduled Castes, 9 Scheduled Tribes and 2 other communities. The Gorkhas have been classified as one of the 18 communities. Also see K.L. Pradhan, 2003, The Gorkhas of Mizoram, in A.C. Sinha and T.B. Subba (eds), *The Nepalis in Northeast India*, New Delhi: Indus Publishing House, p. 295.
2. Imdad Hussain, 2003, Soldiers and Settlers: Recruitment of Gorkhas, in A.C. Sinha and T.B. Subba (eds), *The Nepalis in Northeast India*, New Delhi: Indus Publishing House, pp. 67-69.
3. Nirmal Kumar Pun, 2000, Migration and Settlement in Mizoram, in P. Sunwar, J. Kumar and I.K. Subba (eds), *The Gorkhas of Mizoram*, Vol. I., Aizawl, pp. 12-13.
4. See *North and North Eastern Frontier Tribes of India*, 1983 (Reprint), Compiled by Army Head Quarters, New Delhi, pp. 230-42. Also see K.L. Pradhan, 2004, Settlement of Gorkhas, in Sangkima (ed.), *Cross-Border Migration—Mizoram*, Delhi: Sipra Publication, p. 58.
5. Pun, 2000, *op. cit.*, p. 100.
6. A.G. McCall, 1977 (Reprint), *The Lushai Hills District*, Calcutta: Firma KLM Private Ltd., p. 4. It is recorded that 'I have been asked by the several chiefs to allow the settlement of Gorkhas in their villages'. Also see *Mizo leh Vai Chanchin* (*Mizo and Non-Mizo Story*), 1932, Aizawl, p. 23.
7. Subash Chatterjee, 1986, *Mizoram Under the British Rule*, Delhi: Mittal Publications, p. 13. He states that "these Gorkhas after their retirement from the army and police force took Lushai Hills as their homeland with their hearts and souls and settled there".
8. Pradhan, 2004, *op. cit.*, pp. 258-62. It is interesting to note that some Gorkhas were awarded the privileges and powers of the Lushai chiefs with hereditary rights of succession. For example, Lalsingh Lama was conferred the chieftainship of Hriangmual.
9. Lalrimawia, 1995, *Mizoram-History and Cultural Identity*, Delhi: Spectrum Publication, p. 1.
10. Sangkima, 2004, in his introduction, writes, 'it is needless to say that when the Mizo National Front (MNF) started the movement for independence from India in 1966, a number of Gorkhas joined MNF'. It is therefore presumed that due to this very reason the Gorkhas were exempted from the Quit Mizoram Order of 1982, when the MNF ordered all outsiders to leave Mizoram by 21st June, 1982.
11. Pun, 2000, *op. cit.*, pp. 13-18.
12. Sangkima, 2004, *op. cit.*, p. 13.
13. McCall, 1977 (Reprint), *op. cit.*, pp. 176-80.

14. The first Gorkha who became the President, Village Council of Sriman Tilla (now Zotlang) was Bir Bahadur Limbu in 1958.
15. Pradhan, 2003, *op. cit.*, pp. 63-64. Also see N.N. Kundu, 1995, Gorkha, in K.S. Singh, (Gen. Ed.), *People of India-Mizoram,* Vol. XXXVIII, Calcutta: Seagull Books, pp. 60-661.
16. Sangkima (ed.), 2004, *op. cit.*, p. 13.
17. *Ibid.*
18. *The Mizoram Gazette Extraordinary*, Vol. XXX, 2001, Aizawl, dated 18th May, 2001.
19. The Government of Mizoram's Notification No. J.20011/102/83-POL (ST), 3rd February, 1992.
20. Pun, 2000, *op. cit.*, pp. 27-28. The cancellation of the Gazettee, he states, was due to: (1) 'these days parochialism has become a platform for political aspirants as well as the unsuccessful and disgruntled politicians in India. Parochialism is the last resort for them. Hence, unnecessary and over politicization or parochial issues occur frequently. (2) Some section of the people failed to realize that the conferment was as effective instrument to storm infiltration of foreigners as it was based on the census of the Gorkhas, while providing justice to 0.72 per cent population of the Gorkha permanent residents, and (3) The Government faced a dilemma as to whether to stick to the decision once it made or to protect the lives and properties of the Gorkha minority. The Government has chosen the latter'
21. The Mizo National Front's Election Manifesto (Assembly) 1998, issued by Zoramthanga, President, MNF on 14th October, 1998.
22. The Mizoram Gazette, *op. cit.*, 3rd February, 1992.
23. *Ibid.*, No. C.11011/1/93/-EDN (THE) dated 2nd June, 1999 and 15 July, 2002.
24. The Mizoram (Election to Village Council), 4th Amendment Rule, 2004.
25. The Government of Mizoram's Notification No. F.22015/85/94-HM, Vol. II, dated 17th May, 2001.
26. The Government of Assam's Notification No. TAD/OBC/61/15 dated 12th September, 1961 and No. AAP/7850/4 dated 28th February, 1950.
27. The Government of India, Office Memorandum No. 36012/31/90-ESH (SC) dated August 1990.
28. The Government of Assam Memorandum No. ABP 338/83/14 dated 4th January, 1984 with annexure of OBC lists.
    (a) The Government of Punjab's Notification No. 14980-WC-57/106352 dated 7th and 13th September, 1957 with annexure of OBC lists.
    (b) The Government of Meghalaya, No. SW (5) SC/ST-1/93Pt/113 dated 19th March, 1996 with annexure of OBC lists.
    (c) The Government of Nagaland, Home Department's Notification No. GAB-8/2/9/73 dated 22nd October, 1974.

The Nagaland Government has declared all those Gorkhas/ Nepalis and their direct descendents who have settled in Nagaland permanently prior to 31st December, 1940 shall be treated as "indigenous non-Naga local residents" for equal property rights, educational facilities, licenses and loans.

29. The Mizoram Gorkha Welfare Association, Aizawl, letter No. MGWA/ 23/OBC/(G)MIZ) 2005 dated 13th June, 2005 and a letter from the National Commission for Backward Classes, New Delhi, with annexure of questionnaires for consideration of request for inclusion and complaints of under inclusion in the Central list of OBC.

15

Nepalis in Meghalaya: Diaspora and Identity

AMENA PASSAH

The term 'identity' comes in various forms. Classical theorists like C.H. Cooley[1] speak of the 'looking-glass self' where identities are formed based on what the individual thinks he/she is perceived by others. On the other hand, G.H. Mead[2] introduces the concept of 'I' and 'me' where 'me' is the object of one self formed by the subject 'I'. It is the subject 'I' who reacts to the historical situation as it is perceived by 'I', then seen objectively and assessed by the object 'me' and consequently internalized and incorporated into the formation of 'self' and 'identity'[3].

Collective identity of a people at any given place reflects the sameness of identity that a people with a shared history hold in common and which establishes a cultural belongingness, in spite of superficial differences.[4] Identity is formed basically in the context of differences from 'others'. Other people have to be encountered in order to form one's sense of identity.[5] While writing on the notion of 'identity crisis' Eric Erikson remarks that 'in the social jungle of human existence there is no feeling of being alive without a sense of identity.'[6] In today's scenario, diverse groups are questioning traditional identities that were previously taken for granted. For instance, women are questioning their identity in a previously accepted patriarchal society. The same stand on previously taken-for-granted identities is now being taken by ethnic minorities, homosexuals, dalits and indigenous peoples amongst others. Most social groups are aware of their identities and are reconstructing the same, giving rise to 'identity politics.'[7] In many societies today, 'identity politics' has come to stay. Thus identity helps a people to describe itself in relation to the other.

The spectre of 'identity crisis' rears its ugly head, sooner or later, wherever minority groups have settled, out of their choice, or have been forced to settle by circumstances. This is irrespective of the degree of assimilation with the indigenous community in which they are placed. This has exactly happened in the case of the Nepalis of Meghalaya in 1986-87. This lifted the lid off their complacent lives. With the exception of some, a majority of them is still reeling from the shock and harbour apprehensions of a future backlash again. They have got back into the grind of daily living putting these fears at the back of their minds. The innate friendliness of the majority Khasi-Jaintias, the tribal people of Meghalaya, has to a great extent assuaged their horrible memories.

Meghalaya is one of the smallest states of India and is strategically located in Northeast India. Carved out of the state of Assam, it became a full-fledged state in 1972 with an area of 22,429 sq. kms. Meghalaya has a predominantly tribal population belonging to the three communities called Khasi, Jaintia and Garo. It is one of the Indian states where a large number of Nepalis reside. The tribes of this state had trade contacts with the plains people in the foothills in Assam and present day Bangladesh from the earliest times.[8] As early as 11 February 1835, the Khasi Hills came under the control of the East India Company, when the Political Agency was set up with Cherrapunjee as the headquarters. The headquarters of the Sylhet Light Infantry was also located at Cherrapunjee.[9] It was in 1861 that Shillong as the new headquarters was mooted by the Calcutta Government,[10] which became a reality in 1864. By 1874, it was made the headquarters of the Chief Commissionership of Assam.[11] Thus it became the centre of British administration and of the military forces of Assam right from early times. It soon became the centre for Gorkha forces employed in Northeast India. It is not surprising that the first recorded settlers in Meghalaya were Gorkhas or Nepalis. The Gorkha Association to cater to the social activities of the Gorkhas settled in Mawprem area of Shillong was established as early as 1886.[12]

On the whole, the Nepalis of Meghalaya are living a much freer life than was once possible in their own country. Majority of them have settled in these hills for generations. The Nepali or Gorkha population of Meghalaya is today so indistinguishable a part of the local environment that it is often forgotten that the first settlers arrived nearly two centuries ago.[13] They have long been recognized as sturdy, brave, loyal, honest[14] and industrious people. They came as soldiers, graziers, farmers, porters, traders, sawyers, *chowkidars*, etc. Today with improved financial and better living conditions and benefiting from education, many are playing important roles in the society especially in the educational, administrative and military sectors. For example, some are occupying senior positions in North-Eastern Hill University, Government of Meghalaya, in politics, in the Indian Army, Assam Rifles[15] etc. Some have even contracted matrimonial alliances with the local population. The Nepali adage 'dress according to the land you are in' is reflected in the easy and assimilative character of the Nepalis among the Khasi-Jaintias.[16]

There are cases where the Khasi-Jaintia wives have fully adopted their Nepali husbands' customs and are the very picture of Nepali women in appearance, attire and language. On the other hand, there are Nepali spouses of Khasi-Jaintia women who have totally imbibed the facets of Khasi-Jaintia life and are often mistaken for Khasi men. These are men and women whose ancestors had come to these hills long ago, struggled to start a new life and gradually interacted and sometimes assimilated with the local people. Little did their ancestors imagine that in the distant future, their progenies would be seen to pose a threat to the local people.

Formation of the Nepali Diaspora in the Khasi-Jaintia Hills

In this connection, it is pertinent to understand the logistics that brought the Nepalis to these Hills. They began to settle in this part of the country when they were recruited into the East India Company's armed forces. When we talk of the Gorkha settlements in India in general and in Northeast India in particular, the Anglo-Nepalese War of 1814-16 between the expanding Gorkha power of Nepal and the British power in India assumes great significance. The conflict helped the British to extend their territory and establish a bond with Nepal through signing the Treaty of Segowli in 1816.[17] In the above war, the Gorkha soldiers, though outnumbered, with inferior weapons, had fought valiantly before they surrendered.[18] Though defeated, their fighting qualities and martial talents had been noticed and greatly appreciated by the British who remarked that "we have met with an enemy who shows decidedly greater bravery and greater steadiness than our troops possess."[19] Impressed by their magnificent fighting qualities, the British Army recruited them in large numbers. Nepal realized that the recruitment would be a serious threat to its sovereignty and discouraged its subjects from joining the British Indian Army with measures like putting to death those Gorkhas returning to Nepal on leave and also confiscating properties of those serving in British Indian Army.[20] On the other hand, realizing the situation, the British Government encouraged the migration of Gorkhas from Nepal with their families[21] and established Gorkha settlements in the hills of India[22] since they were hill tribes and preferred the hill areas. In course of time, the 7th and 8th Gorkha Rifles were raised in Assam. The 8th Gorkha Rifles had its genesis in the 16th Sylhet Local Battalion and its headquarters was in Shillong till 1943.[23]

It is very clear that had the British not made inroads into Northeast India in general and Khasi-Jaintia Hills in particular, the Nepali immigration would not have occurred to such a great extent. The Gorkhas came as soldiers and porters with the British armed forces. The Burmese invasion of Assam and the surrounding areas posed a threat to the British power and turned the attention of the British to Assam. The Anglo-Burmese relations deteriorated, culminating in the Anglo-Burmese War of 1824-26. The advance of British troops into Assam marked the termination of the policy of neutrality which the British government had uniformly followed with Assam for the past 30 years.[24]

With the transfer of the headquarters from Cherrapunjee to Shillong, the military units moved likewise but the transfer was delayed till 1867. The 44th Native Infantry Regiment, comprising Gorkhas, along with the Regimental Hospital, moved into their new quarters in the present day Cantonment in 1867. This infantry was later renamed the 44th Gorkha Rifles and stayed in Shillong up to World War II[25] and the hospital's name was changed to the 44th Gorkha Rifles Regimental Hospital. After the 1897 earthquake, the damaged hospital was re erected and renamed the Military Hospital, Shillong.[26]

The British, noting the bravery and loyalty of the Gorkhas, paid special attention to their welfare. Family accommodation was extended to them, their children would, if need be, later recruited into the British Army and retired Gorkhas who wanted to settle in India were allotted lands around the Regimental Centre where, in course of time, Gorkha localities grew up.[27] In fact, there were a series of correspondence between the Army and the British to form a Gorkha village in the Khasi Hills.[28] This village would serve as a home for the women and children when the Gorkhas were out of station. Pensioners and reserved men of the regiment would also reside there. In course of time, the Deputy Commissioner, Khasi and Jaintia Hills, strengthened by the existing treaties with the *Syiems* (chiefs) of Khyriem and Mylliem, cleared the proposal.[29] The dawn of India's independence saw a subtle tussle between the British and the fledgling Indian government to exercise control over the Gorkhas. The matter was resolved in the tripartite agreement in July, 1947 between India, Nepal and Great Britain wherein 6 regiments remained with India and the remaining 4 went to Great Britain. Thus the Gorkhas who stayed back, settled along with their families in India including Shillong.[30]

After the link was established between the Khasi Hills and Nepal through the Gorkhas there were more Nepalis entering these hills. They came as porters, graziers, farmers, traders, hewers of wood, *chowkidars*, labourers, miners etc. By the 1901 Census of India, there were only 1722 Nepalis. But by the 1991 Census,[31] there were 43,574 Nepalis constituting 3.94 per cent of the total population.[32] By the Census of 2001[33] they constituted 4.9 per cent of the state's population.[34] In the past, apart from Mawprem, Jhalupara and Barapathar areas of Shillong, the interiors of Nongstoin, Nongspung and Nongkhlaw had attracted many Nepalis. Today they are found all over the state with heavy concentration in Mawprem, Barapathar, Nongmynsong, Paltan Bazar, Upper Shillong, Laitumkhrah and Umpling areas of Shillong city; Bapung, Lad Rymbai, and Khliehriat of Jaintia Hills; Nongstoin, Mawkyrwat, and Mairang of West Khasi Hills and Nongpoh and the interiors of the Ri Bhoi District.

Questions arise then as to why there was a great exodus from Nepal, Darjeeling, Sikkim and other areas like Darjeeling district of West Bengal into the Khasi-Jaintia Hills? Undoubtedly, Nepal is one of the poorest and most underdeveloped countries in the world.[35] There was also a wide gap in income distribution.[36] The difficult terrain made life miserable and unprofitable for the farmers and graziers.[37] Again the Nepalis whom the writer interfaced with in Shillong, Jowai and Bhoi region of Meghalaya were unanimous in stating that though back home, food was never in short supply yet they felt the pinch because there was no opportunity for ready cash. They candidly informed that Nepalis loved money and would not mind working hard to attain it. This explains the great number of them as traders, coolies, domestic workers, *chowkidars*, labourers in and around Shillong and as coal miners in Bapung and Lad Rymbai of the Jaintia Hills of Meghalaya.

Again, though Prithvinarayan Shah had politically unified Nepal, this had been done 'without weighing the cost in terms of human suffering for one's own people.'[38] The grim poverty made people long for a soldier's life. Apart from being lucrative, adventurous and challenging, the pensions of ex-servicemen did a lot to augment their meagre family income. Many of them chose to stay back in the hills of the present-day Meghalaya and other states of Northeast India because they were granted plots of land by the respective army authorities on their retirement.

Moreover, the oppressive land and labour policies and the obnoxious rural indebtedness threatened the very survival of the low-income people of Nepal.[39] No wonder the Nepalis considered migration as the only way out of their misfortunes and soon made their way to Sikkim, Darjeeling, Assam, Bhutan and beyond. There is no doubt that the Nepalis came with the colonial rule. They were trusted by the British and all the political agents were accompanied by the Gorkha soldiers who were in turn followed by their families.

Apparently, the hills of present day Meghalaya were one of the most favourite destinations for the Nepalis. As early as 1931, the Census Report of that year revealed that the areas most attractive to the Nepalis were the Khasi-Jaintia Hills of Meghalaya, and Lakhimpur, Kamrup and Darrang districts of Assam. The other hill districts and frontier tracts exercised strict control over the immigration of Nepalis making those destinations less attractive for their migration.[40] One of the factors attracting them to Meghalaya was the presence of coal mines that needed plentiful supply of labour and the Nepalis in Nepal, already victims of the population explosion in their country, needed no second thoughts to leave their land and make a beeline for these hills which offered them job opportunities. The increase in the population of Sadar and Shillong subdivisions in 1931 is primarily attributed to their immigration.

The opening of the new road to Sylhet attracted more immigrants.[41] The local chiefs or Syiems themselves had encouraged the immigration of Nepalis.[41]

> The immigration of these graziers is, I am informed, encouraged by the *Syiems* (chiefs) who levy a grazing tax on immigrants—a tax which they cannot levy on their own subjects—and the immigration of Nepali graziers is thus a source of considerable profit to them.

In recent times, the factor which greatly facilitated the exodus of Nepalis to these hills was the series of treaties signed between India and Nepal. The Indo-Nepal Friendship Treaty of 1950, the Tripartite Delhi Agreement of 1952 and the revised Indo-Nepal Agreement of 1956 especially Article 7 of the Treaty of 1950, granted equal privileges in terms of ownership of property, residence, employment, occupation, movement and other similar privileges on a reciprocal basis for both nationals of India and Nepal in both the countries.[42] Again, the non-requirement of a visa or passport for entry into either country, greatly facilitated mobility into these areas.

Finally, industrialization and development of roads and other infrastructure also opened avenues for Nepali employment in Meghalaya. Higher income levels, better educational facilities and the continuing matrimonial alliances with the people from these hills facilitated their migration to the Brahmaputra valley[43] and to Meghalaya as well. Thus, once the Gorkhas and their families had established a link between these hills and Nepal, the initial trickle of Nepalis became a surging stream.

Identity Crisis of the Indian Nepalis

For all their contribution to the Indian society, the Nepalis have long been a submerged identity. This had not bothered them in the past, content as they were with their work and their relations with the local population. But this idyllic existence was shattered in the 1980s with the emergence of the anti-foreigner stir.[44] Their ancestors had settled in various parts of India for generations, had looked upon India as their permanent homeland and had even sacrificed their lives for the country. Suddenly they realized that they were looked upon as 'foreigners' and unwanted intruders. Much to their dismay, they realized they had not been accepted after all these years. A lot of soul-searching took place among them. Many were hurt and disillusioned by the suspicion and apparent hatred of their Khasi friends. Many however realized that it was not only the Nepalis who were targeted but even the Bengalis and Biharis were. It was the proverbial 'sons of the soil' issue, reportedly triggered off by the Bengali community of Shillong who provoked the Khasi Students Union led by Bull Lyngdoh by threatening that the Nepalis of Meghalaya would soon begin to demand for a separate state.[45] But some like Utpala Sewa[46] felt affronted that after being born in India and her father decorated for exemplary service to the country, the identity of the Nepalis is still being questioned. They are troubled that Bangladeshis get away with being regarded as Bengalis coming from West Bengal and hence are accepted as Indians.[47] Some are still apprehensive of a future backlash. Many again feel that they have no roots and an uncertain future. The Nepalis who have settled in India feel they are unwanted and ignored not only in India but also in Nepal. In Nepal they are called prawasis and considered as Indian citizens while in India, they are called 'Nepali immigrants.' The ethnic violence in the past in various parts in Northeast India placed the Gorkhas in a worse position than during the colonial period. The British called them 'domiciled Gorkhas' and had recognized their political and economic rights *vis-a-vis* the Indians but overnight they became 'immigrant Nepalis' and most of their rights were trampled upon.[48]

More than the Nepali Hindus, it is the Nepali Christians who are experiencing a greater 'identity crisis'. On the one hand, the Nepali converts suffered humiliation in the hands of their own Hindu-majority community members.[49] On the other hand, they suffered in the hands of the Khasi Christians, as they were identified as 'foreigners' in Meghalaya. On occasions like a bereavement which involves family and community participation, Christians in many cases were debarred from joining in. Hence a sense of alienation crept in. The Christians were gripped by a feeling of hurt, sadness and being in no man's land. The Nepali Hindus did not expect Nepali Christians to hold Nepali surnames. In fact the Hindu Nepalis ignored their Christian counterparts and refused to regard them as Nepalis, treating them as tribals and outcastes. This is because Nepali Hindus considered Christianity as a tribal religion. It is not a trivial matter to be rejected by your own people especially in an alien land. All Nepali Christians still consider themselves as Nepalis, their contention being that a person's identity is determined not by his religion but by his language. If a person has adopted another religion to experience God, and has still retained his mother tongue, his Nepali identity should not be denied to him.

The Nepali Hindus, on the other hand, feel affronted that the moment their people become Christians, they disassociate themselves from participation in their religious festivals and abandon some cultural habits. However apart from this sense of rejection from their own people and the step-motherly treatment of the Central and State governments the Nepali Christians, on the whole, are happy living in Meghalaya. They have a wholesome interaction with the Khasi Christians. The latter not only extend help in spreading the gospel, but also in setting up schools for them, encouraging them for higher education and providing employment opportunities for such Nepalis. Financial aid is also provided for the poor and needy. There is intermarriage between the two communities. They are free from the bane of caste system prevalent in the Hindu community. The largest church in the Khasi Hills is the Mawkhar Presbyterian Church and a Nepali has been elected to the post of *tymmen basan* (elder), a high and privileged post in the church next only to that of the pastor. The Nepali Christians are invited to all religious and social gatherings of the Khasi Christians and this fosters a spirit of oneness between the communities.

In the 21st century, memories of the 1980s incident have been pushed to the backburner. Things have limped back to normal. Many of the genuine citizens are in the electoral rolls of the state. The unfortunate ones are the daily wage labourers who because of the time factor or total ignorance have not had their names included in the electoral rolls. The uneducated ones do not bother to enroll in the electoral rolls and have a devil may care attitude about the future. The only grouse of the Nepalis is that like other non tribals, they are not allowed to buy land.[50] Nor are they eligible for state services without domicile certificates. The other misgiving is that the Central and State governments have conveniently feigned ignorance of the Indo-Nepal Peace and Friendship Treaty of 1950 and the Nepalis living in these hills do not enjoy the rights outlined in the treaty. In fact, certain groups in the Northeast including the Khasi-Jaintia Hills had demanded the scrapping of this treaty. The Khasi Students' Union had staged a sit-in demonstration in collaboration with the North East Students' Organization in this connection.[51] Politicians like Paul Lyngdoh, who is now a cabinet minister of the state in charge of Urban Affairs, had urged the state government to make the relevant portions of this treaty non-applicable to Meghalaya.[52] In this connection, as has been noted earlier, the genuine Indian citizens or the Nepalis who have been born, brought up and stayed for many years in Meghalaya harbour suspicion for any new Nepali in town fearing that a wrong move by the latter may upset the equilibrium that has set in and bring about a backlash again. In fact, if possible, they discourage any new arrivals. The Indian Nepalis are being encouraged by Lyngdoh's political party, the KHNAM (Khun Hynniewtrep National Awakening Movement) to join hands with it to do away with the treaty.[53] It is apparent that the Khasis are apprehensive of being reduced to a minority in their own state if influx is not checked. Thus some enlightened Nepalis argue that if the Nepalis of Meghalaya pitch in with KHNAM, it would prove their solidarity with the tribals and be beneficial to the Nepalis in the long run.

Most Nepalis are unhappy about the nomenclature 'Nepali' because they conjure up images of being citizens of Nepal and they feel this would hamper any future possibility of ever being accepted as Indian citizens and being given their rightful place in Indian society. Some of them would much prefer the term 'Gorkha' as it is associated with valour, loyalty and integrity of the legendary Gorkha soldiers with their history of exemplary military service. They could at least hold their heads high.

Indeed, the Christian Nepalis have forged a strong link with the local Christians. But there are many highly respected Hindus who have strong ties with the Khasis. One of them, Shradda Pradhan, informed me that the tribal Khasi-Jaintias possess the same character and mindset with the Nepalis and she is more at home with them than with the fellow non-tribal community members. In the aftermath of the 1980s incident, many of them refused to leave Meghalaya because they had nowhere to go since they had made Shillong their home and the more fortunate ones had acquired land before the Land Transfer Act was passed. They also understand that the 'sons of the soil' policy in job avenues is prevalent in most areas and are gearing up for the challenge.

Most Nepalis are honest and sincere as they have always been. It is hoped that the future will see more tolerance, cooperation and understanding between them and the Khasi-Jaintias. The government need only make sure that the rights of the genuine Indian Nepalis are safeguarded.

NOTES AND REFERENCES

1. Leela D'Souza, 2003, "Identity Formation and Pluralism: The Need to Construct Identities", *Social Action*, October-December Issue, pp. 413-17.
2. *Ibid.*
3. *Ibid.*
4. Quoted in Anand Thapa, 2005, *A Critical Appraisal of Nepali Identity among the Nepali Christians in the North Eastern Region*, Unpublished Thesis, John Roberts Theological Seminary, Mawklot, Serampore University, 2006.
5. D'Souza, *op. cit.*, 417.
6. M.F. Bendle, 2002, "The Crisis of 'Identity' in High Modernity", *British Journal of Sociology*, 53(1): 1-18.
7. Y. Stavrakakis, 2001, "Identity, Political" in *Encyclopedia of Democratic Thought*, London, Routledge, p. 334.
8. A.J.M. Mills, 1853, *Report on the Khasi and Jaintia Hills*. Also see J.B. Bhattacharjee (ed.), 1986, *Studies in the History of Northeast India*, Shillong: NEHU Publications, 1986. 9 Bengal Political Correspondence, 23 February, 1835, Nos. 1-2.
10. Assam State Records, Letters received from Government; Vol. 46, 1864, Eden to Hopkinson, 31 December, 1864, No. 6188.
11. E.A. Gait, 1906, *A History of Assam*, Delhi: Surjeet Publications, Indian Reprint, 2004, pp. 387-91. See also P.R.T. Gurdon, *The Khasis*, Delhi: Cosmo Publications, First Published 1907, Indian Ed. 1980.
12. Editor's note, 1986, *The Gorkha Association, Shillong Centenary 1886-1986*, Shillong, the Gorkha Association, Shillong.
13. B.B. Chettri, 2006, 'The Settlement of Gorkhas and Premier Gorkha Educational Institutions in Shillong', Shillong, p. 29.
14. Interestingly, some Nepalis confessed that many of them are no longer honest and sincere as they were in the past. I have come to the conclusion

that these admirable values are somewhat diluted in most cases when they come into contact with other peoples and when they are educated.

15. Amena Passah, 2003, "Nepali Christians in the Khasi-Jaintia Hills", A.C. Sinha and T.B. Subba (eds), *The Nepalis in North East India*, Delhi: Indus Publishing House, pp. 277-78.
16. *Ibid.*, p. 278.
17. Suman Raj Timsina, *Nepali Community in India*, quoted in Thapa, *op. cit.*, p. 7.
18. B.B. Chettri, *op. cit.*, p. 29.
19. Sushila Tyagi, 1974, *Indo Nepalese Relations* (1858-1914), Delhi: O.K. Publishing House, p. 201.
20. B.B. Chettri, *op. cit.*, p. 29.
21. *Ibid.*
22. The first and fourth battalions were stationed in the Punjab Hills, the second at Dehradun and the third in the Simla Hills. See K. Mazumdar, 1973, *Anglo-Nepalese Relations in the Nineteenth Century*, Calcutta: East India Press, p. 157.
23. K.K. Muktan, 2002, *The Legendary Gorkhas*, Guwahati: Spectrum Publications, p. 50.
24. S.K. Bhuyan, 1949, *Anglo-Assamese Relations 1771-1826*, Guwahati: Lawyer's Book Stall, p. 519.
25. H.J. Huxford, *History of the 8th Gurkha Rifles 1824-1949.*
26. *Military Hospital, Shillong, Centenary Health Bulletin*, Shillong, Vol. 1, Issue 1, 20th January, 1997, pp. 6, 7.
27. Muktan, *op. cit.*, pp. 212-73.
28. Proceedings of the Chief Commissioner of Assam, Military Department. Shillong, 1989, dated 23rd January, 21st March and 9th April, quoted in Thapa, *op. cit.*, p. 15.
29. *Ibid.* It is important to note here that Khasi Syiems, unlike the Jaintia Syiems, were actually chiefs, and not kings.
30. For details see Muktan, *op. cit.*, pp. 65-66.
31. *Census of India, 1991, Meghalaya*, Shillong, Director of Census Operations.
32. This population was apparently a seasonal population.
33. *Census of Meghalaya, 2001*, Director of Census Operations, Meghalaya.
34. As calculated by L.R. Lyngdoh, Statistical Assistant, Census Operations, Meghalaya, 2001.
35. Passah, *op. cit.*, p. 279.
36. About 47 per cent of the national income goes to only 10 per cent of the population.
37. John Burbank, 1991, *Nepal*, Singapore, Times Edition Pvt. Ltd., p. 31. For details see Passah, *op. cit.*, pp. 279, 280.
38. Ludwig Stiller, 1976, *Silent Cry*, Kathmandu: Sah Yogi Prakashan, p. 66.
39. N.R. Shreshtha, 1990, *Landlessness and Migration in Nepal*, Colorado: West View Press, pp. 292-97.

40. *Census of India 1931*, Vol. 3, Part 1, Calcutta, Central Publication Branch, p. 53.
41. *Ibid.*, p. 26.
42. Lopita Nath, 2003, 'Conflict-Afflicted Nepalis of Assam: The Reality', *The Nepalis in North East India*, A.C. Sinha and T.B. Subba (eds), *op. cit.*, p. 210.
43. *Ibid.*, p. 211.
44. Detailed information in Passah, *op. cit.*, p. 291.
45. Puran Bista, "Casting ethnic slur on Nepalis", Ekantipur.com, 24th January, 2005.
46. Utpala Sewa is a Reader, Department of English, North-Eastern Hill University, Shillong. Her father, Lal Bahadur Sewa, was an IPS officer and had died in harness. In his honour, his bust was constructed and is still there at the IPS Academy, Hyderabad. A medal instituted in his name is awarded every year.
47. In this connection, it is pertinent to know that the Khasi Students' Union (KSU) is again active and is conducting eviction drives against Bangladeshi intruders. In fact, the Nepalis should know that they are not singled out, but they happen to fall into the category of non Khasis and hence suffer from the same predicament as other non-Khasis do in Meghalaya.
48. Thapa, *op. cit.*, p. 19.
49. For details, see Passah, *op. cit.*, pp. 283, 292.
50. The Meghalaya Transfer of Land (Regulation) Act, 1971, pp. 1, 3, 4, 5.
51. *The Shillong Times*, Vol. LX1, No. 154, January 17, 2006.
52. *Ibid.*, p. 5.
53. *Mawphor*, Vol. X11(17), No. 23, January 28, 2006.

16

History of Nepali Settlement in Assam

NIRA DEVI

It is widely believed by scholars that there were matrimonial and other cultural relationships between Nepal and Assam since ancient times. According to the famous historian Kanak Lal Baruah, Rajyamati, the daughter of the famous King Harshabarman was married to Jayadeva II, a king of Nepal. Similarly, the Nepalese Princess Ratnakumari was married to Biswa Singha, the founder of the Koch dynasty.[1] Srimanta Sankardeva propounded the Vaishnavaite religion in Assam and he asked the people of all castes and creeds to follow his religion. It has been mentioned by Maheswar Neog, ex-President of Assam Sahitya Sabha, the highest literary organization of Assam that Ratikanta Upadhyaya, one of Sankardeva's disciples of Nepali origin was made the *satradhikar* (in charge) of the Nepalu *satra* in Teok.[2]

During the second decade of the 19th century both Assam and Nepal faced a tragedy. In the year 1814 a historic war was fought between the British and Nepal, which is known as the Anglo-Gorkha war. In this war, 4,629 British soldiers armed with modern weapons fought with only 2,600 Nepali soldiers, who were armed only with the traditional weapon *khukuri*. Though Nepal lost the battle, it proved the extraordinary skills of Gorkha soldiers in the warfare. Thereafter the Treaty of Segowli was completed in the year 1916 whereby Nepal had to transfer some of its bordering areas like Darjeeling, Sikkim, Shimla, Nainital, Kumaon and Garwal to the British India. Thereafter the Nepalis residing in those areas automatically became the subjects of the British India. Moreover, impressed by their bravery the British started recruiting Gorkha soldiers in large numbers who mostly settled in India after retirement from service.

From 1817 to 1819 Assam was twice invaded by the Burmese and life became miserable in Assam due to torture by the Burmese invaders, which is locally remembered as *Manar Upadrab* (torture by Burmese). The then king Purandar Singh fled from Assam and requested the East India Company to fight against the Mann (Burmese). The East India Company brought the Assam Light Infantry from Cuttack which comprised of Gorkha soldiers. A war broke out on 5th March, 1824 and the Gorkha soldiers showed extraordinary courage to send back the Burmese forces to their country. The Yandaboo Treaty was completed in 1826 and Assam was brought under the British rule. During that time Assam was covered with thick forest and the Gorkhas were employed for clearing the forest, necessary surveys and settlement activities. Company insisted that the Gorkha soldiers should reside in Assam after retirement so that their sons could also be recruited in the army.

Gorkha soldiers on their periodic visit to homeland were reported to have encouraged youths to migrate to Assam where the prospects of employment as soldiers and labourers in coal and oil fields were bright. They began to migrate to this region with family and livestock population. Assam with its relatively sparse population and extensive grassland along the Brahmaputra River attracted the Nepalis settlers to settle along the riverine tract.

Gangmouthan Gaon Panchayat

The latitudinal extension of the Gangmouthan Gaon Panchayat on which the present article is based is from 26° 45′ N to 26°48′ N and longitudinal extension from 93°18′ E to 93° 20′ E. It is situated in the southwestern part of Behali Development Block and the area occupies a part of interfluves on the north bank of the river Brahmaputra. It is bordered by rivers Borgang on the west and Behali on the east, separating it from Baghmara Block and Telengania Gaon Panchayat respectively. The southern boundary is demarcated by the Brahmaputra itself and on its northern boundary lies the Borgang Gaon Panchayat. The total geographical area of the panchayat is 20.06 square kilometres with a population of 1245 persons as per 2001 census, which accounts for about 11.74 and 9.09 per cent of the block's area and population respectively.

The area comprises 8 revenue villages, viz., Bahbari Pathar, Gangmouthan, Nakania Pathar, Nilbari, Khelmati, N.C. Borgang Chapori and Borbheel Kachari. A portion of Borbheel division of Borgang tea estate has also been included in the study area. The population of the area is composed of five communities, which are Assamese, Nepali, Bengali, tea and ex-tea garden labourers and a few Biharis.

Peopling of Gangmouthan Gaon Panchayat

Nepali: During 1850s sporadic skirmishes occurred in eastern part of Nepal between Bahuns and Chhetris on the one hand and Rais, Limbus, and Magars on the other. The former, who were recent migrants to the region and were numerically less significant had to incur heavy losses due to these conflicts. On the other hand, agriculture held little promise due to the rugged topography, erratic rainfall, lack of irrigation facilities, primitive farm technology and rural indebtedness. This motivated many of the high caste Nepalis to leave Nepal for a new life in Assam.

The early Nepali settlers of Gangmouthan Gaon Panchayat belonged to Bahun and Chhetri castes who had migrated from Ilam, Jhapa, Panchthar, Dhankuta, Okhaldhunga and Taplejung districts of eastern Nepal.[3] They built *khutis* (cow sheds) in Jorkhutimukh, Company Chapori, Naste Tapu, and Arimarakhuti in Kaziranga area. They converted the milk into curd or clarified butter and exchanged them with food items in the local areas. Majority of the Nepalis had their grazing lands in Kaziranga forest for which they paid tax to the British government.

Through these pioneers the news of abundance of luxuriant grassland as well as cultivable waste land available in Assam reached Nepal which further attracted Nepali graziers and cultivators.[4]

The proposal to declare Kaziranga as a reserved forest for conservation of one-horned rhinoceros severely restricted the area available for cattle or buffalo rearing in that area during 1920s. Moreover, occasional cattle disease—Rinderpest—locally known as *goti* spread in the *khutis* causing death of a large number of cattle. So the Nepali *khuti* owners slowly shifted their occupation from dairy farming to agriculture. In due course of time the people of the next generation got educated and took active participation in the Indian freedom movement along with the local people. Two schools—Gangmouthan and Hatibandha—were already imparting education in the area since 1914. With the establishment of Behali High School in 1941 the literacy level of this region greatly increased. These factors caused a considerable shift of occupation from primary to tertiary sector in the latter half of the 20th century.

Assamese: The Assamese are the original people of the village whose arrival dates back to 15th century when Srimanta Sankardeva came with his disciples to Gangmouthan for the propagation of

Vaishnavaite religion.[5] A second large group of them came from the south bank of the Brahmaputra to settle in that area after the Burmese war. The Assamese were basically agriculturists and they cultivated paddy.

There are 1790 households in Gangmouthan out of which Nepali and Assamese households number 460 and 277, which accounts for 25.7 and 15.5 per cent of the total population respectively. 15 per cent of the households were taken as sample for the study on which this article is based and hence, 69 and 42 households respectively of the two communities were surveyed.

Demographic Characteristics

Sex ratio: Sex ratio is an index of socio-economic condition of an area or a population. It is defined as the number of females per thousand males, which are 964 for the Assamese and 1052 for the Nepalis. In other words, the Nepalis have a positive sex ratio whereas the Assamese have negative sex ratio.

Literacy: Literacy reflects the socio-economic, cultural and political levels of a society. This element must be taken into account in any study on human resources of an area. Community-wise and sex-wise variation in literacy is shown in Table 16.1.

Table 16.1: Community-wise Variation in Literacy in Gangmouthan

Community	*Population*			*Literates*		
	Total	*Male*	*Female*	*Total*	*Male*	*Female*
Assamese	271	138	133	244 (90%)	123 (89%)	121 (91%)
Nepali	462	225	237	390 (84%)	206 (92%)	184 (78%)

Source: Computed from field survey conducted in 1999.

Table 16.1 shows very high percentage of literacy among both the Assamese and Nepali communities. The successful spread of education in Gangmouthan is closely linked with the freedom movement. During 1890s the students of this area had to go to Jalukbari Lower Primary School located in Telengania Gaon Panchayat at a distance of about 5 kms from the village. After the establishment of Hatibandha Middle School in 1914 in Gangmouthan, education of children became easier. In the year 1941 the erstwhile Behali High School was established under the initiation of the people of the locality. Here it may be mentioned that Behali High School was the third high school in the then Tezpur subdivision of Darrang District. It was founded by the freedom fighter Chabilal Upadhyaya, Bogiram Saikia, Hari Prasad Upadhyaya, Narapati Muktan, Benimadhab Choudhury, Kumud Sharmah and Bishnulal Upadhyaya who was also the founder headmaster.

With the establishment of Behali High School the level of education among local people rose tremendously. Moreover, the school played an important role in generating social interaction amongst the people of the area lying between the rivers Buroi on the east and Ghiladhari on the west.[6]

Table 16.2: Level of Educational Achievement in Gangmouthan GP

Education Level	*Primary*	*Middle School*	*High School*	*H.S.L.C.*	*Secondary*	*Graduate*	*Post Graduate*	*Technical**	*Non-Technical***	*Total*
Assamese	15 (6%)	34 (14%)	96 (39%)	21 (9%)	37 (15%)	37 (15%)	4 (2%)	–	–	244
Nepali	43 (11%)	68 (18%)	100 (26%)	58 (15%)	54 (14%)	50 (13%)	6 (2%)	2 (1%)	4 (1%)	385

Source: Computed from field survey conducted in 1999.

* Bachelor of Engineering, Bachelor of Technology, etc.

** Doctors, lawyers, etc.

It is evident from Table 16.2 that there is no visible difference in levels of educational achievement between the Assamese and the Nepali. However, the achievements of Nepalis in this gaon panchayat are quite praiseworthy. Till 1943 the number of graduates in Darrang district was zero but by 1971 there were 46 graduates, 5 Master of Arts, 2 BT (Bachelor in Teaching), 1 SDC (Sub Deputy Collector), 2 MBBS, 2 Asstt. Engineers, 1 Magistrate, and 1 Lawyer. There are 92 graduates in Tezpur subdivision of Darrang District whereas in Mangaldai subdivision there is hardly 1 graduate and at present there are only 2 graduates in North Lakhimpur subdivision.[7]

Cultural Interaction

In Gangmouthan the settlement of people belonging to different communities has significantly contributed to the growth of ethnic and cultural diversity and the long and continued interaction among them has significantly transformed the socio-cultural fabric of the area.

The Nepalis of Assam have now accepted Assamese not only as a medium of communication but also as a medium of instruction in the schools from the primary level. Although the erstwhile Behali High School established mainly under the initiative of the Assamese Nepalis, Assamese was adopted as the medium of instruction unanimously. Not a single school in the area has any other language as medium of instruction other than Assamese. Many Nepali students have shown proficiency in Assamese language at different levels of education. Many of them have earned repute in Assamese literary circles for their contribution to Assamese language and culture. The Nepalis have adopted the Assamese language to such an extent that they have even given up the original Nepali words and started using the Assamese words in their day to day communication, as shown in Table 16.3 below.

Table 16.3: Assamisation of Nepali Language

Assamese	*Nepali*	*Modified Nepali*
Kuhiyar	Ukhu	Kuiyer
Darmaha	Talab	Darmaha
Naw	Dunga	Naw
Dalang	Pool	Dolong
Anarash	Bhui katar	Anarash
Haladhi	Besar	Hardi
Kauri	Kag	Kaurhi
Kal	Kera	Kol
Khirki	Jhyal	Khirki
Muna	Jhola	Mona
Siyahi	Mashi	Siahi
Uth-nam	Charnu-jharnu	Uth-nam

Interestingly some Assamese school-going girls have shown exceptional efficiency in singing both Assamese and Nepali songs. Nepali young stars can sing Assamese modern songs, *Borgeet* (religious songs of Assam), *Bihu* (main festival of Assam) songs and perform Bihu dance. There are instances of honouring Nepali girls as *Bihu* kuoris, *mou kuoris* during the cultural programmes held during Bihu. During the *Magh Bihu* festival celebrated during the harvest season the Nepalis of Assam make *Bhelaghar* (a hut made of bamboo and thatch for the festival) and celebrate *Bihu* whereas in other parts of India or in Nepal they celebrate only *Makar-Sankranti* during the season by taking holy dip in the rivers and taking boiled tubers and other sweet dishes. Inter-community marriages between the Assamese and Nepalis have been taking place and are being accepted by both the communities. Economic interaction is also taking place between these two communities to a large extent. Many of the Assamese families have started keeping *khutis* in the *chaporis* (riverine islands) which was absolutely a traditional activity of the Nepalis till 1960 or so.

Economic Organization

In Gangmouthan, where the inhabitants are of diverse ethnic origin, there appears to be wide variation in the proportion of workers and non-workers as also in male-female work participation between the Assamese and Nepalis, as shown in Table 16.4.

Table 16.4: Workers and Non-workers: Gangmouthan

Community	*Total Population*			*Workers*			*Non workers*		
	T	*M*	*F*	*T*	*M*	*F*	*T*	*M*	*F*
Assamese	271	138	133	79 (29%)	73 (53%)	6 (5%)	192 (71%)	65 (47%)	127 (95%)
Nepali	462	225	237	150 (32%)	116 (52%)	34 (14%)	312 (68%)	109 (48%)	203 (86%)

Source: Computed from field survey 1999.

The overall participation rate was found to be more or less equal between the Nepalis and Assamese of this gaon panchayat, but the female workers' proportion is much lower among the Assamese than that of the Nepalis. Obviously the share of female non-workers would be higher among the Assamese than among the Nepalis. The work participation rate among the population also depends on their dependency ratio, which is governed largely by the age structure of the population.[8] The dependency ratio shows the ratio of the inactive population who cannot contribute to the production process but have to be fed and clad. This imposes a great burden on the community's economy. Thus, higher the dependency load, greater is the demographic investment required.[9] The variation of dependency ratio of the sample population is shown in Table 16.5.

Table 16.5: Dependency Ratio: Gangmouthan

Community	Population				Dependency Ratio	Activity Rate (Total)
	Total	Children	Old	Adult		
Assamese	271	61	38	172	58	29.2
Nepali	462	102	60	300	54	32.5

Source: Computed from field survey 1999.

$$\text{Dependency Ratio} = \frac{\text{Number of Children } (<15 \text{ Years}) + \text{Old Peoples } (>65 \text{ Years}) \times 100}{\text{Number of Adults}}$$

$$\text{Or } \frac{\text{Economically Inactive People} \times 100}{\text{Economically Active People} \times 100}$$

It has been observed that dependency ratio of the Assamese is greater than that of the Nepalis. This may be attributed partially to less female participation among the Assamese in different productive occupations, as seen in Table 16.5 above.

So far the work participation of the Nepali females is concerned, there is no inhibition against female employment, and therefore, the participation rate is higher among them in comparison to the Assamese females. The history of female participation in gainful profession outside the family in Gangmouthan is quite old. It was during early 1930s that women of the area started getting exposed to outside world and were trying to learn certain skills along with their males. During mid 1930s some of the women from the Nepali community opened the door for female participation in work force and engaged themselves in teaching. They were followed by the Assamese women in late 1940s. Unlike the Assamese females the Nepali females are engaged in both primary and tertiary activities.

Main Finding

The overall population figures and economic attainments of the two communities have been analyzed by means of a set of indicators like literacy rate, workers-non-workers, and dependency ratio. After analyzing the components ranking is done following Kendall's ranking coefficient method. To examine the relative difference regarding each component the community which scores highest in the case of an indicator has been assigned rank 1. Similarly the ranking for the other community has been done on the basis of the relative strength. Finally, a ranking co-efficient has been obtained by adopting the following formula:

$$\text{Ranking Co-efficient} = \frac{\text{Total of the Ranks}}{\text{Total No. of Items}}$$

The community which has a lower ranking is better off compared to those having higher co efficient. Hence, the Nepalis of Gangmouthan have attained better standard of living than the Assamese in relation to the above mentioned indicators.

Table 16.6: Calculation of Rank Coefficient

Total	*Assamese*	*Nepali*
Total literacy rate	1	2
Male literacy	2	1
Female literacy	1	2
Dependency rate	2	1
Male workers	1	2
Female Workers	2	1
Mean per capita income	1	2
Modal income	2	1
Expenses on travel	2	1
TOTAL	**14**	**13**
Rank coefficient	**1.56**	**1.44**

Conclusion

The Assamese and Nepalis of Gangmouthan started with two different economically gainful activities and despite settling in the Gaon Panchayat later than the Assamese the latter have made a lot of progress educationally and economically. Thus it is evident that Nepalis are making satisfactory progress in Assam. The challenge ahead lies in sustaining the progress of this community, which seems increasingly difficult in view of the shrinking economic and other opportunities as more and more Assamese people are competing for the same resources.

REFERENCES

1. Cited in S.R. Jaisi, 1990, *Itihas Ko Adhar Ma Asamey Nepali Haru*, Digboi: Bodh Kumari Smriti Prakashan.
2. Bishnulal Upadhyaya, 2002, *Nepali Satradhikar Ratikanta Upadhyaya*, Borgang: Author.
3. M.C. Bhuyan, 1972, Immigration to Assam Valley: A Geographical Analysis, *North Eastern Geographer*, 3(1): 177-89.
4. M. Bhattacharya, 1997, *Srimanta Sankardevar Sthapita Gangmouthanar Itibritta*, Borgang: Author.
5. Bishnulal Upadhyaya, 1971, *Asamey Nepaliharu*, Kathmandu: Bhanu Prakashan.
6. *Ibid.*
7. R.C. Chandna, 1986, *Geography of Population*, New Delhi: Kalyani Publisher.
8. B.N. Ghosh, 1985, *Fundamentals of Population Geography*, New Delhi: Sterling Publishers.
9. M.G. Kendall, 1939, "The Geographical Distribution of Crop Productivity in England", *Journal of the Royal Statistical Society*, 162: 24-28.

17

Gorkhas as Colliers: Labour Recruitment and Racial Discourse in the Coal Mines of Assam

TEJIMALA GURUNG

The migration and settlement of the Gorkhas or Nepalis in Northeast India began in the nineteenth century, with the beginning of colonial rule in Assam.[1] The Gorkhas who were brought in as recruits to the British army and as civilian wasteland settlers, who were to 'people' the scantily populated Northeast India, were essentially sponsored by the colonial state. On retirement the ex-soldiers were even given lands by the government to settle in the region. Besides them, there were other forms of migration too—as porters, herdsmen and marginal farmers.[2] The British either created the conditions or sponsored such migrations from outside the region. These migrants undertook diverse occupations to survive in alien conditions. They took to agricultural farming, dairy farming, professional grazing, small time trading and rubber tapping.[3] However one wave of migration of Nepalis, which is not adequately known and highlighted, is to the coal fields of Upper Assam primarily as labourers. This migration too was induced by the colonial state. From the nineteenth century, under colonial intervention, private enterprises in the mining industries had begun in Assam, notable among them being oil and coal. Since labour was not available locally, the coal industry had to depend on migrant labour. But most of the migrant labour, which was mainly indentured from the tribal areas of Bengal Presidency, was absorbed in the tea industry. Plainsmen like the Assamese could not be recruited for the jobs in coalfields for they refused to work as labourers as they were self-sufficient. The Nepalis were then already on the migratory route to Darjeeling tea estates and army recruitment centres in various parts of

India like Shillong, Darjeeling, and Dehradun. They also arrived in the coalfields of Assam to do the jobs that no one else was willing or available to do.

Beginning of Coal Mining in Assam

The British were in search of a local source of coal as fuel from the very beginning of their advent in Assam. This was because the administration had to carry coal from Raniganj in Bengal by railway up to Calcutta from where it depended on river transport. It raised the cost of transportation tremendously. Only a local supply could make it cost effective. The first recorded notice of the existence of coal in Assam was by Lieutenant Wilcox, the Revenue Surveyor posted at Sadiya who in April 1825 discovered coal beds in the Dissang Valley region in Upper Assam. Subsequently he found such belts in the bed of Buridihing River at Supkong.[4] The discovery by Wilcox inspired the first Agent to the Governor General, North-East Frontier, David Scott, as mining coal locally would make the introduction of stream navigation in the Brahmaputra easier and cheaper. In 1826, Wilcox informed Scott about the easy procurability of coal in Upper Assam. A series of correspondences later[5] Scott finally sent some specimens of coal to Calcutta for the perusal of the Government of Bengal. In 1827, Wilcox led a sponsored expedition which resulted in the discovery of a coal mine twenty miles east of Rangpur in Upper Assam. Meanwhile coal was also discovered along the Someshwari River in the Garo hills. However Scott concentrated on the coal mines of Upper Assam. Mining had started in 1828 itself when C.A. Bruce excavated about five thousand maunds of coal.[6]

In the beginning the Fort William authorities in Calcutta gave little encouragement to the mining of coal in Assam. The meagre demand, shortage of labour, transportation problem and the then insecure state of this frontier made them apprehensive of undertaking any large scale mining operation. But the establishment of Assam Company in 1838, and prosperity of the growing tea industry necessitated increasing supply of coal which made the government turn its attention to the coal of Assam. The Assam Company began to quarry its own requirement from the Jaipur mines in Upper Assam from 1840. A Coal Committee was set up by the administration in 1838 to report on the actual deposit and quality of coal in the region. By 1847 Major Hannay had started two quarries in Jaipur. The government started the steamer service in Brahmaputra River from 1847 which enhanced the demand for coal.

By 1867 the coal mines were opened for private operation. However, not much progress in the exploitation of the coal deposits and recruitment of miners was made until the formation of the Assam Railways and Trading Company in 1881. Two years later the coalfields in Upper Assam were connected by railway lines. In 1882 the Makum (Ledo) field in Upper Assam was taken over by the Company on lease. Work in the Tikak, upper Ledo and Ledo valley mines had also begun in the same year and on the Namdang and Tirap grants in 1897-98. In 1893 the stocks of the Assam Railways and Trading Company at Calcutta amounted to 60,000 tonnes. By the beginning of the twentieth century Assam had become self-sufficient in coal. In 1903 the total output was 293,000 tonnes. There were 1200 labourers working under the supervision of European miners.[7] At this stage there were very few Nepali workers whose recruitment started later as detailed below.

As the coal industry was ready to take off, it confronted major problems in its development. Most important problem was that of transportation. To combat this bottleneck railway lines were sought to be constructed, which happened only by the end of the nineteenth century. In 1882 the first railway line was opened from Dibrugarh Steamer Ghat to Jaipur Road. Two years later the coalfields of Upper Assam were connected by railway lines. The other major problem was that of labour. Initially the local labourers and Naga tribes were sought to be engaged as labourers but both were not interested in working as mining labour force. The Nagas were particularly afraid of tunneling or mining. Hence mine workers from the Bengal field were imported. In the early years the colliery labour force not only included men from the then undivided United Provinces, Bihar and Central Provinces, Makranis and Peshwaris but also Chinese. The Ledo and Tikak estates situated in Lakhimpur and Sibsagar districts in Upper Assam on contracts. But the overworked, unhealthy and deplorable conditions in which the labourers worked became a concern. A committee was set up in 1894 to look into the conditions of the colliery labourers which not only recommended improvement in the working conditions but also that only certain classes of people should be recruited in these coal mines as others were not 'racially' suitable for the hard work that colliery required. The committee recommended not to recruit coolies from up-country, i.e., north western region of India as they were unsuitable for the hard work required in coal fields and restrict labour recruitment to the tribal areas of eastern and central India. The communities found suitable for such hard work were mainly tribes like the Santhal, Borah, Bourni and Dhanger from eastern and central India.

It was in this context that the Company thought of recruiting the hardy Gorkhas as colliery labour force.

Gorkhas as Colliery Labour Force

Once it was decided by the committee for reasons noted above to try out 'martial' Gorkhas as colliery labourers, efforts to recruit them started in right earnest. Initially, the Assam Railways and Trading Company recruited Nepali labourers for the coal mines from Darjeeling[8] though importation of labourers from Darjeeling was officially prohibited by the Bengal government vide notification [No. 3293-TC of 1st November, 1907]. These labourers were not placed under any contract. On putting in about 300 days' work the cost of the journey home was paid by the Company. When the Company found that recruiting from Darjeeling, from 1912 the Nepali coolies were recruited by the Company through the Tea Districts Labour Association, Gorakhpur[9] in the United Provinces. But recruiting from Gorakhpur did not suit the Company for it could be done only between January and March, whereas labour was really needed in June and July. In December 1913 the Company was able to recruit only 284 through the sub-agency at Basti, 50 kilometres from Gorakhpur.[10] To attract labourers favourable terms were offered. The recruitment was on 'short term' agreements not exceeding 12 months and the Company undertook to repatriate the men at the end of the term for which they were recruited. Since 1916, the coolies recruited had to be put before the Gorkha Recruiting Officer, Gorakhpur, to prevent recruitment of men of the military castes. The recruitment of Nepalis as coolies was preferred over any other class of men such as the Makranis [from Makran and Peshwar in present Pakistan] and Bengali labours. As G. C. Webster, the Colliery Superintendent, remarked in 1913 'they [Nepalis] will do any kind of work they are put on to do, whereas this cannot be said of any other class of labour'. Also 'they are far more tractable to reasons...make most trustworthy and capable men inside the colliery.' Besides, large numbers of Nepali subjects entered Assam through other than regular recruiting agencies. Many of them were enticed by the *sardars* to the coal mines. Recruitment of labour was thus both through official and private channels.

During the First World War the recruitment of Nepalis for other than military purposes was stopped. In 1918 the Gorakhpur depot was temporarily closed.[11] In 1919 under arrangement made by the Government of India with the Government of Nepal the recruitment of Nepalis for industrial purposes in the forests, tea gardens and coal mines was resumed for temporary employment during the dry and winter months.[12] The orders of the Government of India issued on 9th April, 1919 stated specifically that 'The recruiting of Nepalese subjects for temporary employment during the dry or winter months in tea gardens, forests and coal mines may be resumed provided that no attempt is made to recruit inside Nepal territory. The Government of India also considers it advisable that the employment of Nepalese of the fighting classes who are of military age should be discouraged as far as possible.' The orders did not define what period was intended by the "dry and winter months". The impression created amongst the Company was simply that the recruitment of Nepalis on earlier basis might be resumed. In 1919 the Gorakhpur depot was reopened for recruiting them. Large numbers of them were recruited and contracts were entered into with Nepali coolies on terms inconsistent with the conditions agreed upon by the Government of India and the Nepal Government.

Mode of Recruitment

The system of recruitment of Gorkhas as coolies in the coal mine of Assam was known as the Short Term Contract System. Under this system the labourers were recruited temporarily for a period not exceeding one year within which they were to be repatriated at their employer's expenses. A depot was opened at Gorakhpur at the Indo-Nepal border for the recruitment of the Gorkha labourers for the collieries from where they were then transported to the mines of Upper Assam. The European employers were given strict instructions to scrupulously follow the system. The District Labour Association was provided with the instruction that the coolies were required for a year and they were to be told that they would be employed for ten months and then repatriated. The other two months were to be used as journey time between Nepal and India. The short time contract provided for the repatriation of the coolie within the period of contract. The recruitment was done through *sardars*, *chowkidars* and contractors of Nepali origin who were recruited by mining companies like the Assam Railway and Trading Company. A Nepali *sardar* when required for recruiting purposes was given a license in the Ledo Labour Office by the Assistant Labour Superintendent. A questionnaire was then filled in for the *sardar* in the Ledo Labour Office. The *sardar* took his license in triplicate to the Dibrugarh Court where it was countersigned by the District Magistrate, one copy being kept in the Court at Dibrugarh.

The *sardar* then proceeded to Gorakhpur, at the Indo-Nepal border point, where the recruitment would take place. On arrival there he appeared before the Tea District Labour Association Depot and from there he was sent to the District Magistrate who lent approval of his license. The *sardar* then commenced recruiting and gathered them at Gorakhpur Tea Districts Labour Association Depot. The recruits were examined there by the Civil Surgeon, who was paid 8 annas per head, and provided a fitness certificate. The recruits were then sent to the Military Recruiting Officer who then selected from the gathering some for the army and left the rest for the coal mines. The officer issued a certificate stating that he had examined the recruits and explained to them that they were going to the coal mines and ascertained that they were willing to proceed there. The Tea District Labour Association's local agent at Gorakhpur then forwarded them on after he had made certain that the men understood where they were going and the rate of payment. They were then inoculated and vaccinated and given a full clothing outfit and put on the journey. On arrival at Ledo, they were examined again. They were supplied with a full week's ration and then channeled to their respective *sardars*.

The coolies thus recruited were managed entirely, except for work in the colliery by Nepali staff recruited for the purpose. The colliery labour except fitters was paid a day's wage and received their wages fortnightly on a fixed day. Most of the coal filling was done on *ticca*, or a contract payment and this was the chief work on which the Nepalis were employed. The contract was taken by a head *sardar*. Labourers were generally paid individually. In case of a contract for filling containers with excavated coal, the Company paid each person Re. 1 per day out of the contractor's money and the contractor then paid his people the extra they had earned above the Re. 1 per day. Coal cutting was either on *ticca* or day's work and the coal cutters drew their own wages. The contractors were paid a commission on the number of tubs filled or on the number of *hazrees* or attendance. The coolies worked officially for a nine hour shift excepting *ticca* coal cutters who usually had a six hour shift.

It is evident that the entire procedure was based on a lot of formalities and institutionalized bureaucratic procedures. It had an inbuilt potential for corruption and mis-utilisation which the *sardars*, European officers, and recruiting officers freely indulged in. It was this rampant corruption of the *sardars* in alliance with the European owners which often resulted in mal-treatment of the recruits. On enquiry it was found that the sardars were interested in keeping the labour in the colliery, as they drew a commission on the number of days each coolie worked, and in many cases concealed from the Europeans that they wanted to leave the mines and go home. Some times the coolies were recruited for a term of six months by the recruiting *sardars*, though their instructions were not to take men for less than a term of one year and the Company understood that they had agreed to work for a year. This was a fraud perpetrated on the recruits quite often. A large number of Gorkhas actually agreed for six months during the dry winter season and return home by the advent of rains when they could go back to farming. But once they completed the six months they were told that the contract was for one full year and they could not be allowed to go back.[13]

Opposition to Gorkha Recruitment in Coalmines

There was a murmur of opposition to the recruitment of Gorkhas in the collieries of Assam from the very beginning. It was not just from the Royal Government of Nepal which protested the ill-treatment of its subjects in the coal mines by European miners but also by British army officers who felt that such recruitment of martial Gorkhas in trivial jobs like the coal mines was wasteful of human resources. The issue was reopened in December 1922 when in a demi-official letter to the British envoy at the Court of Nepal, the recruiting officer for the Gorkhas, Gorakhpur, Major Brook Northey informed that the Tea District Labour Association was busy recruiting 2000 coolies for the coal mines in Assam. The classes comprised all the best fighting castes like Magar, Gurung, Thakur, Chhetri, etc.[14] The concern of the military was that such recruitment would lead to a drain of the manpower and the physique of Nepal from where it recruited its fighting men. This would affect recruitment by cutting into the supply of Gorkhas into the colonial armed force. In February 1923 Captain Lal Dhoj, an officer of the Nepal Government, while on a visit to Kamakhya, Guwahati happened to hear about a large number of Nepalis who had been enticed to work in the mines. After a trip to Ledo where he made private enquiries *incognito*, he submitted a petition in March 1923, to the Governor of Assam which highlighted that many Nepalis including ex-sepoys and military castes were working in the coal mines of Makum viz., Ledo, Tikak, Golai, Rangring (Namdang), Lekhapani, and Margherita in very harsh conditions. Many of these coolies had been lured by false inducements and forcibly kept. The point emphasized was that the Nepali labour was not doing well in the coal mines and was anxious to get back to their homes. Lal Dhoj's memorandum highlighted for the first time the fraudulent practices in Gorkha recruitment as well as their plight in the coal mines in Assam.

> I then went to Ledo coal mine and there to my great surprise found even pensioned soldiers working as ordinary coolies. I heard from them and other Nepalis working in the coal mines that they were persuaded to come there on the assurances given by Nepali contractors working under the Company that they would be employed as Commissariat Officers, soldiers and policemen etc on handsome salaries with free clothing and good ration and that they would have never come to coal mines had they known it before hand. I also found several persons of position and means having their homes in Nepal actually working as coolies. I found a Brahmin gentleman who had come with his servant to offer oblations and funeral cakes at Gaya, working as a coolie. As he was a new comer and did not know much about Railway traveling some contractor's men got hold of him telling him that he will be taken to Gaya where they were also going brought him to Ledo. There are several instances like this...I also heard long stories of cruelty and ill treatment which shocked me very much...the condition in which I found the Nepalis was indeed very miserable. They were poorly clad and they all seemed to be in very poor health. I also understand that being unable to endure their lot large numbers escape from the coal mines from time to time.[15]

The memorandum created quite a stir in the British government as it was bound by an agreement with the Government of Nepal on the issue of recruitment of Nepalis in India. It therefore instituted an enquiry into the allegation made by Lal Dhoj. In March 1923, the Nepal Durbar moved the Government of India directly on the above issue. The complaints made by the Nepal Durbar were:

(1) Fraudulent recruitment of the Nepalis.
(2) Forcible detention of the labour and compulsion to work under bad conditions.
(3) Forcible prevention of attempts to escape and punishments of such attempts by corporal punishment or otherwise cruelly treated.
(4) Heavy death rate among the coolies.

(5) Inability of the coolies to find anyone to whom they can make the complaints.
(6) Employment of Gorkhalis of the fighting classes as coolies.
(7) Enticement of boys for employment as coolies.[16]

In the early period of 1923 the issue of Gorkha recruitment in the coal mines in Assam became a subject of governmental enquiry in Assam.[17] On the basis of the complaints of the Nepal Government of fraudulent recruitment and ill-treatment, the Government of India directed the Assam Government to institute an enquiry into the matter. The enquiry was aimed primarily to check the recruitment of certain sections of the Gorkhas whom the colonial state represented as 'martial castes' for commercial or industrial purposes. This would be detrimental for the colonial state which sought to protect its interest as evidenced by the enquiry conducted for the purpose. The enquiry brought into light several aspects relating to the process and terms of recruitment of Nepali labour to the coal mines as well as the condition of labour therein.

Accordingly under instructions from the Government of India, in April 1923, H.C. Barnes, the officiating Commissioner of Assam Valley Division, was ordered by the Assam Government to hold an enquiry into the question of recruitment of Gorkhas of the military classes in the coal mines. The enquiry revealed that the recruitment procedure of the Assam Bengal and Railway Trading Company was in contravention of the provisions laid down in 1919 and highlighted the forcible condition under which the labour was retained at the collieries. The labour had been recruited on false pretences and large number of Gorkhas of the fighting castes and of ex-sepoys was also employed in the mines. The coolies though recruited for a year on the express condition of repatriation within the period of contract were not repatriated, though anxious to leave. The coolies, though technically free, were in reality treated as indentured labour. The total Nepali labour force in the mines in 1921, 1922 and 1923 numbered 1357, 1368 and 1906 respectively. The Company's books showed that in these first two years the numbers of coolies running away from the mines were 305 and 247. In 1922 the Company had repatriated 164 Nepali coolies. The Company on its part pleaded that it misunderstood the resumption of recruitment in 1919 as meaning the earlier practice of recruitment for a year and that the Labour Association was engaging the men for this period. The Company alleged that the true reason for the sudden depletion of a 'well cared for and contented labour force' was because the Nepal Durbar considers it derogatory to the state and to the Gorkha or a Nepali to serve as a coolie in the tea gardens and coal mines.

The outcome of the enquiry was that hundreds of Nepalis working in the collieries had to be repatriated by the Company. The Nepali labour formed the bulk of the labour force of the Company in the mines.[18] The Agent of the Company admitted that the tea industry, oil industry, shipping, Gauhati Waterworks, mills, and mining industries of the province would be ruined at least for the season. Under orders from the Assam Government 598 coolies out of a total of 1900 were repatriated in the month of May 1923 itself. The remainders were to be sent in subsequent batches every month. *The Times of Assam*, in its issue dated 19th May, 1923, gave vent to the fears that such a sudden exodus of such a large number of men would not only directly entail a reduction in the output of coal but lead to a rise in the price of coal and affect all the factories and mills depending upon Assam coal. The Assam Government beyond making arrangements for repatriation of all Nepali coolies did not consider it necessary to undertake a special enquiry into the conditions of labour in the mines.[19] It was felt that it would further unsettle the labour already seriously disturbed by the enquiries and by the repatriation of a large number of Nepali labourers. The Tea Districts Labour Supply Association was to be impressed upon by the Assam government that Gorkhas of fighting classes were not required for recruitment to the coal mines in Assam.[20] Besides the condition relating to temporary employment, no further restrictions were imposed on recruitment for the coal mines of other categories of non-martial Gurkhas. In a demi-official letter to the British Envoy dated 20th December, 1923, the Chairman, Assam Labour Board cautioned against the closure of the recruiting depot at Gorakhpur stating 'nothing but evil can result from doing away with the only agency which recruits in a legal and regular manner and does not attempt to recruit within Nepalese territories' unlike other illegal recruitment carried on at several places contravening government order.

Discourse on Race and Martiality

The above overview of developments relating to the issue of Gorkha recruitment during the period 1923-24 brings to light interesting aspects of how migration of labour to the region was conditioned by the interests of the colonial state. The issue of Gorkha recruitment also brings into focus the wider and an important aspect of colonial thinking or representation on 'race' and 'martial castes' which was assiduously propagated and cultivated from the late nineteenth century to justify colonial rule. The growth and development of the tea industry, railways, mining etc in Assam from the nineteenth century onwards created immense needs of labour in a region where even during the pre-colonial period labour was a scarce commodity. The colonial state sought to facilitate the demand by inducing migration of labour. One such economic migration in large numbers was that of the Nepalis who were induced to come attracted by the economic prospects of earning a livelihood. As the inflow of Gorkha migration became steady certain influential sections within the colonial state began to question the pernicious effect of such recruitment. It was felt that Gorkhas being a martial race their recruitment in the coal mines was a gross wastage of valuable natural resources. The exploitation of a martial race 'who were none too numerous', especially in coal mines would be pernicious in its effects on the manpower and physique of Nepal. It was desired to limit this recruitment or stop it totally if this was possible. Eventually the colonial state had to intervene which prevented the recruitment of certain categories of the 'martial race' to industrial services like in the coal mines.

The Government of Assam was also seriously concerned about the matter as the recruitment outside the province of Gorkhas for the Assam Rifles (a paramilitary force under the Ministry of Home Affairs, Government of India) had been discontinued at the wish of the Government of Nepal and Government of India and supply of suitable recruits from within the province was seriously affected by the competition offered by private employment on more lucrative terms than in the Assam Rifles. Regarding such diversion of Gorkha human resources for non-martial purposes a visibly disturbed high ranking British Police Officer wrote to the Government of Assam,

> I am finding it extraordinarily difficult to obtain recruits of the proper stamp in Assam and if nothing is done to prevent the enticement of Gurkhas into easy and more lucrative menial employments, the efficiency of the Assam Rifles battalions will be seriously impaired. As matters stand the competition in obtaining suitable recruits is most unfair to me: I am restricted to recruiting in Assam, where as the coal mines may obtain recruits both through Darjeeling and Gorakhpur. However careful the Recruiting Officers at these places may be, the presence of recruiters there, unconnected with regiments is dangerous because there are ways of getting good men away without the knowledge of the Recruiting Officers.[21]

There was growing demand from the army and police officials that recruitment of Gorkhas in non-military pursuits should be stopped forthwith. Here of course a distinction was made between the fighting castes of the Gorkhas and the non-fighting castes. The concerned camps had no objection to the recruitment of Gorkhas of non-martial castes into any other pursuits but had strong reservations about absorption of the martial ones for non-military purposes. The Government of Nepal also wanted that recruitment of Gorkhas of the fighting castes should be absolutely prohibited for the future. As regards the prohibition of the future recruitment of Nepal subjects of the fighting classes it was pointed out that, 'So far as recruiting at regular Recruiting Depots such as that at Gorakhpur is concerned the prevention of the recruitment of Gurkhas of the fighting classes could be effected by arrangement with the Tea District Labour Association and the Assam Labour Board. This would indeed be no innovation since all Gurkhas recruited at Gorakhpur are already passed by the Gurkha Recruiting Officer.'[22] As far as employment in the coal mines was concerned the Agent and General Manager were made to issue orders that Gorkhas of martial castes were not to be recruited either locally or through agencies outside the province. But this was done under the condition that non-martial castes of the Gorkhas would be continued to be recruited for the coal mines by private companies like the Assam Railways and Trading Company.[23] However the Government of Assam expressed its difficulty in preventing the recruitment of martial Gorkhas by private companies as it was not under its direct jurisdiction. But it promised to use its influence to pressurize the parties to refrain from such wasteful recruitment and cutting into the man power supply of the colonial army.

It is interesting to note the appropriation of racial discourse by the colonial states and European private entrepreneurs in the labour recruitment process of Gorkhas in the coal fields of Assam. The Gorkhas were recruited through negotiated agreement with the Government of Nepal because they were found to be members of 'martial' race who were tough, industrious, loyal and hence suitable for the hard work required in the mining of coal. But the same attributes were applied for their withdrawal. It was felt that the Gorkhas because of their above qualities were an important human resource which could not be 'wasted' in inane jobs like mining but be reserved for Empire building in which they served as military men. The same argument was used in importing indentured labour force from the tribal regions in Eastern and Central India for the tea plantations in Assam. Initially they tried to employ the local Assamese plainsmen as well as tribals into the growing tea industry. But the indigenous population could not be lured into it despite measures like high remuneration as well as high land revenue demand imposed by the colonial state to coerce them into joining as tea garden labour. Disgusted, the British rejected the Assamese as 'lazy' and turned their attention to the tribals of mainland India. The tribals were found to be tough enough to bear the hardship that the job involved. Again biological attributes were constructed to structure the tribal as 'tough' people.

Such constructions abound in the colonial ethnography.[24] Gorkhas, by their cultural and physical aptitudes were thought to be fitter than others for military service.[25] The fighting qualities of the Gorkhas were 'discovered' in the nineteenth century by the British in course of their imperial wars. Obviously the 'discovery' was based on personal observation and prejudice. The theory was that environment and biology created particular aptitudes. It is another matter that despite the theory, Gurungs and Magars were preferred over other members of similar tribal groups from comparable environments.[26] It is evident that the concept of race included grouping of people which held them to display inherent, heritable, persistent or predictive characteristics and which thus had a biological or quasi-biological basis.[27] Racism occurs when such characteristics are assumed from generalizations and are not verifiable. It implies a ranking according to the biological origins and features.[28] The features included propriety, honour, honesty and duty as accompaniment of race. The Gorkhas were the target of such construction of race theory which was an essential part of the nineteenth century western view of non-western societies. Gorkhas were thus not only seen as martial they were even attributed qualities like propriety, honesty, bravery and loyalty which did not always stand the test of truth. But the construction sustained. It was indeed a part of imperial political expediency. Race theory was therefore a 'self serving intellectual habit rooted in relations of power and exploitation, but this does not mean that there were no actual differences or conditions which also helped explain its deployment in practice. Such practice on the one hand shows adjustment to fit facts and on the other residual gullibility (blindness to contrary data) derived from faith in a revealed system of knowledge.'[29] The engagement in race theory vis-à-vis recruitment of Gorkhas in the collieries of Assam was one such instance.

Acknowledgement

This is an expanded version of an earlier article published in the *Proceedings of NEIHA*, Twenty-fifth Session, Shillong 2004. The author is thankful to SAP-DRS (UGC), Department of History, NEHU, Shillong for facilities extended towards preparation of this paper.

REFERENCES

1. Tejimala Gurung, "Human Movement and the Colonial State: The Nepalis of North East India under the British Empire", in A.C. Sinha and T.B. Subba (eds), *The Nepalis in Northeast India: A Community of Indian Identity*, Delhi: Indus, 2003, pp. 172-83, for details.
2. *Ibid.*
3. Sajal Nag, "Fei-isation of the Nepalis of Northeast India," in Sinha and Subba (eds), *Ibid.*, pp. 184-95.
4. Priyam Goswami, *Assam in the Nineteenth Century: Industrialization and Colonial Penetration*, Guwahati: Spectrum, 1999, p. 87.
5. Bengal Secret Political Consultations, 24th August 1827, No. 13, 26th October, 1827, Nos. 13, 20, 21, cited in *ibid.*, p. 88.
6. *Ibid.*, One *maund* was about 37.5 kilograms.
7. *Ibid*, p. 108.
8. Extract from Agent and General Manager, Assam Railways and Trading Company, letter no. N-5-3830, dated the 12th September, 1912, to Secretary to the Chief Commissioner of Assam, in Assam Secretariat Proceedings, Political-A, March 1924, p. 52.
9. Letter No. 292, dated the 20th January, 1913 from G.C. Webster, Colliery Superintendent, to Agent and General Manager in *ibid.*, p. 54.
10. *Ibid.*, p. 55.
11. Vide Government of India, Commerce and Industry, letter No. 2119, dated 22nd April, 1918, to the Chief Commissioner of Assam.
12. Vide Government of India letter No. 1687, dated the 9th April, 1919, to the Chief Secretary to the Government of Assam.
13. Assam Secretariat Procedings, No. 167C, 6th May, 1923, Political-A.
14. Demi-official letter from Major Northey, Recruiting Officer for Gorkhas at Gorakhpur to Lt.Col. W.F.T. O'Connor, British Envoy at the court of Nepal dated 8th December, 1922, Assam Secretariat, Political-A, March 1924.
15. Captain Lal Dhoj to His Excellency, the Governor of Assam dated Shillong 11 March, 1923, *ibid.*
16. H.C.Barnes, Officiating Commissioner, Assam Valley Division to the Chief Secretary to the Government of Assam dated 5th May, 1923, *ibid.*
17. Assam Secretariat Proceedings. Appointment and Political Department. Political- A, March 1924.
18. Extract from *The Times of Assam*, dated the 19th May, 1923.
19. No. Pol, 1445 A.P., dated Shillong, the 14th July, 1923, from Chief Secretary to the Government of Assam, to the Secretary to the Government of India, Foreign and Political Department.
20. *Ibid.*
21. W.C.M. Dundas, IGP, Assam to Chief Secretary, Govt. of Assam, 12 January, 1924.

22. A.W. Botham, Chief Secretary to the Govt of Assam to the Secretary to the Govt. of India, Foreign and Political Department. Shillong 19th January, 1924.
23. *Ibid.*
24. Peter Robb, "South Asia and the Concept of Race", in Peter Robb (ed.), *The Concept of Race in South Asia*, Oxford, 1997, pp. 1-76 for a discussion.
25. Lionel Caplan, "Martial Gurkhas: The persistence of a British Military Discourse on 'Race' " in Peter Robb (ed.), *ibid,* pp. 260-303.
26. *Ibid.*
27. Peter Robb, *op. cit.*
28. *Ibid.*
29. *Ibid.*

Section 4

Nepali Sub-cultures: Youths, Women, Food and Medicine

18

Indian Nepali Youths and Identity Crisis

ANURADHA SHARMA

Introduction

Identity crisis is all-pervasive. It is located both in the core of the individual and the community. And the struggle to achieve identity is a universally expected part of an adolescent (or youth), regardless of culture and ethnic background.[1] For the young members of ethnic minorities, identification with their own culture is an additional and important aspect of identity development.[2] The development of ethnic identity assumes a critical dimension for minority youths since they have, in addition to their ordinary developmental issues, the added burden of exploring the values of both their host society and their original cultures in the process of becoming members of their own ethnic group as well as the regional mainstream society. Identity is not an end in itself; it is a means through which one seeks to achieve acceptance and respect from the host society.

Speaking of identity crisis among the Indian Nepali youths, more precisely the present generation of the IBCNs, or India-Born Confused Nepalis, the crisis can be seen as one arising due to confused ethnicity and nationality. For most Indians, Nepalis are migrants from Nepal. Others see them as useful and honest *kancha*s and *darwan*s. These are gross generalisations that the people in the sub-continent are so wont to making. Nevertheless, these are definitely a matter of concern because these constitute the collective image of the community.

In the absence of a well-defined and universally accepted historical explanation of the presence of thousands of Nepalis in India and a clear understanding of the mainstream regarding the same, these youths often have to confront uncomfortable questions regarding their origin, answers to which they do not have. What has compounded the crisis is the recent nomenclature debate—the contentious Gorkha-Nepali issue.

Stereotyping comes very naturally to the world and just like the Muslims world over are looked upon as terrorists, in India, Nepalis, irrespective of which country they belong to are a community of menial workers—a stereotype reinforced by a number of Hindi films in which "Gorkha" is often used as a synonym of *chowkidar*. In this context, Nepali "Gorkha" and Bihari "Bhaiya" can be said to be quite similar.

The damage to the Indian-Nepali image is because of the number of Nepalis migrating to India in search of jobs as *chowkidar*s, sex-workers (60 per cent of Indian sex-workers are said to be Nepalis) or as waiters in roadside restaurants, who far surpass the number of Indian Nepalis holding prestigious positions. In modern Indian society, the Indian Nepali youths, often clubbed together with the Northeastern youths, are more associated with fashion, alcohol and drugs. Even in Siliguri, which has a sizeable Nepali population, a good portion of which is well-established, I have heard comments like 'Even though he is a Nepali, he is very much into studies and does not take drugs.' Perhaps, it is because of these kinds of humiliating generalizations that the search for a respectable identity is what is strongly felt by the Indian Nepali youths.

In order to place a balanced view on the subject and to get to know the aspirations of the IBCNs better, I conducted a survey during March-April 2006 with a cross-section of about 50 Indian Nepali youths from different parts of the country. Though the number is very small to make any generalization about such a large and heterogenous community, the basic idea behind the whole exercise was to get the feel of how the IBCNs think and what they aspire for. Aging between 20 and 40, the respondents were from different places like Delhi, Mumbai, Goa, Bhubaneshwar and Calcutta, other than Siliguri, Darjeeling and Sikkim. And their responses were as diverse as interesting.

The To-be-or-not-to-be Question

It is a rather dull question to ask whether or not you are proud to be a Nepali given that the answer is expected to be obvious. But that was not the case. Some respondents said off-the-record: 'Actually, I don't think I am very proud to be a Nepali.' These respondents from Mumbai and Delhi do not reveal their Nepali identities and have been staying there since the past several decades as Assamese, given that they have their roots in Assam. To take one particular example, a 30-year-old girl in

Mumbai is married to a Marwari and is a mother of two children. It is not clear if her husband is aware of or not, but her in-laws do not even have the whiff of her little secret that she is a Nepali.

Needless to mention that these advantages are enjoyed by the Nepalis of the Caucasoid descent. But for the Mongoloids, they have little choice. As a 24-year-old girl studying engineering in Delhi remarks, 'I don't even have that option.'

Youth and Self-evaluation

I asked my respondents what they liked and disliked about being a Nepali. This, I thought, would help us find out where the Nepali community had gone wrong and what the youths perceived of it. And the response was as overwhelming as diverse. Respondents were critical about our laid back attitude and the near refusal of the IBCNs to strive to become a part of the regional mainstream. D.N. Chhetri, an academician from Darjeeling, said: 'We are oblivious to changes taking place in the surroundings. The benefit accrued from the developments taking place around us, like the IT boom, has not touched us at all. We are hardly bothered.'

Absence of long term plans and lack of ambition are two big problems with the Indian Nepali youths. In a place like Darjeeling, which is home to some of the best schools (though they are not like what they used to be earlier), there should have been a large number of people in "good places". Where are the youths in the medical and engineering professions or in administration? And why are places like beauty-parlours, brothels, motor stands brimming with them? These questions need to be seriously pondered upon.

The Nepali youths suffer from an acute inability to dream. Lack of ambition is so strongly outlined that a typical IBCN "is happy strumming the guitar at Chowrasta and wooing his girl, but he does not cherish the dream of becoming an Indian idol." Lack of original thought is not only confined to the youths. It is the overall community trait. 'We are a subservient lot, content with what is given to us. We don't question, leave aside revolt. We are perfectly nonchalant and we will do without water, roads and electricity, but we will not speak out.' Vivek Chhetri, a journalist from Darjeeling, put it this way.

One of the interesting findings of my study was a marked change in the attitude of today's youths. Not very long ago, it was common to see a group of youths huddled together and talking on how the regional mainstream had marginalized us and finding sundry excuses for our own failures. The fact that my respondents were critical of such practice only shows that there has been an attitudinal shift in some way in our youths.

IBCNs and Westernisation

Youths worldwide are seen as a part of society that is most likely to engage in a process of cultural borrowing that is disruptive of the reproduction of traditional cultural practices, from modes of dress to language, aesthetics to ideologies. Everywhere youth subcultures are seen as being implicitly rebellious, born as much from a desire to reject the generation that went before them, as from identification with what they have become. Indian Nepali youths are no exception.

Westernisation, more specifically Americanisation, is something that a good part of the world is battling. The United States is accorded a certain pre-eminence in the field of the 'commercial culture industry' with powerful multinational distributors like Time-Warner, News Corporation and the Hollywood Studios, making the US a highly visible player in the cultural market place. Such a monopoly has significant ramifications on the dynamism of culture and fears, both real and perceived, of homogenisation of the world's cultures.

The modern cosmopolitan societies are characterized by some degree of homogeneity in every aspect, be it food, clothing, career etc. and it is but natural for the Indian Nepali society to increasingly become a part of the new-look cosmopolitan India. But such has been the degree of Westernisation—restricted to clothes and spoken language—that it has also affected the overall identity of the community. All the respondents agreed to the fact that we were over-westernised and said it was a cause of concern for the society in that the very innate Nepali attributes are giving places to confused western characteristics. Traditional clothes and foods are given the go even in typically traditional occasions like marriage ceremonies and festivals like Dashain and Tihar.

The concern is also because it is pseudo-westernisation that the IBCNs are taking refuge to. The West-aping is limited to clothing and all the distorted notions of the Western value system. The actual ideals of the West like dignity of labour, high regard for hard work, etc. are all thrown away like the peel of a banana. Even as many said that the attitude towards Westernisation was because there was nothing in the community to be proud of, many others reasoned that the tendency to look at the West was a manifestation of the perpetual quest for identity. 'It is this quest that sometimes makes us worship Sai Baba and sometimes Bruce Lee,' Vivek Chhetri said.

The Role of Elders

All the respondents I interviewed were very critical of the role played by our elders, who as a matter of fact have not been able to lead the IBCNs "in the right path". Respondents used strong terms like "useless" and "irresponsible" when they spoke about the earlier generation. According to them the Nepali parents, though most of them continue to remain conservative, have not been able to pass on to the present generation cultural values and tradition. A senior official with the Port Trust of India in Goa put it very simply: 'Today I am what I am because of my parents. If all the parents made equal efforts, the whole community would have been different. Our parents are not very serious of their children's careers.' A Kalimpong-based director of a hospitality management school adds: 'Nepali parents are least bothered about what their children are doing in the college. They pay the money and that is where their role ends.'

Yam Jaisi, an employee with a car dealer in Siliguri, puts it rather funnily: 'We have such parents who are happiest to sell off a plot of land to buy motorcycle for their son.' Bad parenting is in fact one of the big reasons for the state of the IBCNs, who are often described as rudderless and, as one of the respondents put it, "lost" generation. What appears from this study is that the elders of our community have not been able to pass on the sense of values and tradition to the youths, which has been responsible for what the IBCNs are today.

Government's Role

Government is everybody's *bete noire*, at least ostensibly. Government's role came in for criticism from everybody during my survey too. It is a common feeling that the central and state governments have not been able to protect the rights of the Indian Nepalis. Though none of my respondents could cite specific example where the government machinery had been outright biased against the Nepali minority, they all said that there was always an "undercurrent" of a step-motherly attitude towards them and it was the government, they said, which was to be blamed. As Vivek Chhetri puts it: 'Even today the government has not been able to give a clear definition of who the Indian Nepalis are. The ambiguity that was sown by the 1950 Friendship Treaty is still there everywhere.'

Recounting one of his experiences that occurred at Naxalbari, near the Indo-Nepal border of Siliguri sub-division, D.N. Chhetri says: 'A block development officer once refused to attest the photocopies of my original documents because I was a Nepali. I had to create pressure on him with the help of local political leaders to get the job done.' 'The caretakers of the government themselves have misconceptions about Indian Nepalis. Even though the government guarantees equal rights to us as a matter of policy, it has not been able to adequately educate or sensitise its workforce at the implementation level, which is why the intended fairness of the policies gets thwarted,' Vivek Chhetri said.

Misplaced Loyalties

The issue of misplaced loyalties also came up during my survey of the IBCNs. More than five of the youths I interviewed had got Nepalese passports. Every year a good number of Indian Nepalis go abroad on Nepalese passports because it is said to be easier to go to the West from Nepal than from India. For them, the lack of clear identity of the Indian Nepalis acts as a blessing in disguise. Though some insist that they are Indian "at heart" some of them make no secret of their thoughts. 'Nepal or India, it does not matter to me. When I am getting a chance to take advantage of certain opportunities abroad only through Nepal why not make use of it and have a good life?' said Rahul Sharma (not his real name) who works at a call centre in Bangalore. He has a Nepalese passport and is trying to make it to the UK some day or the other. The trend is a continuation from our parents' generation. '*Nepal ko nagarikta lei rakhna parchha hoi*' was a common refrain I used to hear as a child, which must be a precaution they wanted to take due to a deep sense of insecurity they suffered from in many parts of India. Earlier it was easy and as a child I knew of many people who had Nepali *nagarikta* (citizenship) despite calling themselves Indian and living in India. Nowadays, I am told that the process is not as easy as it used to be, or perhaps they do not try as hard. Could this be indicative of a higher degree of insecurity the Nepalis experienced in India earlier than it is now? One cannot rule this out completely.

Identity, Development and Gorkhaland

When asked what was on the top of their minds—identity or socio-economic upliftment of the people—majority of my respondents said that they wanted socio-economic upliftment. If for some food, clothe and shelter are top priorities, for others who need not worry so much for such basic needs, the identity question needs to be settled first.

One of my respondents migrated with his family from Mizoram to Siliguri about four years ago. A first class mechanical engineer, who now works with a car dealer in Matigara in Siliguri subdivision of Darjeeling district, says it was not in search of livelihood or money that he went to Siliguri. It was for the sense of insecurity that he felt in Mizoram, which made him leave the state. To quote him, 'We were scared what we would do if we were thrown out of Mizoram the way we were thrown out of Bhutan. Here, we are a sizeable chunk, which makes us hope that nobody would easily dare to throw us out from here.'

Another respondent, a teacher from Gorubathan near Kalimpong subdivision of Darjeeling district, put it this way "*Arka ko barima chha-talla bilding banayera ke garnu*?" Or what is the use of making a six-storeyed building on someone else's land?

Some respondents felt that recognition of the Nepali language in the 8th Schedule to the Constitution of India did not help much towards crystallisation of their identity. 'Language is not identity. The Naga language is not constitutionally recognized, but the people have no problem identifying themselves as Nagas because they have a state.' Language can actually be as important basis of identity as statehood is, but those who consider a separate statehood for the Indian Nepalis to be important would obviously discount the important role that language plays in the formation of their ethnic identity. One of the respondents, who has a restaurant in Goa, perhaps sums up what we go through day in and day out, 'As an individual they all respect me, but the moment I say I am a Nepali, they react in a peculiar manner. Donno how to describe that, but it is bad.'

The issue of statehood, which has taken a beating in the Gorkha-Nepali debate, is also an issue with the youths. Even though some would like to have us believe that the Indian youths are reconciled to the Sixth Schedule status, statehood is in the top of the minds of most Indian youths. One of my respondents even asked why the Nepalis could not have "Sikkim and Darjeeling" together, if not a separate Gorkhaland?

Though there is a section of the youths that strongly believes that a state would be a total solution to all problems, including identity and socioeconomic upliftment, the "progressive" majority wonders if a state could be the answer to their socio-economic problems. Biharis would then have been a different story, and would not be found doing the most menial jobs in most parts of the country. They would not face eviction from states like Assam, Maharastra and Nagaland.

A majority of my respondents said that identity would come with high socio-economic standards. 'Identity is not that big an issue because we are not an altogether obscure community! We need to produce more intellectuals, more doctors and engineers,' Alwin Lama, a Kalimpong-based academician, who has travelled widely in India, said.

I also came across a duality among the youths while speaking to them during my survey. It was interesting to note that there was a need for a 'distinct' identity, an identity which not only separates them from other Indians, but also from the Nepal Nepalis. It is an interesting paradox. In the present set up, Gorkha is the word. It just emanates from the feeling that this word will be able to achieve the desired distinctiveness. Whether it does from the point of view of the others is however a separate issue. To consider a hypothetical situation where we had anything in the name of a state, carved out of any piece of land, which we could call "our own" no matter which corner of the world we are in, it is the land that brings about this distinction. Therefore the name to denote the community becomes less material. In a queerly paradoxical fashion, those respondents who vehemently wanted to be called "Gorkha" earlier said that they did not mind being called "Nepali", if they had a state of their own. This confusion, it can be said, justifies my argument that what we are actually aiming at is being accepted as part of the mainstream and a separate name or a state is just a means of achieving it.

Nepali-Gorkhali

The Nepali-Gorkhali debate is perhaps the most contentious issue of recent times. And the youths are a divided house in this regard. Such debates arise in India perhaps because it is a country where Calcutta is renamed as Kolkata, Bombay as Mumbai, Madras as Chennai, with demands of renaming West Bengal to Bangla toeing the line. Coming to think of this issue, the following questions come to my mind. If Punjabis and Bengalis enjoy a distinct identity in India despite being in two different countries, what is the problem with the Nepalis? Why do Indian Nepalis have to change their name? Is it to please the mainstream by asserting that they have nothing to do with Nepal? Why do they need to do that? It is like saying 'Okay, if you don't like the word Nepali, I will call myself a Gorkha for you!'

Even if the Nepalis of India and Nepal are same, which is what circulates outside the Nepali world, for they speak the same language, eat the same food, celebrate the same festivals and reside in contiguous areas, living under two different nation-states following completely different forms of governance or rules of law for almost two centuries now have made them two different sets of people with different values, norms, degrees of individual freedom, participation in development process, and so on. Even if a distinct name is needed to denote Indian Nepalis, why 'Gorkha'? Is this because this is endorsed by the British? Is it because our martial identity is the only saving grace? Perhaps we are confusing our desire to be accepted with the desire to be identified and respected.

The case of Biharis should serve as an example to us. Nowadays a good number of young English-educated Biharis from the upper-middle class do not introduce themselves as Biharis when they are with others. Here I am talking about a class of businessmen in Siliguri, who introduce themselves as 'UPaids' or from Uttar Pradesh. Though I have some specific cases from Siliguri, I am aware that Biharis elsewhere, except of course in Bihar, pose similarly because the Bihari identity does not evoke any respectability even if it is clearly Indian. Indian imagination of Biharis is not the one a Bihari would like to be associated with.

Why do they have to do that? They have a state of their own. Any corner of India or globe they go to, they do not have the fear of being called "immigrants" or "foreigners". Bihar perhaps produces the highest number of IAS and IPS officers every year, a fact that even the Bengalis, who pride themselves on being educated and cultured, are jealous of. Not only this, Bihar's representation in the central government is quite impressive, with Bihar ministers holding important portfolios in the central government. Why then a good chunk of modern Biharis feel shy of their Bihari identity?

Despite its strengths, Bihar has neglected the socio-economic development at the grassroots. No matter to which heights they have reached, most Indians perceive of them as *panwala, puchkawala* and rickshaw-*wala*. And this is why the few who have made it big do not want to be looked down upon as apart of the "*bhaiya* brigade". There can of course be other interpretations as well, which I do not deny. Is it not possible that the Indian Nepalis will go the Bihar way even if all of their demands, be it of separate state or nomenclature, are met? Being geographically and culturally in proximity through history this cannot be ruled out.

Looking Ahead?

Political debates and deliberations will go on, but it is time now to act on a more tangible and concrete level. India or Nepal, Gorkhali or Nepali, for a community, which lives with the shame of comprising 60 per cent of women in sex trade in India, it is time to deliberate and plan strategies to encourage more Nepali youths to go for higher education in which the Indian Nepalis are sadly lagging far behind most Indian communities, reduce their dependence on drug addiction and alcoholism, and finally train them to take up challenging careers in emerging fields. As Sarita Sharma of Mumbai points out: 'We need more doctors, engineers and bureaucrats. It is only when our people become more visible in respectable places, will we be able to gain respect and acceptance as part of the mainstream.'

One of the respondents, who is a gazetted officer in the Port Trust of India in Goa says it aptly, 'We need to make a collective effort. Since our efforts have been isolated and limited to an individual in the past, we have not been able to make the difference.' The Indian Nepalis also need to communicate with others. So far, the perception others have of them are based on what they have observed and not on what have been verbally or in writing communicated to them. They need to debate and arrive at a consensus and then through proper channels disseminate to the outer world in a sustained and deliberate manner things they would want others to know.

They need to reposition themselves in the perceptual map of others for which they need to develop a model that encourages communication within the community as well as outside. By communication, I mean talking in a collective voice and not in singular voices that had been taking place so far.

There is a need for a strong political platform, and my respondents have all agreed that a political awakening is the need of the hour. What can be said to be a good sign is that some of the youths I interviewed said that there was a need for young people to join politics. They further said that they would themselves like to join politics if that could help the community. This is a good sign given that politics is often avoided as a "dirty-game" though there is a need to create a strong political platform because the existing system has failed to deliver on many counts. Without a strong political movement most of the other initiatives would be limited to rhetoric only.

There is a need for adopting both short and long term strategies to deal with the problem of identity crisis among the Indian Nepali youths today, which is one of the most important factors to shape their personalities. The nomenclature issue needs to be settled at the earliest through a common consensus given that such dissenting voices send wrong signals and miscommunicates our identities adding up to the already existing store of confusions, myths and fallacies. A systematic study into youth behaviour and aspirations in changing times is also required. A SWOT analysis to understand their strengths, weaknesses opportunities and threats is necessary.

Based on the suggestions I got from the respondents it is felt that creating a network of youths across boundaries for mutual exchanges could be an immediate step they could undertake. The immediate advantage of such exchanges is that they would promote the sense of belonging and fellow-feeling. In the long-run, such networks could be used in a number of ways for the overall improvement of the community.

REFERENCES

1. Erik H. Erikson, 1968, *Identity, Youth, and Crisis*, New York: Norton.
2. J.S. Phinney and Linda L. Alipuria, 1990, "Ethnic Identity in College Students from Four Ethnic Groups", *Journal of Adolescence*,13 (2): 171-83.

19

Trafficking of Nepali Women in India

SHARDA CHHETRI

Identity of Nepali Women in India

If Nepali men in India are generally looked down upon, the attitude towards Nepali women is worse. Even in the higher professions, Nepali women have to be doubly good to be regarded as equal to the men they work with. Most people are reluctant to believe that Nepali women can also be educated and can have their own thinking. They are at times even considered to be "easily available." Nepali girls at any Indian college or university in India's metropolises face more problems than the other Indian girls do.

In this paper I focus on the Indian Nepali women who have been forced into sex work in India's metropolises. Many of them had left their homes in remote villages of Nepal as early as 6 or 7 years of age, lived and died here in India homeless and helpless. I am going to discuss in particular the trafficking of young Nepali girls from across the border. The facts and figures are collected from various agencies and NGOs or the Indian Nepali girls who are forced into prostitution in the Red Light areas of Mumbai, Kolkata and Pune. A staggering 60 per cent of the sex workers and brothel owners in Mumbai and Kolkata are Nepalis. The story of girls from Nepal being trafficked is old, but that is no reason for not highlighting it here again. For the past four decades, every year 7,000 to 10,000 Nepali girls are trafficked into India. It has been found out that at least 25 per cent of the 2 lakh Nepali girls in the Red Light areas of India are Indian Nepalis. And, according to Maiti Nepal, an anti-trafficking organisation located in Nepal, most of the 25 per cent girls are from Northeast India, including Darjeeling, Jalpaiguri and Sikkim. This is indeed a very disturbing fact. There is little or no difference between a Nepalese Nepali and an Indian Nepali in a Red Light area and Nepali girls in general are very much in demand, which makes them that much vulnerable to the designs of the criminals engaged in the trafficking.

The widely accepted definition of human trafficking, as proposed by the UN Commission on Human Rights, is: 'Trafficking in persons means the recruitment, transportation, purchase, sale, transfer, harbouring or receipt of persons by threat or use of violence, abduction, force, fraud, deception or coercion (including the abuse of authority) or debt bondage, for the purpose of placing or holding such persons whether for pay or not, in forced labour or slavery-practices, in a community other than the one in which such persons lived at the time of original act described.'

At a consultation in Darjeeling in 2005 on "Tackling newer emerging vulnerabilities leading to traffic of children and women in eastern Himalayas" organized by the Church of North India in collaboration with the United Nations Development Fund for Women (2005), it was pointed out that according to estimates more than 2 million women of Indian, Nepalese and Bangladeshi origin were engaged in the commercial sex trade of India. Of these at least 500,000 are under 18 years of age. This is not surprising since Asia is home to more than 900 million of the world's poor—the most vulnerable of all groups. Trafficking in women and children is the largest source of revenue generation in international organized crime after drugs and arms smuggling. The global trafficking industry generates an estimated 5-6 billion US dollars each year. Trafficking as a contemporary form of slavery not only involves exploitation but also physical and mental abuse of human beings on a massive scale, which is a serious violation of basic human rights.

The Himalayan region being one of the most economically under developed regions in Asia, human trafficking has been thriving at an alarming rate. Nepal has been designated as a "sending country" or country of origin in the regional web of trafficking. India is usually referred to as a "transit," "source" and "destination" country. Girls and women are trafficked both within the country, across the countries within the region, as well as across region and continents beyond Southasia.

Most of the details that I present here are based on a study conducted in Mumbai between 7th June and 19th September, 2004, and in Kolkata between 24th November, 2004 and 14th January, 2005. In Mumbai the locations of the study were the Red Light areas of Kamathipura, Khetwadi, Ghatkopar and in Kolkata the locations were Sonagachi, Kalighat, and Kidderpore. This was a qualitative study and no attempt was made to assess the numbers or sources or persons trafficked, numbers of persons in slavery or debt bondage, numbers of persons in prostitution, or to collect other quantitative data. The study was sponsored by Terre des hommes Foundation[1], which is based in Switzerland. The study focussed on the economic and social system that engenders the trafficking process.

There are two situations in which trafficked Nepali girls and women spend their first two to ten years in the brothel. Girls or women who are placed against their will in a situation of forced labour, unremunerated and penalized amounts to slavery. Girls whose families incur a debt directly to the brothel owner are placed in a similar situation in order to repay the debt. The common term for both is *chhokri*.

The key finding of the study was that almost all Nepali girls had entered prostitution in a situation of slavery or debt bondage under the age of 18 years and at an average age of 14 to 16 years. A majority of them are trafficked by the Nepalese themselves and sold to the brothel owners in India.

Demand for Nepali Women

Almost all respondents were unanimous in their statement that Nepalis were very much in demand because of their 'beauty, fair complexion and youthful appearance even when they grew older', thus prolonging their "working life." Notably, what set aside Nepali sex workers were their honesty, politeness and cleanliness. They were also praised for their "fair business practices" as compared to Bangladeshi and Indian sex workers. They consciously sought to develop good customer relations. Politeness and soft spokenness were repeatedly mentioned as their unique traits. Somewhat paradoxically, clients valued Nepali sex workers because they did not 'act like prostitutes.' Limited data on the sale price of *chhokris* showed that a Nepali *chhokri* in Kolkata fetched approximately Rs. 60,000 to Rs. 70,000 while in Mumbai she would fetch above Rs. 1 lakh for the trafficker. The brothel owner who has 'invested' in a *chhokri* makes at least Rs. 24,000 from her per month. The brothel owner would make up for the *chhokri* cost in less than 6 months, but the time of forceful confinement varied from two to ten years during which the brothel owner made four to twenty times the price of a *chhokri*.

Procurement of *Chhokri*

It appears that almost all trafficking from Nepal is conducted by the

Nepalese, both male and female. Traffickers sometimes work in small groups and certainly in collaboration with community members, employers, local officials, border officials, etc. Traffickers appear to be either "freelancers" selling their products to the highest bidder among a range of brothel owners in a particular locality, or persons (especially women) mobilized by certain brothel owners to "recruit labour".

While almost all the informants had been trafficked against their will and without knowledge of their destination, a couple of them had entered prostitution voluntarily. The traffickers (dalals, as they are usually called) were both males and females. A significant number (approx 1/ 4th) were trafficked directly through someone they knew in their village or workplace. No sex worker respondent discussed being trafficked by or with the knowledge of their families. Nearly one half had been lured by the promise of work, and approximately one fourth followed a man out of love.

Life after Slavery and Debt Bondage

After the life of bonded slavery for two to ten years, the girls are 'free' to go back to their own homes. However, only a small percentage go back home. Social stigma and rejection by family members often force them to remain in the brothels of India. A high percentage of them would have contacted HIV by then and would be left to die unattended.

Trafficking from Darjeeling-Sikkim-Jalpaiguri Region

In recent years there has been an increase in the number of Nepali girls "missing" from Darjeeling, Sikkim, and Jalpaiguri areas of West Bengal. According to Anuradha Koirala of Maiti Nepal, lack of employment opportunities in the Darjeeling-Sikkim Hills has often led to young boys and girls seeking employment in Kathmandu and other Indian cities. The premium that is placed on a young Nepali girl by brothel owners makes them a very vulnerable target group. By very conservative estimates, at least 7,000 Nepali girls are trafficked into India every year. Yet, even this figure "fails to cater to the demand." While Nepal is the source for trafficked girls, India, especially the eastern Himalayan region of it, is a source, transit and destination point for the victims. Most young victims leave home for a "better life" in the Indian cities. Of late there has been a spurt of human resource agencies operating in Darjeeling-Sikkim areas, which promise young girls with house jobs in the Middle East and

Singapore. After investing the savings of their parents or selling off their jewellery and landed property in order to obtain a visa, the girls invariably land up in wrong hands. There are of course a few success stories, but for most of the "dream chasers" it is a horrendous journey, where besides housekeeping, they are expected to physically entertain guests of the family. Most girls do not tell about the ordeal they go through out of shame and stigma.

The crisis in the tea gardens of Darjeeling and Jalpaiguri has led to the closure of many gardens in recent years. In the absence of alternative means of livelihood, the young women of this region have become exceptionally vulnerable to the lures of a better life in the cities.

Because of its proximity with the border town of Pashupati and its easy road facilities and closeness to Siliguri, it is believed that Mirik, a tourist destination in Darjeeling, is fast turning to be a "transit point" from where girls are first brought from Nepal and huddled out of Siliguri once the clearance signal is given.

The Lhotsampa Refugee Problem

According to Kavita Shukla and Michelle Brown of Refugees International (RI), 'As a result of the nine-year Maoist conflict in Nepal, greater numbers of Nepalis are going to India and these new arrivals are being confronted with the same protection concerns that have plagued generations of Nepalis in India. Under the 1950 Peace and Friendship treaty between Nepal and India, Nepalis have the right to live and work in India and have been coming for decades to India in search of employment opportunities. In theory, Nepalis in India have the same rights as Indian citizens, with the exception of voting rights, yet they are often denied their basic legal rights and are vulnerable to labor rights violations and various forms of exploitation.'[2]

Due to the open border between Nepal and India obtaining an accurate count of how many Nepal Nepalis have been migrating to India since 1996 to escape the armed conflict in Nepal in the wake of Maoist violence is very difficult. Estimates of people driven to India as a consequence of the conflict are inexact and vary widely, from hundreds of thousands to millions. Analysts interviewed by Refugees International agree that seasonal migrants who used to come to India temporarily are now moving to India with their belongings. Previously Nepal Nepalis tended to come to India during times of economic and political crisis and would go back to Nepal when the situation stabilized. However, in recent years, these people no longer appear to be returning to Nepal. Based on an assessment of conditions inside Nepal and interviews with around 30 Nepali migrants in India, RI believes that the conflict is now so all-pervasive that it is impossible to separate purely economic migrants from those fleeing the conflict.

In 2005, RI interviewed a group of Nepalis in Delhi, who work as *chowkidars*, or watchmen. According to this group, there has been a 50 per cent increase in their number in Delhi in the last few years. The members of the group are primarily from the far western districts in Nepal, and many belong to the most marginalized groups in Nepal and also most affected by the Maoist violence there since mid-1990s. Whereas previously single men used to come for work in India, now entire families are migrating.

Once in India, the Nepalis become vulnerable to labour and human rights abuses, much like other poor Indians and illegal migrants from Bangladesh. According to the *chowkidars*, they have no legal rights. If they are abused at work and complain to law enforcement officials, their complaints are not taken seriously. In case of robbery, for example, even if they have worked in a neighbourhood for many years, the police assume that they are accomplices. Thus they are increasingly blamed even for crimes they have not committed. While the Nepalis in the formal sector in India enjoy the same legal rights as other Indians, as they join labour unions, the formal sector constitutes a mere 8 per cent of the workforce, and majority of Nepalis fall outside this sector. The lack of membership in any organized labour group hits the Nepali women the hardest, and those working as domestic servants remain particularly vulnerable.

Why is Trafficking Flourishing?

The main reasons why trafficking is flourishing are poverty and desire for a better life. Traffickers exploit impoverished and vulnerable individuals seeking a better life. In countries with chronic unemployment, widespread poverty or lack of economic opportunities, traffickers use promises of higher wages and good working conditions in foreign countries to lure individuals into their designs. Many times the individuals have jobs or advanced degrees but believe the traffickers' promises because they want better lives.

Almost every other day the newspapers are replete with stories of child prostitution and child pornography, especially in areas of throbbing tourist flow. The Southeast Asian region is one part of the globe where sex-related tourism thrives. The idea of sex-tourism has also caught up in Goa and elsewhere in India. Several NGOs in Darjeeling feel that Sikkim-Darjeeling area, being a tourist hot spot, the fear of this region being vulnerable to prostitution and human trafficking would not be misplaced. The process of globalization has opened up new avenues for intensifying the commercial sexual exploitation of children.

The loss of traditional means of livelihood due to the spread of modern forms of entertainment forces many in these communities to allow the exploitation of their girls and women. Women who are in economic distress due to lack of means of livelihood, widowhood, separation of husbands, abandonment by family etc., are much against their choice, forced to become the victim of commercial sexual exploitation. Migrant women and children from within the country or from neighbouring countries are more likely to be forced to become victims. Girls in the fringes of the entertainment industry such as bar girls, cabaret dancers, circus girls, etc. area also vulnerable. But most families and victims are unaware of the dangers of trafficking because of the "success stories", displays of wealth, or remittances back to villages from relatives working abroad or in urban areas that provide powerful incentives for others to migrate for work.

Conclusion: What Must be Done

(1) Advocate and sensitise Nepali women in villages, schools and colleges about this reality.

(2) Promote NGOs and Self Help Groups to act as vigilantes in villages for any new face with suspicious activities.

(3) Set up a 24 × 7 helpline.

(4) Rehabilitate and reintegrate women who have been rescued from traffickers or from the brothels. Counselling is a must for all the rescued girls.

(5) At the moment, all Indian Nepali girls [including those from Darjeeling-Sikkim areas] who have been rescued from brothels in India's metropolises are sent to Maiti Nepal in Kathmandu, wherefrom they are sent back to India for reintegration. This causes a lot of legislative problems. Stree Shakti has been formed with the help of Maiti Nepal with the objective of directly rehabilitating and reintegrating the girls of this region who have been rescued.

(6) Alternative means of livelihood, including vocational training, should be imparted by the government, to the vulnerable groups.

(7) Establish a network of all the NGOs of this region working on anti-trafficking, rehabilitation and other women's issues.

It is very commendable that the Sikkim State Women's Commission headed by Manita Pradhan has seriously taken up the issue of the trafficking of Nepali women in India. The studies and surveys so far carried out by city-based NGOs and organisations need to be authenticated. It will not be an easy task since almost no case is filed under the Immoral Traffic Prevention Act.

REFERENCES

1. Terre des homes, 2005. *Summary of Findings: A Study of Trafficked Nepali Girls and Women in Mumbai and Kolkata, India.* Kathmandu: Terre des hommes Foundation.
2. Shukla, K. 2005. *India: Nepali Migrants in Need of Protection. www.refugeesinternational.org/content/article/detail/6429*

20

Food and Identity: A Study among the Nepalis of Sikkim and Darjeeling

JYOTI PRAKASH TAMANG

Food symbolises the culture of a community and provides it with a distinct identity. The *bhat-dal-tarkari-achar* (rice-legume soup-curry-pickle) is a typical food of every Nepali of Sikkim and Darjeeling, signifying his distinct identity. *Dhenroh*, or boiled maize-flour, eaten with butter-milk is another typical Nepali food. Regarding a typical Nepali's food habits, the morning starts with a full mug of tea taken with sugar or salt with or without milk, and with or without a pinch of black pepper. The first meal eaten in the morning is a simple *bhat-dal-tarkari-achar.* It is followed by light refreshment with mostly traditional snacks and tea in the afternoon. The second major meal is dinner, which is served early in the evening, and which consists of the same *bhat-dal-tarkari-achar*.

Traditional Nepali food is less spicy and prepared in *gheu* (purified butter) and animal fat, but nowadays most of them use edible oils except in remote villages where the traditional medium of cooking persists. Most Nepalis are non-vegetarians but beef is rarely cooked at home except by Tamangs, Sherpas and Yolmos. Newars like buffalo meat. Cooking is usually done by women. Elderly male members of the family are served the meals first and the women eat afterwards. More than 40 varieties of ethnic fermented foods and beverages, 100 types of non-fermented foods and 190 species of edible wild plants are consumed by different groups of Nepalis as staple foods, vegetables, pickles, condiments, and herbal materials.[1] Most of these foods are lesser known outside and confined to particular groups and places. Some ethnic foods of the Nepalis are: *dhenroh, chamray, chatamari, gundruk, sinki, kinema, selroti, chhurpi, dahi, mohi, gheu, maseura, khalpi, mesu, sidra, sukuti, sukako maacha, sukula, sukako masu, phulaurah, somar, phapar ko roti, kwanti, chhwelaa, wachipa, alum, foldong, falki, khoreng, goyong, kodo ko jaanr, bhaati jaanr, raksi,* etc. Some of these foods are described in some detail below:

Alum

Alum is a special dish of Tamangs mostly consumed during festivals. It is a paste of finger millet or buckwheat made into rolls and put into boiling water until it is ready to eat.

Chamray

Chamray is a typical Nepali *pulao* prepared from local varieties of rice. Rice is first soaked with bay leaves and cinnamon and cooked with *gheu* and water. *Chamray* is eaten with potato curry mixed with *til* or sesame seeds.

Chatamari

Chatamari is a rice pancake commonly prepared by Newars. During its preparation rice flour is mixed with water and smooth batter is made, which is spread on hot butter and the pancake is prepared. *Chatamari* is served plain or with a topping of ground meat.

Chhurpi

It is of two types—hard and soft. The hard *chhurpi* is mostly prepared from yak milk in high altitudes (2100 to 4500 m). It has its characteristic gumminess and chewiness and is commonly eaten as a masticator. Two types of hard *chhurpi* are prepared: common *chhurpi* and *dudh chhurpi.* The soft *chhurpi* is a cheese-like fermented milk product, prepared from cow milk as well as yak milk. It has a rubbery texture with a slightly sour taste and an excellent aroma when it is fresh. It is prepared into a curry by cooking in oil along with onions, tomato and chilies, or with wild edible ferns, locally called *ningro* (Diplazium esculentum). It is also used for preparing *achar* or pickle by mixing it with chopped cucumber, radish, chilies, etc. Soup prepared from soft *chhurpi* can be consumed as a substitute for *dal* along with rice.[2]

Chhwelaa

Chhwelaa is a dish of Newars made of boiled buffalo meat. During its preparation, meat is boiled and cut into pieces. It is mixed with a paste of spices, kneaded thoroughly and fried in oil. Fried fenugreek seeds and turmeric are garnished with meat. It is served with *chiura* (beaten rice) during festivals, feasts or special occasions. There are two types of *chhwelaa: haku chhwelaa* is plain, and *manu chhwelaa* is prepared by roasting the buffalo meat on charcoal fire. Besides *chhwelaa*, there are varieties of meat dishes of Newars, such as *sypati, kimila, gorma, chula, tahkha, naga, pupala,* etc.

Bhaati jaanr

Bhaati jaanr is a Nepali word for rice beer. During production of *bhaati jaanr*, glutinous rice is cooked for about 15 minutes in an open cooker, excess water is drained off and the cooked rice is spread on a bamboo mat for cooling. A dry mixed starter culture called *marcha*[3] is powdered, and about 2 per cent of it is sprinkled over the cooked rice, mixed well and kept in a vessel or an earthen pot for 1-2 days at room temperature for saccharification. After saccharification, the vessel is made airtight and fermented for 2-3 days in summer and 7-8 days in winter. *Bhaati jaanr* is made by adding hot water and stirring the fermented mass with the help of a hand-driven wooden or bamboo-made stirrer and is consumed directly. Sometimes, *bhaati jaanr* is stored in an earthenware crock for a week or more after desired fermentation is completed to make yellowish-white supernatant liquor called *nigaar*, collected at the bottom of the earthenware crock which is drunk directly with or without addition of water. *Bhaati jaanr* is an inexpensive high calorie staple food-beverage for the non-Brahmin Nepali post-natal women and ailing old persons who believe that it helps to regain their strength.[4]

Dahi

Dahi, the traditional curd, is produced at home for direct consumption as well as for the preparation of a number of other milk products like *mohi*, *chhurpi*, and *chhu*. Apart from its dietary properties, dahi plays an important role in the social and religious customs of the local people. It is consumed as a refreshing non-alcoholic beverage. Sugar may or may not be added before consumption. It is also consumed with rice or *chiura*.

Dhenroh

Dhenroh is a popular porridge-like Nepali food, which is more filling and nutritious than the common staple diet of rice. It is prepared by boiling the corn-flour with butter and salt and cooking it until the porridge thickens and starts separating from the edges of the pan. It is eaten with vegetables, *achar*, *dahi* and *mohi*. *Dhenroh* and *gundruk* together form the most typical food combination among the Nepali farmers.

Falki

Falki is a special meat-based dish of Gurungs. During preparation, the leg or head of sheep, preferably with more bone, is cut into small pieces and fried with green boiled and dried maize, tomato, onion, ginger, and turmeric powder and cooked to make a curry. It is consumed with boiled rice.

Foldong

Foldong is a rice-ball consumed commonly by Tamangs. Rice is mixed with clove, cardamom, dry fruits and butter, and made into round flat shape. It is consumed as a cake. *Foldong* is an essential food item to be presented to a bride's parents to solemnize a Tamang marriage.

Gundruk

Gundruk is a non-salted, fermented and sun-dried leafy vegetable. This is particularly prepared during October-December when large quantities of perishable leafy vegetables such as leaves of mustard, *rayo-sag*, radish, and other vegetables are available. *Gundruk* is eaten as a soup or pickle. *Gundruk* soup is made by soaking it in water, squeezing it dry and frying it in oil with chopped onions, tomatoes, chilies, turmeric powder and salt and adding water. It is then boiled for a while, and served hot with cooked rice. *Gundruk* is a good appetizer in a bland and starchy diet.[5]

Khapjay

Khapjay is a wheat-based deep-fried sweet or salty snack, common to Tamangs, Sherpas and Yolmos. It is usually prepared during festivals and special occasions. *Khapjay* is also prepared by the other Buddhist tribes of the region like the Lepcha and Bhutia.

Kinema

Kinema is a traditional fermented soybean food having characteristic stringy property with unique flavour, commonly consumed as a curry with cooked rice. *Kinema* serves as an inexpensive high source of plant protein food in the local diet. Delicacy of *kinema* can be perceived by its appealing flavour and sticky texture. Fresh *kinema* is fried in vegetable oil, with chopped onions, tomatoes and turmeric powder. Salt and sliced green chilies are added and fried for a short while. A little water is added to make thick gravy. Dried *kinema* is sometimes mixed with leafy vegetables to make a mixed curry.[6]

Kodoko Jaanr

Kodoko jaanr is the most common fermented alcoholic beverage prepared from dry seeds of finger millet (*Eleusine coracana*), locally called *kodo.* The Bhutias call this drink *chhyang* and the Lepchas call it *chee. Kodoko jaanr* is consumed in a unique way in the Sikkim Himalaya. About 200-500 grams of *jaanr* is put into a vessel called *tongba* and hot water is poured up to its edge. After 10-15 min, the milky white extract of *jaanr* is sipped through a narrow bamboo straw called pipsing which has a hole at the bottom to avoid passing of grits. Water can be poured twice or thrice after sipping of the extract. Guests are served with *tongba* along with fried meat or pickle. Alternately, the thick milky white liquid is pressed from the *kodoko jaanr* and is filtered with the help of a strainer called *chhapani*. Such liquor is believed to be a good tonic for ailments and post-natal care.[7]

Kodoko roti

Kodoko roti is a typical pancake prepared from finger millet and is served with different varieties of pickles.

Kwanti

Kwanti is a special food of Newars. This is prepared by mixing nine varieties of sprouted pulses and beans, such as white grams, dry peas, soybeans, black-eyed beans, white kidney beans, green grams, black grams, lentils and moth beans. Soybeans are soaked in water for 4-9 days, and other beans are soaked for 1-2 days. Sprouted beans are cooked with butter and spices to make a thick soup which is served with boiled rice. It is eaten in the festival called *Kwanti Purnima*, which usually falls in August.

Mesu

Mesu is a traditional fermented young bamboo tender shoot product with a sour-acidic taste. It is eaten as a pickle. *Mesu* pickle mixed with oil, chilies and salt can be kept in a closed jar for several months without refrigeration. It is sold during rainy season, when bamboo shoots are available in plenty in the local markets.[8]

Mohi

Mohi or buttermilk is a liquid fermented milk product. It is usually a by-product of *dahi. Mohi* is a Nepali name. The Bhutias and Lepchas call it *kachhu. Dahi* is churned to produce *gheu* (butter) and the liquid that remains is *mohi*. It is consumed as a cooling beverage during hot days and to overcome tiredness. It is also processed further to produce other fermented milk products like *chhurpi* and *chhu*.

Phaparko Roti

Phaparko roti is a traditional buckwheat bread. It is served with *philingoko achar* (pickle made from seeds of *niger Guizotia* sp.) or *silamko achar* (pickle made from seeds of *Perilla frutescens*).

Phuku-aamchu

Phuku-aamchu is deep-fried wheat flour bread, which is eaten as a snack by Tamangs, Sherpas and Yolmos. It is mostly prepared during festivals and special occasions by Buddhist tribes.

Phulaurah

Phulaurah is split black gram-based fritters eaten as a snack. Split black gram is soaked overnight, the seed coats are removed and the grams ground to paste. *Asafoetida* (*hing*) cumin seed or *jeera*, ginger, chilies, salt and a cup of water are mixed to make a thick batter, which is fried until it becomes golden brown. It is served hot with *silam ko achar* during festivals of the Nepalis.

Raksi

Raksi is a clear distilled wine with characteristic aroma. It is prepared from fermented cereal beverages such as *kodoko jaanr, bhaati jaanr, makaiko jaanr, gahoonko jaanr,* etc. Fermented masses of buckwheat, potato, canna and cassava roots are also distilled to get *raksi. Raksi* is a common term in Nepali meaning alcoholic drink. It is usually stored in bottles capped with a piece of dry corncob. Sometimes, petals of *Rhododendron* sp. are mixed during distillation to give a distinct aroma to it. This type of *raksi* is commonly prepared in few places.[9] *Jhaneko raksi* (*raksi* seasoned on hot oil with spices and herbs) is drunk hot to get relief from cough and cold.

Selroti

Selroti, a ring-shaped, spongy, pretzel-like bread, is prepared from well-mixed fermented rice batter and is deep fried during religious festivals and special occasions. It is served as staple confectionery bread with simiko acchar (pickle prepared from string beans) and meat. It can be preserved at room temperature for a month or more.

Sinki

Sinki, a non-salted fermented radish taproot, is prepared by pit fermentation, which is a unique type of bio-preservation of foods through lactic acid fermentation. It is usually prepared during winter when radish taproots are available in plenty. With a highly acidic flavour, it is typically used as a base for soup and as pickle. The soup is made by soaking it in water for some time, squeezing it dry and frying along with chopped onions, tomatoes and green chilies and salt. Soup is served hot along with meals. It is said to be a good appetizer, and people use it also as a remedy for indigestion.[10]

Sishnu

Sishnu soup is prepared from the leaves of edible wild varieties of nettle grass. It is a typical Himalayan cuisine served with cooked rice. Many wild varieties of nettle grass are grown in these regions. The nettle leaves are boiled with rice, turmeric powder and salt till it is fully cooked. Then oil is heated with sautéed garlic flakes and added to cooked thick nettle soup.

Sishnu soup is ready to serve with cooked rice. This soup is also prepared by directly pouring the unwashed leaves of this nettle grass on boiling water without washing the same. It turns into a thick soup very soon.

Sidra

Sidra is a sun-dried fish consumed by Nepalis. It is served as *achar* or pickle. During pickle making, *sidra* is roasted and is mixed with dry chilies, boiled tomato and salt to make a thick pickle paste. In a typical meal of the Nepalis, cooked rice and *kalo dal* (black gram soup) is served with *sidrako achar*.[11]

Somar

Somar is an indigenous fermented milk product, prepared from cow or yak milk, and is mostly consumed by the Sherpas of Sikkim and the Darjeeling hills.[12] It is a soft paste with a slightly bland and bitter taste and has a strong flavour. It is kept for a long period by cooking it with butter and turmeric to produce a soft-brown paste to form another type of *somar.* It is consumed as soup with boiled rice or *dhenroh*.

Sukako Masu

Sukako masu is a dried meat and is mostly prepared from mutton. It is eaten as such or as curry with *thukpa* or soup noodles and boiled or baked potatoes, and also with rice.

Sukako Machha

Sukako maccha is a typical smoked and dried fish commonly eaten by Lepchas. River fish are collected in a basket, which is made of bamboo strips and tied around the waist of the angler while he is fishing. Fish are kept on a big bamboo tray to drain off the water, degutted, mixed with salt and turmeric powder and kept above the earthen oven in the kitchen. It can be kept at room temperature for 2-3 months. It is cooked with vegetables as curry and eaten with rice.[13]

Sukuti

Sukuti is also a very popular sun-dried fish among the Nepalis of Sikkim and the Darjeeling hills. It is consumed as pickle, soup or curry. During curry preparation, it is fried, mixed with dry chilies, onion and salt to make a pickle.

Tama

Tama is a non-fermented young tender bamboo shoot. Some varieties of bamboo shoots commonly grown in the Sikkim Himalaya are *Dendrocalamus hamiltonii, Dendrocalamus sikkimensis* and *Bambusa tulda* locally known as *choya bans, bhalu bans* and *karati bans*, respectively are edible when young. These bamboo shoots are collected, defoliated and boiled in water with turmeric powder for 10-15 minutes to remove bitter taste of bamboo. It is commonly sold in the local markets during the months of June to September when young bamboo shoots sprout.

Wachipa

Wachipa is a typical Rai food consumed as a side dish. There are two types of *wachipa*: non-vegetarian *wachipa* is rice fried with minced chicken and then mixed with powder made from the burnt feathers of a cock or hen. It is eaten on special occasions. Vegetarian *wachipa* is similar to *wachipa* fried rice except that it does not contain meat or the powder from the burnt feathers. Leaves or flowers of a type of plant called *damlapa* is mixed in place of meat. This type of *wachipa* is usually prepared during May-June and August-September. The Rais believe that consumption of *wachipa* cures body ache.

Antiquity of *Kinema*

The history of *kinema*, a fermented soybean food of Nepalis, throws light on the cultural history of the community. The word *kinema* has been derived from *kinamba* of the Limbu language in which *ki* means fermented and *namba* means flavour.[14] The kingdom of Limbuwan (presently the districts of eastern Nepal—Terathum, Taplejung, Panchthar, Dhankuta and Ilam) was established by the Limbus before the seventh century. They ruled that part of Nepal until the unification of Nepal in 1769.[15] Though there is no historical document on the origin of *kinema*, it is widely believed that the Limbus started its production and consumption. The unification of Nepal and migration of people from one place to another might have popularized this food among the other Nepali groups like Rai, Tamang, Gurung, Magar and Sunuwar. *Kinema* is not traditionally eaten by the Nepali Brahmins. Although the reason is not documented, it is believed that the Brahmins usually regard *kinema* as *basi* meaning stale. Another reason may be its strong flavour. However, for many ethnic communities in the eastern Himalayas and Southeast Asian countries it is a delicacy. The Lepchas call it *satlyangser* and the Bhutias call it *bari* in Sikkim. In Meghalaya, the Khasis call it *tyrumbai*; in Manipur a similar product is known as *hawaijar*; the Mizos call it *bekang-um*; and in Nagaland it is called *aakhuni*. It is called *natto* in Japan; *chungkok-jang* in Korea; *thua-nao* in Thailand; *pe-poke* in Myanmar and *douchi* in China.

Some anthropologists of food believe that the traditional Asian fermented soybean foods eaten even today had originated from *douchi*, the oldest type of fermented soybean dating back to around 300 BC during the Han dynasty in southern China.[16] Some believe that during the Han dynasty, *douchi* spread northward to the northern China, westward to eastern Nepal, southward to Indonesia and eastward to Japan.[17] However, while the nature of the products showed similarities, the method of preparation and mode of consumption vary from place to place. Hara *et al.* reported[18] that plasmid of *Bacillus subtilis* (*natto*) strain (microorganism in *natto*) resembles that of *Bacillus subtilis*, the dominant microorganisms of other Asian fermented sticky soybean foods such as *thua-nao* and *kinema*. Tamang *et al.* confirmed[19] similarity among *Bacillus subtilis* of fermented soybean foods of Asia on the basis of phylogenetic analysis by determining the 16s RNA sequencing. This proved that they might have originated from the same stock. *Douchi* may be the origin of *kinema* and other fermented foods, but until the scientific basis of molecular identification tool of the functional microorganism in these products is known it will be impossible to trace the antiquity of *kinema*. Moreover, anthropologists of food have also not yet traced the antiquity of soybean cultivation in Nepal and adjoining regions in the eastern Himalayas. The origin of fermented sticky soybean could also be accidental. Some cooked soybeans could have been left after the meal which turned into viscous stringy threads with a typical flavour in the next morning. This could probably be the origin of kinema and other similar soybean products, subsequently developed by further innovation and demand of local people depending on agro-climatic conditions.[20] Antiquity of *kinema*, however, is yet to be fully explored and ascertained.

Cultural Importance of Foods

Certain foods have huge cultural significance in Nepali society of Sikkim and Darjeeling. For instance, celebration of festivals is incomplete without *selroti*. It serves as a confectionery during festivals. It is prepared particularly during the *Tihar* festival and is offered by the sisters to their brothers on the last day of this festival. It is also served during marriage and funeral ceremonies.

Among the Bahun and Chhetri castes of the region, the boys after *bratabandha* and the girls after marriage are not allowed to take stale food. As per their customs, food cooked in a roofless place was not allowed to be eaten and this custom still prevails among them. *Dhakaney*, rice cooked in butter and milk is served exclusively to married daughters at their parental house a day before *teej* (a Nepali festival). This is called *dur.* This dish is quite heavy and nutritious and people can fast the following day easily. *Khir* is another dish, which is prepared by cooking rice in milk only. It is served on special occasions to symbolize prosperity. The members of these castes eat *khir* and *phulaurah* on *shradh* (death anniversaries).

Dahi is a sacred item in many of the festivals, religious occasions and marriages of Nepalis. It is also used by Nepalis as an adhesive for rice grains and colour to make *tika* which is applied on the foreheads of the younger members of the family by their elders during festivals and marriages. It is mixed with *chiura* and eaten in *ashadko pandhra* (which falls in the month of July) signifying the beginning of work in the fields for the farmers.

For a Hindu Nepali, *gheu* (purified butter) is a sacred thing. It is used in the rituals related to birth, marriage, and death as also in other *puja*s as sacred offerings. The Nepalis, Bhutias and Lepchas use *gheu* also for lighting the lamps for gods and goddesses in religious places. During *maghe sankranti* (a festival of Hindu Nepalis), a variety of boiled tubers or *tarul, tilko laddu* (sesame balls mixed with molasses), *papadko phulaurah* (buckwheat fritters) are eaten by the Nepalis.

The cultural significance of food among Newars is also interesting. For instance, the most common expression for greeting in Newari is *ja naye dwuno la*? It means, 'have you had your rice?' Meat and alcohol are culturally acceptable to them. Two food items—*dhau saga* and *khe saga* are important in ritual exchange among Newar relatives. *Dhau saga* consists of *dahi* and flattened rice and *khe saga* consists of egg, *chiura,* meat, fish, *wa* (roasted pulses) and *ayela* (distilled liquor). Newars believe that *dahi* is associated with masculinity and purity, and the egg is associated with sexuality and fertility. *Kwanti* has its own connotations. It is related to the mysteries of creation and growth. Nine kinds of pulses and beans symbolise the *nava-Durga* cult, the cult of nine Durga, the goddess of Hindus. Traditionally, it is not eaten by Newars for a year after death.

Traditional alcoholic beverages have strong ritual importance. Social activities like marriage and festivals require consumption of appreciable quantities of alcoholic beverages among the Limbu, Rai, Gurung, Magar, Tamang, Sunuwar, Newar, Sherpa, Bhutia and Lepcha communities. *Jaanr* and *raksi* are essential to solemnize the marriage ceremony of these communities. Elopement is a common practice among Nepalis. Relatives of the boy usually go to the girl's house with bottles of *raksi* to respect the verdict of her parents and pay the penalty for elopement. Once the consent is granted by the girl's parents, freshly prepared *raksi* is served to all and the marriage is solemnised.

Alcoholic beverages are offered to perform the *pitri puja* or *kul puja*, which means worship of ancestors. *Mandokpenaa thea* or *kodoko jaanr*, filled in *tongba*, and *raksi* are among the important materials for performing a ritual of the Limbus called *tongsing*. Those who come to offer condolences at a funeral or a memorial service for the deceased are served with alcoholic beverages, mostly among the non-caste Nepalis.

Drying of *gundruk* and *sinki* in the sun is a remarkable step in the traditional processing of foods. They are preserved for several months without refrigeration and consumed during monsoon when fresh vegetables are scarce. Dry *gundruk* and *sinki* are comparatively lighter than the weight of fresh substrates and can, therefore, be carried easily while traveling. Carrying dry *gundruk, sinki, kinema*, hard *chhurpi, sidra, sukuti, sukako masu, maseura*, etc. is still common practice among the Nepalis of Darjeeling and Sikkim while travelling long distances.[21] Because of the acidic taste, *gundruk* and *sinki* are said to be good appetizers, and people use these foods as remedies for indigestion.

Regular consumption of meat is expensive for a majority of the poor rural people. They slaughter domestic animals usually on special occasions, like festivals and marriages. During *dasain* (a festival of Nepali), goats are ritually sacrificed to please the goddess Durga. After the ceremony, the meat is cooked and eaten. The remaining meat is preserved by smoking to make *sukako masu* for future consumption. Such meat can be kept for several months.

Among Rais, marital status is a very strong determinant in the preparation of certain items. For instance, only widows or unmarried women are allowed to make *marcha,* a traditional dry starter for alcohol production. Those who make it believe that addition of wild herbs gives more sweetness to the product and adding chilies and ginger get rid of devils that may spoil the product. This is actually to check the growth of undesirable microorganisms that may inhibit growth of indigenous microflora in *marcha*.[22]

Conclusion

Today these foods are associated with culture and tradition, and they are consumed during special occasions and festivals. Whatever be their antiquity, there is no denying the fact that *dhenroh, kinema, gundruk, sinki, jaanr, raksi* etc. represent a distinct cultural identity of the Nepalis of Sikkim and Darjeeling.

Compared to fermented foods (which number about 20) of southern and western India such as *dosa, idli, dohkla*, etc there are more than 80 types of common and lesser-known fermented foods and beverages in the Darjeeling hills, Sikkim, and Northeast India. Today, India has one of the largest numbers of food recourses. No doubt the Indian Nepalis or Gorkhas have significantly contributed to the rich dietary culture of India. *Kinema* has already entered in the patent process of India.

The word 'Nepali' has been recognised by the government of India while granting Nepali as an official language in the Eighth Schedule of the constitution. Similarly, the word 'Gorkha' has been officially recognised by the government of India while signing the tripartite agreement in 1988 and memorandum of settlement in 2005. Hence, the government of India, by accepting both Nepali and Gorkha identities, has created further confusion in their minds. Finally, while the government of India has accepted them as Indians, many people of India have not, which is one of the biggest challenges of the Indian Nepalis or Gorkhas today.

REFERENCES

1. A. Rai, R.M. Sharma and J.P. Tamang, 2005, "Food Value of Common Edible Wild Plants of Sikkim", *Journal of Hill Research,* 18(2): 99-103. Also see, J.P. Tamang, 2005, *Food Culture of Sikkim*, Sikkim Study Series Volume IV, Gangtok: Information and Public Relations Department, Government of Sikkim.
2. J.P. Tamang, S. Dewan, S. Thapa, N.A. Olasupo, U. Schillinger and W.H. Holzapfel, 2000, Identification and Enzymatic Profiles of Predominant Lactic Acid Bacteria Isolated from Soft-Variety *chhurpi*, a Traditional

Cheese Typical of the Sikkim Himalayas, *Food Biotechnology,* 14(1 and 2): 99-112.

3. N. Tsuyoshi, R. Fudou, S. Yamanaka, M. Kozaki, N. Tamang, S. Thapa and J.P. Tamang, 2005, Identification of Yeast Strains Isolated from Marcha in Sikkim, A Microbial Starter for Amylolytic Fermentation, *International Journal of Food Microbiology*, 99(2): 135-46.
4. J.P. Tamang and S. Thapa, 2006, Fermentation dynamics during production of *bhaati jaanr*, a traditional fermented rice beverage of the Eastern Himalayas, *Food Biotechnology*, 20(3): 251-61.
5. J.P. Tamang, B. Tamang, U. Schillinger, C.M.A.P. Franz, M. Gores and W.H. Holzapfel, 2005, Identification of predominant lactic acid bacteria isolated from traditional fermented vegetable products of the Eastern Himalayas, *International Journal of Food Microbiology,* 105: 347-56.
6. J.P. Tamang and S. Nikkuni, 1996, Selection of starter culture for production of *kinema*, a fermented soybean food of the Himalaya, *World Journal of Microbiology and Biotechnology,* 12: 629-635. Also see, J.P. Tamang, 2001, *Kinema*, *Food Culture,* 3: 11-14, and J.P. Tamang, 2003, Native microorganisms in the fermentation of *kinema, Indian Journal of Microbiology,* 43(2): 1-4.
7. S. Thapa and J.P. Tamang, 2004, Product characterization of kodo ko jaanr: fermented finger millet beverage of the Himalayas, *Food Microbiology,* 21: 617-22.
8. J.P. Tamang and P.K. Sarkar, 1996, Microbiology of *mesu*, a traditional fermented bamboo shoot product, *International Journal of Food Microbiology,* 29: 49-58.
9. J.P. Tamang, S. Thapa, J.P. Tamang and B. Rai, 1996, Indigenous fermented food beverages of Darjeeling hills and Sikkim: process and product characterization, *Journal of Hill Research,* 9(2): 401-11.
10. J.P. Tamang and P.K. Sarkar, 1993, *Sinki*: a traditional lactic acid fermented radish tap root product, *Journal of General and Applied Microbiology,* 39: 395-408.
11. N. Thapa, J. Pal and J.P. Tamang, 2006, Phenotypic identification and technological properties of lactic acid bacteria isolated from traditionally processed fish products of the Eastern Himalayas, *International Journal of Food Microbiology,* 107 (1): 33-38.
12. S. Dewan and J.P. Tamang, 2007, Dominant lactic acid bacteria and their technological properties isolated from the Himalayan ethnic fermented milk products, *Antonie van Leeuwenhoek International Journal of General and Molecular Microbiology* (in press).
13. N. Thapa, *et al.*, 2006, *op. cit.*
14. J.P. Tamang, 2001, *op. cit.*
15. J.R. Subba, 1999, *The Limboos of the Eastern Himalayas with Special Reference to Sikkim,* Gangtok: Sikkim Yakthung Mundhum Saplopa.

16. T. Bo, 1984, Tousi no genryu oyobi sono seisan-gijutu, *Nippon Jouzo Kyoukai Zasshi,* 77(7): 439-445 (Japanese).
17. M. Horii, 1997, Soybean and fermented food culture in the world, *Farming Japan,* 31 (4): 10-12.
18. T. Hara, S. Hiroyuki, I. Nobuhide and K. Shinji, 1995, Plasmid analysis in polyglutamate-producing *Bacillus* strain isolated from non-salty fermented soybean food, 'kinema', in Nepal, *Journal of General and Applied Microbiology,* 41: 3-9.
19. J.P. Tamang, S. Thapa, S. Dewan, Y. Jojima, R. Fudou and S. Yamanaka, 2002, Phylogenetic analysis of *Bacillus* strains isolated from fermented soybean foods of Asia: *kinema, chungkokjang and natto, Journal of Hill Research,* 15 (2): 56-62.
20. S. Nikkuni, 1997, Natto, kinema and thua-nao: traditional non-salted fermented soybean foods in Asia, *Farming Japan,* 31 (4): 27-36.
21. J.P. Tamang, 1997, Jatiya Khadyaharu: *Kinema, Gundruk* ani *Sinki, Nirman samayik sahitya sankalan* (Eds. Pawan Chamling and Gopal Gaule), Namchi: Nirman Prakhashan, 189-193 (Nepali).
22. J.P. Tamang, 1998, Role of microorganisms in traditional fermented foods, *Indian Food Industry,* 17 (3), 162-167.

21

Herbal Medicinal Culture of the Nepalis of Darjeeling and Sikkim

D.R. CHHETRI

Folklores, traditions, rituals and practices are important features of culture, which are nurtured through centuries. The history of herbal medicines is as old as human history. In the Darjeeling and Sikkim Himalayan region, the common people rarely consult a modern physician for the treatment of their common ailments. Instead, herbs play an important role in the everyday life of the inhabitants of this region.[1]

Darjeeling and Sikkim Himalaya is situated between 87° 59′-88° 53′ East longitude and 26° 31′-28° 10′ North latitude. This region is rich in floral diversity, endemic elements and a number of species which have become rare, threatened or endangered. The tribes of this Himalayan region also have rich traditions of herbal medicine for which a few literature are available.[2] There are different types of sub-tropical, temperate and alpine plants whose medicinal value is not yet known to science. More than 400 species of plants possessing therapeutic properties have been recorded from Sikkim Himalaya alone.[3] Lacking proper studies and measures for domestication, this vast resource has remained untapped and underutilized so far.[4]

The People and their Healing Practices

The major ethnic groups of the Sikkim and Darjeeling Himalayan region are Nepali (Gorkha), Lepcha and Bhutia. Of these, the Nepalis are subdivided into three distinct categories: (i) *Tagadharies*: represented by Bahun, Thakuri and Chhetri castes whose members wear the sacred thread across their chest and who bear Caucasoid features, (ii) *Matwalis*:

represented by the Mongoloid groups like Rai, Limbu, Tamang, Magar, Gurung, Sherpa, and Yolmu. They are traditionally known as "drinking castes", and (iii) Scheduled Castes represented by Kami (blacksmith), Damai (tailor/musician), Sarki (cobbler) etc. Among the Nepalis the Newars constitute a special category because they have the whole hierarchy of castes from the Brahmins to the so-called 'Untouchable' castes within themselves and according to religion are divided into both Buddhists and Hindus. Despite their division into different social groups, cultural interactions and inter-caste marriages are quite common. The Lepchas are one of the oldest tribes inhabiting Darjeeling and Sikkim Himalayan region. They are born naturalists and have separate names for nearly every bird, plant, orchid and butterfly to be found in this region.[5] The Bhutias are the descendents of Tibetans and they practise a form of Buddhism known as Lamaism. Each of the above ethnic groups has its own distinct form of worship, language and tradition, but all of them are exceedingly generous, light hearted and law abiding people. The Nepali language serves all the three ethnic groups as a *lingua franca*.[6]

The main occupations of the people of Darjeeling and Sikkim Himalaya are agriculture, agro-forestry, horticulture, animal husbandry etc. Agricultural practices in these hills are characterized by low input and low yield. The geometric progression in the growth of human population has been exerting pressure on traditional practices and leading to fragmentation of land holding size. Consequently, the people have been pushed to a marginal existence while this region is situated in one of the biodiversity hot-spots of the world and is a virtual gold-mine of medicinal plant biodiversity. Moreover, the indigenous people of this region have a rich local healing tradition and a large number of traditional healers have been practising indigenous medicine for hundred of years.[7] Being close to nature, traditional herbal culture is very well developed in the Darjeeling-Sikkim Himalaya. Traditional medicine in this region is practised by everyone, including the Lama (Bhutia priest), Bongthing and Mun (Lepcha male and female priests), Jhankri, Bijuwa, Fedangba, etc (Nepali medicinemen) all of whom utilize the locally available plants for treatment of ailments. However, despite its rich biodiversity and a rich culture of traditional medicine this Himalayan region is paradoxically inhabited by some of the poorest peoples in the universe.[8]

Why Study Herbal Medicine?

Traditional herbal medicine relates to health practices, approaches, knowledge and beliefs incorporating naturally available plants or plant products applied singularly or in combination with minerals, animal products, spiritual therapies etc. in order to diagnose, treat and prevent illnesses or maintain well-being. Traditional systems of medicine attempt to embody a holistic approach, i.e., viewing an individual in his totality with the socio-ecological system. The socio-ecological system remarkably influences the mental state of an individual which in turn alters the secretions of neurohormones etc. These secretions have profound physiological effects. Therefore, it is worthwhile to devise novel methods to evaluate the intriguing aspects of traditional medicine.[9] About 70-75 per cent of Indian population is dependent on herbal medicine for primary health care because of better cultural acceptability, better compatibility with the human body and lesser side effect. Availability and cost-effectiveness are other reasons for its popularity.

Medicinal plants have high potential for creating jobs and pushing economic growth in resource constrained areas suffering from limited educational opportunities, lack of infrastructure and underdeveloped commercial activities. The conversion of socio-cultural traditions and indigenous knowledge into economic opportunities also has the advantage of preserving the vanishing cultural knowledge and practices which are threatened due to globalization. As the Himalayas are recognized as the treasure trove of biological and cultural diversity there is a need to protect indigenous knowledge and cultural diversity on an urgent basis. In the uplands of Northeast Himalayas, the means of achieving this may be by providing economic value to the traditional and indigenous knowledge.[10]

A huge chunk of humanity is still dependent on herbal medicine for their healthcare needs. This is truer for people living in remote areas away from modern world of activities.[11] A tremendous scope of research is foreseen on the biochemical, pharmacological and pharmaceutical aspects of traditional medicine and the related plants in Darjeeling Himalayas.[12] Knowledge in these aspects may have unforeseen commercial potentialities.

It is believed that at least 25 per cent of modern medicine is of plant origin. Some of the important allopathic drugs of plant origin in Indian market are enumerated in Table 21.1. Furthermore, economic strategies in the herbal sector should be formulated considering the market forces and global impacts of traditional medicine which are as follows:

- 75 per cent of world population is dependent on traditional herbal medicine for its healthcare.

Table 21.1: Allopathic Drugs Originating from Himalayan Medicinal Plants

Botanical Name	*Local Name (in Nepali)*	*Part Used*	*Medicinal Compound*	*Usage/Disease*
Artemisia annua	Titaypati	Plant	Artemisinin	Malaria
Asparagus racemosus	Kurilo	Root	L-asparginase, Rutin	Cancer
Catharanthus roseus	Sadabahar	Leaf	Vinblastine, Vincristine	Cancer
Cinchona officinalis	Kulain	Bark	Quinine, Quinidine	Malaria
Commiphora waightii	Aghori	Gum	Gugulipid	Hypolipidaemic
Digitalis purpurea	Ghantiphool	Leaf	Digoxin	Heart failure
Ephedra gerardiana	Somlata	Plant	Ephedrine	Asthma, congestion
Gloriosa superba	Langaray tarul	Tuber	Colchicine	Gout, cancer
Mucuna pruriens	Kauso	Seed	L-Dopa	Hypertension
Panax ginseng	Salanay	Root	Ginsenosides	Tonic, antioxidant
Rauwolfia serpentiana	Sarpagandha	Root	Reserpine	Hypertension
Taxus baccata	Dhyangre salla	Leaf	Taxol	Anti cancer

Source: Raghav, 2003.

- 25 per cent of modern medicines are made from plants first used traditionally.
- Current global market of herbal medicine is worth US $62 billion/annum and growing steadily.
- In the USA more than US $17 billion is presently being spent on traditional medicine.
- In Europe and North America, over 50 per cent of the population has used traditional medicine at least once.
- Traditional medicine is effective in diseases where allopathic drugs have become resistant, e.g., malignant malaria can be treated with *Artemisia annua* (*Titaypati*) and recalcitrant viral fever with *Swertia chirata* (*Chireto*).

Threats to Traditional Medical System

The Darjeeling and Sikkim Himalayan region is becoming modernized due to increased level of education, travel, interaction with outsiders, influence of religious preachers, politicians, etc. Modernization and globalization have given the people economic freedom, political empowerment and a sense of self-confidence to some extent. However, due to modernization the educated people are moving away from their traditional herbal practices. The young generation is no longer interested in herbal medicine. In order to preserve these practices economic elements must be incorporated with traditions and cultural wisdom.

Increasing demand for medicinal plants from the Himalayan region has resulted in unsustainable harvesting and consequent loss of species. Besides, loss of forest covers due to developmental activities, natural calamities and demographic changes have led to the loss of biodiversity.[13] The main drawbacks of the traditional herbal medicines are:

- Unregulated or inappropriate use of traditional medicine may have dangerous effects. For example, *Citrullus colocynthis* (*Indreni* in Nepali) is still used as a remedy for jaundice in the local therapy while pharmacological studies have confirmed its toxic effects to liver cells.[14]
- A growing herbal market has posed a threat to biodiversity through over-harvesting which may lead to extinction of species.
- A significant number of the people who depend on herbal medicine face alarming danger because of herbal medicine being mixed with allopathic drugs. More than 50 per cent of traditional

medicinal practitioners prescribe allopathic drugs without proper knowledge which is creating health hazards and economic burden to the community.[15]

- At present the protection under the patent law are inadequate and does not protect the interest of the people who nurtured traditional medical system for a long time.

Future Prospects

In the Himalayan region of Sikkim and Darjeeling earning a high return from limited land holding, maintenance of sustainable conditions, preservation of biodiversity, continuance of organic cultivation etc. are the challenges faced by agriculturists. Cultivation of medicinal plants may help to maintain ecological conditions. It may replenish the dwindling stock of wild plants and help in the conservation of species. It may also give high economic return.

Though the global herbal medicine market is worth US $62 billion, the total Indian export is worth US $500 million only. The market is dominated by China. India exports herbal medicines mostly in crude form, quality control is weak, and there is little research on the validation of the drugs. Figure 1 shows the conventional strategy for a modern drug development. It requires about 10 years of research and approximately Rs. 800 crores of investment for a single drug discovery. Under such backdrop the big question is, why should one go for such drug development? The answer may be summarized as:

- Because Darjeeling-Sikkim Himalayan region contains many unique medicinal plants (endemic) which are not available anywhere else in the world and no research on drug discovery involving these plants has been done so far. The research laboratories like the Central Institute of Medicinal and Aromatic Plants (Lucknow), Central Drug Research Institute (Lucknow), Herbal Research Development Institute (Gopeshwar), M.S. Swaminathan Research Foundation (Chennai), National Institute of Pharmacy Education and Research (Mohali), Regional Research Laboratory (Jammu) etc. are not involved in drug discovery research based on Darjeeling-Sikkim Himalayan endemic plants. Other local/state level institutes neither have the infrastructure nor the expertise for such research.

- Because it has been realized that medicinal plants of the Indian Himalayan region offer advantage in having much greater possibilities of providing new molecules used in drugs due to the extreme environmental condition they are subjected to.[16]
- Because instead of random search for medicinal plants, a selective search based on traditional knowledge would be more focussed and productive and certainly more economic.[17]
- Because traditional knowledge can provide great value in selecting plant material for use in drug discovery.[18]
- Because even if a single blockbuster drug can be developed, it will be worth all the trouble. For example, Lipitor, the cholesterol reducing medicine from Pfizer has a worldwide sale of US $10 billion (about Rs. 45,000 crore).[19]

Conclusion

The medicinal plants of this Himalayan region are gradually becoming extinct due to developmental activities. Domestication of these plants is of utmost importance to stop this trend. Some solution to human suffering like cancer and AIDS may lie hidden in the treasure of these Himalayan plants. Considering the fact that traditional knowledge forms the basis for the development of new products and cultural diversity is more threatened than biodiversity, it is an urgent necessity to record as quickly as possible all the information about our natural resources and their usage.

Ultimately, in the modern scheme of drug development it is proposed that priority should be given to the use of medicinal plants used by the indigenous people for specific purpose. Traditional use also means that toxicity studies and clinical trials may be done away with. It may substantially reduce laboratory time and cost. Since in the Himalayan region several herbal remedies exist for each human ailment, some of them will definitely prove suitable leading to the development of a new drug.[20]

In order to translate our natural heritage and cultural wisdom into a tangible economic gain, a multilayered collaboration among the grassroots people, the government and the scientists is a must (Figure 2). The people should conserve their herbal resources and preserve their cultural practices. The government should provide land and seed money to the grassroots people for the cultivation of medicinal plants and should also facilitate marketing of their produce. At the same time, the authorities should provide the scientists with infrastructure facilities in a suitable manner. The scientists should work towards development of agrotechnique packages and transmit them 'from the laboratory to the land'. On the other hand, the scientists should screen the plants for their biological activity, identify the effective chemicals in the plants, isolate and characterize them, and finally work towards developing new drugs following the ethnobotanical leads present in the prevailing healing systems of the people. The international agencies may also be called for collaboration whereby they may participate in the advanced capital and technology intensive stages of drug development. After all, they will also be benefited because the cost of drug discovery research in India is one fourth of that in Europe and the USA.[21]

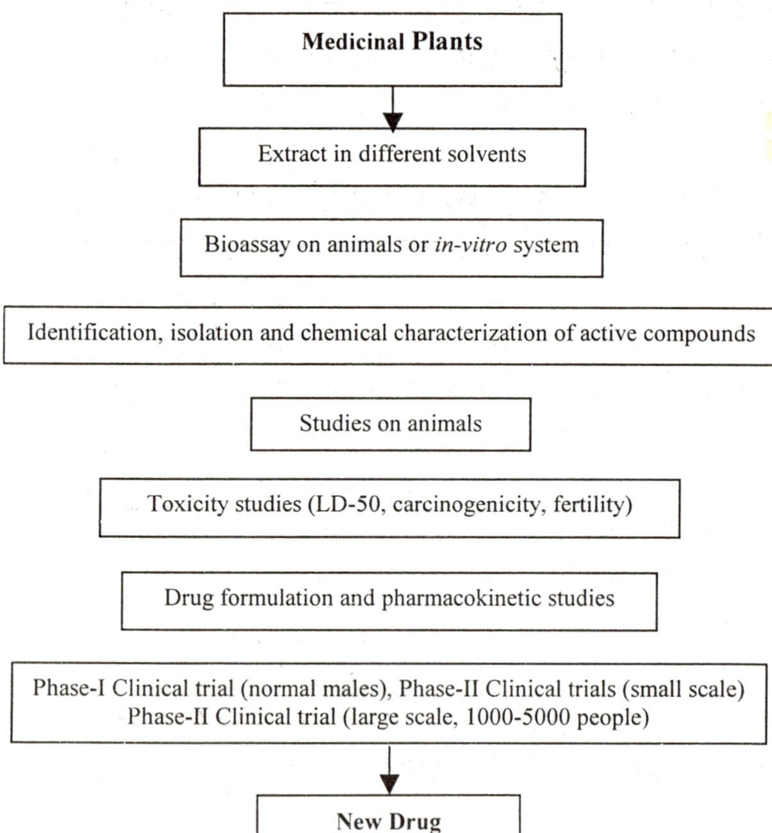

Fig. 1: Conventional Strategy for Modern Drug Development Starting from Medicinal Plants

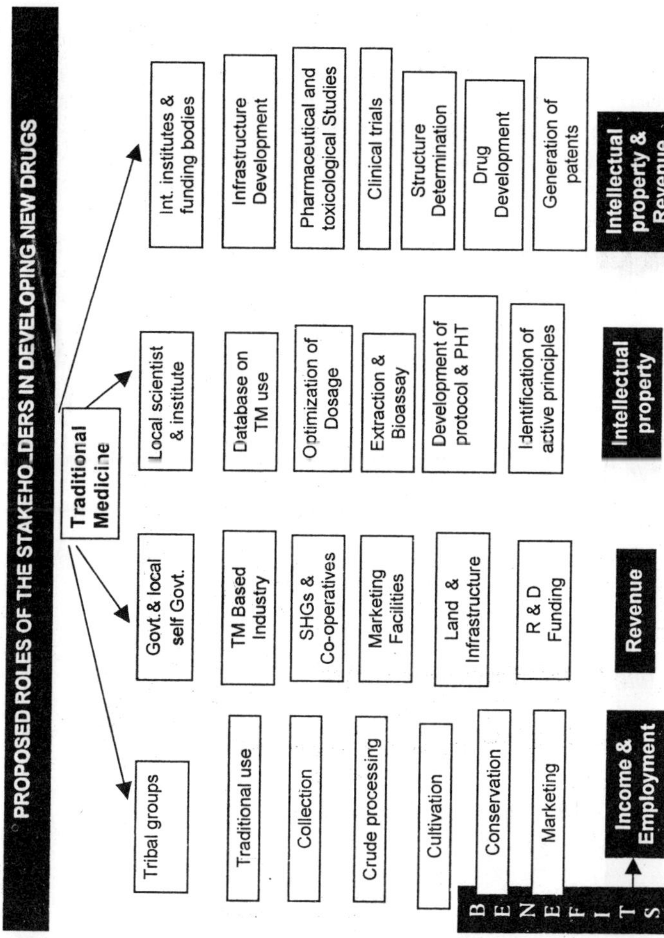

Fig. 2: A Proposed Model for Drug Development in the Darjeeling-Sikkim Himalaya Using Local Medicinal Plants, Traditional Knowledge and Modern Technological Inputs

REFERENCES

1. K. Biswas, 1956, *Common Medicinal Plants of Darjeeling and Sikkim Himalaya,* Calcutta: Bengal Govt. Press.
2. D.R. Chhetri, D. Basnet, P.F. Chiu, S. Kalikotay, G. Chhetri, and S. Parajuli, 2005, "Current Status of Ethnomedicinal Plants in the Darjeeling Himalaya", *Current Science*, 89(2): 264-68. Also see, D.R. Chhetri, 2005, *Lepcha Ethnomedicinal Plants from Darjeeling Himalayas*, P.K. Mukherjee (ed.), *Proceedings of International Conference on Promotion and Development of Botanicals with International Coordination: Exploring Quality, Safety, Efficacy and Regulations,* Kolkata: Allied Book Agency, pp. 234-39.
3. T.N. Srivastava and B.K. Kapahi, 1990, "Resource Survey of Plants of Potential Economic Value of Sikkim Himalaya", *Bulletin of Medicinal and Economic Botanical Research*, 12(1-2): 1-11.
4. D.R. Chhetri, 2005, "Ethnomedicinal Plants of the Khangchendzonga National Park, Sikkim, India", *Ethnobotany*, 17: 96-103.
5. E.C. Dozey, 1989, *A Concise History of Darjeeling District since 1835,* Calcutta: Jetsun Publishing House.
6. D.R. Chhetri, J. Adhikari and S. Adhikari, 2006, "Hepatoprotective Medicinal Plants from the Darjeeling Himalaya", P.C. Trivedi (ed.), *Medicinal Plants: Ethnobotanical Approach*, Jodhpur: Agrobios (India), pp. 207-17.
7. G. Bodeker, 2002, Medicinal Plants: Towards Sustainability and Security. IDRC Medicinal Plants Global Network Sponsored Discussion Paper for WOCAMP III, Chiang Mai, Thailand.
8. D.R. Chhetri, P. Parajuli, and G.C. Subba, 2005, Antidiabetic Plants Used by Sikkim and Darjeeling Himalayan Tribes, India, *Journal of Ethnopharmacology*, 99: 199-202.
9. A. Subramoniam and P. Pushpangadan, 1995, *Ethnopharmacologial Validation of Traditional Medicines/Remedies*, P. Pushpangadan, U. Nyman and V. George (eds), *Glimpses of Indian Ethnopharmacology,* Thiruvananthapuram: Tropical Botanic Garden and Research Institute, pp. 351-60.
10. P.S. Ramakrishnan, 1992, *Shifting Agriculture and Sustainable Development: An Interdisciplinary Study from North Eastern India,* Carnforth: Paris and Parthenon Publishing Group.
11. S.K. Rai and R.B. Bhujel, 1999, Notes on some less known Ethnomedicinal plants from Darjeeling Himalayas, *Journal of Hill Research*, 12: 160-63.
12. G.S. Yonzone, D.K.N. Yonzone and K.K. Tamang, 1984, "Medicinal Plants of Darjeeling District", *Journal of Economic and Taxonomic Botany*, 5: 605-16.
13. D.R. Given, 1996, *How Plants Become Extinct? Principles and Practices of Plant Conservation,* Portland: Timber Press.

14. M.A. Al-Yahya, A.H. Al-Farhan and S.F.I. Adam, 2000, "Preliminary toxicity study on the individual and combined effects of *Citrullus colocynthis* and *Nerium oleander* in rats", *Fitoterapia*, 71(4): 385-91.
15. A.D. Choudhury, K. Sudhakar, K. Abdullah, A. Holla, and C.R. Choudhury, 2002, "Pattern of Drug Use in an Indian Urban Area: A Questionnaire Survey, *Indian Journal of Pharmaceutical Science*, 64(2): 124-28.
16. J.R. Sharma, V. Mudgal, and P.K. Hajra, 1997, "Review Scope and Perspectives," V. Mudgal. and P.K. Hajra (eds), *Floristic Diversity and Conservation Strategies in India*, Vol. I., Calcutta: Botanical Survey of India.
17. B. Rameswararao, M.M. Kesavulu, and C. Apparao, 2003, "Evaluation of Antidiabetic Effect of *Momordica Cymbalaria* Fruit in Alloxan Diabetic Rats", *Fitoterapia*, 74(1-2): 7-13.
18. W.H. Lewis, A. Vaisberg, G. Lamas, and C. Sarasara, 2004, "Elvin-lewis M. Advantage of Ethnobotanically Based Research for Searching New Pharmaceuticals", *Ethnobotany*, 16: 10-15.
19. D.G. Shah, 2005, "Challenge and Opportunity: Ranbaxy's Legal Battle with Pfizer Indicates How Tough and Profitable the Global Pharma is", *India Today*, 30(43): 34.
20. D.R. Chhetri, *et al.*, 2005, *op. cit.*
21. S. Mukherjee, 2004, "Patent Potential: India can Emerge as R & D Hub in Pharma", *The Times of India*, VI(69): 11.

Section 5

India-Nepal Linkage: History, Literature and People

22

Origin and Development of the Nepali Language

MADHAV POKHAREL

Nepali is an Indo-Aryan language of the Indo-European family. It is customary to establish genetic relationship among Indo-European languages by comparing words for hundred. If the word begins with/s/, the language is put into the Satem class and if it begins with/k/, language is grouped under Centum. The words for hundred start with/s/ in both Sanskrit and Nepali to be classed as Satem languages while it starts with/ k/ in Latin to categorize Latin under Centum. Except for the Tokhari language which was being spoken until the 9th century at Xinjiang in Western China, a Centum language, almost the whole of the Eastern group of Indo-European languages are Satem while roughly the whole of Western group of languages tend to be categorized as Centum.

Although the cognates of the Sanskrit word 'aarya' like 'Ireland' can establish distant historical relationship among several Indo-European languages, 'aryana', recorded by Greek historians like Herodotus (5th century BC), should be the precursor of modern word 'Iran'. Therefore linguists like Bloch (1965), Chatterjee (1926), Sen (1960), Masica (1990) and Cardona (2003) consider Iranian and Sanskrit (including its descendants like Nepali, Hindi, Bangla and Assamese) as Aryan languages. Linguists like Bhandarkar (1882), Ghatage (1962) and Siddheshwar Varma and Bhim Dev (1953), who worked on historical and comparative linguistics, have discovered rules of linguistic similarities between Sanskrit and Iranian to establish common genealogical relationship between them. For example Sanskrit/s/ corresponds with Old Iranian/h/ in the following data:

1a. Sanskrit: *sapta, sindhu, asura, sama, shaasaka*
b. Old Iranian: *hapta, hindu, ahura, hama, shaaha*

Nepali language makes use of the Iranian words *hapta, hindu* and *shaaha* together with the Sanskrit words (1a). Linguists, who have worked on Indo-Aryan languages, believe that Nepali is developed not from Iranian but from Indo-Aryan. On this ground Nepali is believed to have developed from Sanskrit.

Beams (1872) and Cardona (1988) are of the view that the language got the name Sanskrit only after Panini (5th century BC). If a linguisti prepares to write a grammar of a language following linguistic principles, he collects data from native speakers of the language, not from learned pundits, but Panini has based his grammar on the language of pundits (*shiSTa prayoga*).

The meaning of the word 'Sanskrit' is 'refined' or 'purified'. On the contrary, since the word 'prakriti' also means 'people', the literal meaning of the word 'praakrita' comes out to be the 'language of the people'. It follows that 'praakrita' was the spoken variety of the language of common people internalized by a child from his family and neighbourhood, but Sanskrit was the variety of language standardized by the works of grammarians like Panini and learned by students at schools. Prakrit being the spoken form of the language was natural to have several nonstandard varieties and Sanskrit tended to have a single variety for being learned at schools. As the standardization of Sanskrit continued, variants of the language were further narrowed down until the language became a single variety. Panini's *aSTaadhyaayii* won the competition of standardizing Sanskrit among grammarians, because it has generalized Sanskrit language used both in the Vedic texts and in the Classical Sanskrit texts with about four thousand algebraic formulae. With this a student can have mastery over Sanskrit language in a limited time as against the grammars of his contemporaries and predecessors like *Pratishakhyas*. Today the variety of language that follows Paninian rules is considered correct and the one which does not is considered incorrect. In this way, the words 'Paninian' and 'correct' have become synonymous. This account shows that the variety of Sanskrit that is being taught in universities today is a variety standardized and developed by grammarians like Panini. The variety thus developed was related to Vedic texts on the one hand and the variety of the language taught in various schools during Panini and his predecessors on the other.

Panini was born in Taxila which is situated in modern Pakistan. During the time of Panini, the spoken language of Taxila may have been somewhat similar to the standardized Sanskrit. Geographical variants of standard Sanskrit were very few, but the spoken varieties must have been many. Patanjali[1] has also noted some of the variant forms. When Sanskrit was used as the administrative language by the kings and emperors from Central Asia to Southeast Asia and when it reached China, Korea, Japan, Vietnam, Myanmar, Malaysia, Indonesia and Cambodia with the scriptures of Mahayana Buddhism it underwent many hybrid and corrupt forms. There are four or five varieties of Prakrit language[2] during Asoka's period (3rd c. BC).

Prakrit languages of several varieties appear in Buddhist and Jaina literatures and Sanskrit dramas. Since they are written varieties, it is difficult to guess which of the corresponding spoken varieties developed into the Apabhramsha language. It is not natural for the written variety to be developed into a spoken form of a natural language. Therefore, Nepali could not have been developed from any of the written varieties of Sanskrit, Prakrit or Apabhramsha languages. On the basis of research works of Prakrit grammarians like Hemchandra, Bararuchi and Bhandarkar (1914), Grierson (1916) and Turner (1931, 1966) believe that Nepali may have developed from the Northwestern variety of Prakrit.

Hoernle (1880) has classified New Indo-Aryan languages into Inner and Outer groups. In his opinion, there is a clear contrast between the Indo-Aryan languages of the Gangetic basin and elsewhere. He has labeled the languages of the Gangetic basin as Inner group in contrast with the Outer group spoken elsewhere. The Outer group comprises Nepali, Gadhwali, Kumauni, Rajasthani, Gujarati, Sindhi and Kashmiri and the Inner group covers languages like Hindi, Bengali, Oriya, Assamese, Panjabi, Maithili, Bhojpuri, Awadhi, Chhattisgadhi, Bagheli, Marathi and Konkani. When I analyzed the comparative wordlists of New Indo-Aryan languages given by Turner (1931), I discovered that nominals (nouns and adjectivals) are o-suffixed in the Outer group of languages which correspond with a-suffixed nominals in the Inner group, e.g.:

2a. Nepali : *mero jeTho choro ayo.* 'My eldest son came'
2b. Hindi : *mera bada ladka aya.* 'My eldest son came'[3]

According to Hoernle (1880) the Outer group entered the Indian peninsula prior to the Inner group. The Gangetic basin facilitated its entry into the Indian subcontinent. There is always a political and military competition among power groups to occupy the most facilitated territory and the winner controls it. With this principle, the Inner group, although it was late to come to the subcontinent, was successful to control the centre by replacing the preceding groups. The Outer group, according to Hoernle, was the one which was replaced by the late-comers. In fact the Outer group Indo-Aryan speakers are seen to have occupied the Himalayan and the Aravalli ranges. Masica (1990) has noted the similarities between the Indo-Aryan languages of these two mountain regions. Major ethnic groups which speak these two stocks of languages are Khasa and Gurjara.

Atkinson (1880), Joshi (1926), Pande (1937), Sankrityayan (1953, 2013 BS, 2015 BS) and Balkrishna Pokharel (2055 BS) have done extensive studies on the Khasas. Sankrityayan (2013 BS) has identified Western Chinese province Xinjiang or the Tarim river basin as the original home of the Khasas. Archaeological studies of Xinjiang (see Mair 1998) reveal that the original homeland of Sakas was the Chinese province Gansu, a neighboring province of Xinjiang, but when the power of Mongols arose around the 1st century, the Mongols replaced the Sakas of Gansu. The Sakas settled for some time in Central Asia to the north of Afghanistan (probably in the present day Tajikistan, Uzbekistan or Kazakhstan republics of the Russian Federation) and finally entered the Indian subcontinent during the reign of Kaniska. Khasas, Sakas and Kushanas were akin to Iranians, but Khasas entered the Indian subcontinent long before Sakas and Kusanas. In the Mahabharata (Sabha Parva, Udyoga Parva and Karna Parva) a group of Khasas were forming a queue in the Rajasuya Yajna of king Yudhisthira with offerings of gold dust (*Pipiilikaa suvarna*) in their hands.[4] They came from their abode, the region of Mt. Kailasa. Until very recent times the Kailasa-Manasarovara region was Nepal's territory, but today it is in Western Tibet, Tibetan Autonomous Region of the Peoples' Republic of China. The snow-clad Kunlun mountain region separates Western Tibet from Xinjiang. With this, we can guess that the Khasas must have entered Western Tibet through some pass that cuts across Kunlun. Sankrityayan (1948) reports that a group of Khasa people live in Western Tibet even today and they are called Khachhe by the local people.[5] Mount Kailasa is noted as the abode of Lord Shiva in the Puranas. In one of the hymns (Shiva-panchaaksara-stotra) Siva is addressed as Yaksa (Yaksa-svaruupaaya). Atkinson (1880) opines that Khasas were previously called 'Yaksa'. Lama Taranath (Chattopadhyaya 1970) has collected two Buddhist stories called 'Divyaavadaana' and 'Ashokaavadaana' which note that two Khasa boys from Western Nepal helped king Asoka while there was a plot against him in Pataliputra (modern Patna). Although the historicity of texts in the Indian subcontinent is a major point of debate, I feel it is better not to ignore these points. Historians and archaeologists of this region need to focus their attention on this issue.

In the Changu Narayana inscription king Manadeva (5th century) is reported to have won the rulers of 'Malla-puri'. In *Raajatarangini*[6] of Kashmir, a story notes that a 7th century king named Jayapida was captivated by king Arimudi of Nepal. These fragments hint that Khasa people were living in Western Nepal at least from the first century, but Yogi Narahari Nath (2012 BS) and Tucci (1956) discovered that Khasa kings came to rule Jumla from Western Tibet in the 12th century. Although these descriptions show that the Khasa kings came to rule over Jumla from Tibet in the 12th century, it cannot be refuted that the Khasa people were dwelling in Nepal as late as the beginning of the 1st century or as early as 3rd century BC or prior to that.

In order to unite Nepali, Kumauni, Gadhwali and Kashmiri, Chatterji (1926) has imagined the existence of Khasa Prakrit through which even Nepali is implied to have developed. Although all the linguists who have worked on Indo-Aryan do not support Chatterji, but when we imagine the existence of various historical and geographical spoken varieties of Prakrit, Chatterji's proposal sounds right.

Sanskrit or Old Indo-Aryan is dated to be in vogue during BC 1500-500, Prakrit or Middle Indo-Aryan (including Apabhramsa) is dated from 500 BC-1000 AD. Asokan texts are not in Sanskrit but in Middle Indo-Aryan, so those who have worked on Indo-Aryan like Beams, Bhandarkar, Chatterjee and Bloch have estimated the period of Middle Indo-Aryan from 500 BC to 1000 AD and New Indo-Aryan languages like Nepali, Hindi, Bengali and Assamese are dated by linguists to have emerged since AD 1000. In the same light, Nepali also may have crossed the Middle Indo-Aryan to the New Indo-Aryan stage. On the basis of Sircar's (1965) research the oldest New Indo-Aryan document (10th century) is found in Marathi. Chanda Baradai's *Prithviraj Rasau* which was dated by earlier researchers as 12th century is now revised to be of 10th century. On this ground, we can assume that Nepali also may have got New Indo-Aryan shape around the same time. Yatri (2039 BS:96-100) has claimed that 'Damupal's inscription' which he discovered in Dullu in Nepal is to be dated as 1038 BS (AD 10th century) and should be thus categorized as the earliest Nepali inscription. Since it was very likely that Nepali took its New Indo-Aryan shape during the 10th century, many scholars accepted Yatri's claim, but when I declared that the Damupal's inscription cannot be earlier than 13th century, scholars are now diverted to the inscription of Asokchalla (13th century) to declare it to be the first inscription of the Nepali language, but the authenticity of Asokchalla's date is to be confirmed by future research.[7]

Although Nepali is basically a Khasa language, due to series of Muslim raids and attacks in the Gangetic basin Rajput kings of Gurjar-Pratihar dynasty, who resisted the attacks constantly, had to finally take shelter in the Karnali region on the basis of Tucci's (1956) genealogy of Atri and Atreya gotra peoples of Nepal. According to Gautam (2050 BS: 23-26) for 500 years since the 7th century there was tremendous influence of Kannauj (Kaanyakubja) in North India. During that period there were two routes linking Kannauj. One route passed through Kannauj, Ayodhya and Shravasti in India; Surkhet, Dullu and Sija in Nepal and Mansarovar and Guge in Tibet. The other route passed through Nimisharanya (Nemsar in present day Sitapur district in Uttar Pradesh, North India). Therefore, the linking routes helped Kannauj to influence the Karnali region.

In any case, the oldest inscriptions in Nepali were issued by the Khasa kings of the Karnali region. Nepali language is being written in the Devanagari script since that time. However, Madhav Lal Karmacharya has discovered some Nepali documents in the Tibetan script. The Roman script was used in the newspaper *Parbate* published initially from Singapore and later from Hong Kong.

Balkrishna Pokharel (2019 BS, 2020 BS) has identified three historical dialects of Nepali. According to him Old Nepali dates from the beginning to 1555 BS (the inscription of Dhavakarmath), Medieval Nepali dates from 1555 BS to 1931 BS (*Divyopadesh* of Prithvi Narayan Shah) and Modern Nepali dates from 1931 BS to the present. The reason why B. Pokharel gave the 1955 inscription as a turning point in the history of Nepali language is that according to him that was the first inscription where vocabularies of Perso-Arabic sources appear in Nepali epigraphy, but the findings of Chalise (2063 BS) show that Perso-Arabic vocabularies appear in Nepali a century earlier in the inscriptions of Malaya Bam (1446 BS). Besides, postposition <ko> is used to connect clauses for the first time from the same inscription. This change in the structure of Nepali can be correlated with the collapse of the Khasa Empire into smaller kingdoms.

Research works of Timilsina (2050 BS), Niraula (2050 BS), Subedi (2051 BS), Acharya (2053 BS) and Dhungana (2054 BS) reveal that there are 12 or 13 dialects of Nepali. Among them the variety of Nepali spoken from the Bheri river basin in Nepal to Dibrugadh in India or in Myanmar is considered variants of the eastern dialect. Even the standard dialect is developed from the eastern dialect. Today although the variety of the Nepali language found in *Gorkhapatra*, Radio Nepal, Nepal Television, universities, Nepal Academy and literary criticism looks very different from the spoken variety it is closer to the eastern dialect. In addition, it is natural that Nepali language spoken in twelve different dialect areas is not homogeneous. On the other hand, varieties of Nepali spoken by bilingual speakers of about 100 languages may approximate around hundred. Each of such bilingual speakers of Nepali from Himachal Pradesh through Nepal to Dibrugadh and Myanmar may speak Nepali at least in two different ways. There are basically two types of native speakers. One type of native speakers' parents speaks Nepali through generations, because their forefathers spoke only Nepali. The other type of Nepali native speakers is those whose forefathers spoke different native languages. Thus, standard Nepali is the common code of unaccountable spoken varieties of Nepali. Every Nepali speaker within Nepal and abroad is sentimentally attached to this common code.

Pieces of Nepali literature prior to Prithvi Narayan Shah cannot be said to have discovered, but since then literary tradition continues. Subananda Das who wrote the oldest Nepali poem to our record was a contemporary of Prithvi Narayan Shah. Translated books from Sanskrit are found older. Nepali literature is classified into four periods: Heroic period, Bhakti period, Sringara period and Modern period. Bhanu Bhakta represents the Rama Bhakti tradition of Nepali literature. According to some critics Modern period of Nepali literature is started by Lekhnath Paudel and Dharanidhar Koirala; according to others, modern period starts with *Mutuko Byatha* (1986 BS) a drama by Balkrishna Sama, while there are some who try to link the modern period with the literary magazine *Sharada* (1991 BS), however, majority of them go with Lekhnath and Dharanidhar. This incident matches with the publication of the newspaper *Gorkhapatra* (2058 BS), literary magazines like *Sundari* (1963 BS) and *Madhavi* (1965) and the grammars of Singh (1969 BS), Pandit (1969 BS) and Sigdel (1976 BS) and the establishment of institutions like Gorkha Bhasha Prakashini Samiti (1970 BS) and Tri-Chandra College (1975 BS).

The establishment of Darbar High School (1910 BS) also contributed to the development of the Nepali language. Jaya Prithvi Bahadur Singh was first to write textbooks in Nepali. He wrote textbooks like *Aksaranka Siksa* and *Bhugol Siksa*. After that Paras Mani Pradhan contributed to this field. Today almost all kinds of textbooks and teaching materials are available in Nepali. In the development of the Nepali language the contribution of the following is seminal:

- **Grammars**: Ayton (1820), Banda (1831), Turnbull (1887), Birendra Kesari Arjyal (1945-1962 BS), Ram Mani Adi (1965 BS), Singh (1969 BS), Pandit (1969 BS), Dixitacharya (1913), Swanr (1975 BS), Sigdel (1976 BS), Paras Mani Pradhan (1920), Nagendra Mani Pradhan (1989 BS) and Sukraraj Shastri (1990-1992 BS), etc.
- **Magazines and Newspapers:** *Gorkha Bharat Jiban* (1943 BS, Varanasi), *Gorkhapatra* (1958 BS, Kathmandu), *Gorkhe Khabar Kagat* (1901, Darjeeling), *Sundari* (1963 BS, Varanasi), *Madhavi* (1965 BS, Varanasi), *Gorkha Sathi* (1912, Calcutta), *Chandra* (1972 BS, Varanasi), *Chandrika* (1918, Kurseong), *Gorkhali* (1972, Varanasi), *Janmabhumi* (1979 BS, Varanasi), *Gorkhamitra* (1924, Calcutta), *Gorkha Sansar* (1926, Dehradun), *Adarsa* (1930, Kalimpong), *Khoji* (1932, Darjeeling), *Sahitya Sammelan Patrika* (1932, Darjeeling), *Gorkhali Ravi* (1933, Darjeeling), *Sharada* (1991 BS, Kathmandu), *Gorkha Sebak* (Shillong), *Nebula* (1935, Kalimpong), *Udyog* (1992 BS, Kathmandu) and *Udaya* (1993 BS, Kathmandu), etc.
- **Dictionaries:** Dravid (1905), Satyal (1916), Kilgaur *et al.* (1923), Turner (1931), Rana (1936-1938, 1998 BS), Chalise (1941, 1942), Cornelius (1944), Pradhan and Pradhan (1947), Dhungana (1950), Pradhan (1951), Sharma (2019 BS), Sapkota (2034 BS) and Pokharel *et al.* (2042 BS), etc.
- **Textbooks:** By Jaya Prithvi Bahadur Singh, Paras Mani Pradhan, etc.
- **Publishers:** Gorkha Bhasa Prakasini Samiti (1970 BS), Nepali Sahitya Sammelan (1924), Bhasanubad Parisad (1992 BS), Apatan Sahitya Parisad (1947) and Royal Nepal Academy (2014 BS), etc.
- **Writers:** Lekhnath Paudel, Chakrapani Chalise, Dharanidhar Koirala, Surya Bikram Gyanwali, Rudra Raj Pande, etc.

Attempts to simplify and regularize Nepali spelling start with Birendra Kesari Arjyal (1947-1957 BS). *Nepali Kasari Shuddha Lekhne?* (1992 BS) published by Nepali Bhasa Prakasini Samiti was the first institutional attempt to standardize Nepali spelling. Sajha Prakasan (2029 BS) tried to regularize spelling by organizing an interaction among grammarians like Balkrishna Pokharel and Taranath Sharma and writers like Balkrishna Sama, but that interaction could not come to any conclusion about regularizing and standardizing Nepali spelling. The Tribhuvan University Curriculum Development Centre made the third attempt in this direction. It brought consensus among those who were teaching Compulsory Nepali subject in Tribhuvan University-affiliated campuses. *Nepali Brihat Sabdakos* (2040 BS) of the Royal Nepal Academy is the result of that consensus. There is a need for further institutional attempts from the scholars of both Nepal and India to standardize Nepali spelling.[8]

Contributions of Calcutta, Varanasi, Darjeeling, Dehradun, undivided Assam, Bhaksu and Sikkim are notable for the historical development of the Nepali language. The recognition of Nepali by Calcutta University, establishment of Gorkha School in Meghalaya and establishment of Nepali Sahitya Sammelan (1924) in Darjeeling have contributed to the development of Nepali. Nepali language was called 'Gorkha Bhasa' in Nepal. The Italian writers Amaduzzi and Adlung or British researchers like Hodgson, historians like Kirkpatrick, grammarians like Ayton (1820) and lexicographers like Turner (1931) were first to call this language Nepali (see Grierson 1916 and Sharma 2056 BS), but it was Darjeeling which taught Nepal to call the language 'Nepali' instead of 'Gorkha Bhasa' and it was Sikkim that played a very significant role behind inclusion of the Nepali language in the Eight Schedule of the Indian constitution in June 1992. Today PhD degree is awarded by Tribhuvan University, North Bengal University and Benaras Hindu University in Nepali medium; Nepali language is taught in various universities of the world and is broadcast from national radio stations of various countries. It is used today in various websites and electronic media like radio, television, cinema, documentary films, and internet and so on.

Madan Puraskar Pustakalaya (2013 BS) is the biggest library of Nepali books. That institution has developed a Unicode font for Nepali. This font can be downloaded freely from the Internet. This has facilitated the users to send emails in Devanagari font. This facility is gradually helping a Nepali reader to read information in the Internet. Under the joint coordination of the High Level Commission for Information Technology of the Government of Nepal, Madan Puraskar Pustakalaya and Microsoft Company represented by Unlimited Software, professors from Tribhuvan University, Kathmandu University, Mahendra Sanskrit University, computer experts and representatives of various government and non-government agencies worked together in 2004 to make computer vocabularies in Nepali. The Microsoft Company has developed a Spellchecker for Nepali based on *Nepali Brihat Shabdakos*. After that Madan Puraskar Pustakalaya's project called 'Bhasa Sanchar', has developed software called 'NepaLenux' in order to facilitate Nepali readers to access computer information in Nepali at low cost. With that programme one can use computer in Nepali language. One can spellcheck about thirty thousand Nepali words of *Nepali Brihat Sabdakos* with NepaLinux. We can Google-search information through the Internet in Nepali today.

At present a comprehensive corpus based electronic dictionary of Nepali is being produced by 'Bhasa Sanchar' project under the coordination of Goteburg University, Open University, Lancaster University, Tribhuvan University, Kathmandu University and Madan Puraskar Pustakalaya. The dictionary project is financed by the European Language Research Association. Up-to-date techniques of lexicography, corpus linguistics and computational linguistics are being applied in designing this dictionary. Entry selections, alphabetic ordering, frequency, collocations, meanings, concordance, word class, illustrations and variant meanings, etc. sare ascertained by computer and computer software. The target of this dictionary is one million words. One of the targets of the project is to produce an online dictionary of Nepali. One can even search synonyms and antonyms of Nepali vocabularies. In order to have access for the blind, the dictionary has a Text-to-Speech component which reads a highlighted text. Now we should be able to provide SMS in Nepali language in the mobile phone sets. The 'Bhasa Sansar' project is believed to work on this as well.

According to the Constitution of Nepal (2047 BS) Nepali is the national and an official language of Nepal. It is also a lingua franca of the Nepalis scattered all over the world. When the Nepali language was included in the 8th Schedule of the Indian Constitution, Nepali attained the status of an international language.[9] Now there is need for conducting joint projects for the uniformity of written Nepali across the international borders. This may be the reason why the Central Institute of Indian Languages (CIIL), Mysore is compiling a multilingual dictionary of Nepali. Besides, the North-East Regional Language Centre (NERLC) has been training high school teachers of various Indian states with a Basic Course in Nepali.[10]

Now, there are about 30 million Nepalis in the world. In the current situation when the Nepali language is taking quantum leaps on various sides, one of its problems is to distribute Nepali books to Nepali speaking people scattered all over the world. Paradoxically, there are big piles of unsold Nepali books covered by dust in the store rooms of Sajha Prakashan and the Royal Nepal Academy. Nepali writers, readers, publishers and book distributors are suffering because many Nepali readers do not have access to Nepali books either due to poor economic conditions or their dispersed habitation in inaccessible areas.

NOTES AND REFERENCES

1. See Shastri 1968.
2. See Mahendale 1948.
3. See Pokharel 2002.
4. See Mani 1975.
5. Professor Wang Yao of Chinese University of Minorities told me in personal communication that all of them are Muslim today.
6. See Stein 1990.
7. See Pokhrel 2057 BS.
8. See Shailaja Pokhrel 2061 BS.
9. See Pradhan 1992.
10. The CIIL, Mysore has already designed such a course.

BIBLIOGRAPHY

Acharya, Bhagabat. 2053 BS. *Allocation of Nepali Dialects Based on Pronunciation* [in Nepali]. MA thesis, Central Department of Nepali, Tribhuvan University.

Ayton, J.A. 1820. *A Grammar of the Nepali Language*. Calcutta: Philip Peraira.

Basham, A.L. (ed.). 1975. *A Cultural History of India*. London: Oxford University Press.

Beams, John. 1872-1879. *A Comparative Grammar of the Modern Aryan Languages of India*. London: Trubner.

Bhandarkar, Ramkrishna Gopal. 1885. Wilson Lectureship: Development of Language and of Sanskrit. *The Journal of the Bombay Branch of the Royal Asiatic Society,* 16a: 245-74.

Bhandarkar, Shridhar R. 1914. *Wilson Pilological Lectures on Sanskrit and the Derived Languages*. Delivered in 1877 by R.G. Bhandarkar. Bombay: Mrs. Radhabai Atmaram Sagoon.

Bloch, Jules. 1965. *Indo-Aryan*. Paris: Libraire D' Amerique et D'Orient (Translated into English by Alfred Master).

Buhler, Georg. 1896/1980. *Indian Paleography*. New Delhi: Oriental Books.

Cardona, George. 1988. *Panini*. Delhi: Motilal Banarasidass.

Cardona, George and Dhanesh Jain (eds). 2003. *The Indo-Aryan Languages*. London and New York: Routledge.

Chalise, Bidur. 2063. *A Study of Evolution of Grammatical Features in Nepali Inscriptions* [in Nepali]. Ph.D. thesis, Tribhuvan University, Kathmandu.

Chalise, Chakrapani. 1941. *Nepali Pocket Dictionary*. Kathmandu: NBPS.

Chalise, Chakrapani. 1942. *Dictionary of Synonyms* [in Nepali]. Kathmandu: NBPS.

Chatterji, Suniti Kumar. 1926. *The Origin and Development of the Bengali Language*. Calcutta: University Press.

Chattopadhyaya, Debi Pd. (ed.). 1970. *Taranatha's History of Buddhism in India*. Translated from Tibetan by Lama Chimpa and Alaka Chattopadhyaya. Simla: Indian Institute of Advanced Study.

Cornelius, A.W. 1944. *Gurkhali-English Dictionary*. Dehra Dun: Jugal Kishore.

Dhungana, Lavanya P. 2053 BS. *Allocation of Nepali Dialects on the Basic Vocabulary* [in Nepali]. MA thesis, Central Department of Nepali, Tribhuvan University.

Dhungana, Ramchandra. 1950. *Concise Nepali-English English-Nepali Dictionary*. Kathmandu: Sajha Prakashan.

Dixitacharya, Bishwamani. 1913. *Gorkha Byakarana Bodh* [in Nepali]. Dilli Bazaar: Author. Dravid, Gangadhar Shastri (1905). Anglo-Nepali Dictionary. Benaras: Vishwaraj Harihar Prakashan.

Gautam, Teknath. 2050 BS. *History of the Rapati Zone and Some Memoirs* [in Nepali]. Varanasi: Ajaya Printers.

Ghatage, A.M. 1941. *Introduction to Ardhamagadhi*. Kolhapur: School and College Book-stall.

Grierson, G.A. 1916. *Linguistic Survey of India* 9.4:1-100. Calcutta: Government of India.

Hoernle, A.F. Rudolf. 1880. *Comparative Grammar of the Gaudian Languages with Special Reference to the Eastern Hindi*. London: Rubner.

Joshi, Laksmi Dat. 1926/1984. *Tribal Peoples of the Himalayas: A Study of the Khasas*. Delhi: Mittal Publications.

Katre, S.M. 1964. *Prakrit Languages and their Contribution to Indian Culture*. Poona: Deccan College.

Kharel, K.C. Prerana. 2058 BS. *An Introduction to the Grammar of Birendrakesari Arjyal* [in Nepali]. Kathmandu: Laxman Kharel.

Kilgour, Robert, H.C. Duncan and G.P. Pradhan. 1923. *English-Nepali Dictionary*. Darjeeling: Government Branch Press.

Mair, Victor H. (ed). 1998. *The Bronze Age and Early Iron Age Peoples of Eastern Central Asia*. Vols. I and II. Washington DC and Philadelphia: The Institute for the Study of Man in Collaboration with The University of Pennsylvania Museum Publications.

Malla, Kamal Prakash. 1980. Amritananda's Grammar A.D. 1831. *Nepalese Language Society*. Kathmandu: LSN.

Mani, Vettam. 1975. *Puranic Encyclopedia*. Delhi: Motilal Banarasidass.

Masica, Colin P. 1991. *Indo-aryan Languages*. Cambridge: University Press.

McCrindle, John W. 1901/1971. *Ancient India as Described in Classical Literature*. Amsterdam: Philo Press.

Mehendale, Madhukar Anant. 1948. *Historical Grammar of Inscriptional Prakrits*. Poona: Deccan College.

Mishra, Tarananda. 2053 BS. Emperor Asoka and his Relationship to Nepal. *Prajna*, 82:57.

Niraula, Yajneshwar. 2050 BS. *Allocation of Nepali Dialects on Verb Forms* [in Nepali]. MA thesis. Kathmandu: Central Department of Nepali, Tribhuvan University.

Ojha, Gauri-Shankar Hirachand. 1894. *Ancient Indian Scripts* [in Hindi]. (3rd edition, 2016 BS). Delhi: Munshiram Manoharlal.

Pande, Badridatta. 1937/1990. *The History of Kumaun* [in Hindi]. Almoda: Shyam Prakashan.

Pischell, R. 1957. *Comparative Grammar of the Prakrit Languages*. Translated by Subhadra Jha. Varanasi: Motilal Banarasidass.

Pokharel, Balkrishna. 2019 BS. *Nepali Language and Literature* [in Nepali]. Kathmandu: Ratna Pustak Bhandar.

Pokharel, Balkrishna. 2020 BS. *Five Hundred Years* [in Nepali]. Kathmandu: Jagadamba Prakashan.

Pokharel, Balkrishna. 2055 BS. *The History of the Khasa People* [in Nepali]. Biratnagar: Author.

Pokharel, Balkrishna (ed.). 2040 BS. *Comprehensive Nepali Dictionary* [in Nepali]. Kathmandu: Royal Nepal Academy.

Pokharel, Madhav P. 2057 BS. Dating of Damupal's inscription. *Prajna*, 90:1-19.

Pokharel, Madhav P. 2002. O-ending nominals in New Indo-Aryan. *Nepalese Linguistics*, 19:17-22.

Pokharel, Madhav P. 2004. State of Lexicography in Nepal. Paper Presented at the International Conference on Indian Lexicography. Chennai: University of Madras.

Pokharel, Madhav P. 2062 BS. Importance of Sanskrit in the world and our duties in Nepal [in Nepali]. Paper Presented Royal Nepal Academy in a Seminar on the Utility of Sanskrit organized by Sanskrit Seva Parishad.

Pokharel, Shailaja. 2061 BS. *Justification of Spellings of Nepali Brihat Sabdakos* [in Nepali]. Kathmandu: Jagadamba Prakashan.

Pokharel, Shailaja. 2062 BS. Social introduction to the Nepali language [in Nepali]. *Sabda-samyojan*, 22:60-64.

Pradhan, Paras Mani. 1951. *English-Nepali Nepali-English Dictionary*. Kalimpong: Bhagyalaxmi Prakashan

Pradhan, Paras Mani and Narendra Mani Pradhan. 1947. *New Standard Dictionary, English-Nepali*. Kalimpong: Bhagyalaxmi Prakashan.

Pradhan, Shiva. 1992. *Language Movement: Until the Road to Success* [in Nepali]. Gangtok: Gangtok Prakashan.

Przyluski, J. 1920/1967. *The Legend of Emperor Asoka in Indian and Chinese Texts*. Translated by Dilip Kumar Biswas. Calcutta: n.p.

Rana, Pushkar Shamshere J.B. (ed.). 1936-1938. *English-Nepali Dictionary*. 2 vols. Kathmandu: Nepali Bhasha Prakashini Samiti.

Rana, Pushkar Shamshere J.B. 1998 BS. *A Dictionary of Proverbs and Idioms* [in Nepali]. Kathmandu: NBPS.

Sankrityayan, Rahul. 1948. *Buddhism in Tibet* [in Hindi]. Allahabad: Kitab Mahal.

Sankrityayan, Rahul. 1953. *Introduction to Himalayas (1): Gadhwal*. Allahabad: Law Journal Press.

Sankrityayan, Rahul. 2013 BS. *History of Central Asia Part I*. Patna: Behar Rastrabhasa Parisad.

Sankrityayan, Rahul. 2015 BS. *Kumaun*. Varanasi: Jnanmandal.

Satyal, Ram Prasad. 1916. *English-Gorkha*. Benares: n.p.

Sen, Sukumar. 1960. *A Comparative Grammar of Middle Indo-Aryan*. Poona: Linguistic Society of India, Deccan College.

Shastri, Charudev. 1968. *Patanjali's Mahabhasya*. Delhi: Motilal Banarasidass.

Sircar, D.C. 1965. *Indian Epigraphy*. Delhi: Motilal Banarasidass.

Subedi, Sakhi Sharan. 2051 BS. *A Survey of Nepali Dialects on Syntactic Features*. MA thesis, Central Department of Nepali, Tribhuvan University.

Timilsina, Yamanath. 2050 BS. *Allocation of Nepali Dialects on Numerals and Pronominals* [in Nepali]. MA thesis, Central Department of Nepali, Tribhuvan University.

Tucci, Giuseppe. 1956. *Prelimanary Report on Two Scientific Expeditions in Nepal. Materials for the Study of Nepalese History and Culture 1*. Serie Oriental Roma-x. Roma: Instituto Italiano per iL Medio ed Estramo Oriente.

Tucci, Giuseppe. 1962. Nepal: *The Discovery of the Malla*. Translated from Italian by Lovett Edwards. London: George Allen and Unwin.

Turnbull, Archibald. 1987. *A Nepali Grammar and English-Nepali Nepali-English Vocabulary*. Darjeeling: L. Roy.

Turner, Ralph Liley. 1931. *A Comparative and Etymological Dictionary of the Nepali Language*. London: Kegan Paul, Trench and Trubner.

Turner, Ralph Liley. 1966. *A Comparative Dictionary of the Indo-Aryan Languages*. London: School of Oriental and African Studies.

Varma, Siddheshwar and Bhim Dev. 1953. *The Etymologies of Yaska*. Hoshiarpur: Vishveshvaranand Institute Publications.

Yatri, Purna Prakash Nepal. 2039a. The oldest Nepali inscription (a bird's eye view). *Language Issues of Twenty-five Years* [in Nepali]. Edited by Balkrishna Pokharel. Kathmandu: Royal Nepal Academy.

Yatri, Purna Prakash Nepal. 2039b. *The Travelogue of King Gaganiraj* [in Nepali]. Kathmandu: Nepal Research Associates.

Yogi, Naraharinath. 2012-2014 BS. *Itihas Prakash*, 2.1: 58-61.

23

India-Nepal Treaty of Peace and Friendship: Nature, Problems and the Question of Identity of Indian Nepalis

B.C. UPRETI

India and Nepal are two neighbouring countries that have multi-dimensional and unique relations. Nature has indeed placed India and Nepal so close to each other that it is in many respects unparalleled any where in the world.[1] The geographical continuity and compactness, shared history, deep-rooted socio-cultural connections and similarities, mutual politico-strategic concerns and economic interdependence have encouraged the development of an intimate relationship between the two countries. It is equally important to note here that India and Nepal not only have formal, politico-diplomatic, relations, but also have informal or people-to-people relations.[2] Therefore in understanding India-Nepal relations it is important to take both into consideration.

The open border is in many ways an important factor in shaping India-Nepal relations. There are very few sovereign and independent countries in the world that have agreed to maintain an open international border.[3] Nevertheless, the various sources of intimacy between India and Nepal have also often acted as a source of irritants in their relations. There are issues like open border, inter-state migrations, politico-strategic concerns, sharing of natural resources, trade and transit, and so on that have often caused constraints and serious deadlocks in the relations between the two countries. Therefore, it can be said that despite intimacy and nearness India-Nepal relations are complex. These relations have a chequered history. The two close neighbours have been often described as uneasy friends[4], uneasy partners[5], friends and strangers[6], and so on.

These complexities demand a broader focus on India-Nepal relations as to understand it in a proper perspective.

The treaty of peace and friendship concluded between the two countries in 1950 forms an important basis of India-Nepal relations. It has regularized the relations between the two countries. But at the same time the treaty has become a source of irritants and obstacles, albeit the treaty has survived over half a century. The treaty is a highly comprehensive document not only dealing with politico-strategic issues but also dealing with economic and social issues in the interest of the people of the two countries. The treaty has taken a number of popular aspects into consideration befitting the nature and dimensions of India-Nepal relations. However, the treaty has been opposed in Nepal as well as India. There are demands for its revision and even for its abrogation. It was opposed by the Gorkha National Liberation Front in Darjeeling during the height of its movement in mid 1980s and it is opposed by some Nepali organizations in Assam today. Where has the treaty failed? Has it become irrelevant in today's context? What are the expectations of the people of the two countries from the treaty? To what extent can the treaty ensure identity of the Indians in Nepal and the Nepalis in India? These are some of the issues, which seem to be significant in the context of an analysis of the treaty. It has also to be understood here that the treaty of 1950 is as much important for India as it is so for Nepal.

Treaty of Peace and Friendship

The treaty of peace and friendship was signed between the two sovereign and independent countries of India and Nepal on 31st July, 1950 after mutual consultations and agreement. The treaty containing ten articles provides a broad framework for the pursuance of mutually beneficial bilateral relations between the two countries. A letter was also exchanged between the two along with the treaty that was not made public till 1959. The letter, which is explicit about the security concerns between the two countries, became a bone of contention and criticism in Nepal. More than any thing else, that the letter was kept a secret has been an issue in Nepal. It was known to the public only in 1959. It stated that neither of the two governments would tolerate threat to the security of the other by a foreign aggressor and the two countries would consult each other to deal with such a threat. There was also a mention about import of arms and ammunitions by Nepal, foreign assistance to and treatment of the nationals of one country in another.

Most of the Nepali criticism of the 1950 treaty is surrounded around the politico-strategic aspects of the same. They allege that India has been more concerned about its strategic and security concerns in the Himalayas but ignored Nepal's sovereignty. There is also a perception in Nepal that India accorded importance to the prevailing political context at the time of signing the treaty. There is also a feeling among many in Nepal that India gave more importance to the political conditions in the Himalayas at that time than the actual needs of the Nepali people. They particularly refer to India's growing security concerns in the Himalayas in this regard. But these criticisms have generally overlooked the economic and social aspects of the treaty. In fact, the treaty has followed a broad and long-term perspective. It reflects the historico-political, geo-economic and socio-cultural dimensions of the relations between the two countries. Therefore, the treaty has to be understood in a comprehensive perspective. There are five important considerations in the context of the 1950 treaty of peace and friendship, which are as follows:

(1) Different aspects of the treaty have been projected and interpreted by the two countries according to their own interests and preference.
(2) The treaty has been made an instrument to realize vested interests in the field of domestic politics, particularly in Nepal.
(3) The treaty has been made an easy target of the hostile postures adopted by the two countries against each other.
(4) Denouncing the provisions or working against the spirit of the treaty has generally been viewed as the assertion of national identity and sovereignty, particularly in Nepal.
(5) There have been too many expectations from the treaty at the popular level but the implementation of various provisions is far short of these expectations.

Context of the Treaty

The question of redefining relations with the Himalayan states became prominent with India's independence after the British withdrawal from the sub-continent in 1947. The British had defined India's relations with Nepal.[7] The independent India concluded a stand still agreement with the Himalayan state. But there was a need to find a durable basis for bilateral relations between these countries. Nepal, Bhutan and Sikkim were all weak, backward and had fragile political structures. They were not in a position to withstand external security dangers that were becoming alarming after the withdrawal of the British power. India itself was exposed to numerous problems. There were serious challenges of socio-economic reconstruction and political stability. Her own security was at stake. She was seriously involved in the post-partition complexities with Pakistan and it had thrown a number of challenges in domestic and regional contexts. India was also in search of a space in the cold war-ridden world politics. A strong neighbour in the north (China) was likely to pose new challenges to India's security and stability. China's ambitions as an Asian giant had sufficient historical reasons. It was certain that India would have to reshape its politico-strategic and diplomatic postures in view of China's emergence and the possible competition with it in future.

In 1949 China emerged as a strong communist power and it began to exert its control over Tibet. It even annexed Tibet, a historically strong state in the north of the great Himalayan range. It was not only an indication of China's intentions but it exposed the security of the Himalayan states badly, and consequently India's security stakes in the region because of the geo-politics of the region. This was when Nepal was passing through a difficult time in terms of domestic crisis and turmoil. A violent movement was in the offing against the hundred-year-old Rana oligarchic political system. The democratic forces fighting against the Ranas had taken an organized shape from the Indian soil and they had close association with the Indian leaders. The Ranas were in search of an external support and it was certain that India alone could have lent that support.

Nepal was equally concerned about the growing Chinese activities in the north. It was not only afraid of growing security threats from the north but there was also a danger of the communist infiltration in the kingdom. It was not in a position to withstand the security threats from the north on its own. Thus, there were some common interests between India and Nepal that brought them together on the issue of concluding a treaty. The Rana rulers also thought that they would be able to win India's support against the anti-Rana movement if they agreed to India's considerations for a peace treaty. It was in the context of these circumstances along with the geographical, economic and socio-cultural considerations that the treaty was signed. Major world powers of the day were also concerned about China's emergence as a communist power and its occupation of Tibet. They were apprehensive of communist infiltration beyond the Himalayas. The poor and backward conditions of the Himalayan states were conducive to communist infiltration. A vacuum had already been created in Southasia after the British withdrawal. The world powers were looking forward to fill up this gap that would also help them in the context of the cold war politics. These developments were posing a challenge to India's security, status and the regional stability. It necessitated India to give a sound basis to her relations with its neighbouring countries. It is true that the treaty was concluded in a given situation but a long-term perspective of the situation was taken into consideration while concluding the treaty.

Nature and Characteristics of the Treaty

The 1950 treaty of peace and friendship along with the letter exchanged with it was aimed at forging a close relationship between the two countries. The treaty recognized the existence of deep-rooted and ancient ties between India and Nepal. It was agreed that the treaty would be an instrument to promote these ties and perpetuate peace and friendship between the two counties. The treaty has three broad dimensions:

Defense and Security Aspects

The defense and security constitute a major aspect of the treaty and the letter exchanged with the treaty further consolidated it.

(1) It is agreed that the two countries will inform each other of any serious friction or misunderstanding with any third country that is likely to cause any breach in the relations between the two.
(2) Threat to the security of either country by a foreign aggressor shall not be tolerated and mutual consultations shall take place between the two in order to envisage counter measures.
(3) If Nepal wishes to import arms and ammunition necessary for its security through the territory of India it shall do so with the assistance and agreement of the Government India.
(4) Both the governments agreed not to employ any foreigner whose activities are prejudicial to the interest of either country.

Economic Aspects

It was agreed that India would help Nepal in her quest for modernization and development. The treaty stipulated that should the government of Nepal decide to seek foreign assistance, preference would be given to the Government of India or the nationals of India, provided the terms offered by the government or the nationals of India are not less favourable to Nepal than the terms offered by any other donor country.

Social Aspects

The two countries agreed to provide nationals of the other, in its territory, national treatment with regard to participation in industrial and economic development, and to the grant of concessions and contracts relating to such development. It also states that the governments of India and Nepal agree to grant, on a reciprocal basis, to the nationals of one country in the territories of the other the same privileges in the matter of residence, ownership of property, participation in trade and commerce, movement of people and other privileges of similar nature.

The treaty shall remain in force unless it is declared terminated by either party by giving one year's notice.

Working of the Treaty

In the years immediately following the signing of the 1950 treaty of peace and friendship, a close understanding developed between the two countries in politico-strategic and economic matters. It was characterized as an era of special relationship. India agreed to provide guards and telephone operators to secure the Nepal-China border. An Indian Military Mission was sent to Kathmandu to modernize the Nepali army. Indian economic assistance and investments began in Nepal in a big way. India also provided assistance to Nepal for administrative reorganization, survey and other related works. There was a clear understanding between the two countries on many domestic and international issues. This intimacy, however, broke with the change of political climate in Nepal and the changed perception of the new political leadership there towards India, particularly after 1960. The treaty became an easy target and people in Nepal began to denounce the provisions of the treaty in several ways.

(1) Nepal cultivated friendly relations with China, signed a treaty with it and sought Chinese assistance for the construction of roads and other infra-structure development. Nepal also started pleading for the principle of equidistance between India and China in place of special relations with India.

(2) Nepal began to play the China card and brought its larger involvement in order to reduce its dependence on India.

(3) Nepal also began to denounce the provision of preference to Indian nationals by giving contracts to foreigners, etc.
(4) Nepal discouraged Indian migration to the country and their large-scale involvement in industries, trade and commerce by revising the laws relating to industries, labour, employment in governmental sectors, etc. For instance it changed the rules relating to the foreign employment in industries. The labour laws were also revised with a view to discouraging permanent employment to foreign nationals in Nepalese industries and business concerns. During 1980s the Nepal government introduced the Work Permit System for the Indian nationals seeking employment in Nepal.
(5) Nepal moved a proposal to declare it a 'zone of peace' so as to make the provisions of the treaty become ineffective, particularly the provisions relating to mutual security interest as envisaged in the treaty because once Nepal was declared a zone of peace all such provisions would be deemed to have become irrelevant. A large number of countries endorsed Nepal's 'zone of peace' proposal but India did not agree to it. So the proposal could not be implemented.
(6) It was made compulsory for the Indian emigrants in Nepal to seek a Work Permit from the Ministry of Home Affairs of the Government of Nepal in order to enter into any employment. This system was introduced with the intention to reduce Indian employment in Nepal. However, Sikkim, one of the federal states of India, also followed, and still does, the same system for the people of Nepal working in cardamom fields in its North District.
(7) In June 1988 Nepal imported arms from China without any prior information and consultation with the government of India.

Thus, Nepal has tried to act against the provisions and the spirit of the treaty in a number of ways: its efforts to diversify its aid and trade programme to other countries particularly to China, Nepal's attempts to prefer private investors/contractors in place of Indians, the attempts to discourage Indian employment in Nepal, purchase of arms and ammunition from China without any prior consultation with and information to India, its quest to declare itself a zone of peace and the introduction of Work Permit System for the Indian nationals, etc.

India has, on the other hand, tried to follow the provisions of the treaty although it has not always been successful. There has not been any kind of opposition at the official or unofficial levels in India pertaining to the working of the treaty except in Northeast India where there have been serious violations of the treaty in the context of the Nepalis. The restrictions over the movement of Nepalis in the region and their forceful eviction from Assam and Meghalaya in the wake of anti-foreigner movement was resented in Nepal as well as by the Nepalis in India, which was tantamount to the violation of the 1950 treaty. The Nepalis have been actually evicted from every part of Northeast India except Tripura and Arunachal Pradesh where they are in very small numbers. They were treated as "foreigners" like Bangladeshis, frisked and asked to go back from the immigration check points like Srirampur Hat in Assam and Byrnihat in Meghalaya. All this continued till some years back, when following a Public Interest Litigation filed by a Nepali advocate at the Gauhati High Court, it was declared that the state actions against the Nepalis were "illegal" as per the provisions of the treaty. As regards the security argument forwarded by some authors behind not allowing the Nepalis to move freely in the region the historical fact is that the Nepalis were settled by the British in strategically important areas of the region so that they could secure the revenue areas of region from the marauding hill tribes.

Changing Perceptions: A Review

It was by the communist government of Nepal during 1994-95 that a demand was raised officially for the revision of the treaty of peace and friendship for the first time. But in the unofficial circles voices were raised against the treaty much before. The Nepalese political leaders who were against the treaty have placed a number of arguments. It has been argued that the circumstances in which the treaty was signed have changed and therefore there is no relevance of the treaty any more. Actually, Nepal's indication has been towards its changed relations with China. Nepal has been in favour of equitable relations with India and China and in this regard the treaty has been viewed as an obstacle. It is true that Nepal has friendly relations with China and the circumstances of the early 1950s do not prevail any more. But the point is the treaty puts no hurdles on closer Nepal-China relations. The fact remains that Nepal concluded border treaty with China despite the treaty of 1950 with India. Nepal also accepted aid and imported arms from China. It opened relations with several other countries as well. The treaty never obstructed Nepal's diplomatic postures. So it is mainly for political reasons that the treaty has been viewed as an obstacle. It has also been argued by some in Nepal that China would also demand similar concessions from Nepal as India has because of Nepal's treaty with India. Here again, Nepal has satisfied Chinese expectations to a great extent, be it the question of linking Kathmandu to Tibet and beyond or the Chinese involvement in sensitive projects. Also while forwarding such arguments the ground realities have been ignored. In fact, India-Nepal relations are much different from Nepal-China relations. Nepal's dependence on India is much more than on China and the kind of multi-dimensional relations that it has with India are not possible with China.

Nepal has further argued that the treaty is unequal as it puts India in an advantageous position vis-a-vis Nepal. It is true that in certain respects India's position has been more advantageous than that of Nepal. As far as the provisions of the treaty are concerned India has looked at the treaty from the perspective of its security interest in that country whereas Nepal has gained a lot from the provisions relating to socio-economic sectors. This is indeed true even without a comprehensive account of who gains more between the two countries. But when facts are not available, perceptions get the upper hand. It has also been complained by some people of Nepal that the treaty was concluded when an authoritarian regime was in power in Nepal. Here again, it has to be realized that the treaty was concluded between two countries. The governments of the day only become instruments to sign the treaty. A treaty cannot be invalidated merely on the ground that a particular government was in power that had signed the treaty.

Therefore, it seems that most criticisms of the treaty seem to be politically motivated. The working of the treaty was smooth so long as there was a close understanding between the two countries. It became an issue of Nepalese criticism against India when the relations between the two countries became strained for one reason or another. We have to take note of the fact that the treaty itself provides for its liquidation. Any party not willing to continue with the treaty may withdraw from it by giving one year's notice. So, at least theoretically, Nepal is free to abrogate it by giving India one year's notice. In practice, this is not easy because the consequences of this on the two countries and their bilateral relations cannot even be imagined.

The question of modification in the treaty or replacing the existing treaty by a new one has been raised by some intellectuals, political groups and think tanks in Nepal as well as some parts of India. But a national debate on the issue is yet to take place in Nepal or in India.

Treaty and National Identity of Indian Nepalis

One very important issue related to the 1950 treaty of peace and friendship is the question of national identity of the Indians in Nepal and Nepalis in India. The Nepalis constitute a sizeable group in India particularly in Northeast India and have a distinct linguistic and ethnic identity. It was nearly 160 years back that the Nepalis began to migrate to Assam as tea plantation labourers, graziers, rubber trappers and agriculturists. This process of Nepali migration to India has continued since then. After 1950 the Nepali migrants began to move to different parts of India but largely settled in various states of Northeast India. They may be broadly divided into two categories: one, descendants of those who settled in India during the British era and are bona fide citizens of India and, two, the recently migrated Nepalis who are scattered all over the country.

The Nepalis of Northeast India lived in harmony with the local people and there was no problem for them for a very long period of time. They learnt the local languages, married with local women and even adapted themselves to the local cultures and traditions. However, after the anti-foreigners movement launched by the All Assam Students' Union in 1979 the local communities have begun to see them as outsiders and have even evicted them from areas where they were in minority and defenceless.[8] It is true that Nepalis of Northeast India in particular and of India in general feel insecure in India. Therefore, the issues of national identity are important for them. This also explains why they have often demanded the abrogation of the treaty between India and Nepal. They say that this treaty puts their national identity in jeopardy because they are always treated as the nationals of the other country. So the treaty is an obstacle to obtaining complete nationhood of the mother country for both Indians in Nepal and Nepalis in India. The fact is that the treaty (Article VIII) provides for two-way migrations and their employment and settlement in the either country. The treaty speaks about equal treatment to the citizens of either country. It of course does not say anything clearly about preservation of their identity and granting of citizenship and autonomy to them. It depends on mutual perceptions and cordial relations between the two countries. These are indeed political issues relating to the governments of respective countries. Therefore, the treaty has to be seen in the given perspective and not to be expected anything beyond its purview. Once citizenship is granted to a migrant community they become the state subjects and have to be dealt within the framework of the domestic laws of the country. If a group of people migrates to either country and demands equal rights and privileges as per the treaty it cannot be denied to them. Once these benefits like employment, citizenship, settlement, etc are given other demands would naturally follow. This has happened in the case of Nepalis in Northeast India as well as Madhesis in Nepal's terai. The demands like autonomy, recognition to language, reservation of seats in the parliament, etc are obvious outcome after a certain stage of group formation and interest articulation among the migrant community. These issues emerge because of a sense of insecurity among these groups, which ultimately leads to a process of politicization of these groups. Their sense of insecurity gets sharpened due to conflicts over resources as a consequence of increasing population and decreasing resources.

How about the Nepalis migrated to other parts of India after 1950? Interestingly, the Gorkhaland movement made a distinction between the two sets of Nepalis in India. They are concerned about the interests of Indian Nepalis. The post-1950 Nepali migrants to India are considered to be 'Nepalese subjects.' They consider these migrants as an obstacle to their national identity. The GNLF leaders were also critical of the 1950 treaty of peace, particularly Article VIII, which provides for two-way migrations and equal treatment to them in terms of employment, ownership of property and settlement. Thus, the question of national identity of Indian Nepalis is an important issue.

Concluding Observations

The 1950 treaty of peace and friendship is a significant aspect of India-Nepal relations. There can be no doubt that the treaty has been a strong basis of relationship between the two countries. Nevertheless, the treaty has also been a source of tensions and conflicts between the two countries. The treaty has been criticized and there is strong resentment in both Nepal and India against its continuation. It is not clear whether the critiques of the treaty in Nepal and India have also taken popular perspectives in view. It is important because it is yet to be properly understood to what extent the treaty has promoted people to people contacts between the two countries and protected their interests.

Does the treaty deserve revision, replacement or abrogation? Apart from political rhetoric the position of Nepal is still not clear. There is no consensus in this regard either in Nepal or in India. Does Nepal want to replace this treaty with some other treaty? In fact, there is a need for a comprehensive review of the treaty, a review of its positive and negative dimensions, a review of its successes and failures, a review of its benefits and losses, and then decide whether the treaty needs revision, replacement or abrogation. It is true that a treaty has to take into consideration the changing dynamics of relations between the two countries. But there has to be clear intentions and a proper perspective. A friendship treaty has limited scope. It can only regulate bilateral relations between the two countries and cannot resolve all possible domestic tangles. The question of revision of the treaty needs a clear consensus on these issues between the two partners.

REFERENCES

1. Ramakant and B.C. Upreti (eds), 2005, *India and Nepal: Aspects of Interdependent Relations,* Delhi: Kalinga Publications, pp. ix-xiii.
2. B.C. Upreti, 2003, "India-Nepal Relations: Dynamics, Issues and Problems", *South Asian Survey,* 10(2): 258-74.
3. B.C. Upreti, 1994, "Indo-Nepal Border Problems", *South Asian Studies,* Vol. 9, January-June Issue, pp. 75-84.
4. S.K. Jha, 1975, *Uneasy Partners: India and Nepal in the post-colonial era,* New Delhi: Manas Publications.
5. B.C. Upreti, 2001, *Uneasy friends, Readings on India-Nepal Relations,* Delhi: Kalinga Publications.
6. Rishikesh Shaha, 1968, *Nepal and India: Friends and Strangers,* Kathmandu: Nepal Council of World Affairs.
7. Asad Hussain, 1970, *British India's Relations with the Kingdom of Nepal,* London: Allen and Unwin.
8. Myron Weiner, 1978, *The Sons of the Soil: Migration and Conflict in India,* Princeton: University Press. Also see B.B. Kumar, 1995, *Tensions and Conflict in Northeast India,* New Delhi: Cosmo Publications.

24

Nepalis and Bangladeshis: A Comparative Study

D.B. CHHETRY

Comparison can at times be misleading and is more likely to be so when the subject of discussion is as contrasting as the Nepalis and Bangladeshis in India. An attempt is made in this article to trace the origin and migration of Nepalis and Bangladeshis with reference to Assam in particular and Northeast India in general, for nowhere else has the issue of Bangladeshi infiltration and Nepali presence raised so much heat and controversy as in this region. A Bangladeshi is obviously a citizen of Bangladesh; the term does not admit of any other interpretation. But a Nepali may not always be a citizen of Nepal. He may be a citizen of India, the US, the UK or even China. And the commonality amongst them all is their mother-tongue—Nepali.

A few scholars have used 'Nepali' to mean an Indian Nepali and 'Nepalese' to denote a national of Nepal. I agree that nothing could be better than having two distinct terms—one identifying an Indian Nepali and the other a citizen of Nepal, but such terms should, at the same time, be distinguishable in other Indian languages as well and not just in English, as the above distinction does.

Nepal, Nepalis and Assam: A Historical Perspective

Ancient Assam had close link with Nepal. The kingdom of Kamarupa then extended upto Bihar which was a part of the Gorkha kingdom.[1] Hutton[2] in his *The Origin of Races and Religion in India*, says: 'The Brahmins and Kayasthas of Assam are all imported from northern India, mostly from north Bihar (Mithila)'. Shyamraj Jaisi[3] observes that Mithila then was inhabited by Nepalis and even now their presence there is substantial. He contends that amongst the Brahmins invited and settled in Assam from Mithila were Nepali Brahmins too. Credible historical evidence is available to establish that ancient Assam had matrimonial alliance with Nepal. In the eight century, ancient Kamarupa King Harsha Deva's daughter was married to Jayadeva II of Nepal.[4] Biswa Singha, who is credited with the establishment of the Cooch Behar kingdom, also married a princess from Nepal and is said to have brought Nepali priests, artisans, sculptors etc. from Nepal. Two other Koch kings—Niladhwaj and Narnarayan—are also claimed to have married with princesses from Nepal.

Tirtha Nath Sharma,[5] ex-President of the Assam Sahitya Sabha, says that during the days of Sankardeva (1449-1568) or a little thereafter there were Nepalis in Assam. There are two *satras* (religious institutions) in Assam even now—one in Nagaon district and the other in Sivasagar, which are known as Nepali *satras*, because both were established by a Nepali Brahmin named Rati Kanta. Jatindra Nath Goswami, also an ex-President of the Assam Sahitya Sabha was, according to Tirtha Nath Sharma, a descendant of Rati Kanta. He further claims that there are many others whose forefathers were Nepali but had completely merged with the Assamese society.

Another aspect that merits mention is the ethnic ties between Nepal and Assam. According to Suniti Kumar Chatterjee[6] Limbus, Tamangs, Lepchas, Magars, Gurungs and Sherpas belong to the Kirata group like the Bodos, Kacharis, Rabhas and Mishings of Assam. The discovery in 1907 in Nepal of a rare book, *Charyapada* containing spiritual compositions made by Sahjani Buddhist Siddhacharyas brings to the fore another ancient link between Assam and Nepal in as much as one of the composers of *Charyapada*, namely Mina Nath, is claimed to be a Kaibarta from Kamarupa[7].

Assam: Colonial and Post-colonial Days

Though one is almost tempted to claim that the migration of Nepalis to Northeast India owes its origin to the Segowli Treaty (1815), Sinha[8] is of the view that 'the first direct contact between Nepalis and this region appears to have occurred in 1817, when 1000 Hindustanis and Gorkhas took part in the Sylhet operation as part of the Cuttak Legion (later known as the Assam Light Infantry). It is actually the Yandaboo treaty of 24th February, 1826 signed between the East India Company and the

Burmese King that actually spurred the migration of the Nepalis to Northeast India.

The open-door policy of the British in the matter of recruitment of Nepalis coupled with the subsequent formal agreement reached with the King of Nepal on the issue, ensured the availability of the hardy, good-natured and faithful soldiers whom the British considered somewhat of an asset to contain revolts and extend and preserve their domain in India, particularly in Northeast India. The Assam Rifles whom Sinha[9] prefers to call 'the custodian of the security of the region' was an indispensable arm of the British administration in Northeast India and the Gorkhas were its integral part. Quoting Col. Shakespear, Sinha writes: 'Whether it was Sylhet or the Shillong plateau, Naga Hills or Lushai Hills, Chittagong Hill tracts or Sadiya Frontier tracts, the Bhutan wars or the Manipur rebellion, the Gorkhas constituted half the Assam Rifles and were always there in operation'[10].

Nepali Settlement in Northeast India

The British adopted a policy of encouraging the settlement of Nepali soldiers particularly in the foot hills after their retirement which served two purposes—one, the ex-soldiers acted as a buffer between the British administration and the restive tribal chiefs and two, families of the ex-army men provided a more dependable source and channel for fresh recruitment of Gorkhas. This, they visualized, would make them less dependent on Nepal for recruitment[11]. Sinha[12] refers to the rehabilitation of Gorkha ex-soldiers in at least 40 sites numbering as many as three thousand individuals. Some of these sites such as Sadiya in Assam, Mantripokhari in Manipur, Aizawl in Mizoram and Mokokchung in Nagaland are as old as one hundred years.

It is, however, not correct to assume that the Nepali settlement in Northeast India in general and Assam in particular composed of the ex-soldiers or their families alone. Once the story of land abundant region with vast expanse of greenery, dense jungles and hills was relayed back home by the soldiers, other fellow Nepalis arrived here to try their luck and took to cattle-breading, dairy farming, sugar-cane cultivation. Many found odd jobs in government offices as *chowkidars*, peons, gardeners and the like. Amongst this group of migrants, mention must be made of the graziers or *khutiwalla*s whose presence was substantial in the Brahmaputra Valley the districts of Karbi Anglong and North Cachar Hills in Assam as well as in Khasi and Jaintia Hills, Garo Hills, Nagaland

and Manipur. It is pertinent to note that during 1919-20, of the 1.25 lakh cattle population in the Brahmaputra valley for which grazing tax was realized, the overwhelming bulk belonged to 6319 professional graziers of whom excepting a few hundred, all were Nepali migrants[13].

'Foreigner' Nepalis

The centuries-old cordial relation between the Nepalis and local people in Assam and Northeast India came under severe strain after 1978. Suddenly they found themselves labelled as 'foreigners'. Although initially the Assam Movement spearheaded by the AASU (All Assam Students' Union) during 1979-85 on the foreigners' issue, was directed against the Bangladeshis, as days rolled by the Nepalis too could not escape their wrath resulting in their large-scale displacement. As Lopita Nath says[14] it was suggested by the AASU that a 'monstrous problem' had been created by the infiltration of illegal foreigners from Bangladesh and Nepal finding their way into the electoral rolls. Consequently, during the intensive revision of electoral rolls prior to the 1985 General Elections in Assam, thousands of Nepali names were unceremoniously struck off. A sense of injustice and deprivation pervaded the community.

The harrowing experience and trauma caused on the Nepalis by the Assam Movement had hardly been left behind when the Bodo agitation loomed large in the horizon. Like the AASU and following its methods the ABSU (All Bodo Students' Union) spearheaded the movement since 1986. To prove their majority the Bodos started an ethnic cleansing operation[15] and the Nepalis in the interior of the districts of Kokrajhar, Bongaigaon, Nalbari and Darrang were evicted or victimized, because 'Boros consider(ed) the Nepalis as foreigners inhabiting India'.[15] Afflicted by a feeling of terror, insecurity, deprivation and displacement the community lost its emotional moorings.

It would be perhaps not wrong to say that the Assam Movement was the precursor of similar agitations in other states of Northeast India in which Nepalis were principal targets. Lopita Nath[16] gives some vivid account of what transpired in these states:

> In 1980, Nepalis who were accorded domiciled status as back as 1947 in Manipur became targets of attack compelling them to flee for safety. Similarly, during 1987, violence erupted in Meghalaya, and Nepalis living in Shillong, Jowai and other parts of the state became the targets. *The Sunday Weekly* magazine

> reported that dozens of innocent children of Nepalis working in Jowai coalmines died of hunger because their parents did not return home even weeks after the incident. The Khasi students and the Government of Meghalaya together deported about 7000-10,000 Nepalis in February-March 1987...In Mizoram and Nagaland where the Nepalis were domiciled for years also suffered atrocities and eviction. In the early 1990s, all Nepali settlers were categorised as 'foreigners in Mizoram' and in 1992 government withdrew certain benefits extended to the pre-1950 settlers. As a result, many families left Mizoram...In Nagaland, in 1980s, extortion was used as a means to terrorise the Nepalis who had settled in the state before 1940 and were treated as indigenous non-Naga local residents. Consequently, they were forced to resort to distress sale of their property. In the Merapani region located on the border of Wokha of Nagaland and Sibsagar district of Assam, about 200 Nepalis lost their lives in clashes.

The Bangladeshis

As is well known the erstwhile East Pakistan broke away from Pakistan and metamorphosed into Bangladesh in 1971. The same people who were known as Pakistanis became Bangladeshis overnight. Today, the word "Bangladeshi" is anathema to the psyche of the people in the region in general and Assam in particular. The Assamese people and the AASU have been in the forefront of a somewhat sustained campaign, though now on a low-key, for identification and deportation of Bangladeshis since the late 1970s. It is worthwhile to mention that the old PIP (Prevention of Infiltration from Pakistan) scheme which was in operation in Assam after the partition, continued even after the emergence of Bangladesh for detection and deportation of Pakistanis/Bangladeshi till the enactment of the IMDT (Illegal Migrants-Determination by Tribunals) Act in 1983.

The present issue of Bangladeshi infiltration has a long history. Muslim exodus from erstwhile East Bengal (present Bangladesh) started in 1920s. This is what the extract of the proceedings of the Government of Assam in the Revenue Department contained in order No. RC8/42/19 dated 6th March 1942 has to say:

> The problem of immigrants is not by any means a new one, and has been exercising the minds of district officers ever since

> cultivators from East Bengal began, over 20 years back, to arrive in large numbers and to settle in the districts of Lower Assam, spreading subsequently upto the districts of Upper Assam. Things went sufficiently well so long as these cultivators were engaged in filling up the vacant spaces in the riverine area. But as they drew nearer to the areas held by the indigenous people signs soon became apparent of the clash of interests between them and the local people and of the dangers to the internal life and habits of the latter.[17]

The Government then introduced what is known as the "Line System" to contain the influx of immigrants, but the Muslim League Ministry which assumed power considered it as being unfair and illegal. Lt. Gen. (Retd.) S.K. Sinha[18], the then Governor of Assam in his report to the President of India in 1998, refers to an observation made by the Viceroy, Lord Wavell, in the Viceroy's Journal thus: 'The Chief problem is the desire of the Muslim Ministers to increase this immigration into the uncultivated Government lands under the slogan of Grow More Food but what they are really after is Grow More Muslims'.

The sheer number of Muslim immigrants seemed overwhelming. Besides, because of professing a different religion and culture, at least in outward manifestations, the Muslim immigrants could not relate themselves well to the host communities in the region. These perceptions immensely contributed to a sense of fear of being swamped by a demographic invasion from across the border.

This is in sharp contrast to the position of the Nepali migrants not only in the colonial days but also during a long spell after independence till the explosive events of the late 1970s overtook both sense and sensibility. The contention is that the influx of immigrant Muslims which commenced before partition from East Pakistan is continuing even after the emergence of Bangladesh and though at the beginning the reasons for such influx were primarily economic, as in most other cases of migration, over the years, political factors are claimed to have come into play.

Extent of Muslim Immigration

Revealing statistics, Governor Sinha avers in his above mentioned report that the much higher percentage growth rate in Assam for 1911 to 1971 over the all India and Bangladesh figures indicate high migration to Assam. He stresses that during 1971-91 the growth rate of Muslims in Assam was much higher than the all India average, suggesting continued large-scale illegal migration of Muslims. Quoting 1991 census report he reveals that four districts in Assam have already become Muslim majority districts and two other were on their way. The 2001 census report has since proved the Governor right. Sinha thus focusses on the extent of Bangladeshi immigration to Assam and calls for measures to arrest the same.

Indian politicians from time to time are known to have indicated the numerical strength of the Bangladeshi immigrants. Governor Sinha, in his report of November 1998, points out that on 6th May 1997 the Union Home Minister informed the Parliament that there were 10 million illegal migrants in India. Later basing on Home Ministry/Intelligence Bureau sources *India Today* magazine in August 1998 gave the breakup showing Assam's share of 4 million. The break-up was revealing in that even Delhi, the capital, and states like Rajasthan and Maharastra were not free from Bangladeshis.

Prior to this, Chief Minister of Assam Hiteswar Saikia[19] on April 10, 1992, making a statement on the floor of the state assembly informed the members of the house that there were 30 lakh Bangladeshis in his state. A hue and cry was raised by the state's immigrant Muslim leaders and politicians. Two days later, he retraced his statement on the plea that his information was not based on accurate report and that there were no Bangladeshis in his state. D.N. Bezborua[20], the then editor of *The Sentinel* remarked that 'the jubilation in Bangladesh over Histeswar Saikia's last statement that there were no Bangladeshis in Assam could almost be heard all the way upto Guwahati!'

The Minister of State (Home), Government of India, informed the Indian Parliament in 2005 that there were 50 lakh Bangladeshis in Assam. He also gave similar statistics for West Bengal and other States. The statement raised a furore in Assam and its Chief Minister impressed upon New Delhi that it was factually incorrect and baseless. The Union Government ultimately withdrew the statement!

Nepalis and Bangladeshis: Are They in the Same Boat?

What is the position of the Nepalis in Northeast India vis-à-vis Bangladeshis? On the strength of the 1950 treaty between India and Nepal even a Nepal Nepali has the right to residence, business or trade, own property, move out freely in Assam as well as in any other states subject to any legal and constitutional restrictions imposed and enforced on other Indian citizens as well. This is apparently a unique privilege for them.

But irrespective of whether they are Indian citizens or citizens of Nepal they have come to be identified as 'foreigners' like Bangladeshis and are subjected to uncalled for harassment and injustice at the entry points of states, railway stations, bus-terminus etc. There are several instances of Nepalis in Assam being hauled up under the IMDT Act even when the same was not applicable to them.

A Bangladeshi is in a more comfortable position than his Nepali counterpart. Although a Banglaseshi cannot legally enter the territories of India without a passport and visa, he has always been doing so. He can even avail himself of what is euphemistically called 'Dhaka Passport', i.e., get pushed across the border (*Desh*, April 2, 2006). No wonder as many as 39,476 Bangladeshis should be detected in Assam between 1993 and 1998. But the most revealing fact is that out of 39,476 infiltrators, Bangladesh refused to accept as many as 30,223.[21]

Compare this with the deportation and dumping of thousands of Nepalis from Assam, Meghalaya and other states of Northeast India without following any legal procedure whatsoever. *Desh* (17th December, 2005), a leading Bengali magazine, has also revealed that 11 lakh Bangladeshis who entered West Bengal between 1972 and 2004 have not returned to Bangladesh and in the government records they are simply shown as 'untraceable'! According to a newspaper report (*Amar Asom*, 25th February, 2007) between 2004 and 2006 as many as 5,263 Bangladeshi passport holders who entered Assam did not go back to their country. Obviously they did not vanish.

I have already alluded to the statement of the Assam Chief Minister and that of the Union Home Minister of State in this paper to stress how both the state and the central governments meekly surrendered on the issue of Bangladeshi immigration. Compare this with the atrocities inflicted on the Nepalis and their forceful deportation in 1980s and 1990s, be it from Meghalaya, Mizoram, Manipur, Nagaland or Assam. Since the Government of India maintained a stoic silence and considered it expedient not to intervene on behalf of the beleaguered and hapless Nepalis of the Northeast in the spree of violence against them continued in many parts of Northeast India.

The Government of Bangladesh is not tired of saying that there is no illegal emigration to India. Most immigrant Muslim leaders and politicians in Assam view the issue of Bangladeshi infiltration as a myth. Nor are they convinced that the census data and intelligence reports are neutral and true. They have not lost sight of the fact that in electoral politics numbers count and count the most. They need not be reminded either that so long as democracy is the catch-word, power comes not through the barrels of guns but through votes. On the contrary, there has been practically no migration of people from Nepal after the early 1970s to Northeast India. In fact, writing in the Assamese daily *Amar Asom* demographer Jogesh Bhuyan[22] says that the fact that the growth rate of the Nepalis in Assam has come down between 1971 and 1991 is indicative of out-migration of the community. And yet, it is not the non-Nepali intellectuals and organizations but our own Nepalis, who have been in the forefront of a demand for abrogation of the 1950 treaty or scrapping of the so-called 'culprit' Clause 7 and even for sealing the border with Nepal, and all this at a time when Bangladeshi intellectuals like Sadeq Ali Khan[23] and others are known to be rooting for 'borderless competitive trade of labour' so that their 'bulging population might find a welcome in adjacent lands inhabited by kindred peoples'.

One could not agree with Subba[24] more when he says that there is perhaps no other tribe or community which is distributed all over the seven states of Northeast India as the Nepalis are. But what exactly is their demographic size? Table 24.1 below provides the answer.

Table 24.1: Nepali Population in Northeast India

States	*Nepali Population*	*% to Total Population*
1. Assam	4,32,519	1.93
2. Meghalaya	49,486	2.77
3. Nagaland	32,274	2.67
4. Arunachal Pradesh	81,176	9.39
5. Mizoram	8,247	1.20
6. Manipur	46,498	2.53
7. Tripura	3,082	0.11

Source: *Census of India*: 1991-Part IV B(I) (A), (C) Series, Language Table C-7.

Although the language data for 2001 census are yet to be released by the Government of India, there are no indications of any alarming increase in Nepali population in any of the seven states. Subba[25] has pointed out that in none of the states except Arunachal Pradesh the Nepalis constitute even 3 per cent of the total population. Even in Assam where the community has the largest concentration, they are just 1.93 per cent which is not formidable by any standard and yet this has not deterred a minuscule section in the state to raise the false alarm of a Nepali uprising for political power in the north bank of the Brahmaputra River. Certainly things will not improve by brandishing *khukuris*. The need of the hour is not expression of emotionally surcharged sentiment but a restrained, analytical and pragmatic approach.

Conclusion

Nepalis have centuries-long relationship with the people of India. While the British played a pivotal role in introducing the Nepalis to this region, the community's inherent qualities of adaptability endeared them to the host societies. But with the passage of time and the burgeoning population competing for scarce resources, fissures developed in their otherwise close link and rapport with the local communities. Consequently, thousands faced eviction and deportation like the Bangladeshis but, unlike them, who could be driven out only under the provisions of the laws of the land, namely, the PIP and later the IMDT Act, the Nepalis could be simply evicted by some local youth organizations, and with the connivance of the policemen carted off and deposited at the other side of the Indo-Nepal border. In the game of survival and proliferation even under a hostile environment, the Bangladeshis are unique, leaving Nepalis miles behind. Bangladeshis are "politically" not there but they are everywhere to be seen. Nepalis are likely to remain a docile minority group doing its bits to withstand the forces inimical to them, primarily because number is not on their side. Of course number is not always important. No one will perhaps dispute that though their population is only 0.01 per cent of the total population of India, Parsis dominate the country's industry, business, science and art. But it is wrong to compare the Nepalis with Parsis for obvious reasons. The future of the Nepalis in India apparently lies in consolidating in the field of education and adoption of a pragmatic approach to all issues, be they social, economic or political.

REFERENCES

1. Lopita Nath, 2002, *Ethnicity and Cross Border Movements in the North-East: A Study of the Nepalis in Assam*, Kolkata: Maulana Abul Kalam Azad Institute of Asian Studies, p. 58.
2. J.H. Hutton, 1973, cited in Moheswar Neog (ed.) *Studies in the Early History of Assam*, Guwahati: Assam Sahitya Sabha, p. 26.
3. Shyamraj Jaisi, 1996, in *Itihas Adharat Asomor Nepali* (Trans. Agni Bahadur Kshatry), Guwahati: Art Printers and Stationers.

4. Kanak Lal Barua. 1933, *Early History of Kamrupa*. Shillong. 1933. p. 11, cited by Lopita Nath. *op. cit.*, p. 56.
5. Tirtha Nath Sharma, 2006, "Asomot Nepali" in Rudraman Thapa and Sobhit Kumar Chetry (eds), *Asomor Thaluwa Nepali*, Dibrugarh: Kaustabh Prakashan, p. 2.
6. Suniti Kumar Chatterjee, cited in Nath, *op. cit.*, p. 57.
7. Maheswar Neog, 1986, in *Complete Works of Maheswar Neog*, Guwahati: Assam Sahitya Sabha, pp. 277-78.
8. A.C. Sinha, "Indian Northeast Frontier and Nepali Immigrants" in A.C. Sinha and T.B. Subba (eds), *The Nepalis in the Northeast India*, New Delhi: Indus, 2003, p. 42.
9. Sinha, *ibid.*, p. 43.
10. Sinha, *ibid.*, p. 8.
11. K.K. Muktan, "Gorkhas' Contributions to External and Internal Security of India" in Sinha and Subba, *op. cit.*, p. 128.
12. Sinha, *op. cit.*, p. 44.
13. Amalenda Guha, 1988, *Planter Raj to Swaraj*, New Delhi: People's Publishing House, p. 93.
14. Nath, *op. cit.*, p. 90.
15. Nath, *op. cit.*, p. 99.
16. Lopita Nath, "Migrants in Flight: Conflict-induced Internal Displacement of Nepalis in Northeast India", *Peace and Democracy in South Asia*, Vol. 1, January 2005.
17. *Government Land Policies in Recent Times: A Compilation from 1942 to 1989*, Revenue Department (Settlement Branch) Dispur, Guwahati, 1990, p. 1.
18. Lt. Gen (Retd.) S.K. Sinha, Report to the President of India as published in *The Sentinel* dated 18-27 December, 1998.
19. D.N. Bezborua, "Our Land, Their Living Space", *The Sentinel*, March 17th to 20th, and 22nd March to 27th March, 2000.
20. Bezborua, *ibid.*
21. Lt. Gen. (Retd.) S.K. Sinha, *op. cit.*
22. Jogesh Bhuyan, 1999, "Asom Musalman Pradhan Raijya Howar Sambhavana Asene?" *Amar Asom*, November 1.
23. Bezborua, *op. cit.*
24. T.B. Subba, "Nepalis in NE India: Political Aspirations and Ethnicity" in Sinha and Subba (eds), *op. cit.*, p. 60.
25. *Ibid.*

25

Shared Destiny: Indians of Nepalese Origin (INO) and Nepalese of Indian Origin (NIO)

A.C. SINHA

The cultural map of ancient India refers to *Jambu Dwipe Bharat Khande*, recited on all auspicious occasions among orthodox Hindus, which had concept of India from the (Indian) Ocean to the Himalaya, known as *Asetu Himalaya*. That classical image of Bharatkhand among others prominently described the Himalaya as the abode of gods, sages, rishis, Yakshas, Kinnars, Kirats and holy citadel of Lord Shiva, one among the Hindu trinity of Gods, and from where, the sacred rivers such as Ganges, Yamuna, Saryu, and Brahmputra originate. One of the best poetic descriptions of the Himalaya may be discerned from a Sanskrit classic of the great bard Kalidasa, who termed it 'Devtatma Himalayo Nama Nagadhiraj'. In that image of the Himalaya, there was no distinction between Kashmir, Himanchal, Uttaranchal or Nepal parts of the Himalaya. They were/are all Himalaya, which were considered holy land of retreat, penance, and shrines of the sacred beings. The Hindus from all over had/ have an abiding desire to go on pilgrimage to the holy sacred centres among others Pasupatinath in Kathmandu. In the same spirit, denizens of the Himalayan region used to go on pilgrimage to *char dham* (four holy centres) on four directions, and seven *tirtha*s or *puri*s at different locations all over India. The great reformer, Swami Sankaracharya, undertook a pilgrimage to Pasupatinath with a view to establishing his school of Hinduism there. The sacred specialists from southern India officiate as priests in many of the holy shrines in the Himalaya inclusive of Pasupatinath at Kathmandu.

The Magadh Empire under Ashoka the great or Gupta rulers and many other dynastic rulers in eastern India in ancient period of the south Asian history spread their sway in present day Nepal. Ancient Mithila, the land of mythic kings, Janaka of Videha, invariably extended to the hills and major parts of the eastern terai of Nepal. And many of the rulers of the regional dynasties of Mithila, and mid and eastern Nepal had their sway in the hills as well as in the plains and the terai in particular. In this context, two small republics of Lichchavis and Shakyas, located in the northern Bihar, eastern Uttar Pradesh and Nepal terai in the pre-Maurayan period of the Indian history are of historical significance. Needless to mention that Sidharth, who came to be known as Gautam Buddha after his enlightenment at Bodh Gaya and who was the originator of Buddhism, was born at Kapilvastu in terai. Nepal has tried to appropriate Buddha as Nepalese without his Indian context. Since then, most of the rulers at Pataliputra, Kanauj, Delhi and elsewhere in north India, extended their sway up to Nepal. Even in the medieval period of Indian history, Delhi rulers desired to rule over the Himalaya region. In this context, even in the bad days of Mughal period, Baisi and Chaudisi principalities in western and middle Nepal were under some sort of sovereignty of the great Mughal Empire. The claim of the great Gorkha king, Prithvi Narayan Shah, that the Gorkha kingdom was the 'real land of the Hindus' (*asal* Hindustan) should be seen in a cultural sense, as bulk of India had by then come under the alien—read Muslim or the British rule. By then, the British had begun to consolidate their stronghold on rest of India and naturally, Nepal got busy in carving itself an autonomous image of the Hindu kingdom, distinct from the British India.

History of INO and NIO

Hrishikesh Shaha, a noted scholar of Nepal, writes that in ancient times, terai contained several well-known centres of Vedic and Buddhist learning—Janakpur, Biratnagar, and Niglihava. The Buddhist republics of Shakyas and Kolis such as Kapilvastu and Ramgam were situated in the central terai. In the east lay the famed seats of Vedic learning such as Videha and Vestadipak. Kautilya's *Arthashastra* took note of the black woolen blankets from Nepal, which were used as excellent raincoats. The earliest rulers and dynasties such as Gopalas (cow-herds) and Mahisapalas (buffalo-herds) may suggest pastoral and nomadic stage of their society prior to the wider use and prevalence of agriculture.[1] One learns from D.R. Regmi that, 'From 50 AD to 350 AD, i.e., for a period of 300 years, Nepal seems to have lost its independent status on the regular domination from Patliputra.'[2] There is a consensus among the scholars that Lichchhvi rule in Nepal commenced in the first or second century AD and continued till the end of eighth century. Needless to mention here that major concentration of the Lichchhvis was at Vaisali in north Bihar.[3] In 1200, a new king, Ari Malla, was the first to adopt the suffix 'Malla', a honourific title which was probably initially used by the Pallava dynasty of southern India. The 600 years prior to Prithvi Narayan Shah's conquest of the valley (of Kathmandu) in 1768-69 are consequently referred to as the "Malla Period".[4]

After the fragmentation of the Khasa empire, located in present day Uttaranchal in India, south-eastern Tibet and bulk of western Nepal, in fifteenth century, a series of petty principalities emerged in Karnali basin (*Baisi*—twenty-two) and Gandaki basin (*Chaubisi*—twenty-four). Among them, 'while some new rulers were genuine refugees from the plains, others were really of Khasa or Magar origin, though claims and counter claims make it impossible to be sure of true origin of any particular family. The Sen rulers of Palpa and Makawanpur are referred to as Magars in documents from the Kathmandu valley and Sikkim. The Shahs of Gorkha were also some times described as Magars and the names of Kancha and Micha, which occur in the genealogy linking the dynasty to the brother of a Chittar ruler (of Rajasthan in India) perhaps, support this. The ruler of Baldeng (near present-day Butwal), overthrown by Palpa and other Chaubisi states around 1700, was also supposedly a Magar.'[5]

Moreover, it is not true that all Rajputs were simply fleeing away from the Muslim wrath in the medieval period. This period also saw a general consolidation and agrarian expansion in Southasia as a whole, together with monetization of the economy. Against this background, 'individual families failing to find a niche in the plains areas immediately south of Nepal may have decided to carve out lordships for themselves in the foothills. The founder of the Palpa Sen dynasty may be an example of this. According to one version of the story, he moved from Allahabad into terai and then into the hills rather than directly from Rajasthan.'[6]

To take the above argument further, Rishkesh Shaha[7] records that as early as sixteenth century, Sen Rajas of Makwanpur in eastern terai had managed to set up dynasties in the kingdom of Chaudandi and Vijaypur, which covered the entire eastern terai region of Nepal. If the rulers in the hills were in a position to snatch away the terai land by force, they would always do so. If it was not possible, they would persuade the rulers in the plains to give the terai on payment of rent. In the last decade of the eighteenth century, the Raja of Palpa obtained the zamindari of Kapilvastu, Rupandehi and parts of Nawal Parasi districts from the Nawab Wazir of Awadh. However, coming to the present status of the Nepal terai, as a result of the Treaty of Segowli, on December 2, 1815, Nepal was to surrender the entire terai from east to west to the British. However, Nepal recovered eastern and central terai in 1817 and the western terai was returned to it as a reward of its services rendered to the British during the Sepoy Mutiny of 1857. Incidentally, the sepoy mutiny also resulted in an extensive immigration of plains people from India to the terai with a view to running away from the British harassments.

The Treaty of Peace (Segowli), 1815 envisaged under Article 3 that all terai lands and the hills eastward of the River Mechi including the forts and lands of Nagree and the pass of Nagarcote were to be ceded to the East India Company. Similarly, Article 5 presumed that the rulers of Nepal would renounce all their claims on the territories west of river Kali in the west. The treaty binds Nepal as per Article 6, which says 'never to molest or disturb the Rajah of Sikkim in the possession of the territories' and agrees for the arbitration of the British in case of differences, if any. The rulers of Nepal were given 40 days to vacate the territories east of River Mechi and as soon as it was accomplished, the British got their acts together to carve out a buffer state of Sikkim between Nepal and Bhutan. Sikkim Durbar and the East India Company signed a ten article treaty at Titaliya on February 10, 1917, by which the British agreed to cede all the Sikkim land secured from Nepal to the former. Consequently, the British issued a *sanad* on April 7, 1817 granting Sikkim rule of all the above territories, but Sikkim was reduced to a feudatory of the British in effect. Very soon, the British tricked the ruler to part with Darjeeling hills on plea of turning it into a sanitarium for the sick British residents. Growth of Darjeeling town turned out to be a contest between oriental and occidental approach to human affairs. While the British were busy turning it into a thriving hill station in a systematic manner, the adjoining feudatories were worried about controlling their run away slaves, serfs, peasants, and tenants, who were attracted to remunerative works in Darjeeling. All these resulted in the Treaty of Tumlong, 1861 between the Company and the Sikkim ruler and in the Treaty of Sinchula, 1865 between Bhutan and the Company, by which the territories of the district of Darjeeling were secured. It may be kept in mind that Darjeeling and the Duars eastward of it were very thinly populated at the time. And incidentally, this was also the time British were busy laying out tea plantations and railway tracts for an effective commercial exploitation.

Apart from inexpensive, willing and industrious Nepali labour for clearing the dense, undulating, mountainous forests of Northeast India for tea plantation and laying out roads and rails, the British also invented a myth of the Gorkha martial race. It may be pertinent that in the aftermath of the Sepoy Mutiny of 1857, the British were determined to prove that the Bengalis and high caste Hindus from the Gangetic plains were effeminate and thus, unsuitable for the armed forces. This explains the extensive immigration of coolie as indentured labour from Bihar and Uttar Pradesh, the theatre of the revolt, to far away British and other European colonies across the oceans for plantation work. Meanwhile, Gorkhas, Sikhs, Marathas and others, who did not take part in the Sepoy Mutiny, were elevated to the status of 'martial race' by creating many real and putative myths and thus, they were recruited to armed forces. Coming to theme of our present concern, the Gorkhas or the Nepalis, 'the Gurkhas seemed to have an additional quality associated with those who led them: the special combination of traits (courtesy, humour, sportsmanship) which defines persons' breeding. They were, in short, not simply warriors, but gentlemen as well; hence their depiction akin to public school boys'[8]. Despite being Easterners, they are as if honourary Europeans. And like all martial peoples, the Gorkhas were invariably brave, though in an unthinking, instinctual, some what simple, unimaginative character, encapsulated in a permanent state of juvenile.

As long as the British were in India, they treated Nepal as a farm for breeding coolies and soldiers. There was so much stress on Gorkha recruitment from the Nepal hills that even the progeny of the same Gorkha settlers in and around the army cantonments (termed as the lines boys) were considered unfit for the recruitment in the armed forces. In the same way, the British were certain that the Gorkhas would not like to serve under the Indian officers in the event of India gaining independence in 1947. It was a myth, which was punctured when as per Tripartite Agreement between Great Britain, India and Nepal, 6 Gorkha regiments out of 10 opted to serve India, and naturally under the Indian officers. A significant step was undertaken by Nepal and India, when the Treaty of Peace and Friendship was signed by the representatives of the two governments on July 31, 1950 at Kathmandu. Article 6 of the treaty 'undertakes to give to the nationals of the other in its territory' same treatment, which it gives to its citizens. Similarly, Article 7 stipulates that: 'the governments of India and Nepal agree to grant, on reciprocal basis, to the nationals of one country in the territory of other, the same privileges in matters of residence, ownership of property, participation in trade and commerce, movement and other privileges of a similar nature.' We shall see how the INOs see Article 7 as detrimental to their interests as Indian nationals and how a section of the Nepal Nepalis feel that the treaty has out-lived its relevance with changing times.

Locating the INO and NIO

Before we begin to analyze who are the INOs and NIOs, it is pertinent to clarify a significant point. It is normally claimed in Nepal that the NIO or Madheshis are the land-hungry emigrants from the Indian plains, who went to Nepal terai after the Sepoy Mutiny with a view to clearing the forest and claiming the fertile agricultural fields. Similarly, it is maintained in India that the INOs were invited by the British to develop Darjeeling and to mine copper and mint coins in Sikkim some 150 years back. These claims are partly true. But the fact is that ancestors of the Madheshis in terai and Kirati Nepalis in Sikkim were already there even before 1814-15 Anglo-Nepalese war. The point to be noted is that not all Madheshis and likewise not all Nepalis in Sikkim (which earlier included Darjeeling district of present day West Bengal) were migrants and, in fact, some of them have a better claim to be the "sons of soil" than many others in their respective places. The Royal Government of Nepal since 1960 has consistently maintained that terai is inhabited by a variety of castes, who speak Maithili, Bhojpuri and Awadhi, and are, in fact, Indians residing in Nepal by taking advantage of open border. They are oriented towards India in every walk of life such as social, economic, religious and political and in fact they create a strain on limited Nepalese resources. To Nepal, except their self-interest nothing binds them together with the rest of the Nepalese. The Nepalese state mentions of terai as the southern-most territory of Nepal, 200 metres above the sea level, 10 to 30 miles wide and about 500 miles in length from west to east. Its significance was noted by Rishikesh Shaha thus: 'The terai has an area of 9,437 square miles or 14.4 percent of total area, and a population of 34.56 percent of the total...It contributes 58.9 percent of GDP and 75.6 percent of government's revenue...It represents 62 percent of Nepal's cultivated area and 71.8 percent of Nepal's private industries are located in the terai.'[9] Further, the terai has 18 out of 75 districts from east to west: Jhapa, Morang, Sunsari, Saptari, Siraha, Dhankuta, Mahottari, Sarlahi, Rautahat, Bara, Parsa, Newar-Parasi, Rupadehi, Kapilvastu, Banke, Bardiya, Kailali, and Kanchanpur. Though Nepal does not recognize it, Hindi is the lingua franca of the entire terai.

Between 1860s and 1951, the Nepal government encouraged economic development in the terai and made efforts to settle hill people there. But the response from the hill people was poor due to hot, humid and unfamiliar malarial climate. The Rana regime of Nepal had no choice, but to depend on the migrants from across the border to invest in clearing the dense terai forests and turning them into thriving agrarian economy. There was another development in Nepal since 1950s. And that was the existence of the political parties, which functioned as "melting pots", not only for regionally and culturally diverse groups but also for the urban modernizing elite, the traditional rural elite and for the large number of non-elite groups as well. But 'people of nationally dominant hill culture (read Bahun-Chhetri-Newar) and people of regionally important plains culture have lived separate existences until the last several decades, often with suspicion of each other. Citizenship legislation framed by representatives of the nationally dominant hill culture during the 1960s reflects this suspicion, for it makes the acquisition of citizenship more difficult for the people of the plains origin living in the Terai.'[10] For example, the 1962 Constitution framed under King Mahendra, stipulated, in Article 8, section 2, that 'While making laws in pursuance of clause(i) it shall be, *inter alia,* stipulated that a foreigner may qualify for acquisition of citizenship if,

(a) he can speak and write the national language of Nepal (i.e. Nepali);
(b) he has resided in Nepal for not less than a period of two years in case of a person of Nepalese origin, and for not less than a period of twelve years in case of a person other than of Nepalese origin.'[11]

In this way, 'elimination of the party system in 1960 has(d) returned Nepal to political system in which the traditional elite can assert its influence more exclusively. Although education has become an increasingly important factor in determining political influence, in the absence of direct elections and of political parties to compete in those elections, landownership and high caste status, factors monopolized by the traditional elite, remain more decisive in the political process.'[12]

In this context, the *Jana Andolan* 1 (People's Movement 1), 1990 re-oriented the Nepalese polity from absolute authority of the king to a dual sovereignty of the constitutional monarchy and parliamentary democracy. And it made the people the ultimate source of the power. The

Jan Andolan II (i.e., the unprecedented mass uprising of 2006) has led to restructuring of the Nepalese state, 'there is no space for accommodating the monarchy, at least an active and exclusive king. There is a clear indication of the erosion of the legitimacy of the Nepali monarchy. The recent declaration of Nepal as a secular state is a conscious attempt to hammer at the claim of the divine right by the monarchy of Nepal.'[13] No doubt, this has led to a wild explosion of expectations at all levels. However, significant among them are two: assertion of ethnic identities (*janjati* movement) at various levels and an ethno-regional identity of Madheshis in the terai. However, there is a marked shift in recent Madheshi movement, as terai dwellers cannot be equated with the Madheshis. 'The term "madhesi" literally means a dweller in '*madhes*' (Madhyades) or the plains. In theory any one living in terai could be considered a Madhesi, but it has assumed an ethnic meaning (just like Parbatiya or Pahari, meaning "hill-dwellers"). It refers to plains-dwellers of Indian, Hindu, origin. Usages differ, but it seems clear that the Tharus and other groups do not wish to be included in the category. The Parbatiyas, who are settled in the plains are definitely not included, and Muslims are not members either.'[14]

Right from 1769, variously termed as the Gorkha conquest of Kathmandu Valley by Prithvi Narayan Shah or unification of petty principalities into Nepal by him, the Nepalese rulers projected themselves as the true Hindu rulers by divine right and guardians of Hinduism vis-à-vis India, which was allegedly defiled by alien Muslim or British rulers. Moreover, it was touted as the only Hindu kingdom in the world against the enslaved or secular India, to prove its distinct identity. The Janajati elements in the east and north and Madhesi ethnic groups in the southern terai were played down as if they were aberrations to the dominant Bahun-Chhetri-Newar hill culture as the national icon. Furthermore, the Nepalese ruling class either made strenuous efforts to balance early historical influence of India on Nepal by referring to some shadowy contacts with the north, i.e., Tibet or China or empathizing Prithvi Narayan Shah as unifier of the Nepalese nation, as if it had always been a historical reality. In this context, 'the revival of Hinduisation by King Mahendra in the 1960s is another example of a ruler who does have a secular base invoking traditional legitimacy. By staging a coup in December, 1960, Mahendra ended the multi-party system and instead introduced a party-less panchayat under his leadership. The Panchayat Constitution of 1962, unlike the constitutions of 1951 and 1959, made Nepal a Hindu state.'[15]

The Nepalese hill elite allegedly disdain the Madhesis as merchants or landless labourers. The tragedy is that even Bihar and Uttar Pradesh treat them as uncouth (*bhade*) and avoid even marital relationships with them. C.K. Lal, a noted journalist of Kathmandu, provides example of a high caste Madhesi Bhumihar family, which had best of both the regimes, Indian and Nepalese. But even this family was subjected to social disdain from their Indian counterparts. It so happened that Bhadrakali Mishra and Ram Narayan Mishra held office of the Minister in the Royal Government of Nepal in 1950s and 1960s. Their other brother, Shyam Nandan Mishra, became the Minister of External Affairs in the short-lived government of India headed by Chaudury Charan Singh in 1979. It is said that their grandfather once went looking for a groom for his daughter among some of the reputed families of his caste in Bihar. He not only found the going tough, but was also told that while Mishras of Pipra may be rich they were subjects of the Ranas, whereas the Bhumihars of Bihar were independent zamindars under the British.[16] This example discounts the significance of what the Madhesis call "*beti-roti ka rista*" (bread and bride relationship) from across the border.

With reference to the INOs some clarifications are needed. First, it must be accepted that Kirati elements who now speak Nepali and are identified as Nepalis were already in Sikkim, which then included the present district of Darjeeling under West Bengal, before an extensive immigration of the Nepalese to India occurred after the treaties of Segowli and Titaliya. Second, prior to the British colonization of India, Nepalese traders, pilgrims, roving holy men and sundry marital partners moved from Nepal to India and vis-a-vis. Third, there were seasonal migrants in search of manual work during agriculturally lean months of year, who returned home after a short stay in India. Fourth, the Gorkha soldiers were encouraged to return to Nepal after their superannuation. Fifth, hill communities from Nepalese ethnic commonwealth felt more at home in Northeast India and invariably they preferred to stay back, if opportunity arose. Sixth, it appears that they moved in a systematic way: first, it was Darjeeling, then Sikkim, followed by foothills in western Bhutan, and finally the British Assam hills. Seventh, herdsmen and dairymen moved in search of grazing grounds on river banks, degraded forests, and dry farmsteads right from 1850 onwards and they were encouraged by forest department which charged grazing fees.

The earliest contact of the Nepalese with Northeast India was in 1817, when 1,000 Hindustanis and "Gurkhas" took part in Sylhet expedition as a part of the Cuttack Legion (later known as the Assam

Light Infantry). I have noted elsewhere, 'The story of Nepali involvement in the consolidation of the region under the British Empire is ably presented by Col. Shakespeare's *History of the Assam Rifles* (1977). Whether it was Sylhet or the Shillong plateau, Naga Hills or Lushai Hills, Chttagong Hills Tract or Sadiya Frontier Tract, Bhutan War or Manipur rebellion, the Gurkhas constituted half of the Assam Rifles and were always there in operation. Their important role in the Assam Rifles was recognized in 1865, when the Nepali khukuri replaced the short sword, which used to impede their progress through the dense Assamese jungles. It may be appropriate to inform the readers that in course of time, the crossed khukuri was accepted as the emblem of the Assam Rifles, the custodians of the security of the region.'[17]

Apart from the Assam Rifles, the Gorkha Training Centre and various battalions of the armed forces were stationed in and around the district towns and the strategic locations in the hills of Northeast India. A number of them got settled around these places after their release from their service. The Assam Rifles alone has rehabilitated its Gorkha ex-soldiers in at least 40 sites in the region. In fact, some of these sites such as Sadiya in Assam, Matripokhri in Manipur, Aizawl in Mizoram and Mokokchung in Nagaland are as old as hundred years. Among such sites Assam alone has 13, Manipur 8, Mizoram and Nagaland 7 each, Arunachal Pradesh 3 and Meghalaya and Tripura have one each resettlement colonies of the ex-soldiers. And it goes without saying that these colonies predominantly belong to the INO. Most of the settlers have well adapted to the local social and cultural environment and they have turned out to be inseparable part of the local economy. Apart from the ex-soldiers, there are considerable number of herdsmen and dairy men, lumbermen, and sundry occupational castes such as Kami, Sarki, Damai, and the omnipresent Brahmin priests. Though there is no authentic statistics available on the INOs in the region, their number is estimated to be any thing from three and a half million to six million in Northeast India inclusive of West Bengal.

There is a predominance of what is known as Kirati ethnic groups in Sikkim, Darjeeling, Bhutan Duars and North-eastern region of India. Eastern Nepal has been traditional home of the Kirati communities, which naturally extended to erstwhile Bhutia principality of Sikkim. So the Kiratis like Limbus and Magars claim to be indigenous settlers of Sikkim. The Brahmins among the INOs came predominantly as herdsmen and dairy hands, which invariably turned to farming as and when the opportunity came their way. Ex-soldiers, who decided to settle in Northeast

India, were a mixed group of Chhetris, Magars, Gurungs, Rais, Limbus, and Tamangs. Hindu occupational castes like Upadhyayas, Kamis, Sarkis, and Damais naturally followed the Hindu INO settlements in this region.

Invisible, Yet Exploited: Characteristics INOs-NIOs Share

I. Both INOs and NIOs receive little academic attention in their own countries. The managers of the Nepalese hill culture make all efforts to distance themselves from its southern dominant neighbour, India, and consequently, presence of Madhesis, who proudly trace their cultural roots to the south.[18] One of the best examples of deliberate playing down of the Madhesis may be cited from the celebrated work of Dor Bahadur Bista, *People of Nepal*.[19] In the book running into 252 pages, the author allots only 12 pages to 'Brahman, Rajput and Occupational Castes of the terai'. He writes, '...the terai people speak languages akin to those spoken to the south and practice Indian social and religious customs. But in terai the diversity is great, encompassing several very different languages... (But) the social and economic organization of the terai people is similar to that of Brahmans, Chhetris and other occupational castes of the hill region of Nepal, but by virtue of their Indian influence their way of life is much more like that of North India than that of the Nepal hills. The vast majority of them are Hindus, but there are many Muslims. In contrast to liberal Hindu hill people, these people of terai and border areas are orthodox in their beliefs following Hinduism and caste rules as closely as possible to the classical Hindu pattern...For marriage and other socio-economic relations, the border is ignored. Social and kinship ties are much more important to them than the political boundaries.'[20]

II. Both INOs and NIOs have a share of full-fledged citizens and people who are yet to acquire citizenship of the country they have settled in. In this context, it may be noted that as many as 35,000 stateless INOs were given citizenship 15 years after Sikkim's merger with India.[21] So far Madhesis are concerned Nepal had discriminated against them as a policy, because incorporation of the Madhesis with a relatively sophisticated cultural background in the hill culture as a distinctive mark of Nepal was almost impossible. So the Government of Nepal made it almost impossible for an extensive number of Madhesis to possess citizenship documents and in the absence of such documents, they were not only forbidden from political participation, but also deprived economically and administratively. For example, in the absence of citizenship documents, no Madhesis could sell or buy a property, secure license for starting a business, get admitted to the educational institutions and so on. In this context, the report of the High-Level Citizenship Commission, BS 2051 (1995), found more than three million Madhesis without citizenship certificates.[22] However, to be fair to the present political dispensation in Nepal, having realized the enormity and seriousness of the problem, the present interim government sent teams of functionaries to distribute citizenship certificates to the Madhesis.

III. Both have inadequate voice/representation in the affairs of the state administration. So far as INOs are concerned, they rule the state of Sikkim as per the laws of land. It is they who decide all the significant issues in the district of Darjeeling in West Bengal. They have been represented in state legislative assemblies of Assam, Meghalaya, Manipur and West Bengal as per their population. So far the Indian national legislature is concerned, there are hardly about half a dozen representatives from the community out of a total number of about 750 in both the houses of the parliament. It is not that the community representation is inadequate, but the representatives do not have sophistication and stature to effectively participate in the affairs of the Indian Union. Thus, the community has no effective political voice; they hardly matter in terms of economic clout and very few of them have excelled in print, audio-visual, or other forms of mass media. Thus, when the community is in problem, they do not have spokesmen and their issues are simply ignored by the power to be.

So far Nepal is concerned officially about 35 percent people are of Madhesi origin, apart from an extensive number of residents, who do not possess citizenship certificates. A current estimate suggests that as much as 48 percent Nepalese are of Madhesi origin. But there are a number of ways through which Nepal denied them a genuine representation in its parliament. For example, demographically, terai constituency is much larger than that of the constituencies in the hills. Second, division of the constituencies has been done from north to south ostensibly with a view to including hill people and excluding dominance of the terai people, and not from east to west, which is natural and which favours the Madhesis. The 1990 democratic constitution allotted 83 out of 205 seats in the Pratinidhi Sabha (Lower Chamber of the Nepalese Parliament). Consequently, various political parties put up candidates from the hills from the terai constituencies, who could be elected as per party principles. Consequently, Madhesi representation was always much below their numerical strength. As for illustration, only 40 Madhesis irrespective of the political parties were elected to the last parliamentary election held in 1999.

IV. Both suffer from crisis of identity and carry a negative baggage from the past. So far as INOs are concerned their main grouse is that they are mistaken with the visiting Nepalese. Otherwise, there is no overt effort to suppress them, their voice, their language and their culture. Since 1992, Nepali is recognized as an Indian language and listed among the Indian languages under the VIII Schedule of the Indian Constitution. And for a long period of time, Sahitya Academy, the official body of the Government of India, did recognize the Nepali literature and Nepali authors have duly been awarded as per their merit. Nepali language is taught in a number of universities at different levels and, in fact, there is a huge corpus of literature produced in India. Moreover, there is complete freedom to the various communities to develop their own languages and scripts, as is evident in Sikkim, where various Kirati communities are engaged in enriching their languages.[23]

Coming to Nepalese situation, the first population census, conducted in 1952-54, recorded 58,181 NIOs. Since then, the practice was stopped and a policy to enumerate the speakers of the dialects at the local level with a view to displaying the linguistic differences and to sow the discord among Maithils, Bhojpuris, and Awadhis was implemented. Though Hindi language is taught at Tribhuwan University, Kathmandu, its non-recognition by the state discourages students to study it. Further, against the over-whelming demand of the Madhesis, Nepali is the only medium of competitive examinations for various positions in the government. Moreover, Hindi was not even permitted to be spoken on the floor of the parliament till 1990. Same was the case with their dress—*dhoti-kurta*, the natural attire of the Madhesis—which was again not recognized as proper dress for a Nepalese for a formal occasion. Similarly in the absence official non-sanction of government advertisement, the Hindi periodicals die a natural death.

V. Both suffer from discrimination at various levels and are thus engaged in struggle for securing justice for their members. The oldest INO forum, All India Gorkha League (AIGL), was established at Dehradun in 1923 and it demanded a Nepali speaking state within India. In course of time, the AIGL concentrated mainly in Duars and Darjeeling district. So much so that during the emotionally surcharged phase of Indian history, the region inclusive of Duars, Sikkm and Darjeeling was demanded to be integrated to Nepal in the event of Assam going to Pakistan. Even then the AIGL remained a formidable political party in Darjeeling and the Duars, but very soon it turned out be a rudderless party without a clear political agenda for its followers. In such a vacuum, the Gorkha National Liberation Front (GNLF) led by a former soldier and small time author, Subhas Ghishing emerged with its aggressive demands for a Gorkha homeland in Darjeeling in 1980s. The GNLF populist movement turned violent and intimidating, cutting Darjeeling hills and Sikkim from the rest of India in terms of communication for days together. In an enigmatic and dramatic way, Ghishing termed the INOs as Gorkhas, their language as Gorkhali, and their imagined state, Gorkhaland. This led to further controversy and confusion among the INOs. At long last, Ghishing's agitation resulted in establishment of the Darjeeling Gorkha Hill Council (DGHC) in West Bengal and since then he remained the chairman of that body until March 2008.

The Gorkhaland movement settled for a DGHC for the Darjeeling hills. This was the time trouble started for the Lhotshampas in Bhutan. Many of the former GNLF members assisted the Lhotshampas in a variety of ways. However, Ghishing's autocratic and personalized style of functioning did not endear him to a universal respect and love from the community for him. The ethnic movement with a view to championing the cause of the INOs and spear-headed by him was split into Gorkha and Nepali, from which it is yet to recover. Presently, there are parallel Gorkha and Nepali associations at political, social, cultural, literary, and other forums purportedly espousing the cause of the INOs. Occasionally, one learns the existence of an All India Gorkha Parishad, which holds its sessions at various places in the country and tries to distance itself from Subhas Ghishing. Right now, it appears that the community suffers from absence of creditable leadership to take up the issues of the community's interest.

VI. Both have contributed immensely to the economic prosperity of the states of their domicile, which remains unrewarded. Frederick Gaige, writing in 1975, gives figures for revenue generated in terai for the year 1965-66 for timber, land revenue, customs and excise to be 76 percent of the total income. 'To sum up, although the terai accounts for only 17 percent of Nepal's land area and 31 percent of its population, it contributes approximately 59 percent of Nepal's GDP and 76 percent of the revenue.'[24] He found as much as 72 percent of Nepal's smaller industries located in the terai (p. 34). Moreover, 'except for several stainless steel and synthetic-fabric factories, one cotton mill (not operating at the time) and one steel-rolling mill, nearly all of Nepal's industry, whether large-scale or small-scale, processes timber and agricultural produce are grown in the terai.'[25] India is demographically a big country, in which the INO population is really a miniscule. Moreover, their location in Sikkim, Darjeeling, Duars and Northeastern states is mired in regional ethnic conflicts. Incidentally, these are industrially, commercially, and politically marginal areas in the Indian Union and have an image of predominantly "tribal states" with a number of constitutional guarantees on their land, culture, and other resources. However, contribution of the easily and cheaply available INO labour for infra-structure development of the region is universally acknowledged. Similarly, services rendered by the Gorkha soldiers to armed forces are a well-established reality and Indian nation is indebted to its soldiers for their services at large.

The theatre of the anti-Rana agitation, launched in 1951 by the Nepali Congress, was central and eastern terai, the "land of the Madhesis". It was the Madhesis, who fought with the autocratic Rana regime as the soldiers of the Nepali Congress along other Nepalese and the Indian political class. The Ranacracy was removed, but before democracy could be established, King Mahendra introduced a retrograde panchayati system, which made efforts to negate any democratic achievements made for the terai region during the chaotic democratic phase of 1952-1960. King Mahendra issued a directive in January 1958, making it mandatory in all schools to teach through the medium of Nepali. Vedanad Jha, a Madhesi Nepalese, had organized Nepali terai Congress as early as 1951 with following demands: (i) establishment of an autonomous terai state, (ii) recognition of Hindi as a state language, and (iii) adequate employment of terai people in the Nepal civil service. He pleaded that Hindi was the language of all the residents of terai. The problem was that in the universally illiterate state of Nepal, every body spoke in mother tongue at home and when they had to formally communicate with the authorities, it was in Hindi. But the state did not recognize this reality and declared terai people as speakers of a set of mother tongues—Mathili, Bhojpuri, Awadhi, Tharu, and so on. Vedanad Jha did not do well electorally but he was incorporated in the ruling system as a minister and then as an ambassador.

Another political outfit emerged in terai in 1980s called Nepal Sadbhawna Party (NSP) led by Gajendra Narayan Singh, who was elected to the Nepalese parliament more than once and was elevated to the office of a minister. After his demise, the NSP got divided into two. But the dominant faction headed by Anandi Devi, Singh's widow, continued to be represented in the parliament and even in the national cabinet. This party is one of the constituents of the ruling seven parties' alliance along with the Maobadis in Nepal. Once the Maobadis joined the government in Nepal and the process of instituting a Constituent Assembly was on, patience of the Madhesis gave way, as they saw it as continuation of the same old game of politically ignoring the terai. So a number of violent forums such as Madhesis Janadhikar Forum, Janatantrik Terai Mukti Morcha (Jwala Singh), Janatantrik Terai Morcha (Jai Prakash Goit) sprang up and took the violent route followed by the Maoists to make their point heard by the established democratic political parties. They were finally heard. The present care-taker regime is worried about the anti-state violence in terai and the international community is looking at the events as they unfold there. The Madhesis have been able to send a clear signal that whosoever may control the destiny of Nepal, Madhesis will take it no more lying down and they will not accept the old appellation of "*Timiharu Madhesi*" (You are Madhesis) any more.

There are charges that the palace might have instigated the violence in the terai. There is another school of "wise men" who feel that Madhesi agitation is inspired by the Hindutva brigade from India. Yet another speculation is rife that the force behind the Madhesi movement is that of the intelligence agencies controlled by the Government of India. All these wise men/women still refuse to give any credit to the Madhesis that can take their own decisions affecting their future. Naturally, the present regime of seven parties plus one (Maoists) headed by Girija Prasad Koirala is worried the most. The Maoists, who had incorporated the Madhesis in their grand redesigning of the Nepalese system on ethnic and regional criteria, are terribly upset and intelligentsia of Nepal are worried for the future of democracy in Nepal. But need of the hour is to politically engage and incorporate the various segments of Nepalese society into a mosaic. Political commentator C.K. Lal cautions: 'The government must listen to all groups. If they listen, they will realize that no major political party has a Madhesi chairperson or secretary; that out of 500 or so political appointments since the Jana Andolan (II), less than one percent have been Madhesis. Right now, the situation is at the level of grievances. If not heeded, it will translate into demands, which will soon become conditional and then turn non-negotiable. The state must remember that no one is willing to die for a bright future, but there is no dearth of people willing to die for (ending) a bleak past.'[26]

VII. Both express themselves in their lingua franca, i.e., Nepali and Hindi. Both the communities write in the same Deonagori script, and both speak mutually intelligible languages and, thus, there is a need for making a common cause to sensitize the states on common heritage and convince the power to be about how negligence has led to a fruitless suspicion and sterile conflict of interests. There is another aspect, which needs to be looked into mainly by media and intelligentsia. And this is an atmosphere of suspicion on the simple folk struggling to make a living by their sheer helpless toil and indirectly contributing to building nation strong. Both the Nepamul Bharatiya and the Madhesis have been charged by their compatriots that they represent the advance guards of their cultural founts from across the borders. INOs are suspect in India and the Madhesis are charged to be Indians in Nepal and this has gone on for the last six decades at least. This must stop, because this type of sinister charge has no foundation. Both the regimes, Nepalese and Indian, should ponder over the fact that they are opening a new front, where except the goodwill no rancour exists. Both the regimes, which claim to be open democratic systems, should incorporate the ethnic, linguistic, economic and political demands of their citizens. In this context, demand for a Gorkha homeland deserves all serious consideration. Similarly, had there been concern for treating the Madhesis fairly as proud partners in the affairs of Nepal by the successive governments since 1951, violent upsurge in Terai would not have emerged and so many lives would not have been lost. Still there is time to take positive steps and not treat the democratic upsurge as a criminal act of some anti-national hotheads.

Looking Ahead: Prospect for the Future

It was simply pettiness and narrow pride on the part of the state of Nepal in its treatment of Hindi, the natural language of the millions of terai people. Hindi and Nepali would both enrich one another as media of instruction in the Nepalese schools. By failing to do so, the Nepalese state created a hostile, discontented and worried citizen out of law-abiding and hard working simple Madhesis. It is a universally known fact that Hindi is an apex language out of Awadhi, Bhojpuri, Magadhi, Maithili, Bundelkhandi, Brajbhasha, Rajasthani, Haryanvi, and so on. It is also a known truth that some of these languages have created very rich literature in spite of being linked with Hindi. Hindi has a huge readership, a vast publishing industry, and an honoured tradition of literary movement. Similarly, Hindi cinema has come to stay at international level as an effective means of knowledge, information and entertainment. Moreover, it is recognized by the United Nations as an international language for use in many countries beyond Indian shore. The unique thing about Hindi is its script, Devanagri, which it has proudly inherited from its mother language, Sanskrit, and which it shares with about a dozen of sister languages: Nepali, Marathi, Konkani, Gujarati, Rajasthani, Punjabi,

Dogri, Maithili, Haryanvi and so on. So the Nepalese policy pursued by King Mahendra of "*ek raja, ek desh, ek vesh*" (one king, one country and one dress) was extended to the "principle of one language" (*ek bhasha*) also. Nepal created a myth that no body speaks Hindi in Nepal in the same way now Bhutan is trying to convince itself that no body speaks Nepali in Bhutan and Lhotshampas speak only their mother tongues: Rai, Limbu, Gurung, Magar, Tamang, and so on. One wonders what will be officially approved 'mother tongue' of the Lhotshampa Brahmins, Chhetris, Kamis, Sarkis, Damais, etc. But one Bhutanese[27] scholar with a fertile mind has coined an unheard term, "Lhotsham-mi-kha" as the language of the left-over Lhotshampas in southern Bhutanese foothills.

While Nepal tried to divide Madhesis among Maithilis, Awadhis and Bhojpuris, it is the INOs themselves, who are controverting on Gorkha and Nepali as their appropriate nomenclature. It is the fact that there is considerable language loss among the migrants, especially when they reside among ethnically mixed settlements. The Newars, Limbus, Magars, Gurungs, Rais, Tamangs, Sunuwars, Sherpas and others have invariably ceased to speak their mother tongues at home in Northeast India and have naturally adopted Nepali as their mother tongue as well as their language of formal communication at home and outside. There are other associated issues with this development. Some of the languages of the INOs had a rich body of literature and scripts of their own. Once these communities left their ancient traditional habitat in Nepal, their myths, legends, folk tales, etc. got lost. Moreover, there is a popular misconception in India that any body associated with Nepalese socio-cultural commonwealth is necessarily "Nepali" and must speak Nepali. The simple INOs, who invariably live a deprived life, hardly find time to correct various misconceptions and misgivings about themselves. Moreover, the issue of an appropriate nomenclature of the INOs is mixed with real or imagined history of community's migration, need for a clear Indian identity distinct from the Nepalese, representation of their past Indian heritage, and an equally representative status along with various socio-cultural groups and sub-nationalities in India.

Nepal and India both continue to treat Madhesis and INOs in typically colonial style by denying the basic democratic rights and invariably treating them as non-existent citizens. The problem in India is that it is an open system, in which every ethnic group/ sub-nationality is to compete with others for political space and all types of resources. Though there are constitutional and political guarantees for equality among the communities/nationalities, this does not automatically ensure equality to be translated in reality. Thus, in practice, some are more equal than others in terms of their political role, economic affluence, cultural attainments, and over-all indicators of social development. The INOs represent a miniscule community tugged in an economically backward corner in India, who is suspected with Nepalese citizenship in the eyes of many Indians. Their problems too are not taken seriously as worthy of national deliberation, as they are considered transient settlers. Needless to add that the community itself has not been able to help itself by tactfully articulating its grievances in a democratic and peaceful way to persuade others to come round to the community's stand point. The INOs must know that in an open society such as India, no body is ranged against them; rather rest of the ethnic groups/nationalities are engaged in enhancing their own bargaining power. The best people to learn from are their Nepalese counterpart, the Madhesi under-dogs, who have forced the hill Bahun-Chhetri-Newar power wielders during the last six months to take note of the Madhesi demands and ensure corrective steps for their redressal.

Most of the countries in Southasia are so busy with nation-building exercises around their dominant politico-ethnic ethos that marginal, minor, deviant, discordant and alleged historically antagonistic entities are seen as threat to the system and thus, are considered outside the "national concern" in an opaque way. Thus, one finds Hindus, Christians, Ahmedias, Muhajirs in Pakistan, Lhotshampas in Bhutan, Hindus and ethnic tribesmen in Bangladesh, Tamils in Sri Lanka, hill tribes and Rohangia Muslims in Myanmar, Nepamul Bharatiya, illegal Bangladeshi migrants, Kashmiri Hindu refugees in India and so on are just tolerated by the powers to be and their demands are considered to be "audacious". These ethnic groups are so much tied to the struggles for their daily existence that they hardly have time to think of ameliorating their miseries by taking up their issues at the institutional level. In fact, they neither have a spokesman for raising their voice, nor a leadership effective enough to fight for their cause. The welfare and non-governmental organizations come up in their favour, when there is a dramatic event to make it visible for their presence. In the normal day to day life, these groups are left to themselves. Even in the most democratically open systems, issues associated with these stocks do not find a mention, when national, regional or humanitarian problems are being debated. Moribund SAARC has not even considered the issues associated with these ethnic groups worthy of their deliberations. Nor is there a possibility of such thing happening in the near future, as such moves will immediately arouse national sentiments to guard itself against an alleged sovereign authority to deliberate on the 'national issues' like these ethnic groups. So the question that may asked at this juncture is this: In this apathetic situation, what do the INOs do to end their plight? They do not have very many options to exercise and they do not look ready for any.

REFERENCES

1. Rishikesh Shaha, 1975, *An Introduction to Nepal,* Kathmandu: Ratna Pustak Bhandar.
2. Delli Raman Regmi, 1969, *Ancient Nepal,* Calcutta: Firma KL Mukhopadhyay, 3rd edition.
3. Kumar Pradhan, 1991, *The Gorkha Conquests: The Processes and Consequences of Unification of Nepal with Particular Reference to Eastern Nepal*, Calcutta: Oxford University Press, p. 13.
4. John Whelpton, 2005, *A History of Nepal,* Cambridge: University Press, p. 21.
5. *Ibid.*, p. 23.
6. *Ibid.*, p. 23.
7. Shaha, *op. cit.*, pp. 41-42.
8. Lionel Caplan, 1995, *Warrior Gentleman· "Gurkhas" in the Western imagination,* London: Berghahn Books.
9. Shaha, *op. cit.*, p. 40.
10. Frederick H. Gaige, 1975, *Regionalism and National Unity in Nepal,* New Delhi: Vikas Publishing House Pvt. Ltd., p. 87.
11. Ministry of Law and Justice, *The Constitution of Nepal*, the Royal Government of Nepal, Kathmandu, pp. 3-5.
12. Gaige, *op. cit.*, p. 197.
13. Krishna Hachhethu, 2007, "Legitimacy Crisis of Nepali Monarchy", *Economic and Political Weekly*, May 19, pp. 1830-31.
14. David N. Gellner, 2007, "Caste, Ethnicity and Inequality in Nepal", *Economic and Political Weekly*, May 19, p. 1825.
15. Krishna Hachhethu, 2007, *Ibid.*, p. 1830.
16. C.K. Lal, 2003, "Culture Flows Across a Blurred Boundary" in *State of Nepal* edited by K.M. Dixit and S. Ramachandaran, Kathmandu: Himal Books, 5th print, p. 110.
17. A.C. Sinha, 1990, "The Indian North East Frontier and the Nepalese Immigrants" in *Himalayan Environment and Culture* edited by N.K. Rustomji and C. Rambles, Shimla: Indian Institute of Advanced Studies.
18. Gaige, *op. cit.*, pp. 159-60.
19. Dor Bahadur Bista, 2004, *People of Nepal,* Kathmandu: Ratna Pustak Bhandar, 3rd Edition.

20. *Ibid.*, pp. 129-30.
21. Jigme N Kazi, 1994, *Inside Sikkim: Against the Tide*, Gangtok: Media Publication.
22. Permanand, 2007, "The People of Bhratiya Mul in Nepal and their Problems and Prospects", MSS.
23. A.C. Sinha, *et al.*, 2005, Ethnographic Report on Sikkim, MSS, Government of Sikkim, Gangtok.
24. Gaige, *op. cit.*, p. 28.
25. *Ibid.*, p. 38.
26. Preshant Jha, 2007, "Nepal's Perplexing Moment of Opportunity", *Himal Southasia,* 20(2), February, p. 56.
27. C.T. Dorji, 1994, *History of Bhuṭan Based on Buddhism*, Thimpu: Mrs. Sangay Xam, p. 9.

Acknowledgement

The author thankfully acknowledges the input provided by Prof. Permanand, Department of Political Science, School of Open Learning, Delhi University, Delhi on the Madhesis.

26

The Last Word So Far...

T.B. SUBBA

In Retrospect

I begin my search for the last word on Indian Nepalis with some retrospection on what happened at the national conference on Indian Nepalis that we organised in Gangtok in April 2006. The reason is simple: that occasion was a lot more representative of the views of Indian Nepalis than what is contained in our select list of 24 articles included in this volume. Further, the retrospection on the conference includes the papers contained in this volume although one of the contributors to this volume could not be present at the conference due to the extraordinarily violent situation then prevailing in Nepal. Out of 66 presentations made over three days with two or three simultaneous sessions 43 were in English and 23 in Nepali. This ratio is interesting in view of the fact that the invitees had the option to choose either English or Nepali as the medium of their papers and presentation. I may like to read the above statistics as indicative of the fact that Nepali intellectuals are deliberately using the English medium for reaching out to a larger audience. But in the process they seem to be losing their grip over their own language. The 23 presentations in Nepali were rarely without English words.

The papers presented in English not only appeared to address a wider audience than the papers presented in Nepali, but also looked at the issues of Nepali identity and nationality from cross-cultural perspective, keeping the community in question at some distance and looking at their trajectories a little critically. The papers presented in Nepali, on the other hand, were—barring a few—more inward-looking, introspective, and at times even self-eulogising. The presentations in English also indicated that Indian Nepalis were passing through a crisis of national identity whereas a few Nepali presentations contested this position. Those who took such a position were from Sikkim and Nepal while those from Northeast India insisted that the crisis not only existed but was a grave one. This indicated that the crisis of Nepali national identity was not perceived as a major issue where they were numerically and politically dominant, although theoretically there is no reason why this should have been so. And this was confirmed during the recent Sony TV sponsored competition for Indian Idol in which the Nepalis in Darjeeling and Sikkim, who are in majority there, exhorted other Nepalis to vote in favour of Prashant Tamang for the sake of "national identity".

Actually speaking, identity crises not only afflict minority communities but also follow numerically dominant communities. The minority communities use their identities to wrest away as much of privileges from the control of the majority as possible and the majority communities hang on to their identities to protect their powers and privileges. Further, identities are more often than not given by neighbouring communities or outsiders and are rarely self-given. The people either overgrow such identities or find such identities derogatory over a period of time. They start to strive for a new identity, an identity that suits them most in a given time and space, and they sometimes succeed in getting the acceptance of the neighbouring communities or the state as well. In Northeast India, tribes like Adi, Nishi, and Karbi have successfully abandoned their old identities like Abor, Dafla and Mikir respectively within a relatively short period of time. Other tribes like the Khasi and Garo of Meghalaya are not yet successful in their struggle to be renamed as Hynniewtrep and Achik respectively. No one knows how long they will need to continue the struggle for their desired change of identity and whether or not they will one day be successful. This also pertains to names of places and cities, which are being nativised.

Most presenters at the conference agreed that Indian Nepalis have a nomenclature crisis and they need to have a new name for their community and language other than Nepali and Gorkha because, while some of them argue in favour of Nepali or Gorkha or even both, they are aware of the fact that neither of the two names completely disconnect them from the neighbouring country called Nepal, which is religiously believed by other Indians to be the source of all Indian Nepalis and the country to which they belong. That is why the labels like "foreigners", "migrants", "aliens" and so on used liberally to refer to Indian Nepalis. They are not only labelled so but are even treated as such. Until some years ago they were detained at the immigration check-posts in Assam and Meghalaya and allowed to enter these states only after some harassment and some bribe. They have sometimes been asked to "go back to Nepal" when they pleaded for some legitimate demands like primary education in their mother tongue. They have even been evicted from several parts of Northeast India where many of them continue to live as second class citizens of India. Their sense of belonging to India is doubted by the very people who do not allow themselves to feel as Indians. These predicaments of their life as Indian Nepalis may remain even if they succeed in finding a name that secures their national identity as Indian citizens. And there may immediately be no perceptible change in the perceptions and attitudes of other Indian communities towards them. However, it will begin to make them internally a lot more secure than they are today. Hence the need to secure them with an Indian identity is the uppermost need of them and has been rightly emphasized so by almost every Indian Nepali scholar.

Indian Nepalis know that there are many migrants among them. That is why they seek the state's help to segregate them from those who cross the border everyday and melt into their society and suddenly leave leaving behind a mess for the Indian Nepalis to clean up. Indian Nepalis also argue that many among them are descendants of the original inhabitants of Indian territory, viz., Sikkim and Darjeeling, which is now a part of West Bengal. Further, most present generation Indian Nepalis have several generations of history in specific locales of Sikkim and Darjeeling or elsewhere in India like Meghalaya, Assam and Dehradun. Actually, Indian Nepalis are fighting against two kinds of labelling: one, the labels like "foreigners", "migrants" and "aliens" that eat into their very claims of legitimacy as Indian nationals and at another level the labels like "Kancha" (read household servant), "Daju" (read porters), "Bahadur" and "Gorkha" (*chowkidar*). That such racist labels are not fictions was proved by a Radio Jockey of Red FM Radio in New Delhi who made racist remarks in late September 2007 that resulted in ethnic clash in Siliguri on 26th of that month between Nepalis and Bengalis forcing the administration to call army and Border Security Force to control the situation. Thus this fight is not easy and is not entirely up to them to win. They also need the support of other Indian communities in this fight against what may be called "double labelling".

It is such a situation that is driving Indian Nepalis to search for a label that would be acceptable to all sections of them living in different parts of India. A word, a name for their community and language, which would clearly segregate them from Nepal Nepalis who come and go and who have no roots in Indian soil, but who look no different from Indian Nepalis. They are not stake holders in India and allegedly commit crimes and just go back to Nepal leaving the Indian Nepalis to face the consequences. Indian Nepalis do realise the difficulty that other Indian communities face while trying to draw a distinction between Nepal Nepalis and themselves for the differences are rather difficult to be appreciated by others, as they have to do with dialectical and emotional differences both of which are not easily visible to an ordinary citizen of any country. Indian Nepalis are also aware of the fact that such a name must be acceptable to those living in villages, tea gardens and towns alike, to the semi-literate majority as well as the middle class. Such a name must clearly indicate their Indian-ness. Will someone be able to find or create such a name? Efforts made in the past in this direction have not met with any success. But the effort in this direction must be made for the effort is worth making. One of the editors of this volume has made such an effort, but has himself admitted that it has not been accepted by the target people. "Indians of Nepalese Origin" or INO, as he calls it, repeatedly reminds them of the most important thing they would like to erase from their memory, that is, they are of Nepalese origin. This is perhaps why his co-editors of this volume, while appreciating the effort made by him, have not been able to accept the nomenclature suggested by him.

When I was fine tuning this volume over the past several months I first toyed with several words that could replace, with some effort, Nepali and Gorkha but was enormously conscious of the grounds on which they would be rejected rather than the bases on which they could be accepted. An easy option at this juncture of our history is to endorse the hyphenated "Indian-Nepali" in English and "Bharatiya-Nepali" in Nepali for the community and "Nepali" for the language because while nationality and citizenship make sense only within nation-state boundaries, languages have no such boundaries. I also think that no matter how much we shout from the roof of our house we cannot completely stop others from calling us by the names they have been calling us for so long. Nor can we deny the historical, social, linguistic, religious and cultural linkages between Nepal Nepalis and Indian Nepalis. I further argue that the hyphenated identity is flexible enough to take care of the regional identities in both English and Nepali languages like "Assamese-Nepalis", "Sikkimese-Nepalis", "Bhagsu-Nepalis" and so on.

But the above option does not take Indian Nepalis any further from where they are standing for the past couple of centuries. Hence, an effort must be made to try and push their cart a little ahead. Whoever makes this effort, however, must first consider the bewildering variation in the history, culture, language, religion, and social ecology of Indian Nepalis. The effort must make sense to the Nepali youths in particular for it is they who are most concerned about their national identity today. While they vie for every opportunity with other Indian youths they are burdened with the extra responsibility of defending themselves as Indian citizens wherever they go and whoever they meet. With Prashant Tamang winning the race for Indian Idol it might have appeared easier for them to do so for a day or two but soon the situation was same for them as before.

The Gangtok conference also indicated that both "Nepali" and "Gorkha" have strong constituencies of supporters and they do not seem willing to give up calling themselves and their language by the names they consider to be appropriate. There are merits and demerits in both the nomenclatures and their ardent followers may continue to use them, but if the issue is to seek solution to the crisis of national identity of Indian Nepalis neither of the word fits the bill. A third name must emerge, sooner or later, which can accommodate the aspirations of about five million Indian Nepalis. The past failures and the present fight between followers of the above two constituencies should not deter one from the option to find or create a third nomenclature that will unite the two warring groups rather than divide them.

To find or create such a word is not difficult, but for such a word to be accepted by majority of Indian Nepalis is extremely difficult. Some will oppose a proposed name on political grounds, others will oppose it on caste or religious grounds, and still others will oppose a word on regional grounds. Most people in Sikkim do not think that the word "Nepali" needs to be replaced and many in Darjeeling and Mizoram think that "Gorkha" is the most appropriate name for them. If Assamese-Nepalis suggest a third name it may not be acceptable to the Nepalis of Sikkim and Darjeeling and vice versa on regional grounds and their own sense of who are more advanced or backward. Even within Assam the Upper Assam Nepalis and Lower Assam Nepalis may not agree on the same terminology although they would certainly agree on the need for one. The simple reason for this is the enormous variation of all sorts within Indian Nepalis.

It must be further remembered by one who is proposing a new name that the currency of a name in a given locality, region, or country for whatever historical or political reasons cannot be wished away easily. Nor is it always easy to replace one word with another, especially in government records. The place names like Bombay, Calcutta, Madras and Bangalore continue to be used despite the fact these names have been changed through the due process of legislation. After all every community has to negotiate its identity in a given time and space in order to maximise its chances of survival and development. Only members of a community living in a particular locale know what is in their best interest to call themselves at a given point of time. It is not proper for the Nepalis of Sikkim or Gorkhas of Darjeeling to tell the Nepalis of Manipur or the Gorkhas of Mizoram what name they should call themselves by unless the former are ready to shoulder the consequences, if any, of such an action. Similarly, Nepal Nepalis should have no objection if Indian Nepalis would not like to call themselves "Nepalis" and would like to change the name of their community and language.

Between local compulsions and national aspirations I would opt for the former. The Nepalis of Darjeeling and Sikkim, leave alone the Nepal Nepalis, can do precious little if a Nepali village in Meghalaya or Arunachal Pradesh is set on fire by a group of angry youths belonging to a locally dominant community. Requests from Pawan Chamling to protect "his" people may be replied by his counterparts with assurances, deployment of security personnel, and setting up of relief camps if things go out of control, which they often do. The Nepalis living in a particular place must sort out their differences with other local people and find solutions at the local level. If that fails the Nepalis living there will have to suffer and the Nepalis living elsewhere can do very little about it. Nobody knows that better than Indian Nepalis living in Northeast India in general and the Nepalis living in Meghalaya in particular, where the communal tension following the Sony TV sponsored Indian Idol programme in September 2007 gave them sleepless nights. Like elsewhere they were a divided community with one section supporting Prashant Tamang from Darjeeling and another supporting Amit Paul of their own Shillong until they were forced to realise that they were all believed to be voting for the former because they belonged to his community. That many among them appreciated the beautiful voice of the latter and actually voted for him was rubbished. Some ruffians closed the PCOs in Nepali-dominated localities and even pulled out a few landlines so that they would not be able to vote for Prashant Tamang. The threat to send them back to Nepal or Darjeeling in case Prashant Tamang won was also circulated across the state of Meghalaya.

Several scholars at the Gangtok conference emphasized on re-writing the history of Indian Nepalis and making that history part of the school curriculum so that their children as well as other Indian children know the facts about Indian Nepalis. Apparently the participation of Gorkha soldiers in the massacre of Jalianawala Bagh is not erased from the memory of Indians whereas they have forgotten the role of the same Gorkhas in saving the lives of thousands of people during the Calcutta famine in 1940s and the partition of India in 1947, leave alone their role in protecting the international border or fighting against armed insurgents after India's independence. Therefore, as some scholars at the conference mentioned above rightly argued, writing their own history may erase some misconceptions of their neighbouring communities about Indian Nepalis. Both Darjeeling and Sikkim being favourite tourist destinations, the people there could use the advantage of their locations to rectify the notions of other Indian communities about their history, culture, religion and so on. The tourist brochures are in fact the first texts that need to be rectified in this regard.

To some other participants at the conference, rather than history Indian Nepalis should harp on their language and literature in order to find a less controversial space and voice for themselves within India. Their language and literature, especially their fiction and poetry, have such substantial Indian roots and flavour that they could as well consider this as the basis of their national identity. Like history, literature could of course be one other front rather than an alternative front that Indian Nepalis could open in order to achieve their ultimate goal of establishing themselves as bonafide Indians.

Some presenters reported that Indian Nepalis suffer in many ways in various parts of India, especially in Northeast India, mainly due to the fact that people from Nepal continue to come and settle there under the provisions of the 1950 Treaty. According to them, the solution to this problem lies in segregating the "Treaty-Nepalis" from "Indian-Nepalis", which they say can be achieved by abrogating the treaty and introducing the passport system for those who come from Nepal. But abrogation of this treaty needs to be debated from a holistic point of view and by Indian Nepalis as well as Nepalese Indians for the treaty concerns both these categories of people who A.C. Sinha calls INOs and NIOs in the previous chapter. The abrogation of the treaty must also ensure that the crisis of national identity suffered by Indian Nepalis and Nepalese Indians is taken care of, which it is not very likely to happen because national identity is a lot more complex construction than what most Indian Nepalis think it is.

The various presentations at the conference also indicated that the Indian Nepalis, especially those living in small minorities in different parts of India, share a common complex, which I might like to call, for lack of a better expression, "victim syndrome": victim of Indian ignorance about them, victim of print and electronic media, victim of regional and national politics, victim of the Indo-Nepal Friendship Treaty of 1950, victim of increasingly hostile dominant neighbours, victim of history, and so on. To be recognised as Indian Nepalis and given equal opportunities in the fields of education, employment, and ownership of property without the fear of having to comply with "quit notices" of some local youth or underground organisations is their ultimate wish. Such a wish, however, is increasingly being difficult to fulfil in some parts of Northeast India and is apprehended to be more difficult in future.

We are all aware of the tension within Indian Nepali community—tensions arising from their racial, linguistic, religious, and political diversity, from different constitutional identities like Scheduled Castes, Scheduled Tribes and Other Backward Classes accorded to the various constituents of this community, and other such sources. However, the presentations showed that the internal tensions are not important or not important enough to write about, or to share them with everyone. This was also confirmed by the voting behaviour in Darjeeling, Sikkim and elsewhere during the recent Indian Idol competition. The internal differences based on caste, religion, language, and political affiliation seemed to have been ignored by all of them. But once this euphoria was over the ugly realities began to resurface. Hence, it is perhaps not quite all right to downplay internal tensions. They actually need to be addressed, debated and fatigued not hidden or suppressed. Only from such an engagement may emerge a stronger, more integrated Indian Nepali community. I am happy that there is such an engagement going on and there is at least one article by Shrawan Acharya addressing this problem in this volume.

Furthermore, some of the presentations conceived of identity in a monolithic sense. Its multiplicity, resilience and adaptability have however been attended to some extent in the articles finally included in this volume. Similarly, the fact that ethnic boundaries are ever evolving and they are always blurred and overlapping has received more attention in the volume than they did at the time of conference. Identities are always negotiated differently in different situations and times, which is a grim reminder to those who seek, rather innocently, to have a non-ambivalent identity for a large and heterogeneous population called Indian Nepalis. Their economic, vocational, religious, linguistic, cultural, educational, political diversities have increased so much over the past 200 years or so that it is indeed very difficult to find a single name that subsumes all of them to their satisfaction.

It is true that Indian Nepalis began to experience the crisis of their national identity only after they became literate and began to look out for white-collar jobs. So long as they were pastorals, miners, soldiers, agriculturists, tea-labourers or household servants, there was little opposition to their existence anywhere in India and there was limited spread of identity consciousness among them. Such consciousness came with education, with the emergence of the middle class in the Nepali society and with increased competition for various resources with other Indian communities. This aspect of their identity issue somehow has not received adequate space in this volume.

Allow me to dwell briefly on surnames as expressions of identity adaptation that was highly evident at the conference. The Brahmin participants from Northeast India spelt their surnames as "Sarma" or "Sarmah", whereas those from Darjeeling and Sikkim spelt it as "Sharma". The reason is obvious: the Bahuns in Assam in particular have adapted their surnames to suit the local environment, thereby showing the inclination to assimilate themselves with the Assamese Brahmins rather than identify themselves as Nepali Bahuns. Several presentations also indicated how well-versed the Indian Nepalis were in the languages and literatures of their neighbouring communities and how deeply steeped they were in local cultures without forgetting their own. The Assamese Nepalis have, for instance, added "Bihu" to the list of their festivals and Assamese cuisine to their cuisine, and contributed a lot to Assamese literature. Some of them have even held the highest post of the highest literary organisation of the Assamese, viz., Assam Sahitya Sabha.

The various issues dealt in this volume—be they abrogation of the Indo-Nepal Friendship Treaty of 1950, inclusion of the Nepali language in the VIII Schedule to the Constitution of India, the demand for a separate state called Gorkhaland within the Union of India, or use of local surnames—indicated that unlike many communities in Northeast India or elsewhere, Indian Nepalis seek acceptance of and integration with the great Indian nationhood and not secession from the same. Their orientation is integrative, which should be welcome and celebrated by any nation-state and certainly by India. This is also a conclusion arrived at by various contributors to this volume.

I would also like to state that in this vast country called India each community has to discover itself differently. Once a community is born in India the space must exist for it somewhere. It need not be as big as one wishes or where one wishes, but it does exist nonetheless. This space needs to be discovered and negotiated. However, this space will be visible only when the people attain a certain height, a certain depth of insight, and a certain broadness of mind, which may come (not necessarily it does) only with higher, technical and professional education. Even if some communities have been lucky to get such space on a platter they constantly need to struggle for protecting the same. Those who have been denied such space need to struggle for it, rather than expect it to be given on a platter or complain about why the more fortunate Indian communities have got it so easily. Those who have arrived in India earlier would certainly be luckier than those who arrived late. This principle works even at the village and clan levels. Let Indian Nepalis accept this fact and move on.

A Plea for a New Name

Finally, as someone who has engaged himself with the issue of identity of Indian Nepalis for several years now allow me to suggest a new nomenclature for them. And that is "Sakhaa", which means "friend" in a large number of Insdo-Aryan languages including Nepali. Let me make a few points in its defence. First, it is free from any geographical, cultural and territorial identities like Pahadi, Madhesi, Nepali, Gorkha, Manipuri, Mizo, Bengali, Marathi, etc. and that is, to my mind, its biggest strength. Truly speaking, Indian Nepalis need a de-territorialised (see Bidhan Golay's article in this volume) and de-ethnicised identity for they are not only themselves de-territorialised in India but also have frequently experienced ethnic anger of the locally dominant communities. Second, they live in towns as well as villages, hills as well as plains, speak their language as well as those of their neighbouring communities, celebrate their festivals as well as those of their fellow Indian communities, and are found in almost every state of India. A Sakhaa has no nation and has no territory. He is neither a hillman nor a plainsman. He is not a Hindu, or a Buddhist or a Christian. He can be anywhere and from anywhere—Manipur, Mizoram, Darjeeling, Sikkim, Dehradun, Bhagsu, Mumbai, Delhi, or Karnataka. A Sakhaa does have a history, a religion, a language, a culture, a custom, and a ritual but he is a Sakhaa inspite of all this. He cannot do harm to anyone and no one would like to do any harm to him. A Sakhaa will be there whenever he is needed and will stand by one even when one is found to be wrong.

If the English language, with few dialectical variations, can be called American in America, or the Swedish language called Norwegian in Norway, there is no reason why the Nepali language, which is dialectically different from the Nepali language written and spoken in Nepal, cannot be called Sakhaa Bhasa. The word Sakhaa needs to be used voluntarily for symbolising all Indian Nepalis. The formala "Indian Nepalis+Gorkhas = Sakhaa" needs to be memorised. Initially, such symbolising process will appear awkward, but with a little voluntary effort on the part of all it is possible to adopt the new name by them and for them. May be they will, may be they will need to, may be they will have to sooner or later. There is no great haste. Let the new name be tossed around in the fields and forests, tea gardens and towns, cowsheds and coalmines, towns and metros, or wherever they live, but let something decisive emerge one day. I for one look forward to see that day.

Index